THE DRAGON
SYNDICATES

D1351809

THE DRAGON SYNDICATES

THE GLOBAL PHENOMENON OF THE TRIADS

MARTIN BOOTH

BANTAM BOOKS

LONDON · NEW YORK · TORONTO · SYDNEY · AUCKLAND

THE DRAGON SYNDICATE
A BANTAM BOOK : 0 553 50590 4

Originally published in Great Britain by Doubleday,
a division of Transworld Publishers

PRINTING HISTORY
Doubleday edition published 1999
Bantam Books edition published 2000

3 5 7 9 10 8 6 4 2

Typeset in 11/12 pt Bembo by Hewer Text Ltd, Edinburgh

Bantam Books are published by Transworld Publishers,
61-63 Uxbridge Road, London W5 5SA,
a division of The Random House Group Ltd,
in Australia by Random House Australia (Pty) Ltd,
20 Alfred Street, Milsons Point, Sydney, NSW 2061, Australia,
in New Zealand by Random House New Zealand Ltd,
18 Poland Road, Glenfield, Auckland 10, New Zealand
and in South Africa by Random House (Pty) Ltd,
Endulini, 5a Jubilee Road, Parktown 2193, South Africa

Printed and bound in Great Britain by
Mackays of Chatham plc, Chatham, Kent

This book is dedicated to the memory of my mother,
Joyce Booth, a true China Hand

CONTENTS

ACKNOWLEDGEMENTS

No study of this sort is possible without the very considerable assistance of a large number of people, many of whom must, understandably, remain anonymous. To those others whom I may openly identify, I express my gratitude: they include Professor Terry Boyce, Geoffrey Briggs, Simon Elegant, Assistant Commissioner Michael Horner, Chief Detective Inspector Peter Ip Paufuk, John Keep, Professor Ko-lin Chin, Mark Craig, Alan Wright, Stuart McDonald, Sterling Seagrave, Vincent Chapman, Arthur Hacker, Richard Frost, John Colmey, Johan Fourie, Stefan Pretorius, Liz Thomas, Dr Loretta Pang, Lucien Wong and Ursula Mackenzie (my editor).

Organizations to which I owe a debt of gratitude include the Royal Hong Kong Police (known since mid-1997 as the Hong Kong Police), the Independent Commission Against Corruption (Hong Kong), the Government Information Service (Hong Kong), the governments of Albania, Germany, the People's Republic of China, The Netherlands, Russia and the Republic of South Africa, Interpol, HM Customs and Excise (London), the Metropolitan Police (London), Merseyside

Police (Liverpool), the HongkongBank Group, Master-Card International, Granada Television, the Federal Bureau of Investigation (USA), the Criminal Intelligence Agency (USA) and the Drug Enforcement Administration (USA).

AUTHOR'S NOTE

The English pronunciation and spelling of Chinese words can be confusing. I have used the latest Pinyin system of spelling for all places which exist today (for example, Peking is called Beijing) but reverted to the former Wade–Giles system in referring to places in antiquity, fictitious places or where the identity of a place is not certain. Where proper nouns and personal names are concerned, I have used the Pinyin spelling where appropriate but kept to Wade–Giles for nouns and names more likely to be recognized in that other form: for example, I have referred to Mao Zedong, not Mao Tse-tung, but to Chiang Kai-shek (as he is mostly known outside China) rather than to Jiang Jieshi, as he is referred to in China. I have not differentiated between Cantonese, which is predominantly spoken in southern China and is the language most spoken by Triads, and Putonghua (Mandarin) or other Chinese dialects, but have used either as appropriate. For information, Chinese surnames precede given names.

PROLOGUE

It was the early evening of Sunday, 4 May 1997. A light breeze was blowing in from the South China Sea. The air was warm and just a little too balmy, typical for that time of year in the Pearl River delta area, when the gentleness of spring has already half given way to the oppressive humidity and heat that are high summer in coastal southern China.

Along the Rua da Praia Grande, once the ancient waterfront esplanade of Macau, the lights were coming on in the shops, hotels and blocks of apartments. The pavements were crowded with workers returning home, evening shoppers, tourists out for a stroll in the exotic Orient, or local people making for the many restaurants of the tiny Portuguese enclave. In the pedestrianized Leal Senado, young couples walked hand in hand past elderly women on their way from an evening service in the cathedral. Around the entrance to the Lisboa Hotel, the evening's gamblers were arriving at the casino, whilst across the arching span of the bridge to Taipa Island the luxury residential blocks lining the far shore coruscated in the warm air. Overhead, the identification strobe lights of a jet turning into its final approach to Macau's brand-new international airport flashed against the developing night.

The oldest European settlement in China, Macau seems to have been bypassed by the modern world. Founded in the 1550s and once the most important trading post in the Orient, grown rich on silk, tea, silver and opium, it was diverted into a mercantile side-water when Hong Kong was founded in the 1840s and the British became the world's dominant trading nation. Whilst the former British colony, forty-five minutes away to the east by high-speed jet-foil, has become a vibrant cosmopolitan twenty-first-century metropolis, Macau has remained in the nineteenth century. Parts of it look like an orientalized quarter of Oporto, and the pace of life has a Latin gentility. Roman Catholic priests walk through alleys and up steps little changed since George Chinnery, one of the first Western painters to work in China, set up his easel there in 1825.

With such a historical ambience, Macau has retained something of the Orient's mystique, long since lost in skyscrapered, multi-corporate Hong Kong or Singapore. One has the feeling that there might just still be opium divans tucked away up narrow thoroughfares with quaint names, or white slavers hiding in the shadows, eager to abduct young women into concubinage in the imperial Chinese court. The atmosphere has a sense of louche anticipation.

As usual the streets, designed two centuries ago for horse carriage, handcart, palanquin and rickshaw, were that evening clogged with traffic at a virtual standstill. The only vehicles able to move through the jam were motor-cycles, which wove in and out between the cars, buses and lorries, their throttles revving and their exhausts pumping out noxious high-octane fumes. No-one paid any attention to the two Japanese motorcycles which pulled up on either side of a pale-coloured Toyota saloon car stuck in the traffic. No-one saw the pillion passengers pull Chinese military-issue automatic pistols from their jackets or from beneath their T-shirts. Hardly anyone even threw themselves to the pavement or ducked into a doorway as, a moment later, the riders emptied their weapons into the car at point-blank range, riddling it with a deadly crossfire. The windows shattered. It was all over in less than twenty seconds, the motorcycles racing off, jiving through the stationary traffic. Inside the Toyota, the two Chinese men sitting in the front were killed outright. A third, in the back, writhed for several minutes before dying. The assassination was well timed, meticulously planned and professionally conducted. It was more than fifteen minutes before the police could arrive through the congested streets.

Of the three men killed, one was Shek Wing-cheung, thought by the Macanese police, their law-enforcement counterparts over the border in China and those in Hong Kong to be the close associate and right-hand man of a gangster known as Broken Tooth Kui, considered by the Macanese police to be the much feared and consequently much revered Dragon Head of the enclave's most notorious and powerful Triad society, the infamous 14K. The hit was the latest in a series of gang-related bombings, knifings and shootings; and was, police believed, intended as a warning to Kui from the smaller Wo On Lok Triad society, which was seeking to raise its profile and muscle in on the considerable criminal activity for which Macau has had a reputation for decades.

15

The Portuguese governor of Macau, General Vasco Rocha Vieira, was quick to calm public concern. The problem was being dealt with; there was no real need for anxiety; tourists need not stay away, for the violence was restricted to the criminal underworld. Yet he did not remind the Macanese population of the similar attempted hit on his top anti-Triad law officer six months before. Nor did he mention that, between January and May that year, fourteen people had been killed in Macau, and those were only the fatalities for which the police had details and a corpse to prove the crime.

Four days later, when I arrived in Macau, security was tight. Flak-jacketed police squads armed with sub-machine guns wandered the streets around the Lisboa. At the ferry terminal, all passengers arriving from Hong Kong were closely scrutinized by immigration and police officials who normally paid scant attention to passports. Despite the precautions, a grenade attack was launched upon a gold dealers' shop 200 metres from where I was having lunch one day and a rich merchant's house was bombed half a kilometre from where I was staying.

The real cause of this blood-letting is not to be found in the immediate past. Macau has been a haven for Triad societies for over two centuries and the rivalry which materialized that May night was merely the latest chapter in a story which pre-dates the Roman empire. To discover its roots, and to appreciate the Triad philosophy of secrecy, power and avarice that today rules so much of that part of the international criminal underworld to which they lay claim, one has to go back over two millennia, to the very foundations of Chinese society.

16

PART ONE

THE ANCESTRY OF DRAGONS

1

IMMIGRANTS TO BARBARIAN LANDS

Today there are approximately 60 million Chinese living outside China. Excepting those Africans whose ancestors were slaves, or later willing migrants, they are the largest single expatriate minority nationality on earth, accounting for about 5 per cent of all ethnic Chinese. There is hardly a country in which they are not represented and yet they are not an obvious international community. Wherever they have migrated, or fled, or been driven by natural forces or political upheaval, they have quietly settled, by and large keeping themselves to themselves, maintaining their national and cultural identities with a low profile, even in countries where they have become important contributors to the economy. Only in South-east Asia, where they are either the largest ethnic minority or have even grown to outnumber the indigenous people, have they become conspicuous.

No matter where these migrants have established their communities, Triad societies have set themselves up. For centuries they have been an integral and unequivocally inseparable part of Chinese society.

This massive diaspora is not a recent phenomenon,

although its growth has accelerated considerably in the last two centuries. It has been going on for at least two millennia and the only reason it is so little recognized is that it has been, for most of that while, a gradual process rather than a sudden exodus. It is as if China has, with infinite Oriental patience, been leaking her people across the globe rather than sending out invading armies of soldiers, traders or missionaries. To understand the causes of this mass migration, one has to look back to the very beginnings of Chinese history.

The Zhou dynasty, which was the third, following the Xia and Shang dynasties, was the classical age of Lao Tze and Confucius, the most important of all Chinese philosophers. Starting in 1027 BC, it was at first a time of social order strengthened by a ruthless legal system: the rule of law seems to have been to execute and ask questions afterwards, which focused minds and established the fundamentals of the Confucian system of government which has prevailed in China up to the present day, notwithstanding the introduction of Communism.

The main tenet of Confucian philosophy is that people should live according to the principles of good conduct, practical wisdom, statecraft and correct social relationships. To the philosopher, social and political order were synonymous and should control the lives of both the governors and the governed. The family unit was deemed the basis for society, respect for one's elders and ancestors being cardinal. Confucian ethics centred upon the concepts of *ren*, the main essence of goodness in human relationships, the supreme human virtue manifested in

20

zhong, the basic loyalty of one man to another and *shu*, which encompassed the ideal of doing unto others what you would they did unto you. Amongst other seminal ideals were those of integrity and filial piety.

Under Confucian influence, society was structured and submissive. The emperor kow-towed to his ancestors and the gods whilst the courtiers kow-towed to the emperor; officials kow-towed to the court and the rest of the population kow-towed to the officials, who were, in effect, the world's first civil service. In general, the lower down the social order you were, the more you kow-towed, and the name of the game was tribute offered up the social ladder out of a sense not merely of obeisance and fealty but also of fear. It was a social system founded in the very roots of Chinese culture.

The imperial government was made up almost exclusively of members of the Zhou clan, who considered themselves the only people in the land to be true Chinese; everyone else was considered a peasant of impure, dubious stock. In such a tightly controlled system, government became a sort of precursor of a modern multinational family corporation. There was little or no official advancement for anyone who was not related either by blood or by marriage to the executive, which, by keeping power in the hands of a comparatively small clique, maintained stability both for itself and for its subjects. This is not to say that heads did not roll within the administration: no-one was exempt from the executioner's blade. Nevertheless, by and large, tribute was paid, submission was maintained and order prevailed. China prospered. A money economy was founded, agriculture improved with the discovery of iron smelting and plough forging, laws were written down, and learning and the arts flourished.

As the centuries went by, however, the system began to collapse. Whilst the structure of social order remained more or less intact, it was subverted by extensive corruption. In the Spring and Autumn Era (722–481 BC), codes of honour were undermined by greed and conspiracy. From 403 to 221 BC, the dynasty passed into the Warring States Period in which local powerbrokers set up their small domains and internecine civil war broke out, each fighting the next, joining and breaking treaties at will and trying to gain the upper hand.

During the latter centuries of the Zhou dynasty, merchants came to be resented and regarded as competition by the increasingly mercenary dynastic 'corporate bosses'. The merchants created wealth and this gave them a power-base which was perceived as a threat. A good many of those who were not executed, systematically bankrupted or otherwise driven out of business were banished to the land of Yueh, a part of China south of the Yangtze River which was considered to be very much on the periphery, if not actually outside, the heartland of the people known as the Celestial Kingdom. Once in Yueh, however, the banished merchants found themselves presented with an opportunity which they had been denied further north. They were now within reach of China's long coastline and this meant they could start to travel. These displaced merchant migrants became the first members of the Chinese diaspora.

In order to survive, the merchants – be they simple shopkeepers or men of substance dealing in commodities such as silver, rice or wheat – had only two real means of self-protection by which to curry favour or hold their ground with the imperial administration which controlled the military and the judiciary. One was to become corrupt themselves, which they did with considerable alacrity and proficiency, although this was often insufficient to save them. The other was to follow the example of Confucian ideology and form family, clan, place or name associations, or trade guilds – like brotherhoods – many of which were, by necessity, secret or quasi-secret. Safety, it was considered, lay in numbers: the best way to survive was to group together and watch each other's back. Such mutual looking-over-of-shoulders has been an integral part of Chinese life ever since.

It was not long before the banished merchants began operating ships and cargoes, either using their own capital or investing that of wealthy families in the north who kept quiet about their retained links with the exiles. Their trading was primarily coastal, but it ranged from Siberia, through Korea, across to Japan and down as far as modern-day Indonesia. A few even traded in the Indian Ocean, along the western side of the Malay peninsula and across to the Indian sub-continent itself. Substantial profits were made by all.

They were not the only ocean-going risk-takers. In 472 BC, the ruler of Yueh ordered a fleet of deep-sea rafts to be built (it is thought they were constructed in the vicinity of Hong Kong). When completed, the fleet set sail into the Pacific. It was never heard of again, but anthropologists believe remnants of it might have reached as far as the Hawaiian islands and even the western coast of North America.

In 221 BC the Zhou dynasty fell, to be replaced, for just

fourteen years, by the Ch'in dynasty. The emperor Shih Huang-ti united the whole of China, shook up the administrative process, standardized the written language, built roads, dug canals and raised much of the Great Wall. In 207 BC he lost control and, after a few years' interregnum, the Han dynasty was founded, lasting until AD 220. Yueh, having fought for itself in the Warring States Period, was invaded by Chinese settlers from the north and subjugated: the original inhabitants, who had lived there since time immemorial, either fled west into Indo-China or were assimilated. Today, those who remained make up the ethnic minorities of south-western China, Vietnam, Laos and Thailand. The settlers increased the population enormously and, simultaneously, boosted the number of people seeking to engage in trade.

The Han dynasty was a time of further unification and consolidation. The bureaucracy continued as before, still all-pervading and powerful, if less corrupt and somewhat more lenient. Nomadic invaders from the north, the Hsiung-nu, threatened the borders and attacked settlements on the fringes of China. Although they were brutal and well organized, they posed no real threat; the emperors nevertheless took them seriously and it was through seeking to defeat them that the next major impetus to the diaspora came. It was not a mass migration but the work of a small party of men led by one envoy, Chang Chien.

The emperor Wu-ti sent Chang Chien on a diplomatic mission to investigate the intentions of and spy upon the Hsiung-nu. With a party of 100 men, he set off across the Takla Makan and Gobi deserts. He was not the first Chinese to come this way: merchants had long been dealing with the nomadic enemy, selling them arms despite imperial edicts against the trade and mass executions for those caught involved in it. At last, Chang Chien reached enemy territory, was ambushed and taken before the Hsiung-nu chief, who held him captive for ten years. During his captivity he was given a nomad princess as a bride and, as time passed, he was granted more liberty: it was thought he was inured to his situation. Once his captors were lulled into a false sense of security, however, he escaped with his wife and faithful Chinese servant.

Chang Chien did not head back to China, but turned west. He had a secret agenda: to discover the whereabouts of a tribe called the Kushans which the Hsiung-nu had displaced and encourage them into an alliance with China to defeat the nomads. Travelling through Ferghana – now Tadzhikistan and Uzbekistan – he found them. They had successfully conquered Bactria, which stretched eastwards from the Caspian Sea and southwards as far as the modern-day Afghanistan–Pakistan border. Their arrival had filled a local power vacuum left by the Greeks, who had not long since abandoned the area as the empire of Alexander the Great ended. Through Chang Chien, for the first time, the Orient had come into direct contact with the rest of the Old World.

The Kushans had no interest in fighting the Hsiung-nu. Although Chang Chien's mission was therefore a diplomatic failure, what he did not gain in terms of military alliance he more than made up for in knowledge. When he returned to China, by way of Tibet and after many other adventures, he told of cities in a land called Persia; of Mesopotamia, the shores of which bounded a great landlocked sea, beyond which was another great ocean

25

stretching to the edge of time, to countries of unimaginable beauty and strangeness, populated by giants, dwarfs and bizarre creatures. Yet there was more. Even as far as Bactria, he discovered goods from the land of Yueh which had been traded through India.

Some years later, Chang Chien was again sent west. This time, his mission was different. He travelled with a vast array of wealth and treasures with which to suborn local kings. The reasoning behind this was simple: if the kings were shown how rich China was, they would want to share in her bounty and, in order to do so, would form alliances with her. At the same time, the Chinese emperor's fame would be spread and the world would kow-tow to his splendour and majesty. The strategy worked, but it did more than arrange a few treaties. It established a Chinese presence, and an awareness of China, eastwards from the Mediterranean. The Hsiung-nu, now caught between allies, were defeated. The Silk Road trade routes were established to the north of Tibet, the Jade Road was established to southern Indo-China and Burma, which was already famous for its jade and gemstones, especially rubies. From there, it was only a short sea crossing to India. Along these corridors of trade, Chinese merchants moved westwards under the protection of Chinese soldiers. Foreign traders heading eastwards were similarly safeguarded. It was only a matter of time before Chinese silks became the luxury fabric of ancient Rome.

For 1,000 years, through the rise and fall of the Roman empire, through the upheavals of the Dark Ages and into the Middle Ages in Europe, the Chinese traded with the western Barbarians, as they called all non-Chinese: anything not Chinese was deemed inferior and barbaric. Silk, jade, porcelain, silver, spices and herbs all moved westwards. In the other direction travelled religion (especially Buddhism), technology and scientific discovery, ivory and opium, which was traded predominantly by Arabs. That trade was so great was remarkable, and not just in its magnitude. China being an insular nation, it was illegal to trade outside the national boundaries: indeed, it had been so since the Zhou dynasty when merchants were perceived as a threat and the proscribing of their activities a means of curbing their wealth and power. However, with true Chinese pragmatism, officialdom looked the other way so long as the luxury goods the traders imported found their way into the homes of the courtiers and mandarins and the imperial apartments. In short, corruption ruled.

The dynasties came and went – the expansionist Tsin; the unifying Sui; the T'ang with its unprecedented and magnificent explosion in learning and the arts; the Sung, during which both explosive fireworks and tea-drinking became prominent; the Yuan governed by the Mongol invaders Genghis and Kublai Khan, whose forces swept over the vast country like a plague of locusts and drew China into a colossal, brutal empire which spread from Central Europe to Korea. Yet even they were defeated after a mere 100 years by revolutions in Mongolia and southern China.

Outwardly, China seems to have been a comparatively stable land, yet it was not. Dynasties were usually overthrown by force rather than by social metamorphosis and there were times, such as the Five Dynasties and Ten Kingdoms period (AD 907–60), when civil war killed millions through starvation or by the sword. The system of government remained intrinsically corrupt, outside invaders continually nibbled at the borders and internal dissension was commonplace. The need for self-protection was always uppermost in people's minds and the brotherhoods that had come about before the time of Christ continued to play an important part in Chinese life.

The Mongols were succeeded by the Ming dynasty. Founded in 1368 by a peasant named Chu Yuan-chang, who proclaimed himself the emperor Hung Wu, the Ming was considered the first truly Chinese dynasty for hundreds of years. Disgusted with the corruption of government, Hung Wu set about cleaning up the administration. Corrupt mandarins and ministers were caned to death. Bribery ceased. Favours were no longer for sale or barter. The wealthy had to keep a low profile. Many feigned poverty whilst actually sitting on considerable riches, reinvesting these in order to make further profits. The best way to reinvest was to put money into business ventures overseas, which, whilst illegal, were beyond the scrutiny of the imperial bean-counters.

It was during the early years of the Ming dynasty that the next great impetus to the international migration of Chinese came about. Once again, it was prompted by one man.

Hung Wu's heir died young and the mantle of succession fell upon his grandson, Chien-men, whose position was consolidated by his grandfather's assassinating all opposition. When the boy ascended the throne at the age of sixteen, he nevertheless faced a rebellion led by an uncle who successfully took the capital, Nanjing, in 1402. The imperial palace was razed, the boy emperor disappeared and the uncle proclaimed himself the new emperor, taking the name Yung Lo. Partly as a show of seeking to rescue his nephew, who was said to be living in exile overseas (but who was, in all likelihood, murdered when Nanjing fell), and partly in order to stamp his presence on subject nations, Yung Lo assembled a mighty fleet of ocean-going junks which he sent out on seven voyages to gain tribute and to strengthen his own credibility at home. This fleet was commanded by one Ma Ho.

More commonly known as Ma San-bao, he was a eunuch, lacking both testicles and a penis (*san bao* means three gems: the nickname was ironic for he had lost his 'little jewels') and was a favourite of Yung Lo. A Muslim of Sino-Mongol-Turkish blood from Yunnan province, he was highly intelligent, fluent in both Arabic and Chinese and widely educated in geography. Emasculation before puberty had destroyed his hormonal balance and he grew to well over 2 metres, becoming a mighty military warrior and strategist and helping in the capture of Nanjing. Put in charge of the imperial household of over 1,000 eunuchs, he took a new surname, Cheng, becoming known thereafter as Cheng Ho.

Between 1405 and 1433, Cheng Ho voyaged extensively in his fleet of junks. His first armada consisted of 317 ships carrying 28,000 men. The vessels were state-of-the-art with navigational manuals and charts and compasses consisting of magnetized needles floating in bowls of water. During the twenty-eight years of his maritime wanderings, Cheng Ho visited all of South-east Asia, India and Ceylon, the Persian Gulf and the Red Sea, Zanzibar and Madagascar, the African coast down at least as far as Durban and probably to the Cape of Good Hope. He established puppet-governments near to home and set

29

up alliances with Arab traders in Africa. To this day, remnants of his influence survive in many places, not least at Lamu and Malindi, on the coast of Kenya. At the ruined city of Gedi, only rediscovered in dense jungle near Malindi in the 1920s, were found a pair of distinctive Chinese scissors dating from the fifteenth century. On his last voyage, on which he embarked in 1430, he returned with a giraffe, an elephant and, just as remarkably, artefacts he had traded with Arabs. They were the products of the Italian Renaissance: amongst them were magnifying lenses in the form of spectacles.

After Yung Lo's death in 1424, Cheng Ho came under attack from many quarters in the imperial court because of his and his eunuchs' stranglehold on foreign trade. Under his leadership, they had built up a well-organized cartel which ensured that all foreign trade passed through their management – despite the fact that trade outside China was, in theory, still illegal. Upon his return from his last voyage, he disappeared from public life. His fate is unknown, but he was probably discreetly assassinated. However, he is remembered still in South-east Asia: images of him exist in a number of temples in Thailand and Indonesia where he is revered. In the West he lives on in legend as Sinbad the Sailor, the father of navigation and, long before Vasco da Gama and Magellan, the greatest explorer of them all.

Cheng Ho's voyages opened the eyes of many Chinese to the possibilities that lay overseas. Foreigners may have been barbaric, but they were also ripe for trade and exploitation, and in the years after Cheng Ho's disappearance thousands of Chinese traders set up in business, even though it was illegal to build an ocean-going junk: it branded one a buccaneer and the punishment was execution. With such a threat hanging over their necks, many merchants began to leave China and, although she could have become the most important trading nation on earth, she soon lost her maritime capability.

Old habits die hard. Wherever the Chinese merchants went, they took with them more than silk and scissors. Ever aware of their insecurity, ingrained with centuries of having to watch their own or their brothers' backs, they migrated with their system of Confucian-inspired family and clan, name and place associations intact. This served not only to protect them from the tentacles of the imperial administration, but to bring them security in foreign lands where, on unfamiliar territory, they considered themselves still in danger. In whatever city or town they settled, they maintained their traditions and religions, their cultural identity and, often, their aloofness. They mixed with the locals but they did not integrate with them.

Amongst the many associations and brotherhoods they took with them were those secret societies from which, in time, the Triads sprang.

2

OF RED EYEBROWS AND IRON SHINS

The Triad societies of today are historically, if distantly, descended from those secret associations and groups which fit into the long tradition of self-preservation through unity and patriotism dating back to the authoritarian Zhou dynasty. The need to club together to look after each other's interests is easily understood. The aspect of patriotism is somewhat more complex.

The emperor of China was considered divine, the Son of Heaven whose mandate was god-given. An absolute monarch, he ruled not only by heavenly right but also by personal example, morally and spiritually expected to gain the respect and loyalty of his subjects by his own probity, piety and benevolence. Should he fail to maintain high standards of behaviour, he was considered to have forfeited the Mandate of Heaven, his subjects justified in rising up and deposing him: indeed, such action was deemed their duty to the gods. Floods, famines, earthquakes, tidal waves, typhoons, droughts, eclipses and comets were all taken as omens sent by displeased deities to indicate that the emperor was not living up to his responsibilities and were considered just cause to overthrow him. From the earliest periods of Chinese history, therefore, rebellion has been part of the very fabric of national life.

The first secret society to be recorded originated in Shandong province. It was called the Chih Mei, or Red Eyebrows, because members painted their eyebrows scarlet to look more terrifying: demons had red eyelids. Their leader, Fan Tsung, was a patriot who set out to depose Wang Mang, a usurper who overthrew the Western Han dynasty in AD 9. The Red Eyebrows played a major role in Wang Mang's downfall, leading to his assassination and the establishment of the Eastern (or Later) Han dynasty in AD 25. After his demise, the Red Eyebrows continued to exist as bandits, becoming an embarrassment to the imperial administration they had assisted to power. The army was sent to suppress them, the bandits thrown into confusion by a wily general, Feng Yi, who ordered his troops to paint their eyebrows red, too. In the chaos, the outlaws were annihilated.

With the wiping out of the Red Eyebrows, a historical precedent was set. A secret society had responded patriotically and served the nation well, only to be subsequently persecuted by the regime it had supported.

The Red Eyebrows were not unique, for other secret societies existed in, or soon after, their time. The Tieh Ching (Iron Shins), Tung Ma (Copper Horses), Iron Necks, Green Groves and Big Spears also took part in various political activities, later degenerating from patriotism to outlawry or vanishing from sight.

Beyond self-interest or patriotic politics, however, lay another facet of Chinese life which encouraged the founding of secret societies: the administration of the

33

country itself, regardless of who might rule it. China's geographical vastness made absolute rule impossible. It had to be governed in autonomous provinces or districts. In the Early or Western Han dynasty, a civil-service bureaucracy was created which, although directly answerable to the emperor's central authority, seldom communicated with it. These local administrations were perfect bases for corruption and, being independent, autocratic and undemocratic, were virtually impossible to dismantle. This form of government lasted for 2,000 years, finally abandoned only with the foundation of the Republic of China in 1911. Even now, it lingers on in Communist China, with party cadres, local committees and regional assemblies.

To be a member of the civil service was to be highly respectable and feared. Commonly referred to as a mandarin, the civil servant had power over life and death, for he was tax collector, magistrate, judge and jury in his domain. Yet there was more to the job than ruling. There was profit. Being tax gatherers, and living in a system where tribute was common, mandarins became very rich and powerful. It is no wonder that competition in civil service examinations – the only method of recruitment – was extremely fierce. Hundreds of thousands of men sat the examination annually. Inevitably, many candidates failed to make the grade, yet to be eligible for entry in the first place they still had to be highly educated. The result was a large number of literate and erudite – but unemployed and unemployable – men who were disaffected and disenchanted with the system. They formed a subversive sub-class keen to attack the government which had refused them.

For most Chinese, life was basic and rural. China remained until modern times a peasant agricultural economy. Living a hand-to-mouth existence, peasants were quick to grasp anything which brought stability or security to their lives. One means of security lay in uniting with others. Private associations sprang up to protect rice- or wheat-growers from market exploitation; metalworkers, weavers, stonemasons and livestock farmers formed similar guilds. These became ideal platforms from which failed civil-service candidates could nurture dissent.

Once these associations became quasi-political and dissident, it was essential that they become secret. Throughout Chinese history dissension met with little response other than the executioner's sword, so survival depended on the loyalty of members which could only be guaranteed if it was well enforced. Ritual initiation, imposing religious as well as moral obligation, was the means employed. Three primary religious or philosophical foundations were drawn upon: Taoism, Confucianism and Buddhism, each with a vast lexicon of symbols, images, ceremonies and magical vocabularies.

Taoism, founded by Lao Tze, combined shamanism, alchemy and ancestor-worship. With Confucian precepts moulded on to it, it was just what the secret societies needed, for it emphasized the continuity of the family or clan, loyalty and respect for one's elders, and justice. What was more, Taoism was in part subversive and was occasionally proscribed, as was Buddhism. Both religions periodically became secret sects in response to suppression.

Around AD 170 a popular leader emerged in north-eastern China named Chang Chueh. Regarded by his followers as divine, he claimed supernatural powers as a healer, professing descent from Lao Tze. His reputation quickly spread and, by 180, his disciples had formed a society, the Yellow Turbans. Three years later, under the command of thirty-six generals, it had control of most of northern China. Originally inspired by political disaffection, the Yellow Turbans became not so much a government as a religious movement with selfish motives. Patriotism was not their *raison d'être*: like many religious cults throughout time, their leaders sought personal wealth.

The Yellow Turbans' revolt threw the imperial government into disarray and the Han dynasty fell. Anarchy ruled and the period known as the Three Kingdoms began. For forty-five years China was divided into the states of Wu, Shu and Wei. Yet out of this anarchical interregnum, three figures appeared who were to become mythical national heroes. According to legend, three of the thirty-six Yellow Turban generals, Chang Fei, Kwan Yu and Liu Pei (a member of the imperial Han royal family, the Chihli), met in a peach orchard where they sacrificed a white horse and a black ox, signifying good and evil, and swore a blood oath to be true to each other. Liu Pei became emperor of the Shu state, establishing his seat at Cheng-du. Kwan Yu, who was subsequently murdered by Liu Pei's enemies, was deified by the Ming emperor Wan Li in the late sixteenth century as Kwan Ti, the god of war, wealth, literature and – significantly for Triad history – oath-taking brotherhoods.

When the Three Kingdoms collapsed, the Western Tsin empire was founded by a Wei general. Then, in about AD 304, northern China subdivided again into the Sixteen Kingdoms, while southern China became the Eastern Tsin empire. In 581, the Sui dynasty briefly reunited China, re-established the temporarily banned Taoism and Buddhism, strengthened the Great Wall and paved the way for the first of the truly great dynasties, the T'ang. During the centuries of T'ang rule, however, Buddhism was thrice proscribed, going underground to establish its own secret organization, rich with symbolism and ritual which have remained a seminal part of Triad ceremonies ever since.

The T'ang dynasty's collapse in the early tenth century heralded forty years of disunity, an age known as the Five Dynasties and the Ten Kingdoms period. This was superseded in 960 by the Sung dynasty, in which Confucian values were reaffirmed and the civil service reorganized along traditional lines. Secret societies continued to thrive: the rise of one such group under the command of two rebel leaders, Lu Chun-yi and Sung Chiang, was chronicled in the reign of Hwei Tsung (1102–19). Towards the end of Sung rule, China came under threat from the Mongols. They deposed the Sung emperor and in 1280 Kublai Khan proclaimed himself the first emperor of the Yuan dynasty. Once again, China was ruled by foreigners.

Resistance to Mongol rule was widespread yet lacked cohesion and was centred in the south, where pro-Sung sentiments were strongest: the last Sung emperor and his brother had fled there, establishing a travelling court on the Kowloon peninsula in Hong Kong. Gradually, however, the anti-Mongol factions coalesced into a rebel alliance under three powers: a pirate called Fang

Kuo-chen, a Buddhist monk named Chu Yuan-chang and the Pah Lien or White Lotus Society.

The Pah Lien was, according to legend, founded in the fourth century by the famous Buddhist teacher Eon (Hwui-yin) at Rozan, south of the Yangtze River, where he set up a community worshipping the Amitabha Buddha, the Buddha of the Pure Land, a mystical plane attained by meditation. The community revolved around eighteen monks, the Eighteen Sages of Rozan. It survived the many persecutions of Buddhism over the centuries by – as was common amongst secret fraternities – changing its name to avoid discovery or infiltration, becoming the White Yang Society, the White Lily Society or the Incense Smelling Society. It also affiliated with other religion-based groups, such as the Eight Diagram (or Celestial Principles) Sect, the Nine Mansions Sect and the T'ien-ti Hui or Heaven and Earth Society, which was also known as the Hung Society.

In 1344, the White Lotus Society was revived by Han Shan-tung, who, in collaboration with four other rebel leaders, Liu Fu-tung, Li Erh, Tu Tsun-tao and Su Shou-hui, rose against the Mongols with an army recruited by fraudulently claiming blood descent from the emperor Hwei Tsung and declaring the imminent reincarnation of Buddha. This army, known as the Red Turban Rebels because of their scarlet headbands, destabilized the Yuan dynasty. The society was then joined by a Buddhist acolyte, Chu Yuan-chang. An experienced strategist, he overthrew the Mongols and in 1368 became Hung Wu, the first Ming emperor. Never before had a secret society overthrown an entire administration to found a new dynasty, which, in this instance, was even named by the White Lotus Society after two prophets sent by Buddha to establish peace and order from revolutionary chaos.

That Hung Wu was Chinese was of vital importance. At last, China was ruled by one of her own, a true Chinaman from the provinces south of the Yangtze River: the nearer a man's ancestry to the ancient land of Yueh, the more Chinese he is considered – a distinction still good today. His being Chinese also vindicated the White Lotus Society, which was seen as a gallant and honourable defender of the nation.

For most of the three centuries of Ming rule, the White Lotus Society remained politically detached, neither officially recognized nor proscribed. However, in the reign of Tien Ki (1621–8) it supported a rebel called Su Hung-yu. Quite why it took against the emperor is uncertain, although patriotism of a kind must have played a part: China suffered severe droughts and famines during his reign, throwing his righteousness into question. Northern invaders also stirred up insurrection and Tien Ki was killed in battle. The society remained dormant through the following years of civil strife, which came to an end in 1644 when China was conquered by the Manchus, whose tenure of the Mandate of Heaven, the Q'ing dynasty, was to last into the twentieth century.

The next documented record of the White Lotus Society is in an imperial edict issued by the second Q'ing emperor, K'ang-hsi, in 1662, which rigorously proscribed secret societies along with Buddhism and Taoism. Temples were closed, monasteries shut. Taoists were branded superstitious charlatans and priests caught selling charms were executed. K'ang-hsi painted himself into a political

39

corner: he controlled China, but Ming sympathies ran high, remaining so throughout the whole dynastic period. Other edicts followed banning other societies: the White Lily Society, the Incense Burning Society, the Origin of Chaos Society, the Origin of the Dragon Society and the Hung Society were specifically named. The secret societies went underground and became a focus for pro-Ming insurgence; they formed alliances and began to develop common rituals, secret signs and passwords.

The White Lotus Society gradually disappeared. However, it seems not to have died but to have metamorphosed into or joined up with the Hung Society (sometimes referred to as the Hung League). It was last heard playing a major role in 1814 when a mutiny amongst eunuchs in the imperial palace in Beijing was blamed on the White Lotus Society – or the Three Incense Sticks Society, the White Feather Society, the Rationalist Society or the Eight Diagram Sect, all of which were interrelated. Planned by Li Wan-cheng and Lin Ching and assisted by corrupt eunuchs, it coincided with uprisings in Henan and Shandong provinces. Loyal palace eunuchs held the rebels at bay but provincial towns fell to them and officials were massacred before imperial forces quashed the revolt, putting whole populations to the sword. In the town of Hua, 20,000 citizens were executed, although most were innocent of insurrection. It was the last time the White Lotus Society openly instigated a rebellion, although members joined other occasional uprisings and the society certainly did not become extinct. It still existed in 1900, in the far north of China where it was called the Tsai Lin Society, adherents forswearing wine, tobacco and opium.

As the White Lotus Society transmuted, it was renamed the Sam Hop Wui, or the Three United Society. Members saw the world as tripartite, a unity of the three main powers of nature: heaven, earth and man. Many of the early society flags, used in ceremonies or paraded into battle, bore a triangle. Both the name and the emblem are the origin of the modern term for all Chinese secret societies – the Triads. That said, it is predominantly the non-Chinese world which uses this name: the Chinese themselves refer to the societies either under their individual names or, collectively, as Hak Sh'e Wui, the Black Society.

Exactly when the Hung Society (the Hung Mun in Cantonese) formed is unknown. It just emerged by the organic aggregation of other societies into a united whole. Whilst a society of the same name did exist in the fourteenth century, it most likely came into being – in this incarnation – in 1674, in the thirteenth year of K'ang-hsi's reign: it was certainly well established by 1700. The centres of its activities were the provinces of Fujian and Guangdong, especially the city of Guangzhou formerly known as Canton. At first it was predominantly religious, its main deity being Kwan Ti, who was by now revered by a number of secret societies. To protect itself from infiltration by Manchu agents, the Hung Society, in time-honoured fashion, took a variety of cover names.

One figure who undoubtedly fought for the Ming cause was the son of a Ming official, the famous pirate Cheng Ch'eng-kung. Known in English as Koxinga, derived from his title Kuo Hsing Yeh (Lord of the Imperial Surname), his influence was extensive in his native Fujian. Despite some military success, he was

41

forced to retreat to Taiwan, where, in 1661, he drove out the Dutch settlers, establishing a base from which he sought support from Chinese settlers in the Philippines. He died in 1662, aged thirty-eight, his military ambitions unrealized. Some believe the Hung Society was founded by Cheng with values developed from two classical Chinese novels, *San Kuo Yen Yi* (The Romance of the Three Kingdoms) and *Shui-hu-ch'uan* (The Water Margin), the latter concerning a band of outlaws living in a marshland called Liang-san Po. However, this is unproven.

The third Q'ing emperor, K'ang-hsi's son Yin-chen (1722–35), furthered his father's proscription by publishing edicts against specific secret societies, including the White Lily Society, the White Lotus Society and the T'ien-ti Hui (Heaven and Earth Society), the Hung Society's most widely used alias. Under this name, the society proclaimed its aims of moral reform, the furtherance of religious belief and practice, the encouragement of Chinese nationalism and coined the famous catchphrase which has echoed down the years of Triad history, *Fan q'ing – fuk ming*: 'Overthrow the Q'ing – restore the Ming'.

It was during Yin-chen's reign that the true historical beginnings of the Triads lay. The pivotal event was the destruction of the Shao Lin (Shiu Lam or Siu Lam) monastery although the actual date is unknown and the subject of conjecture. The monks, superb strategists and martial-arts experts, assisted the emperor in a campaign against the Eleuths, a Mongol tribe from the far north-west. However, once they had defeated the Eleuths, they were perceived to be a political threat, suffering the same fate as the Red Eyebrows 1,500 years before. It is on this event, as we shall see, that the Triads base their traditional history and legend.

Other rebellions came and went. In 1761 the emperor Kien-lung issued an edict against the Hung Society, the Ming Tsuen (Illustrious Worthies) and the Pah Yün (White Cloud Society). In 1775 a White Lotus Society official, Liú Sung, started to raise a following which led to an insurrection in 1794. Commanded by Liu Chi-hieh, it raged across western China, putting up a young man called Wang Fa-sheng as rightful claimant to the imperial throne by declaring his descent from the Ming emperors. The rebellion lasted a decade. Thousands were killed and the imperial exchequer spent a fortune. Wang vanished without trace. At the same time, another society official, Wang Lung, raised a revolt in Shandong. Over 100,000 died by the sword as a result and he was executed.

The Hung Society, however, survived.

3

THE T'IEN-TI HUI

By the mid-eighteenth century, the evolution of the
Heaven and Earth Society was well under way. A secret
political underground movement was forming, bound
together by religiously inspired ritual, headed by members
of the educated, literate, disaffected Chinese élite who
were patriotically dedicated to the concept of *fan q'ing –
fuk ming*. However, whilst it has been regarded by many as
primarily a political organization, it was in fact far more a
society similar to the present-day *kai fong* associations
which are common in Hong Kong and Chinese communities around the world. These are philanthropic
mutual-aid or friendly societies, which today run hospitals, orphanages, temples, schools, old folks' day centres
and other charities, collecting money through flag days
and by donation from altruistic businessmen.

The T'ien-ti Hui was just such an association. Life in
China was, at best, harsh. Under the Q'ing rulers, the
Chinese were well and truly subjugated: it was under
Q'ing law that Chinese men had to wear their hair in
plaited queues as a sign of their inferiority and submis-
sion. (The English slang for a queue – pigtail – comes

from the Manchus, who referred to Chinese as pigs.) The rural economy teetered from calamity to disaster and the borders of China were extended outwards – the Manchus were expansionist colonials. Simultaneously, the Chinese population increased dramatically, undeveloped areas coming under agriculture until all viable land was saturated. China's vast problem of overpopulation, still one of the greatest social and environmental dilemmas on earth, was instigated by the Q'ing emperors who required peasants to work the land and maintain the economy.

The peasants who lacked land or could find no work were in dire straits and turned for assistance to such societies as the T'ien-ti Hui, with their religious obligations to help the underprivileged. As land pressures rose, the peasants were forced to migrate, away from their clan or home areas. Once in strange country, where they were outsiders, they banded together for protection and mutual support or, where societies already existed, they joined them. History repeated itself. As in the Zhou dynasty, self-interest fraternities sprang up based upon clan, family or place of origin. In southern China, where at the beginning of the migration there was still land to be had, migrants not only set up brotherhoods but built their own villages, many of them fortified.

When the T'ien-ti Hui appeared, it was a boom time for the birth of secret societies. Its founders came from Zhangpu county in Fujian province, from which they migrated to Sichuan. There they allied themselves to a probably Taoist monk or priest called Ma Jiu-long. With him, they set up a mutual-benefit society the name of which has not survived. Returning later to Fujian, they took their society with them. Another monk, Zheng Kai (or Tixi), who had joined them, settled at the Kwan Yin temple in Gaoxi where he recruited three disciples. They, in turn, initiated more members and extended the society through Fujian and into Taiwan. As migration increased, the society spread to Guangdong and Guangxi provinces. Membership covered a wide social spectrum, from merchants and coolies to educated scholars, illiterate farmers, priests and monks. Some were migrants, some local residents. The T'ien-ti Hui became an important agent of social integration, joining disparate men in a common aim.

As a mutual-benefit organization, the T'ien-ti Hui promised more than philanthropic support. It offered a means of identity for migrants and, in turn, protected them, setting up a social-security network throughout southern China, acting for its members as a *hui guan* – a place association exclusively for those who come from a common village or county. For the Chinese, to be able to relate back to one's family village or area is of paramount cultural and spiritual importance: many overseas Chinese, even those born and raised as expatriates today, harbour a dream of returning 'home', if only to be buried with their ancestors. For the dislocated peasants, the *hui guan* provided social gatherings, lodging houses or business premises, financial assistance in the form of loans and a primitive banking system for the transference of funds. It also provided a marriage-arrangement service, organized funerals, fixed travel tickets or warrants or passes, managed properties it owned and, like a trade guild, regulated business. It was, in short, a social corporation which raised funds from prosperous members and worshippers of the *hui guan*'s patron god in the association's own temple.

The T'ien-ti Hui was more open than the usual *hui guan*. It did not have such strict membership qualifications, but it nevertheless provided the same services, initiating members at ceremonies before a patron deity and images of Tixi. All members were bound to be loyal to the society, abide by its aims, protect their brothers and further the society by introducing new members. Once joined, a member was given his *hua ti* or membership certificate (usually printed on cotton or silk) and the society's secrets, consisting of hand signs, passwords and esoteric prayers, were revealed to him.

Yet there was another side to the T'ien-ti Hui's provision for members. It was typical of the way many such societies developed. In 1788, a senior official in Taiwan stated, 'At first, people were eager to join the society because, if they had a wedding or a funeral to give, they could obtain financial assistance from other society members. If they came to blows with someone, fellow members would help them. If they met with robbers or bandits, as soon as the robbers heard the secret code of their society, they would leave them alone.' Financial help aside, the strong arm of the society was available to avenge its members on thieves, competitors or anyone – including the authorities or people of another province or clan (and, therefore, of another society) – who sought to extort or cheat them. In other words, the society operated a semi-benevolent protection racket and it was not long before this facility became, across southern China, the primary reason for members to join.

The T'ien-ti Hui quickly became a means of exercising

what is known as *xie dou*, the southern Chinese version of the vendetta and some T'ien-ti Hui branches were established solely for this purpose. A perpetual state of violent social conflict between clans, families and *hui guan* groups developed and rumbled on into the nineteenth century, providing the Q'ing authorities with a continual law-enforcement problem.

T'ien-ti Hui finances came from a number of sources. Cash offerings to the society's temples, income from properties rented or leased and interest on loans all flowed into the coffers, but by far the greatest source was membership dues. New recruits had to pay not only the society entrance and subscription fees but also a tribute to their referees for promoting their membership. Office-bearers gained a steady income, for they were the only people who could propose candidates. Fees and tributes could be the equivalent of a month's wages for an ordinary peasant: in 1808, initiation fees in Taiwan were as high as 2 *yuan* in silver, the cost of a valuable beast such as a ploughing buffalo. In some provinces, members had to pay separately to receive their *hua ti*. Therefore it was in the member's interest not only to join for protection but also to enrol others to offset his own outlay and turn a profit.

The society, therefore, which was set up to fight (amongst other things) the extortion of its members, soon took to exercising its own extortion on them. From here, it was a short step into downright criminality and some T'ien-ti Hui societies were established specifically as criminal fraternities involved in robbery, especially in Taiwan and Guangdong, by the late eighteenth century. They did not rob their own members but those of rival clans and societies, often conducting their crimes in the name of *xie dou*. This penchant for robbery was another motive for joining: become a member and avoid being robbed.

Additionally, the T'ien-ti Hui also took on a political dimension. This was a conscious decision made by society leaders, yet criminality was again involved. As early as 1767, Lu Mao, the leader of the first T'ien-ti Hui uprising, recruited members who, after they were sworn in, were informed that they were to pillage the local official warehouse and treasury, as well as the homes of the gentry and landowners, to raise capital to finance a revolt against the Q'ing authorities. Needless to say, Lu made a profit on the deal, charging initiation fees and taking a cut 'for the society' of the loot acquired. In the name of a member and a supposed descendant of the Sung dynastic royal line, Zhao Liang-ming, the uprising was held the following year. It was an abysmal failure.

In 1802, in Guangdong, revolt flared up again when a T'ien-ti Hui society attacked some rival villages. Imperial troops were sent in. Later troubles arose when different societies joined battle or seized the day. In 1832, for example, the Chinese garrison in Guangzhou was sent to suppress a Yao tribal uprising in Guangxi, caused by the Yao minority complaining that society members had been rustling their cattle and stealing crops. With the army *in absentia*, a society moved into the region around Macau, levied their own stiff taxes on local farmers and faced a peasants' revolt as a result. Yet most of these so-called political revolutions were little more than *xie dou* skirmishes. The restoration of the Ming dynasty had little to do with any of them. *Fan q'ing – fuk ming* was far from members' minds: turning a quick *yuan* was what really counted.

In 1807, in response to one of the revolts, an imperial edict was published to suppress a society named the T'in Han Hui, or Family of the Queen of Heaven, which was reported to be involved in criminal activity. Imperial troops were posted south and the society engaged. Soon after, it was reported that the society had been suppressed. This was a lie. The military commanders were telling their emperor what he wanted to hear to save their own hides. The emperor, however, knew the truth: the society existed right across China and even into neighbouring states such as Siam, Cochin-China and, to the north, Korea. Another effort was made to eradicate it. Those in charge claimed they had executed every member, but this was further procrastination. To slay every member would have been to decimate the population, for hundreds of thousands had sworn the society's oaths.

For a few years, the society kept a low profile but later re-emerged, first in 1813 as the Ts'ing-liu-Kiu then as the T'ien-ti Hui once more. It did, however, now restrict most of its activities to Guangdong province and Guangzhou, the regional capital and the biggest city south of the Yangtze. Here it went under the name of the San-ho Hui, or sometimes, the Three Rivers Society, an apt name as Guangzhou stands on the confluence of the Xi Jiang, the Bei Jiang and the Dong Jiang – the West, North and East Rivers. Being based in a major port, it was not long before the society expanded overseas to Chinese communities in Java, Malaya and as far as India and Ceylon.

The bigger it grew, the more the imperial powers tried

to suppress it. They failed. It was impossible to fight secrecy. The society was driven further underground, its members becoming increasingly marginalized, outlawed, desperate and dangerous.

4

THE BIRTH OF THE TRIADS

The T'ien-ti Hui established by Fujianese migrants was not unique. The Cantonese from Guangdong also had their own societies. Merchants, stevedores, shroffs (merchants' accountants and tallymen), clerks, compradores (mercantile middle-men), farmers, carpenters, herbalists, doctors – every profession or trade had its society, usually clandestine. The authorities regarded them all as potential trouble so most hid behind legal fronts. Alongside the legitimate societies were those of pirates, brigands or professional criminals, who used them, including the T'ien-ti Hui, as organizations through which to control gambling, extortion, protection and even kidnapping. With some T'ien-ti Hui lodges being criminalized in any case, it was not long before all societies became corrupt.

There were rich pickings for criminal fraternities. Initiation fees, gambling and other criminality apart, there was, from the late eighteenth century, also opium. Strictly illegal in China, it was being imported in ever-increasing amounts by foreign traders, predominantly British, French and American, who were shipping it through

Macau and Guangzhou, ports where business with foreigners was permitted. Chinese merchants accepted it and joined the business with foreigners, back-handing mandarins right up to provincial gubernatorial and vice-regal level. The actual landing of the drug was carried out by criminal organizations or associations of junk and sampan operators who had the river and civil servants attached to the regional mandarin's *yamen*, or administrative headquarters in their pockets. Distribution from the merchants' godowns or warehouses was often conducted by professional criminals. Those who did not assist in the trade made substantial gains by robbing, or taking protection money not to rob, vessels bringing it ashore.

As with the countless clan or family associations and *hui guan*, these many societies were disparate organizations with no central committee or binding power. Yet there was an overall slang word for them: Men of Hung. The name was of considerable significance, for it was that of the first Ming emperor, Hung Wu, who frequently appeared in Buddhist texts prophesying doom and whose name was often used as a meditative incantation. So sacred or secret was the word *hung*, it was rarely spoken aloud and was dissected into its constituent parts. The left side of the written character consisted of three dots; at the base were two dots rather like the character for 8 (the number signifying wealth); at the centre was the single line meaning the number 1; whilst the top consisted of a contraction of the number 20. To avoid uttering it, members would speak of 3–8–21 or 5 and 21. The Men of Hung were further separated into three divisions, the Tien-ti Hui, the San Tien Hui (Three Dots Society) and the San-ho Hui or Three Harmonies Society.

53

In China, a secret society was generally known as either a *hui* – an association – or a *chiao*, meaning a sect. The authorities had other names for them: *hsieh-chiao* (vicious sects), *wei-chiao* (false-god sects), *chiao-fei* (bandit sects), *yin-chiao* (obscene sects) and *yao-chiao* (perverse sects). All the *hui* were politically dissident and opposed to the authority of the emperor, regardless of what their other activities encompassed. The leaders' authority, in lieu of the emperor's, was absolute and members were bound to them not only by oaths of allegiance but also because they often came from the same clan or place. Some Triad societies even called themselves a family rather than a *hui*.

In many instances, especially amongst overseas Chinese communities, the *hui* became the dominant controllers of society. Where authority was weak, the *hui*s acted in its stead. They organized their own courts, tried their own felons and executed, beat or fined them, arbitrated in disputes, witnessed contracts of business and marriage, carried out social-benefit activities, acted as go-betweens in confrontations between the Chinese community and the local government, and provided relief in times of hardship.

Above all, however, they were ruthless outlaws who robbed, pillaged, killed, kidnapped and extorted from the landowning and merchant classes under the slogan of *Ta fu – chih p'in* (Hit the rich and help the poor). Yet these were no Robin Hoods. They attacked *yamen* buildings, imperial supply convoys, government stores, imperial cargo junks on the rivers and canals, barracks and prisons to release their comrades, but it was to their own coffers, or those of their leaders, that the bulk of their loot was directed.

54

Occasionally, civilian victims struck back, but this was rare. It was not just because the Triads were powerful and vengeful but because their victims believed, as did many, that they had an almost divine right to do what they did: they were religiously constituted, rooted in Chinese history and legend. The medieval outlaw heroes of *Shui-hu-ch'uan* were known to everyone and gave the Triads an aura of tradition: in China, tradition counts for much.

The *huis'* dissidence ran to religion as well as politics. Their religious precepts were still Confucian, but contrary to official Confucianism for they mixed Confucian teachings with Buddhist, Taoist and pagan doctrines. Spirits and demons, prophets and fortune-tellers, magicians and sages, necromancy and geomancy mingled with Taoism and Buddhism in the rituals of all the societies, offering members, through this pool of religious ideals, immortality and a better after-life.

This religious aspect, the hunt for eternal happiness, appealed to the peasant recruits making up the bulk of Triad membership and whatever the societies could do to bolster the religio-magical aspects of their organizations, the better. Meetings were always held at night, the hours when devils roamed the world, and if possible took place on sparsely populated hills or mountain tops, away from the plains and valleys where imperial power held sway amongst the agricultural society. Of course, night also hid the gathering and upland was usually forested, inaccessible and underpopulated, but these were minor considerations. Mountains were also where the gods lived and those seeking eternal life or their company went to commune with them. The most senior official in a Triad society is still referred to as the *shan chu*, the Master of the Mountain.

As the nineteenth century progressed, Triad societies started to attract a wider range of membership. Along with the traditional disaffected scholars and peasants, new sections of society started to join. Merchants entered the ranks, partly as insurance against robbery. *Yamen* officials joined to bolster their inadequate earnings: civil-service salaries have always been low in China, officials expected to improve on them by other means, thus encouraging corruption. Demobilized imperial soldiers signed on, partly because they were only employed crisis by crisis and, between conflicts, were reduced to vagrancy which was punishable by execution. With the gradual opening up of more Chinese ports to Western trade in the early nineteenth century, there was a mass migration to the coastal cities of Guangzhou, Xiamen (then called Amoy), Fuzhou, Ningbo, Shanghai and, later, Hong Kong. Mostly rural agricultural peasants, the migrants were out of their usual environment, the only stable factor in their lives being secret societies. They were recruited in droves.

Many of the merchants or landowners who joined had motives other than insurance. They saw the Triads as a way to increase their own wealth. In simple terms, they invested in Triad activity, bankrolling robbery heists, providing arms or safe houses, fingering potentially lucrative kidnap victims, acting as spies in imperial circles, engaging heavily in the opium trade, bribing officials who were their social peers and fencing stolen goods through their legitimate businesses. Everyone in or associated with a Triad society was a winner. The presence of the wealthy was crucial. Cash flow was always a problem and subscription or initiation fees rarely sufficient. Triad societies were rather like pyramid savings schemes: they had to keep expanding to avoid collapsing. By 1890, participation by the wealthy in Triad activity was so great that it had become a major factor in the developing economic structure of China.

The imperial authorities had one reaction towards the Triads. If they caught them, they killed them. Execution of members was mandatory. Associates, agents or those aiding or abetting were systematically and imaginatively tortured for information before facing a public beheading. In practice, however, things were different. *Yamen* clerks were frequently Triad spies. Mandarins not infrequently looked the other way to avoid being murdered in retribution. In places, they even encouraged the Triads in order to gain more imperial financial aid, a percentage of which automatically disappeared into their purses with a cut going to the Triads. It was not unknown for local governors to carry out fictitious or premeditatedly unsuccessful attacks on Triad societies, with their connivance, in order to keep their credibility intact.

In short, the Triad societies were all things to all men. To the Q'ing rulers, they were cut-throats and dissidents of the worst kind, threatening social order, attacking garrisons and perpetually stirring rebellion. To the peasants, they were heroes who protected them, supported them, gave them an identity and often employed them. To the wealthy, they were a thorn in the side but, simultaneously, an opportunity to gain further riches. To the religious community, they were dissidents, but they kept religion alive and had done so historically when

57

the various faiths were proscribed. To their members, they were a source of spiritual and material enrichment, a secure environment of self-interest.

The first disturbance to be carried out by one of these outlaw societies, which are now considered to be Triad societies in the modern sense, took place in Taiwan in 1787. Concentrated in the mountains east of Changhua, it was organized by one Lin Shuang-wan. A second rebellion occurred in 1814, prompted by the capture and execution of a leader called Chung Ti-kang, with a third in 1816, under the leadership of Hu Ping-yao, who, with his Pure Water Society, put up a pretender to the throne and was put to death for his effort. The following year, a purge in Guangzhou was conducted with little effect. It was not until 1827 that the Q'ing authorities believed they had made a breakthrough after a victorious battle: they were, of course, mistaken. The Triad octopus merely lost one sucker from one tentacle. More insurrection occurred in Guangxi province, commanded by two men, Li Lap-ting and Hung Chun-nin, during the reign of Hsien-feng (1851–61). Like the others, it failed, resulting in mass reprisals and thousands of society members having to flee into exile.

By the middle of the nineteenth century, then, the Triads had become a massive alternative subculture thoroughly integrated into Chinese society, addressing imperial injustice, righting imperial wrongs, and appearing both indispensable and invincible.

5

HUNG HSIU-CH'UAN, YASOO
AND THE RED TURBAN REBELS

During the Opium War (1839–42), Guangdong was in turmoil and, over the following decade, began to disintegrate. Triad societies encouraged the collapse, recruiting widely, inciting mayhem, stirring up anti-foreign sentiments (but also provisioning foreign ships) and promoting their patriotism by announcing their anti-Q'ing dogma. Whole villages came over to the Triads, especially in remote areas lacking clan or place associations. Village elders' responsibilities for social order were handed over to the secret societies, which brought in new values appealing to younger men – the glamour of secrecy, the camaraderie of brotherhood, the promise of a bit of action and the tough-man stance of an organization in which the martial arts were encouraged.

Emboldened by success, the Triads demanded protection money from mandarins and regional governors. They paid up to keep the peace and their lives, ignoring anti-secret-society legislation and conveniently forgetting to report the state of affairs. When, in 1846, the news of the protection racket finally leaked out, a huge drive to suppress the Triads was instigated, using locally raised militia. It failed. The militia was paid by local merchants, many of whom were in league with the Triads, who, to maintain the status quo in Guangdong, quietened down for a while. Further up the coast, it was Triad business as usual. In Xiamen, a Singaporean Chinese merchant, Chen Ching-chen, started the Small Sword Society. He was captured, tortured and executed by strangulation, but his society survived under a successor, Huang Wei. In 1853, the society played havoc with Xiamen, holding the city for some months before moving on to Shanghai, which it virtually controlled for two years under the command of a Cantonese Triad leader, Le Li-ch'uan. It was only with the aid of foreign troops that Le was eventually driven out. His hold on Shanghai had lasted so long because the imperial forces were simultaneously struggling with a far greater problem. They were busy fighting the Taiping Rebellion.

The Taiping Rebellion (*tai ping* means universal peace or harmony) was instigated and led by Hung Hsiu-ch'uan (1814–64), the son of a Hakka farmer from the village of Guanlubu, 50 km north of Guangzhou. He was a bizarre figure, yet his rebellion almost succeeded in toppling the Q'ing dynasty, something the Triads had been aiming at for decades. They had not triumphed partly because they were primarily looking out for their own ends, their followers not united. Hung's disciples were.

Hung was an educated man; he had been a candidate in the civil-service examinations in 1836 but had failed them, his failure not necessarily due to inability. He was a Hakka, a 'guest person', one of an ethnic group which had migrated south from central China in the 1680s, and was therefore not considered a local Cantonese; despite compensations allowing Hakkas less of a handicap in the exams, there was still much racial resentment against them. Furthermore, he sat the examinations in Guangzhou where the examiners were dubious about his peasant background. His failure embittered him, just as failure had embittered generations of candidates, but he did not revert to a secret society to assuage his anger. He took a different course.

Christianity was gaining a foothold in Guangdong. In Guangzhou and Macau, foreign missionaries were at work, publishing tracts and making converts. One of the proselytes of the teachings of Yasoo (Jesus) was a man called Liang A-fa, who, having been baptized by no less a figure than the great Robert Morrison, translator of the Bible into Chinese, spread the Word of Christ by handing out pamphlets to civil-service candidates at the Guangzhou examination hall. Hung got hold of one and decided to start a holy war against the emperor, the local landowners and the established religions. He formed the Society of God Worshippers, the religious basis of which was a hodgepodge of Christianity (Protestant and Roman Catholic), Confucianism, Buddhism, Taoism and his own invention. He interpreted, reinterpreted, twisted and manipulated whatever he needed to fit his doctrine until, by 1848, after some initial setbacks and brushes with the Q'ing authorities, he had a powerful army under his command. The appeal of the Taiping movement was threefold: it was patriotically anti-Q'ing, had a revolutionary religious foundation (of sorts) and sought to overthrow the avaricious landlords.

At first, the Q'ing authorities considered the Yasoo-worshippers nothing more than a temporary fringe sect undeserving of military attention. The Triads were keeping them busy enough, having recently held a large recruiting campaign in Guangxi and the Pearl River delta area, re-arming themselves with modern Western weapons purchased through traders in the embryonic British colony of Hong Kong. Under the audacious command of a famous Triad leader, Ling Shih-pa, they besieged the town of Wuzhou, established toll stations on the rivers feeding from the west into the delta south of Guangzhou, and levied taxes on every passing vessel. As the rivers were the highways of the area, this proved to be a highly lucrative enterprise. Gambling, which was illegal but ubiquitous in Chinese society, was transferred from Guangzhou, where the authorities constantly disrupted it, to Guiping in Guangxi, 350 km up the Xi Jiang. Faced with such brazenness, the authorities directed their attention to the Triads and pirate fleets moving upriver to escape a concerted British anti-piracy drive around Hong Kong. By the time the Taiping Rebellion got under way, it was too late for the authorities to act and the uprising spread like a cane fire across southern China.

All was swept before the Taiping tide. Despite only a rudimentary understanding of Christianity, Hung and his followers had become fanatical Yasoo believers, their zeal directed both at China's established religions and at imperial authority. Temples were destroyed, monasteries sacked, clan halls burned, idols desecrated and monks massacred. All opposition was met with less than Christian charity: if you supported the rebels, you joined them; if you did not you were killed. The fear of God took on a special connotation.

Within three years, the Taiping army reached the banks of the Yangtze River and, in 1851, the capital Nanjing fell. Renaming it Tianjing, the Celestial Capital, Hung proclaimed the Heavenly Kingdom of Great Peace with, of course, himself as emperor of the Taiping Tien Kuo dynasty, which was not finally put down until 1864, when Hung committed suicide. It is estimated that over 35 million people died as a result of the Taiping Rebellion, much of China being laid waste in the process.

To what extent Hung's Heavenly Kingdom of Great Peace had been aided by the Triads' Heaven and Earth Society has long been a puzzle. The Q'ing authorities believed that they were in league, but the Taiping leaders denied any connection. They wanted, they claimed, to establish a completely new ruling dynasty, not to bring back an old one. Hung, who made up his own Ten Commandments, actually hit out at the Triads by making drinking alcohol, smoking opium and gambling a sin. He even went so far as publicly to accuse the Triad societies of being evil. Yet the truth is not quite so clear cut.

The Taiping rebels and the Triads had a lot in common. Both were anti-Q'ing and used the lucky colour red in their banners. Even the phrase *tai ping* was incorporated into Triad ritual, referring to the Tai Ping Market (the Market of Universal Peace), a place in their legendary history. Triads sometimes even called themselves 'men of Taiping'. There were other, closer links forged by rank-and-file Triads joining the Taiping forces. At least one Triad society leader, Luo Dao-gang, who was a Pearl River opium runner, fought with them and the Taiping rebels received some Western weapons which they most likely obtained with the connivance of Hong Kong Triads.

Whatever alliances did occur, they were temporary. The Triads had no desire to associate with the eclectic, eccentric Taiping disciples, who quoted from the 'Yasoo Book' during ceremonies, made Taoist offerings at clan altars and acknowledged the Eighteen Hells of Buddhism but also burned down every Buddhist and Taoist structure they came across, slaughtering the priests and monks. Nevertheless, the Triads were also pragmatists and did not actively turn against the Taiping rebels. It would have been bad for business. Besides, the Taiping Rebellion drew the imperial Q'ing dogs off their tails for a while.

While the imperial army was occupied with the Taiping rebels, the Triads were busy massing an army in the south. As well as Le Li-ch'uan and the Small Sword Society taking Xiamen and Shanghai, other Triads besieged Guangzhou and Guilin. Yet, although these gains could so easily have been consolidated, no effort was made to build upon them. Why this advantage was not grasped is another puzzle. Possibly the Triads and the Taipings did have a loose alliance: to consolidate would have meant crossing Hung. Perhaps they overstretched themselves and were short of funds or manpower. Or maybe they were already losing their political will, the ideal of *fan q'ing – fuk ming* diluted by the success of their criminal endeavour.

The Taiping rebels may not have been in alliance with the secret societies, but they offered them aid when it suited their purpose. They had close links with a movement which held sway over the plains of northern China and Manchuria for fifteen years – the Red Beards, who painted their faces black with a red beard, making them look like the fearsome demons in popular theatre. Formed in 1797 and supported by peasants, they took advantage of China's turmoil to rise to regional power, which they exercised with more justice, social awareness and compassion than the official government until they were finally toppled in 1868.

Harried by the Taiping Rebellion and paranoid about the Triads, the Q'ing authorities in Guangdong and Guangxi, hoping to deal with both errant birds with one stone, decided to act with a heavy hand. A campaign of suppression was mounted but proved financially disastrous. With foreign trade down because of the troubles, tax and customs receipts were low and it was not long before the imperial forces ran out of money. To make ends meet, they demanded contributions from rich landowners and merchants, who were obliged to pay up but, in turn, raised their rents on tenant farmers, who had already suffered a succession of poor harvests caused by typhoons and flooding. Many peasants moved to Guangzhou, only to discover the city in a state of semi-anarchy. Supplies were cut off from the north by the Taiping forces. Foreign traders were either doing little business or had sailed for safety to Macau or Hong Kong. It was not long before there was open revolt against the authorities and their tax regime. The official backlash was severe. Whole villages were ordered to hand over Triad occupants: when they refused, their entire populations were executed and the buildings razed. Nothing could have been more calculated to cause unrest: it gave rise to a veritable regiment of vengeance-seekers under the leadership of a well-known pirate, Ho Lu.

This, in 1854, began the famous Red Turban revolt. Within weeks, the whole delta region, from Hong Kong up to Guangzhou, down to Macau and along the coast to Chixi, was in the hands of a dozen rebel units wearing red headbands. They attacked schools run by the Q'ing administration, wealthy landowners, local barracks and *yamen* buildings. At their instigation, villages set up their own Triad societies and joined in. The authorities armed the biggest landowners from the Guangzhou armoury and a small number resisted the rebels, but most did not interfere: after all, some of them were Triad allies. By the summer of 1854, the Red Turbans had complete and uncontested control of the Pearl River delta.

All looked favourable for the Red Turbans – but it was not. They were united in cause but disunited in fact. It was not long before both food and money started to run out. Squabbling broke out over how to raise funds and who had the right to loot where. With no central command, looting often did more damage than good. Weak leadership in the rebel units permitted looting in order to buy loyalty from the 'troops'. This disenfranchised and annoyed the locals, who had misguidedly thought they were being rescued from the overbearing, over-taxing Q'ing. Places of strategic importance were pillaged rather than captured and garrisoned.

One Triad leader, Chen Kai, realized the error of looting. He captured Foshan, an important town south-west of Guangzhou, and knew that if he held it, he could control the western approaches to the city. He forbade looting, instead taxing the richer locals. The locals, seeing him to be fair, transferred their loyalty to him; the imperial army, meanwhile, realized he was smarter than the rest and therefore posed a real threat. The result was the heavy bombardment and destruction of Foshan, forcing Chen to raise taxes, which, in turn, diverted local loyalties away from him.

With local resistance to the rebels increasing, the authorities gained the upper hand. The Red Turbans were defeated in battle on 7 March 1855 at Huangpu, east of Guangzhou. There followed a period of blood-letting as the authorities embarked upon an extensive eradication campaign. Mass executions became a daily feature, with rotas of executioners employed to keep up with the demand. Informers were everywhere, some making good money by betraying their neighbours to save their own necks or settle old scores. *Xie dou* was the order of the day.

During this reign of terror, many Triads realized there was only one way to survive. They had to find a safe haven, beyond the reach of imperial power. There was one ideal place to make for and they did so, in droves, travelling as boatmen or coolies.

That safe haven was Hong Kong, where, protected by British law, they settled, establishing new societies alongside existing ones, initiating locals in nocturnal ceremonies on the many summits of the mountainous island. It was only a matter of months before they were thoroughly assimilated into the local population.

6

VEGETARIANS, RICE CHRISTIANS AND FOREIGN DEVILS

As the nineteenth century advanced, the imperial powers faced new problems. In 1863, Chinese Muslims revolted; seven years later, Chinese Turkestan erupted in rebellion. These two insurgencies were the greatest of nearly 100 outbreaks of unrest between the end of the Taiping Rebellion in 1864 and 1885. Some were Triad-inspired but most were not. Many societies had reverted to protecting members and organizing trade-union-type groups. Many others, no longer political, existed as criminal fraternities, racketeering and thieving as before. Yet at the same time they also found a new cause to espouse: opposition to the increasing presence of foreigners in the Celestial Kingdom.

The Portuguese were the first European traders to arrive on the China coast. In 1514, they built a small fort and trading post near the fishing village of Tuen Mun, 23 km west-north-west of Hong Kong island. This was attacked and destroyed by local inhabitants, and its occupants massacred. No other permanent settlement was raised until 1557 when imperial permission was granted to establish a base at Macau, whereafter trade with the West gradually increased.

The Europeans wanted much from China. Amongst the items traded were tea, silk, mother-of-pearl, sugar, paper, camphor, gold and silver, lacquer- and enamel-ware, rhubarb, precious oils, bamboo and porcelain. In return, the Chinese purchased such goods as cotton and woollen piece-goods, metals, diamonds and pearls, watches and clocks, coral and amber beads, birds' nests and sharks' fins for soup – and opium. This last commodity was introduced because the balance of trade was too one-sided: the foreigners wanted to export more than insular China wanted to import, so opium was used to create a market, which it inevitably did. As we have seen, opium was introduced to China not by Europeans but by Arabs, who were trading in it as early as the ninth century. The Chinese also grew their own in Yunnan province, but its quality was not nearly as high as that imported by foreigners from India or Persia.

The emperor K'ang-hsi officially sanctioned China's foreign trade in 1685 when he opened Guangzhou to European Barbarians, yet they were strictly controlled, living and working in a small enclave from which they could not stray. All business was governed by the Eight Regulations, under which foreigners could not deal directly with the Chinese population but had to go through the Co-Hong, a cartel of eight to twelve Chinese merchants with exclusive rights to traffic with the foreigners. The Co-Hong members obtained their permission to trade from a *hoppo*, a mandarin who earned huge sums for his emperor (and himself) by issuing operating licences, demanding bribes to allocate them and exacting fines on the Co-Hong for transgressions made by Barbarians for whose actions they were legally responsible. The cost of a licence was the modern equivalent of around £50,000, excluding the purchase bribe, but it was worth it. The cartel members became fabulously wealthy. Wu Bing-jian, who went under the name of Howqua and was the leading cartel merchant in the 1830s, was upon his death worth in excess of £5 million *at contemporary value*.

Opium was the Co-Hong's main import and the British East India Company, which had been established in Macau since 1664 and held a monopoly on all British trade with China until 1833, was their main supplier. The Chinese authorities knew all about opium's insidiousness. In an edict in 1729 the emperor Yung-cheng prohibited its use other than as a medicine. Illegal possession was punished with up to a hundred lashes of a bamboo cane and imprisonment in a cangue (a mobile pillory). Few survived. Dealers and opium-den operators were executed by strangulation, their employees lashed with canes, imprisoned then internally exiled. Traffickers suffered the same fate. However, the edict did not prohibit importation and imported opium cargoes were subject to an excise tax. Business continued as usual and the emperor collected his share of the customs duty until 1799, when the emperor Chia-ch'ing prohibited importation, the use of opium and poppy farming.

Organized smuggling began immediately, conducted by the traders and the Co-Hong merchants, who merely bribed the Q'ing officials to ignore it. Ships with opium cargoes were disguised, sailed under flags of convenience, and were often armed and crewed by marines as well as sailors. Before 1799, opium had been landed at Huangpu but, with this no longer possible, it was transferred to a floating depot consisting of two vessels permanently anchored off Macau; later, a large receiving ship rode offshore near Huangpu. Moving the opium ashore was easy, the Co-Hong merchants paying the necessary bribe, which was euphemistically known as 'tea-money' (because tea was the biggest export) or, more appropriately, 'squeeze'.

In 1820, the penalties for importing opium were tightened further and the receiving ships, of which there were by now a number, set sail for Neilingding Dao, an island in the Pearl River estuary 130 km south of Guangzhou and 35 km east of Macau, which became an entrepôt opium port. This arrangement gave the Barbarian traders a sense of security but presented the Chinese importers with a headache: how to get their opium ashore. This was achieved by a fleet of armed, two-masted Chinese tunks (a type of riverboat-cum-barge) equipped with fifty oars and nicknamed 'centipedes', 'scrambling dragons' or 'fast crabs' because their oars looked like legs. They formed a shuttle service, dodging or engaging imperial patrols. As the Co-Hong could not outwardly employ the tunk crews, they turned to others to manage them.

The opium trade and the cartel system played right into the hands of the Triad societies. They had the manpower to crew the tunks, their pirate comrades knew every creek and gully in the Pearl River delta, they were armed fighters, their involvement could be interpreted as vaguely coming under their doctrine of *fan q'ing – fuk ming*, they were well paid for their efforts, it was not unknown for them to steal a consignment and they knew they could trust their employers. If any Co-Hong merchant ratted on them, they would get him, or his first son, and execute him. This rarely happened. The Co-Hong were often investors in Triad enterprises.

It was not only the Co-Hong who benefited – or benefited from – the Triads. Each Barbarian company, such as the famous Jardine Matheson & Company, dealt with the Co-Hong through a comprador. He was a Chinese fixer-of-all-things, a middle-man *par excellence* who arranged everything from a sampan ride out to a visiting clipper to the supply of everyday provisions. Like the Co-Hong, the compradors were well placed to make a lot of money. They not only worked for their Barbarian employers, they also set up in business themselves. The domestic trading firm owned by Ho Kan-t'ang, a Jardine comprador, was represented in every major Chinese port. Ho Tung (later Sir Robert Ho Tung, the first Chinese to be ennobled by a British monarch, in 1915, and also a comprador) was a director of eighteen companies and ultimately a major shareholder in his former employers, Jardine Matheson.

Being a comprador also carried risks. The son of Liang Yen-hing, the Jardine comprador in Tientsin, was kidnapped by Triads who beat him to death so viciously that his body was identifiable only by the Jardine go-down keys in his pocket. Something had clearly soured in the relationship between Liang and the local society: perhaps he had not met the ransom quickly enough, not put sufficient business the society's way or failed to pay his protection money on time. There again, his son might have been abducted by a rival society from the one to which Liang regularly showed obeisance. Whatever the case, it is clear indication that the compradors were well connected – voluntarily or otherwise – with the Triads.

Few Barbarians ever had direct dealings with Triads. Most would never have come across one. Triads tended to keep clear of foreigners, at least in China. In Hong Kong, matters were different. There, Europeans did come across Triad members, for the societies conducted marches on festival days and organized religious events such as lion or dragon dances. To the colonials, Chinese secret societies were just another part of the Oriental scene, although the trouble they could cause was acknowledged. Some of the earliest ordinances made by the colonial government (numbers 1 and 12 of 1845, the year after Hong Kong was founded) concerned Triad societies.

In time, however, Barbarians in China were also to meet Triads, with terrible consequences.

By the late nineteenth century, Europeans had penetrated far into China. Trading posts and treaty ports were established on main rivers and commercial agents travelled throughout the land buying and selling. The Chinese economy was fast coming under outside influence and capitalism was raising its head for the first time. As they were in the process of doing with Africa, the trading nations of the West started to divide up the Orient amongst themselves. The Russians moved into Turkestan and the north-east, seizing vast areas north of Amur. The British (Hong Kong apart) held sway over the Yangtze River, annexed Burma and took tribute from Nepal. The French sequestered Annam, Cambodia and Cochin-China to form French Indo-China. The Portuguese officially announced their possession of Macau. The Germans claimed pieces of Shandong province. In each of their regions, the foreigners established trading monopolies and started to build roads and railways, maintaining garrisons for their protection.

The stand of the Q'ing government towards this foreign invasion was, for the best part, conciliatory, which angered large segments of the Chinese population. Merchants in particular were infuriated by the authorities, accusing them of encouraging opium importation, allowing Barbarian infiltration, draining the exchequer of silver (true: because of the imbalance of trade, silver was used to pay for the opium), betraying their nation to outsiders and breaking faith with their ancestors, against the teachings of Confucius, Taoism and Buddhism. That many merchants grew wealthy on foreign trade seemed coincidental.

The peasants had little to gain or lose from the presence of Barbarians: whoever ruled the land was immaterial to them. Their agricultural lives were largely unaffected, only those in the cities or treaty ports really benefiting from the increase in trade and small-scale industrialization. Under the influence of the secret societies, however, they did come to disdain the Barbarians.

The accusation of national betrayal struck home with the Triads, the 'patriotic defenders' of the people. They regarded the Barbarians as a blight, but they knew that where there were Barbarians there was business to be had: successful trade meant rich merchants and opportunities for graft and extortion not to be missed. Yet there was one class of Barbarian they could not abide. It was not the trader in goods but, as they saw it, in souls. It was the missionary.

Under the tenuous protection of their national powers,

Christian missionaries flooded into China, building mission hospitals and schools, tending the sick and seeking converts who were generally called 'rice Christians': they espoused Christianity to keep their rice bowls full. This was an unfair appellation: some of those converted became devout Christians, though they were a considerable minority.

The Triads disliked the missionaries for several reasons. First, the Christians posed a threat because they offered an alternative religion to those of the secret societies. Quite possibly, the success of the quasi-Christian Taiping Rebellion was another indication of Christianity's potential. Second, the missionaries worked under the protection of their governments which were close to the Q'ing throne: the missionaries were therefore regarded as Q'ing sympathizers by proxy. Third, missionary doctors were often successful in healing where traditional Chinese medicine failed. Finally, missionary teachers educated children contrary to clan or family traditions, especially undermining the concept of ancestor worship. That the Christians, so few in number and spread so thinly across China, were so well organized also concerned the Triads, who believed that, if they gained a strong following, they would spell the end of secret societies.

It was not long before the Triads were putting about rumours that Chinese women entering the missions were raped, that the missionaries ate babies in their rituals, took their eyes out to make potions and chopped their bodies up for alchemical experimentation. As infant girls were often abandoned in China, and as missionaries were always keen to accept them into mission orphanages, the rumours seemed, to the ignorant peasant, feasible.

The Triads also proclaimed – and this was no rumour – the fact that missionaries engaged in the repugnant opium trade. Almost all missionary doctors used opium as a medicine for fever and dysentery – this was common practice across the Western world. Yet there were some who traded in it as a means of raising revenue for their work. Others provided opium to addicts on condition that they attended prayer meetings: in effect, there were 'opium' as well as 'rice' Christians. So prevalent was the perceived link between Christian preachers and opium that the drug was often referred to as *yasoo nga peen* – Jesus opium. In the light of such hostile rumours and unpleasant truths, attacks upon missionaries seemed inevitable, their isolation in far-flung missions leaving them all the more vulnerable.

Feeling against missionaries and foreigners in general was whipped up by a number of secret societies, all of them allied to Triads if they were not in fact actual Triad groups. They went under a variety of names – the Golden Elixir Society, the Eight Diagram Sect, the Nine Palaces Society, the Observance Sect, the Joss-stick Sect, the White Lotus Society (although it is unclear if this was the original society resurrected or another borrowing the name), the Society of Elder Brothers and the Vegetarian Sect. By the 1880s, there were reckoned to be over 3,600 societies across China, although many were limited to just one village or clan and the statistics, compiled by the Roman Catholic bishop in Hong Kong, were no doubt exaggerated for propaganda reasons.

Of these, the Vegetarian Sect was the most notorious. It was a large society founded in Fujian and divided into nine groups under individual leaders in charge of peasant followers. Religious in nature, it was not made up of vegetarians in the modern sense but of men who followed herbal medicinal practices as well as the usual Triad amalgam of ancestor reverence, Buddhism and Taoism. It was said that its disciples were able, through herbal medicine, to cure opium addiction, which gave them not only a positive anti-foreign credibility but also the cachet of doing social good. They raised funds by charging initiation fees and living, much as Buddhist monks do, begging for alms, although their benefactors were obliged to make offerings to save their skins rather than their souls. Their main ritual was different from the normal Triad ceremony. Offerings were made to the gods of eight 'vegetables': dried melons and melon seeds, red and black dates, kumquats and candied orange peel, ground nuts and dried *leng-keng*, a sort of bean nicknamed *lung yen* (dragon's eyes). Dragon's eyes were the sect's symbol.

From 1885, anti-foreign and -Christian attacks began to occur, gradually building in number. Missions were attacked, Chinese converts beaten or murdered and churches burned. By 1887, the Big Sword Society, in collaboration, it is thought, with the White Lotus Society in Shantung province, was foremost in a campaign of terror directed against foreigners and Christianity in particular. They were rapidly successful in whipping up support by claiming that missionaries' knives and stones could do members no harm if they went through an initiation ceremony involving chanting, the drinking of magical libations and the wearing of a talisman. Many thousands joined and, for a while, struck fear into the hearts of foreigners in isolated missions and trading posts. In 1890, the Catholic church at Lungshui, in Szechuan province, was attacked by a horde of 30,000 people. However, in time this campaign started to fizzle out, its leaders were executed and its members drifted back to their peasant lives.

As the Big Sword Society waned, another society waxed. This was the Ko Lo Hui, or Elder Brothers Society. They recruited widely but no-one appreciated just how widely until September 1891, when imperial authorities made a fascinating arrest. The imperial Chinese customs service was staffed at senior levels by foreigners, over half of them British, who were deemed incorruptible. James Mason was an exception. A former officer in the customs inspectorate, he had been using his contacts to run guns, ammunition and explosives to the Elder Brothers Society, of which he admitted he was a member. Quite possibly he was the first foreigner in China to become an active participant in a Chinese secret society. His arrest showed the authorities how far the situation had moved.

By the end of 1891, anti-Christian attacks were widespread across China and were blamed by the foreign press in Guangzhou, Macau and Hong Kong on secret societies. Complaints were made to the imperial authorities but they took little action. Partly they did not want to stir the Triad hornet's nest and partly they knew they were impotent against them. They also did not want to be seen siding with Barbarians against their own people, no matter how disenfranchised or antagonistic to imperial rule those people might be.

Foreign diplomats considered the hostility towards the missions to be primarily political, aimed at disrupting the good relations which, since the suppression of the Taiping

Rebellion, had existed between themselves and the Q'ing throne, and at isolating the emperor, who remained the primary target of the secret societies. Yet this interpretation was wrong. The secret societies were not so well organized. They were merely using the missionaries as a means to an end, to create chaos from which they might somehow be able to benefit.

Little is remembered of the anti-Christian massacres, for the simple reason that there were seldom any survivors to tell the tale, but a few graphic eyewitness accounts did reach the West. One such is the story of the murder by Vegetarians of missionaries working for the Church of England Zenana Missionary Society at Hwa-sang, 80 km west-north-west of Fuzhou, on 1 August 1895. Hwa-sang was the Chinese equivalent of an Indian Raj hill station, 2,000 feet up a mountain south of the walled city of Gutian (then called Kuching) where the missionaries were based. Close to Hwa-sang, the missionaries had built some bungalows, and it was here they met their fate. The Vegetarians approached early in the morning along the track to Gutian. Some of the missionaries' children were in the woods picking flowers at 6.45 a.m. One of them, eleven-year-old Kathleen Stewart, described what happened:

Mildred and I were just outside the house on a hill we called The Garden, picking ferns and flowers because it was Herbert's birthday, and we were going to decorate the breakfast table. We saw men coming along, and at first I thought they were *dang dang* [coolies]. Milly saw their spears and told me to run, but I was so frightened I lay on the grass, thinking perhaps they would not see me.

> The men did see me, and took hold of me, and pulled me
> by my hair along towards the house. Just as we arrived
> there I fell down. Then they began beating me.

She managed to break free and ran into the house, the
Vegetarians following. Inside, they murdered the girl's
parents, badly wounded her brother Herbert, and slaughtered the nanny, Helena Yellop, who was trying to
protect an infant. Two sisters, Nellie and Topsy Saunders,
were next to be caught and hacked to death. Mildred and
Kathleen were hunted down, the former being severely
slashed with swords. Kathleen had her leg nearly severed
at the knee. Despite being wounded, they struggled to the
nursery and rescued the infant, Evan. The Vegetarians,
finding a drum of kerosene, then set fire to the house. The
children escaped, although Herbert died of his wounds
the next day.

So far, the attack was simply a mass slaughter engendered by hatred of the Yasoo religion, but it took a new
turn in an adjacent bungalow, where five women missionaries were trapped. A band of about eighty Vegetarians surrounded the house and peered in at them. The
women knelt in prayer, waiting for the end to come, but
it was not quite so quick in arriving. At first, the Vegetarians broke in, looted the building and smashed up the
remaining contents. Then one stepped forward and demanded payment to spare the women. One of them, Miss
Codrington, explained that they had no money and an
elderly Chinese servant pleaded for them, but at that
juncture a Vegetarian leader arrived and ordered their
execution. They were chopped to death with swords and
the house torched. Miss Codrington, however, survived

and regained consciousness in time to drag herself free of the fire and pull her dead companions out as well. As the Vegetarians left, they took a bed sheet from one of the houses and painted their slogan upon it: 'The Dragon of China fights the Christian Jesus'.

What had started out as a religiously inspired attack characteristically ended in looting: it was a pattern followed on many occasions, the initial moral justification for the attack soon deteriorating into an orgy of self-interest.

The Triad societies had made a miscalculation. They had assumed that attacking missions would break the Barbarians' spirit, making them leave and cease their presence in the Celestial Kingdom. Yet the attacks had the opposite result. The Barbarians strengthened their resolve and the massacres provided the foreign governments with a new excuse for intervening in Chinese affairs. The retort to the Hwa-sang massacre and the Vegetarians' banner indicates the thinking of the missionaries: 'The son of God goes forth to war also. We know who will be the victor. The Great Overcomer will yet lead captive in the train of His triumph those who, subdued by His will and reconciled by His redeeming love, shall build again the faith they once destroyed.'

Not only missionaries and merchants suffered in these decades of strife. Anti-Q'ing feelings also ran high. In 1886, 3,000 Triad members went on the rampage amongst the Hakka population of Guangdong, whipping up feeling against oppressive government officials. They were easily routed, the leaders fleeing into exile in Hong Kong and Singapore or turning their hand to piracy along the south China coast. Six years later, an identical uprising was similarly quashed.

These were minor disturbances – as, in the cold light of history, were the attacks on foreigners – yet they set the stage for an uprising which was to change the attitude of foreign powers towards China and help to change the course of her future.

The I Ho Ch'üan, or Righteous Harmony Fists, were founded in the mid-eighteenth century in Henan province. A branch of the Eight Diagram Sect, their early (possibly first) leader, Kao Sheng-wen, was executed in 1771. On his death, the society dispersed, members founding lodges in Henan, Jiangsu, Shandong and Shaanxi provinces. Westerners called them Boxers, the name coined by missionaries who wrote for the *North China Daily News* in Shanghai, because they practised a form of martial arts kick-boxing in which both the hands and feet are used in unarmed combat. It is similar to the modern sport of Thai boxing.

The Boxers became the embodiment of secret-society violence. The political situation in China contributed greatly to their rise. Despite the fact that after the suppression of the Taiping 'dynasty' the Q'ing authorities had concentrated on building up the nation's military strength, they were thoroughly beaten in a brief war against Japan in Korea in 1894. More than face was lost. Russia, France and Germany had aided the Chinese in a campaign and, in return, they demanded that China take a loan for the modernization of the country. Britain objected, but the loan went through: 400 million gold francs at 4 per cent interest per annum. The Russians, pressing the advantage, also negotiated permission to run the

Trans-Siberian railway through Manchuria to Vladivostok.

More treaties, conventions and accords were signed, with China obliged to make more concessions. The British extended their landholding in Hong Kong with a 99-year lease on the New Territories, as they were called, in 1898. They also gained more treaty ports, a realignment of the Chinese–Burmese border, permission to join the Chinese railway network to the Burmese and authorization to finance large sections of the national railway-expansion programme through the British-owned Hongkong & Shanghai Bank. France demanded more treaty ports and concessions. Germany requested the lease of Kiaochow as a coaling port; when this was refused, the Kaiser ordered his fleet to take it. The Chinese caved in and also agreed to German mining- and railway-construction rights. Russia insisted on being leased Talienwan and Port Arthur, and on joining these to the Siberian railway. These *faits accomplis* belittled China.

A reform movement sprang up, arguing that if China modernized along Western lines, as the recently victorious Japan had done, she would be a great, unassailable nation within a decade. The reformists persuaded the emperor, Kuang-hsü, of their case and on 19 July 1895 a decree was issued demanding that viceroys and governors reform and modernize. There was opposition from hard-line traditionalists and members of the ruling clan, including Prince Kung, the emperor's brother, and Tzu Hsi, the empress dowager. Nevertheless, in 1898 the reforms started to appear: civil-service examinations were to be restructured; commerce, agriculture, mining and industrialization were to be promoted; a university was to be opened and education reformed; some provincial governorships were to be annulled and monasteries and temples surplus to requirement were to be closed. These decisions were sure to antagonize certain sectors of the Q'ing administration, the people and the secret societies.

With the situation becoming volatile, Tzu Hsi felt she had to act. By October, fearing intervention by the army, she had assumed control and set about dismantling the reforms, imprisoning the emperor on an island in the middle of the Forbidden City and promoting as heir apparent P'u Tsün, the son of one of Tzu Hsi's xenophobic favourites, Prince Tuan. It was deemed that the way ahead was to be militarily powerful, not reformist. Foreign policy, and domestic policy towards foreigners, was now cast in stone. China would not go looking for a war but she would not accept any outside aggression.

With such a policy publicly acknowledged, it was no small wonder that the secret societies became active. Here was a chance to fight for China, eradicate foreigners and missionaries, gain face and national honour, and maybe – just maybe – topple the Q'ing regime at the same time. Also to be taken into consideration was the parlous state of the land. In August 1898, in Shandong and Chihi (modern-day Anhui) provinces, the Yellow River broke its banks, drowned thousands and laid waste vast acreages of wheat and vegetables as well as killing livestock. Disease followed the flood, with outbreaks of cholera and typhoid. The following year, the harvest failed and a plague of locusts swept through China. Even Beijing suffered shortages. In time-honoured tradition, the emperor was seen to be at fault and the people were inclined to rise up against him, but modern politics was now playing its part in China's psyche. The emperor might be to blame, but perhaps the Barbarians were more so. They were doing untold damage by importing their own God, which was upsetting the Chinese pantheon. Chinese Christians were not allowed to attend 'native' festivals, take part in any community event with a religious aspect to it and were forbidden to worship their forebears. Not only the gods were angry – so were the ancestors.

At the same time, foreign aggression increased. Near Kiaochow, the Germans frequently mounted incursions into neighbouring China, burning villages at the least provocation. The Japanese, then the British, occupied Weihaiwei. Near Port Arthur, peasants complaining at the sequestering of their land came under fire from Russian troops: ninety-six were killed.

In May 1898, secret society activity in Shangdong province, the birthplace of Confucius, had begun to intensify. The provincial governor, Chang Ju-mei, was instructed to investigate and maintain order. He did so and, for the first time, the Boxers appeared in an official document. They were not, however called the I Ho Ch'üan but the I Ho T'uan, the Righteous Harmony Corps or Brigade. The society considered itself to be a militia. For five months it did nothing but agitate and hold public demonstrations, broadcasting slogans such as 'Force out all foreigners'. They also distributed pamphlets with titles like 'Death to the Devils' Religion'. Christianity was frequently referred to as *T'ien Chu Chiao*, which translates as the Squeal of the Heavenly Pig. (Christ was commonly portrayed as a pig on a crucifix.) Several phrases covered the term foreigner, including white ghosts, barbarians, foreign pigs or big-noses.

Thousands of peasants were initiated into the I Ho Ch'üan, although most were not active: they joined to avoid a beating, or worse. Rituals included oaths of allegiance, incantations and magical formulae, as well as exhibitions of boxing, which was considered sacred because it promoted concentration, physical fitness and spiritual advancement. Mass hypnosis was part of the process, during which charms were issued to protect the wearers against Barbarian bullets. Members claimed to be able to control the natural elements, especially rain: for this reason, some Westerners referred to Boxers as Rain Processionists. It does not seem to have dawned on anyone that if they controlled the rain they might have averted the devastating floods and droughts of the time.

A Boxer wore a simple uniform. On top of his ordinary clothes he tied a red bandanna around his forehead, a red sash around his waist and red ribboned gaiters around his legs. Around his neck, hanging on either side of his chest rather like a Christian priest's stole, he wore another strip of red cloth similar to the paper prayer banners one sees outside Chinese houses. Upon this, in black ink, was written a slogan, usually 'Protect China – Kill Foreigners'.

Not only men were recruited. Young boys from the age of twelve were initiated into youth branches, while girls aged between twelve and eighteen joined the Hung Teng K'an, or Red Lantern Shrines groups, under the leadership of a woman professing magical powers known as the Huang-lian Sheng-mu (Sacred Mother of the Yellow Lotus). The Red Lantern Shrine members walked everywhere carrying small red paper lanterns, which, it was claimed, would set fire to any building, near or far, if thrown into the air.

Over the winter of 1898–9, Boxer troubles festered, then in March 1899 the whole Boxer movement underwent a sea-change. The governor of Shandong was replaced by a brilliant but anti-foreign and anti-reformist official called Yu Hsien. He was personally appointed by the empress dowager, who vetted all senior appointments. Throughout the summer and into the autumn of 1899 Boxers went on the rampage, killing Christians and burning Christian property. When a number were arrested, Yu Hsien imprisoned the officer who had apprehended them. In early December, under pressure from foreign diplomats, Yu Hsien was recalled to Beijing but his replacement was just as lenient. He was instructed so to be.

On New Year's Eve 1899, the Boxers killed their first foreign missionary, a priest called Brooks. The British rounded up his assailants, tried them under a British consular official, found them guilty and promptly executed them. The Chinese authorities formally expressed regret but did nothing.

To the north, in Anhui, a series of decrees was published allowing villages and towns to form self-protection militia: it was *carte blanche* for the Boxers to organize. In May 1900, a serious anti-Christian riot took place at Kaolo, 1,000 Boxers killing sixty-eight mainly Chinese Christians. The viceroy, Yü Lu, did nothing but suggest the leaders be apprehended. The imperial authorities advised him to pussy-foot: rash action, he was told, could lead to catastrophe. The official policy was that foreigners had to be protected but Boxers were not to be suppressed by force.

The Boxers, emboldened by their success, surged

north, destroying whatever traces they could find of foreign influence. Buildings were sacked, Christians killed, railway tracks uprooted, railway stations burned, factories looted and telegraph lines cut. By the end of the first week in June, the situation was out of the authorities' control. The army was ordered in to annihilate the Boxer movement but it was too late. They were marching on Beijing.

On 1 June, a multinational force of just 340 British, American, Russian, French, Italian and Japanese troops arrived to defend the foreign legations contained in one small diplomatic enclave in the city. South of Beijing, the Boxers murdered two British missionaries, whilst the grandstand at the Beijing racecourse, a real symbol of foreign influence, was razed. Boxer groups started to fight other secret societies. Shops were looted and people stoned or hacked with swords.

The empress dowager had at first been reluctant to carry out any anti-foreign actions. The wily old woman was cautious of the Barbarians and well aware of what they were capable. A foreign military force of 1,000 could wipe out ten times as many Chinese soldiers. She had already bowed to diplomatic pressure by heeding a semi-official communication from Sir Claude MacDonald, the British minister in Beijing, who had cautioned her against quietly doing away with the imprisoned emperor. Yet despite taking his advice, Tzu Hsi was becoming increasingly anti-foreign. On 6 June, she published a decree seeking to appease the Boxers although authorizing their suppression if they rioted. At the command of Kang I, a leading councillor and Boxer sympathizer, the 'rebel' leaders were summoned to a meeting at which they requested the army be withdrawn from attacking them and be employed, instead, to attack foreign troops at Tientsin. Whilst Kang I did not turn the army on the Barbarian forces, he conceded the other demand, as well as reprimanding two anti-Boxer magistrates. The Boxers were all but dictating policy.

Three days later, Prince Tuan ordered the army to prevent a joint allied force, gathering in Tientsin under the British admiral Sir Edward Seymour, from entraining for Beijing. On the same day, 10 June, the Boxers moved into Beijing in large numbers and anarchy ruled the streets.

Seymour's force of 2,129 troops, half of whom were British, left Tientsin by train on 11 June, met a Boxer force at Langfang, defeated it, moved on towards Beijing and were then halted by a huge Boxer ambush: they were pinned down and had to retreat. In Beijing, Mr Sugiyama, the head of chancery at the Japanese legation, was murdered in the street by Boxers. The Boxer Rebellion had officially begun.

Foreign property and churches were torched, legation guards attacked. Foreign residents were relocated to the legation quarter, from where armed parties ventured into Beijing to attempt to rescue Chinese Christians. Some were saved, many were not. On 16 June, a patrol of British, American and Japanese legation guards came upon a massacre by Boxers who were disembowelling and decapitating Christians in a temple. Forty-six Boxers were shot, six of them by Dr George Morrison, an inveterate traveller and the Beijing correspondent for *The Times*. Imperial troops looked on as the fight progressed and survivors were rescued.

The next moves made by the authorities were merely overtures to war. The legations were told to call off Seymour's force, something they could not have done even if they had wanted to: the Boxers had cut the telegraph lines. A grand council was convened, with Tzu Hsi taking the chair. A decree was published: all young, strong Boxers should be recruited into the army.

Diplomatic relations with the Barbarians collapsed. Ambassadors were told to leave China or face military consequences. Tzu Hsi, convinced by now that the Barbarians had started the aggression and that China's extinction was nigh, was not going to surrender before her ancestors. On 21 June, war was declared on the Barbarians and the Boxers became a part of the 'united' effort to drive them out of the Celestial Kingdom once and for all.

For those in the legation quarter, the declaration of war meant little. They had been besieged since 18 June by a force of predominantly Boxers who attacked in waves. (They also fell in waves, their magical invulnerability to Barbarian bullets proving singularly ineffective.) The siege lasted fifty-five days, until a multinational force of 17,000 troops reached Beijing, routed the Boxers and pillaged the Forbidden City. During that time, 66 foreigners had been killed, 8 had died of disease or natural causes (6 of them infants) and just under 200 had been wounded. Over 300 Chinese died in the legation. Outside the barricades, at some points in the siege, the Boxers and imperial troops lay dead three deep. How many were killed in all will never be known, but the number was certainly in the thousands. This is hardly surprising, as most of the Boxers were armed with swords, Chinese traditional pikestaffs or spears; even the imperial troops and those Boxers who had modern rifles had little idea how to use them. Most of the guns captured or taken from the dead were found to have their sights incorrectly set.

Tzu Hsi and the Q'ing court were also routed and fled westwards to Xian. On 7 September 1901, a peace treaty was signed, under the terms of which the Chinese government was obliged to pay reparations of 450 million silver taels (approximately £68 million by contemporary reckoning) over forty years, to concede more trading rights, permit the stationing of foreign troops on Chinese soil to prevent a repeat of the Beijing débâcle, and maintain a corridor from the coast to the capital.

With the imperial court on the run and ousted from its capital, the I Ho Ch'üan simply dissolved. The peasants returned to their fields and missionaries were left comparatively unmolested. Merchants moved once more into the heartlands of China. Some Boxers joined other criminal fraternities; others associated with political Triads, taking with them an even stronger desire to see the Q'ing dynasty fall for having humiliated China.

The Boxer Rebellion was the greatest surge of secret-society activity in China's history. Not since the monks of the Shao Lin monastery helped the emperor rid his kingdom of foreigners had a secret society been officially in alliance with the government. It failed, and it is no small irony that it was put down by the intervention of the accursed Barbarians. The rebellion had, however, shown the potential of the secret societies, which were soon to play an important new role in China's history, one in which they would no longer be politically subversive but central to the very decision-making processes of government.

PART TWO

POLITICIANS, WARLORDS AND GANGSTERS

1

DR SUN AND THE NEW EMPIRE

In the aftermath of the Boxer Rebellion, China entered a period of flux. The imperial family grew more distant, politicians and powerbrokers vied for position and the old order gradually disintegrated. It seemed inevitable that Q'ing rule would soon end, a new China rising from the confusion.

The changes under way were due in part to foreign influence. Chinese students travelled abroad for their education, Chinese men in cosmopolitan cities such as Hong Kong and Shanghai wore the American fedora hat in addition to traditional robes. Overseas, Chinese expatriates felt it was time for a new order to be established, with China adapting to forward-thinking modernization against which the moribund Q'ing dynasty reacted.

The story of how the Q'ing dynasty finally fell, and the part the Triad societies played in this, began twenty-five years earlier with the birth of a peasant's son.

Sun Yat-sen was born Sun Wen in 1866, the youngest of three sons. His father was a subsistence farmer and watchman in the village of Tsui Heng in Guangdong, north of Macau. Sun Mei, his older brother by fifteen years, emigrated to Hawaii in the early 1870s and prospered. At first he worked as an agricultural labourer but then opened a shop catering for migrant Chinese, ploughing his profits into land on the island of Maui and turning this over to cattle. When he returned to Guangdong in 1878 to marry his father's choice of a bride, he persuaded his mother to let Sun Wen, aged twelve, return with him to Hawaii.

In Hawaii, Sun Wen attended an Anglican school in Honolulu, then graduated to Oahu College, where he studied hard, took an interest in Christianity and determined to be a doctor. Sun Mei was appalled at his younger brother, for whom he was responsible, studying Christianity, so he packed him off to China. Back home, Sun Wen was a misfit. With an overseas education, he was restless and joined a local branch of the San-ho Hui or Three Harmonies Society, partly out of boredom and partly out of defiance. At the time, there were a number of societies in the area, stirring up trouble amongst the peasants. With his new-found brothers, Sun studied the martial arts and, in a fit of pique and contempt, desecrated the local temple, for which he was cast out of the community. He travelled to Hong Kong, where he lodged with friends, attended an Anglican diocesan school, then entered Queen's College. At eighteen he was baptized a Christian by an American missionary in Hong Kong, D. Charles Hager, who gave him the Mandarin name I-hsien which, in Cantonese, was pronounced Yat-sen.

Sun Mei, believing his brother needed a firm hand, ordered him back to Hawaii, where he employed him as a clerk in his store. Sun Yat-sen hated it and, joining the

Kwok On Wui Triad society in Honolulu, borrowed money from friends and Triad brethren and returned to China against his brother's wishes. At the age of twenty he enrolled in the Po-chi Hospital Medical School in Guangzhou. Sun Mei, impressed by his determination, forgave him and paid his fees. From Guangzhou, Sun Yat-sen transferred to the recently opened College of Medicine at the University of Hong Kong. It was to change his life.

British Hong Kong was a hotbed of Chinese revolutionary thinking and a haven for Triads for whom China had become too dangerous. In the colony they flourished, controlling – or with a finger in the pie of – almost every aspect of Chinese life. Dock coolies, rickshaw and sedan-chair coolies, street hawkers, opium-den operators, brothel-keepers, shopkeepers, itinerant barbers, even street entertainers, were all 'protected' by or were members of Triad societies. Temples were run and religious festivals organized by them. They smuggled opium, which was legally available, to avoid the excise duty, placed a levy on rice and flour being offloaded from ships in the harbour, operated coolie doss-houses and controlled the markets.

Sun Yat-sen joined a Hong Kong branch of the Three Harmonies Society and was befriended by Dr Ho Kai, a doctor of medicine and British-educated lawyer who was also a Triad, but of the old school: he was an ardent exponent of *fan q'ing – fuk ming*, frequently lecturing on the evils of the Manchus. Sun also fell in with a fellow medical student, Cheng Shih-liang, with whom he shared a strong dislike of the Q'ing dynasty. Cheng, whose family came from Hakka peasant stock in Guangdong, was a Triad and well connected throughout the southern China Triad network. Well versed in Triad mythology, he propounded the uses they could have in time of revolution. Another man Sun befriended was Chen Shao-pai, who became his right-hand man for the next ten years.

Two others with whom Sun was to associate were Yang Ho-ling and Yu Lieh. Yang was the *shan chu* of the Hong Kong-based, politically motivated Chung Wo Tong Society, whilst Yu was a *sheung fa*, a senior official, probably in the same society. They too persuaded Sun of the political potential of secret societies. Together they organized the Chung Wo Tong into a headquarters-in-exile for their political struggle. Connected to all the other Triad societies, criminal or otherwise, it developed into an efficient intelligence-gathering operation.

On graduating in 1892, Sun set up a herbalist shop-cum-clinic in Macau, but it was closed by the authorities. Moving to Guangzhou, he opened a chain of apothecary shops, franchising these out to friends who were often Triad brothers, dispensing both Western and Chinese traditional medicines and performing simple surgical procedures. He perfected the manufacture of home-made explosives upon which he had embarked in the medical-school laboratories in Hong Kong. Despite this clandestine activity, he was not yet a full-blooded revolutionary and tried to enter the Chinese civil service, writing a petition to Li Hung-chang, grand secretary to the emperor and as such head of the civil service. Sun knew that the way to power lay in the official position of mandarin. In 1894, deciding to press his case for appointment in person, he travelled to Tientsin for an audience with Li.

En route in Shanghai, one Sunday morning outside the Moore Methodist Church, he was introduced to a Chinese businessman, Charlie Soong.

Soong and Sun were two of a kind. Both were from southern China, Western-educated, Christian, ambitious and spoke English fluently. They were also both Triad members.

Soong's background was bizarre. His real name was Han Chao-shun and he hailed from Hainan Island. As a youth he went to America, where he was raised by a former Confederate army officer, the famous Methodist philanthropist and 'Bull Durham' tobacco multimillionaire Julian S. Carr. Carr believed this Chinese youth, who expressed a devotion to Christianity and was baptized Charles Jones Soon on 7 November 1880, was ideal missionary material. He planned to educate him then return him to China to preach Methodism. He paid for Soon's education at Trinity College, Durham, North Carolina, and Vanderbilt University. In January 1886, now an ordained Methodist minister, Soon returned to China to commence missionary work.

With Carr's backing, Charlie Soong (as he now called himself) founded the Sino-American Press, publishing Bibles, hymnals, prayer books, Methodist tracts and educational textbooks in English and Chinese. Unknown to Carr, Soong was also an official in several Shanghai Triad societies which also bankrolled the press. Amongst these were the Three Harmonies Society, of which Sun was a member, and the powerful Hung Pang or Red Gang. In 1892, he resigned from the Southern Methodist China Mission. He had a new mission, as an active supporter of the republican cause.

The Hung Pang was more than a criminal or political fraternity. It was the most influential secret society in China with untold power in Shanghai and along the Yangtze River system, controlling everything from the employment of coolies to the operation of river craft. With substantial funds behind it, it was outwardly a mutual-benefit society with patriotic leanings; in fact, it was a well-organized, ruthless criminal association. Its senior members were merchants, traders, mandarins and financiers and, to succeed in Shanghai, one needed to be a member or close to someone who was. Charlie Soong printed the Hung Pang certificates, lodge tablets and, in time, seditious broadsheets.

During Sun's brief stopover in Shanghai, Soong introduced him to Cheng Kuan-ying, a wealthy comprador, and Wang T'ao, an influential journalist. Both were very senior members of the Hung Pang.

Travelling on to Tientsin, Sun waited in vain for his audience with Li Hung-chang. Disheartened, like generations of disillusioned men before him, he returned to Shanghai, stayed with the Soong family and embarked upon a career as a revolutionary which was to make him world-famous and irreversibly destroy China's dynastic history.

Sun was quick to realize the potential and prestige of Triad society membership. He was not the only one. Constitutional monarchists also tried to gain Triad support through Triad members who were merchants or landowners and had joined the societies for protection. Once inside the societies they exerted some influence, but it was insufficient. The republicans held sway.

Both Soong and Sun knew they needed to start their revolution where they could count on substantial support, where they were at home in the local culture and there was every chance of success. The obvious place was southern China and its regional capital, Guangzhou. Not only was the region solidly Han Chinese, and therefore anti-Q'ing, but it was Sun's home, where he was known. If the revolutionaries could take Guangzhou, it would give them a strong foundation upon which to expand.

Gradually Sun prepared his revolution, but circumstances overtook him. In spring 1894, an important pro-Japanese Korean politician was murdered in Shanghai. Who killed him is uncertain but the Hung Pang were more than likely involved, for the corpse was taken by a Chinese naval vessel crewed by Hung Pang members to Korea, where it was dismembered and publicly displayed. The Japanese were incensed and, on 1 August, war was declared.

With the Q'ing army busy fighting in the north, Sun knew that in the south the coast would be clear to start an uprising, but he was not yet ready. He had insufficient funds, hardly any followers and a low political profile. To boost all three, he sailed for Hawaii, knowing that, if the revolution was to succeed, it had to find its initial impetus overseas where Chinese communities harboured republican sentiments. In late November, Sun founded a patriotic quasi-secret society, the Hsing Chung Hui or Revitalize China Society. It quickly took hold and captured the Chinese imagination. One hundred and twenty paid to join and support the cause. One wealthy farmer, Teng Yin-nan, an official in the Honolulu-based

101

Splendid Equality Society, was so confident of Sun's eventual success that he sold his entire business and sailed for Hong Kong. He was to play an important part in the revolution and was rewarded with the magistracy of two key regions in Guangdong, from which position he recouped all his revolutionary 'venture capital' to die a rich and successful businessman.

There were sound reasons for making the Hsing Chung Hui – China's first revolutionary association – a clandestine organization. Secrecy ensured survival. Yet there were other motives, for if the movement looked like a secret society it would attract secret-society members, of which Sun estimated there were 35 million in China – a ready-made revolutionary army. The society was based for safety in Hong Kong and financed by sympathetic Hong Kong as well as Hawaiian Chinese, all of them intellectuals who wanted China to modernize along Western principles. Its stated aim was to overthrow the Q'ing authorities in Guangzhou by mobilizing Triad and bandit societies and exploiting peasant dissent in the Pearl River delta.

Almost the entire membership consisted of natives of the south-eastern Chinese provinces where secret societies had existed for centuries: the area was, after all, the birthplace of the Taiping Rebellion. Cheng Shih-liang was appointed recruiting officer and, with his Triad links, he gathered secret-society members to the revolutionary cause. The Hsing Chung Hui initiation ceremony in part mimicked the Triad societies, stressing in its 36th oath:

> After Entering beneath the Hung Gates, I shall be loyal and faithful and do my utmost to overthrow the Q'ing

and restore the Ming by co-ordinating my efforts with those of my sworn brothers, even though my brothers be of a different profession: our common aim is to revenge the Five Ancestors.

To this was added the phrase 'and establish a democratic government'.

With the Hsing Chung Hui up and running, good news arrived in a telegraph from Charlie Soong. The Q'ing army was being badly beaten by the Japanese in Korea. The public were up in arms at China's humiliation. It was time to act.

Sun sailed for Hong Kong with a handful of recruits. Once there, he met up with one Yang Ch'u-wen, a fellow revolutionary thinker and activist, but Yang had only a small band of followers and finances were still insufficient.

Throughout the spring of 1895, the Chinese army was defeated again and again. By the summer, Sun still had only 153 men. He and Yang decided they had to strike by staging a *coup d'état* on the ninth day of the ninth lunar month in the Chinese calendar, which fell on 26 October and which was an auspicious choice, as this is the day of the festival of Chung Yeung when everyone pays homage to their ancestors, sweeps clan graves clean, visits temples to burn offerings to the forebears and has family get-togethers. Not only would the coup be seen as a paying of homage to the Ming ancestors, but it would benefit from taking place on a public holiday when the authorities' guard would be down.

Sun addressed the problem of undermanning by conscripting 3,000 Triad fighters, Red Poles (the Triad equivalent of non-commissioned officers), and 49s (ordinary members or foot soldiers) to the Hsing Chung Hui. They gathered in Hong Kong, the plan being for them to sail for Guangzhou as ordinary ferry passengers. Their arms were to be smuggled in barrels of cement from the Portland Cement factory in Kowloon. Upon arriving in the city, they would form small units, murdering officials in their homes or taking them captive. Other units were to approach Guangzhou from the maze of tributaries and creeks south of the city. This diverse force was made up of pirates, bandits and Triad members from the North River region commanded by a notorious bandit known as Big Gun Liang. All the rebels wore red sashes or headbands for identification.

Sun and Yang Ch'u-wen, who was overall commander of the uprising, expressed initial concern that the mercenaries would not be true to the cause. Yet both men convinced themselves that, once the bullets flew and the blood oozed, the mercenaries would spontaneously catch the revolutionary zeal and bring with them Triads from the countryside, building a popular army.

Despite their small number, Sun was quietly confident that they would capture Guangzhou. Things did not, however, go as planned. News of the plot leaked out, but the Q'ing authorities thought it was a hoax. Then the invading army missed the boat – quite literally. Standing on the dock in Hong Kong, the mercenaries started arguing over who got the best guns; so engrossed were they in the quarrel that they failed to see the ferry sail. Sun was in trouble. His Guangzhou Triads were ready to go but could not act without the reinforcements. He reluctantly paid them off. Yang, unaware, sent the mercenaries on the next ferry, SS *Powan*, the following day. The Hong Kong police, ever heedful of Triad activities, discovered the plot and cabled Guangzhou. When the ferry arrived, the Q'ing army was waiting. Fifty rebels and the mercenaries' leaders, most of them Three Harmonies Society members from Hawaii, were arrested. Two were decapitated, one was beaten to death with a heavy cane whilst another was hacked to death with swords.

The uprising in tatters, Sun fled from Guangzhou. After hiding in a Christian priest's house, he went to Macau disguised as a woman, then sailed to Hong Kong by ferry. It was the start of a sixteen-year exile.

Until now, Sun had looked like a typical Chinese. He always wore a *sam* jacket and baggy *fu* trousers and had his hair in a long queue. In Hong Kong – where he stayed only briefly, as the police were after him on behalf of the Q'ing authorities – he bought a Western suit. Sailing to Japan, where he would be beyond Q'ing reach, he cut his queue off.

From Japan, he headed for Hawaii. In 1884 or 1885, he had married a girl named Lu Mu-chun from his ancestral village, who for much of their marriage had remained in the village, living with Sun's parents whilst he travelled the world. With the uprising pending, he had shipped her and their two children off to his brother in Hawaii for safekeeping. Now it was time to join them, to regroup and gain wider support. One sure source of support was the Triads.

In the spring of 1896, Sun joined the Che Kung Tong, or Achieve Justice Society, entering as a Red Pole: he skipped the rank of 49 because of his proven experience.

His rapid passage up the ranks was also assisted by an uncle on his mother's side, Yang Wen-na, a senior official in the society. Founded in Guangdong, the Che Kung Tong was a society which had concentrated on recruiting Pearl River pirates and bandits and had been active in the Taiping Rebellion, after which many of its members were forced to escape overseas. Most had fled to Hawaii and North America, taking their society with them to make it one of the most powerful in the continent.

With his new membership, Sun went to San Francisco, where, apart from having his photograph taken – a copy was acquired by Q'ing sympathizers who sent it to Beijing, giving away Sun's new Westernized appearance – he started to connect with all the Triad societies of the USA. In this enterprise he had the tacit support of the Che Kung Tong *shan chu* in San Francisco, for whom he rewrote the society's constitution in such a way as to tighten its control over sub-branches which were being set up all over the American west. However, he was not as successful as he had hoped. Many of his Triad contacts were apathetic about his aims, uninterested in domestic Chinese politics, disenchanted with what was happening in China and distanced from it. Nevertheless, they contributed financial assistance to the cause, if not to the extent Sun had hoped. In his autobiography, Sun noted how 'in America, the "Hung-men" societies naturally lost their political colours, and became benefit clubs. Many members of the "Hung-men" societies did not rightly understand the meaning and exact aims which their society pursued'. In this, Sun was both right and wrong. They had lost their true political colours and some had become mutual-benefit associations, but a good many knew exactly what their aims were: to extort money from their fellow countrymen.

From the USA, Sun moved to England, where in 1896 the Chinese embassy was successful in kidnapping him with the intention of shipping him back to China to stand trial and inevitable execution. He was freed, however, not by Triads but by the efforts of his former professor of medicine in the University of Hong Kong, Dr James Cantlie, a world leprosy expert.

Like North America, Britain produced little support either in manpower or in finance: Chinese immigrants were simply too few in number to make an impact. In Europe, however, Sun's next port of call, he was more successful in gaining minds if not money. He lectured to Chinese students, of whom a considerable number were studying in universities in France, Belgium and The Netherlands. He was also successful in gaining political support in the USA, which was trying to extend its sphere of influence in the Far East, and from European nations who wanted to see a stable, modern China.

The following year, 1897, Sun returned to Japan, where he lived for eight years with the support of a powerful Japanese ultra-right-wing secret organization, the Black Dragon Society, which saw in him a way to destabilize China, drive out its imperial family, establish it as a modern Oriental state in close alliance with Japan and, misguidedly, expel foreigners. Its leaders envisaged an Oriental renaissance: it was they who sowed the seeds which was to lead to the bombing of Pearl Harbor in 1941.

Sun was unable to visit China. Even Hong Kong refused him entry on the grounds that he was a dissident and a Triad. Throughout the Boxer Rebellion and into its aftermath, Sun stayed in Japan. He was not, however, ignorant of what was going on in China. Charlie Soong kept him well informed.

When the Boxer Rebellion failed, Sun gained considerable public support. China had been humiliated in the extreme. What was needed was a true Chinese to take over. As a proven if unsuccessful revolutionary with a price on his head, and as a Han Chinese, Sun seemed just the one. In Tokyo, on 30 July 1905, he called a meeting and founded his Tung-men Hui, or Sworn Society, under the umbrella of which he collected all the groups seeking to overthrow Q'ing rule.

The Tung-men Hui was not a stand-alone secret society as such but an affiliation of pressure groups. Merchants with businesses to protect, landowners, radical thinkers, disillusioned students and disaffected intellectuals, demobilized soldiers and patriotic republicans all joined. So did the Triads. Yet it was the students to whom Sun particularly addressed himself, because they possessed the potential for change. Young idealists were, he considered, better revolutionary partners than self-serving elders. Returning from their overseas studies, they could form a national army of intellectual agitators. He set about impressing upon them the tenets of republicanism and the important role the Triads played in the movement. He stressed the value of Triad societies and requested students to become members. In this way, they would enter into the wider brotherhood and automatically swear loyalty to him as a senior Triad official. Furthermore, he argued, the Triads were a very destructive power which could be turned into a constructive one if they had an adequate,

108

thinking leadership. The students could provide it, their role being to introduce new ideas into Triad societies which would filter down to the peasant masses. This would, he declared, lead to the secret societies' ensuring that the revolution was popularly received. Finally, he lectured, the Triads were not to be looked down upon. This was important, for most students were from the wealthy classes who had traditionally regarded Triads as a criminal rabble-rousing nuisance which preyed upon them.

Sun wanted to bend the Triads to his political will, but in time he realized this was impossible, conceding that whilst he might use them, he would never reshape them. He had to accept that they were primarily self-serving. Instead of reforming them, he left them undisturbed but infiltrated his ideas into them whenever he could, thankful when these occasionally stuck.

Over the next six years, Sun Yat-sen was a thorn in the Q'ing rump. He travelled widely across the Far East and South-east Asia, raising funds and preaching republicanism amongst frequently well-heeled overseas Chinese expatriate communities. He was like a spider, weaving an ever more complex web of support and agitation.

Sun's travelling was partially brought about by necessity. The Japanese government, concerned at the den of Chinese political intrigue existing in their country, quietly but firmly asked him to leave in 1907. He agreed, but did not go empty-handed. The Japanese bought him off with a sum rumoured to be around US$5 million, paid in instalments. He was also kept on the move by the Q'ing embassies, for whenever he arrived in a new country the ambassador would immediately start seeking his expulsion.

In French Indo-China, he raised large sums from the massive Chinese communities in Hanoi and Saigon where Triads provided him with extensive introductions. The French colonial government was sympathetic. They earned a substantial tax revenue from the opium trade with China and were also intimately involved with the Union Corse – the 'French Corsican Mafia' – in Shanghai, which, in turn, was in close collaboration with the city's Triad societies. In effect, the entire French colonial administration was criminalized. Sun used French-backed jungle fighting units, which purchased opium in the mountains of northern Laos, to mount incursions into Chinese territory. They were joined by Triad units. In Singapore and Sumatra, he beat the republican drum. In Bangkok, in December 1908, he really caused trouble. The Siamese government, under pressure from the Chinese embassy, ordered his deportation. He asked for a week to get his affairs in order and to consult with his own ambassador. This rather bemused the Siamese: they pondered over who could be his national representative. Sun promptly presented himself at the US embassy and claimed he was an American citizen. Hamilton King, the US ambassador, was confounded. Sun possessed affidavits from people claiming to have known his father in Hawaii where he had been born. Hawaii was not then an American state, but it had been annexed in 1898 and was therefore under American jurisdiction; that it had been an independent kingdom when Sun was 'born' seems to have been irrelevant. To back up the affidavits, Sun produced a Hawaiian birth certificate and a US passport. Both were fakes manufactured by Triads in Honolulu, but they did the trick.

Now an 'American', Sun was able to travel extensively with fewer diplomatic problems. His web extended. He joined more Triad societies, becoming not only a fund-raising revolutionary but also a *de facto* roving Triad ambassador. Wherever he went, he introduced them into political circles, giving senior society officials the certain cachet of revolutionary respectability.

While Sun circumnavigated the globe, all was not dormant in China. After the rout of the Guangzhou coup, some comrades filtered back to southern China. In 1899, Chen Shao-pai unobtrusively returned to Hong Kong and re-opened a local branch of the Hsing Chung Hui. Cheng Shih-liang, also living quietly under British rule, cultivated his links with Triad societies both there, in Macau and over the Chinese border. Simultaneously, Sun despatched Triad society agents across China to link up with the Ko Lo Hui (Elder Brothers Society) in Henan and Hubei. It has been rumoured that Sun was a member of the Ko Lo Hui, but no proof exists; on the other hand, he joined every society he could if it was likely to gain him support, so it is not inconceivable that his agents were also fraternal emissaries.

Like many a typical Triad official, especially those in criminal societies today, Sun was never lax at seizing the opportunity to extend his own personal power. Abjuring oath 24 and its stipulation that no brother should promote himself, he ousted Yang Ch'u-yun from the Hsing Chung Hui by gaining the advocacy of the Ko Lo Hui in the Yangtze River region. The Ko Lo Hui 49s even started referring to Sun as their 'president'. In the cause of fraternal solidarity, and so as not to rock the political sampan, Yang obligingly agreed to stand down.

Chen Shao-pai and Cheng Shih-liang consolidated their activities with the Hsing Chung Hui in Hong Kong, keeping other Triad societies sweet with cash payments. The buying of allegiance was more effective than relying upon political or ideological sympathies. To further strengthen links, Chen Shao-pai was initiated into the San-ho Hui, although, it is reported, with a much abbreviated ceremony because he was dismissive of secret societies and the mumbo-jumbo of their ritual. He was interested only in political alliance and in the ability of the San-ho Hui to provide 49s with fighting prowess. Once he was sworn in, however, his credibility rose in the eyes of all the other societies with which he had ties.

Some time in the midwinter of 1899, a party of senior Ko Lo Hui officials referred to as *lung tau* (literally, Dragon Heads, a common colloquialism for a society leader), including those of the powerful Golden Dragon and Soaring Dragon branches of the society in the Yangtze River region, visited Hong Kong. Under the sponsorship of Chen Shao-pai, they met the *shan chu* of the main southern Chinese Triad societies to form a grand alliance with the Hsing Chung Hui. Sun was proclaimed chief executive. A full Triad ritual was performed and a bowl of wine mixed with the blood of a cockerel was shared, the delegates swearing fealty and the upholding of the anti-Q'ing credo. The alliance was appropriately named the Hsing Han Hui or Revive Han Association.

The Hsing Han Hui was not a Triad society but a free association. None of the parties lost its integrity or autonomy. There was not even any solid political basis

112

to their assembly. Indeed, the loyalty of some of the delegates – especially those from northern China where societies were more open to infiltration by Q'ing spies – was doubtful. This doubt was later proven when some broke away on being offered more money by opponents. All the delegates were given packets of *lai see* (lucky money). It was the Triad way. The Hsing Han Hui may not have been a Triad society but it behaved like one to achieve its purpose, providing Sun with a nation-wide presence.

The Ko Lo Hui had other uses than as a public-relations facility. It was constantly in touch with Sun, no matter where he was, feeding him information on affairs in China, tipping him off about military or official matters and receiving, stockpiling or distributing the weapons Sun was buying whenever and wherever he could.

Co-operation between the secret societies and the republicans was, throughout the years of Sun's peripatetic exile, very close. They did not just support him and receive his pay-offs and smuggled arms. They also disseminated his ideas to the peasants who made up the bulk of their membership, distributed Charlie Soong's political publications and kept the cause alive. Republicans frequently joined societies, while Triads often attended republican rallies to assist with recruitment. When the republicans had any dirty or dangerous work to be done – political assassination or the shake-down of opponents – the Triads acted for them.

The republicans learned important lessons from the Triads, who were efficient fighters and good guerrilla strategists. To gain loyalty and a sense of sombre occasion and seriousness, the republicans adopted Triad-style oath-taking initiation rituals, with the full panoply of Triad conspiratorial techniques. Passwords and phrases were used, secret handshakes and signs devised to foster secrecy and fraternal oneness. Rice shops, inns and teahouses were utilized as fronts for political intrigue and to provide safe houses.

By 1900, China was ripe for revolution. The Japanese had shamed the nation in Korea and the Boxers, shouting their anti-Christian slogans, were attacking foreigners. Foreign bankers were closing in on the country's economy. Taxes soared. The peasants had had enough and were ready to act, but lacked unified leadership. The Triad societies could have gone to their aid but they were either too busy looking after their own business or too disordered.

In Guangxi, matters took a slightly different turn. Here the peasants were being more highly taxed than elsewhere to pay off a local foreign debt burden, the Q'ing officials were particularly corrupt and the Xi Jiang burst its banks two years running, destroying crops, washing away whole villages and drowning hundreds. In 1897 and 1898, Triad societies in Guangxi organized two uprisings, under the leadership of a *shan chu* called Li Li-t'ing. Sun tried to get his people to join in but they arrived too late on each occasion. Neither uprising lasted long, but they showed Sun how he might gain political capital and kudos by staging another rebellion on the back of the regional misfortunes.

In July 1900, Huizhou was chosen as the starting point for the second revolutionary campaign, which, it was hoped, would bury the Guangzhou fiasco of five years before. It was probably Cheng Shih-liang who picked the venue. Huizhou, on the East River, 100 km north-east of Hong Kong and east of Guangzhou, was in a predominantly Hakka area and Cheng was a Hakka. Furthermore, although Triad recruits came from all over Guangdong, the majority came from around Huizhou. To amalgamate the disparate societies, Cheng imported someone with authority but no prior axe to grind – a smart move considering customary Triad rivalries. The man he called in was Huang Fu, an experienced *shan chu* from a north Borneo society, who took temporary charge of the Hsing Chung Hui until Cheng arrived from Hong Kong.

The rebels were a rag-tag army. A third of them, before the ranks were swelled by militant peasants, were not Triads but Christians: some were of both persuasions. Considering what was going on across China, with secret societies and the Boxers massacring Chinese Christians wholesale, the situation was paradoxical, yet it proves that Triad societies were not specifically anti-Christian, or even anti-foreign: most attacks on Christians were incited by individual leaders rather than the result of heartfelt Triad principles. Moreover, Sun's leadership, albeit by proxy, was strong enough to override the popular xenophobia. Under him, traditional anti-Q'ing motivation was retained.

The republicans may have raised a substantial army from the Hakka but they needed thousands more. To appeal to the peasants, they published a manifesto promising sweeping educational reforms, local government restructuring, constitutional change and an end to corruption. Every opportunity to convince them was exploited, including their gullibility. Near Yichang, on

115

the Yangtze, stood a large conical hill facing the town, upon which huge characters had been cut in the turf and painted white. The first three read *Q'ing kui wan* (The Pill that Fortifies): it was a huge advertisement for a popular tonic. However, when read aloud, the phrase sounded like 'The Q'ing shall soon end'. The Triads made capital of this and many peasants believed the political interpretation. Yichang became an important mustering point for republican sympathizers. Sales figures of the tonic to pro-republican peasants are not recorded.

The republican manifesto was music to peasant ears, pandering to their seething hatred of officials; it also appealed to foreign sympathizers and, therefore, investors. Wherever the revolutionary army moved, it was pasted on temple walls and in markets or proclaimed to gatherings. For the benefit of overseas readers, both sympathizers and foreign governments – the latter already edgy over the Boxer situation and the recently lifted Beijing legation siege – the revolutionaries referred to themselves as the Chinese Republican Association and admitted their Triad involvement. In order to put foreign minds at rest and gain sympathy abroad, and especially in nearby Hong Kong, they published a press statement on 10 October 1900, the day fighting broke out. It appeared in the Hong Kong English-language press and stated, quite categorically: 'We are not "Boxers". We are members of the Great Political Society of Masons, commonly known as Triads.' The image they projected of themselves was that of an army of reforming Ming monarchists, Triads and patriots. They did not proclaim their anti-Q'ing monarchist stand because many overseas governments recognized the imperial dynasty.

Cheng Shih-liang and Huang Fu were good organizers. Their lines of communication were excellent and the timing of the uprising, in the autumn after the rice harvest, when the peasants were less busy and the weather was turning milder, was perspicacious. The rebellion quickly took hold and, within a fortnight, had spread eastwards from Guangzhou, across the East River system and up the coast of China to Fujian. Yet it could not be sustained. The wider the rebellion spread, the more protracted became the lines of communication and, as the troops were told to buy their food rather than pillage the countryside, money started to run out. The uprising was suppressed but it taught an important lesson in revolutionary fighting. It also established the value of the Triads not just as a means of raising fighters but also as a network which had survived to be used again.

The networking capability of the Triads which Sun used so effectively was not merely something which came about through their ties of brotherhood. It was an extension of the particularly Chinese concept of *guanxi*, which arises from the Confucian ethos of revering one's ancestors and forming family, clan, place or name associations. Wherever Chinese go in the world, they never lose touch with their roots and are always open and welcoming to other Chinese if they share something in common with them. The result of this is the global perpetuation of ancient social structures.

It began with the foundations of Chinese society, before the introduction of currency. A farmer would give a sack of rice in order to borrow a plough. A poultry-keeper would give a few eggs to a neighbour

117

who watched for the fox on both their behalfs. Favours were swapped and gradually bonds formed between like-minded individuals. They brought their families or villages together, intermarriage further strengthening and extending the bonds. Down the centuries, clans have built up considerable networks of *guanxi*, which has come to take on an abstract but definite value. It cannot be sold but it can be hoarded, inherited, shared, extended and passed on.

When Chinese started to emigrate, they took their *guanxi* with them. Some even carried written records so they would not forget who owed them a favour, to whom they owed a favour and with whom they were – or were not – connected. In strange lands, *guanxi* enabled them to strike up relationships, found mutual (and Triad) societies, set up schools and banks and forge partnerships, several of which have come down to the present day as some of the world's largest multinational companies. Little business is done without the exercise of *guanxi* and the success of an overseas Chinese frequently depends upon it. Within modern China, little business can be conducted without a stock of *guanxi*, something which has foreign non-Chinese businessmen at a considerable disadvantage until they tap into it by forming their own contacts.

Sun Yat-sen's stock of *guanxi* was vast. Above all else, his Triad *guanxi* was such that it ensured, no matter where he went, there would be someone to give him succour. In addition, he also had *guanxi* because of where he and his family came from. More than 90 per cent of all Chinese emigrants hailed from Guangdong and Fujian provinces, but the majority came from what was termed the Sam

Yap or the Sze Yap – the Three and Four Districts of Punyu, Shuntak and Namhoi, and Sanwui, Toishan, Yanping, and Hoiping respectively, close to Guangzhou and west of the Pearl River delta. Sun's ancestral village was just inside the southernmost range of the Sam Yap district of Shuntak. With so much *guanxi*, Sun was in an exceptionally strong position to network widely. It also meant, of course, that he stocked up a lot of reciprocal *guanxi*: those who did favours for him and his cause might well expect a payback in the future.

While Sun travelled the world, exercising *guanxi*, Charlie Soong was similarly busy. Going to the USA on business, he mixed freely with both US senators and Triad societies: over the winter of 1905–6, he raised over US$2 million for the cause. As a result, he was appointed treasurer of the Revolutionary Alliance, as the Tung-men Hui was now called.

In October 1911, Sun Yat-sen's republicans organized an insurrection at Wuchang. It was the start of a revolution which spread rapidly throughout China. Once again, Triad participation was a seminal ingredient, to such an extent that, in some regions, Triad officials set up spontaneous local administrations with themselves in key positions. The Revolutionary Alliance, now based in Shanghai and Nanjing, was reconstituted into a new, all-encompassing Chinese national political party known as the Kuomintang or KMT.

On 1 January 1912, after the fall of Nanjing, the Republic of China was born, with Sun Yat-sen as its provisional president, although he soon resigned in favour of the commander of the army, Yüan Shih-k'ai, who was better placed to form a coalition of all the interested political factions represented in the new government. No sooner had Sun relinquished his post than the Triads transferred their support to Yüan, who imposed a rigorous tax system to raise revenue to build the new republic. When peasants rose up against it, he sent in troops, equipped with the latest modern Western weapons, to quell them. Units of Triad mercenaries operated at their side.

In Nanjing, on the day after his election as president of the Republic of China, Sun conducted a solemn celebration to honour the spirits of the Ming emperors who had made the city their capital in the fourteenth century. *Fan q'ing – fuk ming* was, at last, a reality. This ceremony was also generally regarded as a sign of homage to the secret societies which had, for over two centuries, fought the Q'ing overlords. A month later, on 15 February, one of the last acts of Sun's brief presidency was to go to the tombs of the Ming emperors and publicly declare to the people and the imperial ancestors that the Q'ing dynasty had ended.

The downfall of the Q'ing dynasty, the overthrow of the last emperor, Henry Aisin-Gioro Pu Yi, and the establishment of the Republic of China, could not have been achieved without the Triad societies. Afterwards, however, Sun rarely acknowledged the vital part they had played and hardly ever admitted his membership of a Triad society. He knew the Triads had been at best uneasy republican bedfellows and was always keen to state that their connection with republican ideals had been tenuous. In public, therefore, he pretended they were a minor factor but in private he knew otherwise and remained in close collaboration with them. He had to. They could easily unseat the republic, or cause it some severe political and social headaches.

Glorying in victory, Triad influence became all-pervasive. In the following years, they greatly increased their membership. Their assistance in the republican cause was rewarded by the virtual recognition of the Triad societies. Triad officials held senior government posts, given to them by Sun in payment for their services, and they became so powerful that most non-Triad officials were obliged to join: in order to gain promotion in the civil service or the armed forces, it was essential to be a Triad. Officialdom turned a blind eye to Triad activity and the Triads acquired exclusive territories where they could get on with their criminal activities unmolested by the authorities.

An example of the kind of accommodation that could be reached was the deal struck in Qingdao, the German treaty port, between a local Triad society and the chief of police. The latter gained his promotion through the intervention of the *shan chu*. Once in his post, he withdrew and virtually disbanded the vice squad. The Triads had a free rein in running all the brothels in the vicinity of the docks, with the result that prostitution rose sharply and venereal disease amongst foreign sailors reached epidemic proportions. Some foreign shipping companies refused shore leave to crews: for a time, Qingdao was nicknamed 'Clapdoh' by foreign sailors. The situation only improved when the chief of police was promoted again, out of the town.

Others, particularly employers who relied upon large bodies of labour, found Triad membership increased

121

security and, pro rata, profits, for the Triads ran most coolie guilds. Merchants, bankers and businessmen quickly discovered that Triad membership oiled the machinery of commerce in a remarkable way. To Westerners this was graft and corruption on a grand scale; to the Chinese it was a well-established facet of public life, an extension of *guanxi*.

China was now a different country, emerging from a system of government 2,000 years old into a new, untried and essentially alien political structure. The imperial era was over: there was no question of restoring the Ming dynasty. The historical mission of the Chinese secret societies, which had in any case become increasingly less important to them, had come to an end. With their new-found power and freedom they quickly degenerated from pragmatic patriots into out and out criminals running sophisticated syndicates funded, ironically, by China's new success. Trade and industry boomed and the Triads reaped huge profits. As the businessmen's success increased, so did the level of their protection money and backhanders.

The next stage in the Triads' history was about to begin.

2

NATIONALISTS, COMMUNISTS AND CROOKS

The establishment of the Republic swept away the old order, yet the underlying tensions in society remained. The peasants were still poor, still exploited, still charged exorbitant rents by avaricious landlords, still oppressively taxed and still preyed upon by secret societies. Droughts, floods and accompanying famines were still common.

Reaction from the peasants took the form of uprisings, but uprisings with a difference. Whereas before these had been spontaneous eruptions of anger, or rebellion spurred on by secret societies or republicans, now they were induced by political parties, of which hundreds sprang up.

These uprisings, mostly shortlived and readily put down if they did not subside of their own volition before the troops' arrival, rolled over the country in waves, like the wind over the rice paddies. Known as *yün-tung*, they were little more than transient movements involving public demonstrations, riots, temporary withdrawal of labour and, on occasion, the boycotting of foreign goods. From the mid-1920s, however, they were to be superseded by a new form of political agitation which evolved into full-scale civil war between the Kuomintang and the

123

Chinese Communist Party (CCP). Supported primarily by peasants, this differed from the *yün-tung* unrest by being better organized by specific political parties which allied armed combat with political dogma.

In this new era of comparative political liberty, secret societies were marginalized. Their role, previously in support of revolutionary reactionists, had become an anachronism. In the minds of many people, they had served their purpose: the Q'ing dynasty was over and they were obsolete. In the big cities, like Shanghai and Guangzhou, the new political parties stepped into their shoes.

The main party, Sun Yat-sen's Kuomintang Nationalist Party, had a struggle keeping both itself and the country on an even keel. Yüan Shih-k'ai started to develop 'dynastic tendencies'. With his presidency ratified in late 1913, he set about marginalizing both Sun and the Kuomintang, dissolved parliament and set himself up as a dictator. In 1915, he oversaw plans to restore the monarchy and, a few months later, declared himself the new emperor.

In his spiritual and ancestral homeland, the southern provinces of China, Sun led a popular rebellion against Yüan, forcing him to surrender his newly acquired throne in April 1916. Two months later, Yüan was dead. This victory was achieved by the Kuomintang with Triad society assistance: there was no way Sun could operate without Triad involvement. The societies were heavily involved with the Kuomintang, which they regarded as 'their' party. Not willing to risk the fickleness of the masses, Sun called upon them to provide muscle, experienced Red Poles taking command of military units.

During his time in the political wilderness, Sun had done more than continue to consolidate his power-base with the Triads. He had married into the Soong family, by now the most powerful in China.

Charlie Soong had six children. Of his three sons, two became powerful financiers, instrumental in the development of the Chinese Republic, whilst the other became China's prime minister. The daughters, Ai-ling, Ching-ling and Mei-ling, were just as important: it was said of them that one loved power, one loved money and one loved China. Ai-ling, who loved money, was a skilful financier and shrewd speculator who married H. H. Kung, the minister of finance, and founded a business dynasty in America. Mei-ling was the one who came to love power. Ching-ling, who loved China, married Sun in 1914. She had, for some time, been his personal assistant and confidante. There was one hitch to their relationship: Sun had not divorced his first wife. This created a degree of unpopularity both in China and with foreign investors, but it did not seriously undermine him. Besides, he had greater problems to face.

For a decade after Yüan's demise, much of China entered into what is known as the Warlord Period. The central government was impotent and local regions came to be ruled by the modern Chinese equivalent of medieval European barons. To keep their positions, they recruited local armies or hired mercenaries, many armed with the latest Western weapons sold to them by itinerant Western arms traders for whom China was, for some years, a boom market.

In political allegiance, the warlords covered the full spectrum. Some were outright monarchists, some republicans, some independence-seekers. A few were Triad leaders. All ruled by charisma rather than charm and, their rule being based upon personality rather than doctrine, their grip on the countryside was tenuous.

To raise finance for their domains, they taxed peasants' agricultural output, placed tolls on rivers and roads, raided each other's little kingdoms and, above all else, grew and traded opium. A good many were little more than localized masters of a manor, but a few grew powerful and had extensive realms. Chang Tso-lin controlled Manchuria, T'ang Chi-yao ran Yunnan and made a small fortune in opium, Yen Hsi-shan held Shanxi. One warlord in Hunan, the self-styled General Feng Yü-hsiang, was a Christian who forbade his troops to drink alcohol, smoke tobacco or deal in, or use, opium. Any who did were shot. Civilian opium dealers in his towns were publicly flogged then paraded in a cangue with a label round their necks outlining their sins. Addicts, on the other hand, were treated for their addiction. Needless to say, Feng was not popular with the Triads.

To counteract the warlords' developing belligerence, especially in northern and central China, Sun set himself up in Guangzhou, strengthening his army with military aid from Russia, which led to a brief alliance between the Kuomintang and the Chinese Communist Party, who were represented at the first national congress in 1924.

The congress elected Sun head of the Kuomintang government, but he was hardly president of China for the party was powerful only in southern China, especially around Guangzhou, where it garnered support from peasants, intellectuals and students, and in Hong Kong and with the army. And, of course, among the Triads.

For several years, Sun tried to reunify China, defuse the warlord situation and persuade them to abandon their ambitions for the sake of the common good. He failed and died in March 1925. His failure is not surprising: China is not and has never been a land where democracy could easily take root. There is too much in the national psyche militating against it. Sun died a hero, but he had only been as successful as he was because of the solid support of his Triad brothers.

With Sun dead, China was ready for her next leap into the political unknown and the Triads were ready for whatever it might bring them. The man who was to lead her through the next turbulent decades, like Sun, served his apprenticeship to power in the ranks of the Triads.

Chiang Kai-shek was born Chiang Jui-yuan on 31 October 1887 in the town of Chikou, in Chekiang. His mother was the third wife of a salt merchant above whose business premises the family lived. His father died when he was a young child and his mother subsequently lived a widow's hard existence: the chances of a widow remarrying in China were slim. Chiang was a disturbed child, his behaviour unpredictable, prone to fits of unbridled rage and periods of ill-health. He was ridiculed by his peers because of his high-pitched voice and peculiarly shaped head, which, in later years, caused the American intelligence services to codename him 'Peanut'.

After his father's death, the family became a target for unscrupulous landlords and Chiang a scapegoat for local petty crime, being arrested for wrongs he had not committed. On one occasion, he was accused of reneging on a debt incurred by another man against a rice merchant:

Chiang was forced to pay the miscreant's debt under a Chinese legal ruling which could hold citizens liable for the wrongs of their family, relatives and even neighbours. He developed a large chip on his shoulder and sought protection from the cruelties of the world. The Triads were his sanctuary. He joined a small group, little more than a street gang, which made a meagre living by extortion; but it served its purpose. Chiang was an ideal recruit. He had a vicious streak, bore grudges and was driven by revenge. Within the security of a brotherhood, the bullied could become the bully.

At the age of fourteen, he was married to a seventeen-year-old local girl called Mao Fu-mei; it was an arranged marriage and he was not in love with his bride. When he was eighteen, he decided against following his father's profession and, with his mother's savings, moved to Fenghua where he enrolled in a small school called the Pavilion of Literature. The school formed his character: he left it a year later, instructed in meditation and determined to succeed in life. For a few months in 1906 he attended a middle school, then, cutting off his queue to show his defiant independence, left to undergo military training in Japan. On arrival, however, he discovered that only Q'ing-government-sponsored Chinese could enter a military academy. Suddenly he was without an aim, adrift in a foreign country, and he gravitated towards the nearest Chinese expatriate community to fall in with the republican followers of Sun Yat-sen. One in particular, Ch'en Ch'i-mei, befriended him. Ch'en, one of Sun's most ardent recruiters, was a member of the especially ruthless and powerful Triad society in Shanghai, the Hung Pang (or Red Gang), the leader of which was Huang Chih-jung, also known as Pockmarked Huang.

Under Ch'en's guidance, Chiang returned to China, sat the army entrance examinations, passed them, attended a military academy in Hebei then obtained permission to be transferred to Japan for further training. In 1908, he embarked on a three-year course at the famous Shimbu Gakko Military Academy, leaving behind his wife – whom he frequently beat and sexually abused – and their first son, Ching-kuo. Upon his arrival in Japan, Ch'en put Chiang up for membership of Sun's political movement. He was accepted.

From time to time, Chiang returned to China, ostensibly to see his mother, though he spent much of his time in Shanghai with Ch'en. It was during one of these visits that he was enrolled into one of the city's powerful criminal syndicates, the Green Gang. Involving himself in its general activities, taking part in extortion, armed robberies and a jail break, he gained a reputation as a skilful and ruthless assassin; his police record in the International Settlement, that area of the city occupied and controlled by foreign nationals, lengthened by the month. The police in the British quarter were especially keen to catch him, yet, despite being frequently indicted, he was never brought to trial. He had powerful friends.

In 1911, now graduated from the Shimbu Gakko school, he joined Ch'en for the revolution in October. Ch'en was in command of the 83rd Brigade, a unit of Sun's republican army made up entirely of 3,000 Green Gang 49s under the control of a number of Red Poles. Chiang, who had quickly risen through the Triad ranks due to his assassinatory proficiency, was one of them. As the revolution gathered pace, Chiang was put in charge of a hand-picked commando unit of 100 men which stormed Hangzhou to assist local republicans who were under fierce attack. Chiang and his men routed the imperial forces and liberated the town. With the success of the revolution – and as one of the Triads who had aided Sun – Ch'en was appointed military governor of Shanghai. With his elevation, Chiang, the hero of Hangzhou, was made commander of his own regiment.

In December 1911, Chiang turned his hand for the first time to political assassination. A Shanghai revolutionary and leader of a Triad society called the Restoration Society, T'ao Ch'eng-chang, appeared to be trying to take over Ch'en Ch'i-mei's position as military and, therefore, political, master of the city. When T'ao fell ill, Chiang went to the hospital and, waiting until T'ao's bodyguards were absent, entered his room and shot him. This was such a high-profile killing that Ch'en deemed it best if Chiang lay low for a while, so Chiang went into self-imposed exile in Japan until late in 1912, when he reappeared in Shanghai and returned to his old ways.

Chiang lived a dissolute, self-indulgent life for which Shanghai catered better than any other city on earth. It was reckoned in 1912 that one in every dozen houses was a bordello and one in every fifty women made her living by immoral means. Just as many young men were also engaged in the same game: homosexual brothels were abundant. Chiang started to drink heavily, which exacerbated his fits of temper during which no-one dared cross him. He lived with 'sing-song' girls in brothels in the French Concession – a part of the International Settlement controlled by the French colonial government in Hanoi – enjoying their company and sexual favours (sing-song girls were prostitutes who visited punters' tables, singing to them as well as joining them in a drink). His favourite haunt was the Maison Bleu, which housed over 100 whores and a resident Chinese classical orchestra; in the 1920s it had a resident jazz band as well. Like every single brothel across the International Settlement, it was operated by the Green Gang, which also controlled by extortion all those elsewhere in greater Shanghai which it did not own.

In this milieu of decadence and crime, Chiang came into contact with every Triad official in the Green Gang. One of them was to become arguably the most important person in his life and one of the most important in the history of China in the twentieth century. His name was Du Yueh-sheng, otherwise known to the police as Big-eared Du.

Du was the consummate Triad criminal. He was born in Kaochiao in Pootung district, across the Whangpoo River from Shanghai, in either 1887 or 1888. Pootung was considered the worst slum in the nation. His father owned a rice shop, but it was only a makeshift affair and he was also his own coolie; his mother was a washer-woman. When Du was three his mother died, at which time, as was the custom, his baby sister was given away. In later life, Du spent a large sum of money attempting to trace her, but without success. His father moved in with another, younger woman but died himself in two or three years. Then, in 1895, Shanghai suffered an earthquake followed by a city-wide cholera epidemic. Du and his 'stepmother' survived both and she continued with the rice shop. Being a vulnerable widow, she was kidnapped by local Triad thugs and sold into one of Shanghai's many brothels. Now about ten years old, Du was put under the guardianship of an uncle who physically abused him and used him as a servant.

By the age of twelve, Du was a hardened, streetwise delinquent, an inveterate gambler with a ruthless reputation. His police file described him as a sinewy youth with long arms, the eyes of a rat and yellow teeth. It was in his early teens that he was initiated into the Red Gang. His sponsor was a fellow gambler and pimp nicknamed Lot Drawer whom Du helped as a runner in a numbers racket. Once a member, Du moved into the Red Gang-managed Tian Song doss-house and began to frequent the home and headquarters of Pockmarked Huang, who was not only the most powerful underworld figure in Shanghai, a major opium dealer and co-owner of the bizarre, world-famous Great World Amusement building on the junction of what is now Nanjing Xi Lu and Xizang Lu, but also chief detective for the Sûreté (French CID) in the French Concession.

At fifteen, Du abandoned his uncle and worked for a while as an assistant at the Da Yu fruit company trading in the French Concession. It was not his only employment. Pockmarked Huang's mistress, Gui Song, was an opium dealer in her own right. On one occasion, a delivery of raw opium was stolen but, after a rickshaw chase across Shanghai, Du recovered it. For his perspicacity, he was taken before Huang to be praised. The astute leader quickly recognized Du's potential and he became Huang's main opium runner, bringing illicit opium into the city whilst acting on the side as a contract killer.

132

Now in his late teens, Du ensured that his physical appearance was both distinctive and disturbing. He shaved his head, which gave even more prominence to the large ears from which he acquired his moniker. His face was round, his eyes coldly inexpressive and narrow, his nose broad; his lips were full and pulled tight over protruding upper teeth, which further accounted for his being compared with a rodent. His neck was short, thick and covered with hard bumps, subcutaneous scar tissue caused by his uncle's savage beatings. His left eyelid hung down in a permanent semi-wink for the same reason, giving him a lizard-like look.

By the time he was twenty-one, Du controlled half the opium dens in the French Concession, through the Opium Pipe Company, ran his own opium business on the rue du Consolat and was the sole proprietor of the up-market jewellers Mei Tsung Hwa Kee. He also operated a loan company with clients ranging from local Chinese storekeepers to foreign expatriates, quite a number of the latter having their homes mortgaged to him.

It was not long before Du was promoted to Red Pole and Huang started to take him into his confidence. Although it was not his position to make such suggestions, Du proposed an amalgamation of the three main Triad societies operating the Shanghai opium trade, the Red, Green and smaller Blue Gangs. Huang agreed that the merger would make good sense and Du was told to instigate his plan. The Green Gang leader saw no point to an amalgamation, so Du murdered him and appointed himself leader in his place. The Blue Gang leader, Chang Hsiao-lin, considered his options in the light of the fate of the Green Gang leader and endorsed the coalition. The opium trade was now under the control of a cartel consisting of Huang, Chang and Du. Their joint criminal territory extended to Zhejiang and Jiangsu and up the Yangtze River as far as Chongqing, giving them direct access to the poppy-growing regions of China.

Within the International Settlement, the provision of opium had long been controlled by the Three Harmonies Society, made up of Teochiu (sometimes referred to as Chiu Chau or Chiu) Chinese from Swatow under the leadership of a Cantonese called Wong Sui. Du approached Wong, who, realizing discretion was the better part of valour, combined his society with the Green Gang. The Three Harmonies Society membership, which included Sun Yat-sen and Charlie Soong, seems not to have objected. It was through this takeover that Big-eared Du came into close contact with the republicans.

Du then disbanded the Three Harmonies Society in Shanghai. By the time he was twenty-one, he had swallowed up all the Shanghai Triad societies with the exceptions of a peasant league in the rural areas around the city, which nevertheless owed complete allegiance to him, and a patriotic society which retained the Red Gang name but engaged in little criminal activity, though it still paid tribute to Du. What remained was a cartel which came to be known just as the Green Gang.

Pockmarked Huang remained the overall *shan chu* of the cartel, but Du was either the *fu* (or deputy) *shan chu* or Incense Master. He rapidly grew exceedingly wealthy, his personal fortune estimated to be around US$40 million at contemporary values by the time he was thirty. Shanghai was his private fiefdom, his citywide network of spies as good as that of any secret service. He even had access to the mail, which would be delayed and opened if he deemed it worthwhile. He bribed the press and, where necessary, not only the Chinese and venal French Concession police forces but also those in other parts of the International Settlement, including the British quarter. By extortion, threats and bribery, Du had in his thrall most of the foreign traders' compradors, which gave him considerable but invisible influence over foreign business interests. One such comprador, employed by the Hongkong & Shanghai Bank in their main office on the Bund, arranged for senior tellers to pass both foreign and Chinese merchants' credit information to Du. With such intelligence, he had his finger on the pulse of the mercantile city.

In 1915 Du married, but much to his disappointment his wife was found to be infertile. They adopted a son and Du took on two fifteen-year-old concubines. They all lived in an opulent colonnaded mansion on the rue Wagner in the French Concession; all senior cartel officials lived in the French quarter, protected by Chief Detective Pockmarked Huang of the Sûreté. The concubines bore six sons for Du, who, ever conscious of the risk of kidnapping, employed White Russian bodyguards. Sexually vigorous into his late thirties, despite his addiction to opium, Du later employed two more concubines.

In his virtually unassailable position, Du mixed with high society. Through Charlie Soong, he was introduced to many influential businessmen, as well as to Soong's own family. He befriended Soong's daughter, Ai-ling, whom he frequently met on her way home from the Methodist Church in the French Concession. The Soongs lived securely under French rule, also watched over by

Huang. Through Ai-ling's marriage to H. H. Kung, Big-eared Du was well known to the banker. As a result, the Kung banking empire, which was controlled by the Soong family, was secretly combined with the Green Gang. This, in turn, gave Big-eared Du an entry into the foreign business community, his credentials given added respectability because of his alliance with the Christian Soongs. For a quarter of a century, until 1940, this connection amassed a staggering fortune from banking, stock-market dealings, property speculation and company asset-stripping. Between them, the Soongs, the Kungs, their political allies and Du had near-complete control of the Chinese economy. It was only with the advent of Communism in 1949 that this control was finally wrested from them.

Well connected he may have been, but Du was still first and foremost a gangster with all the trappings of a master criminal. In his study, *The Shanghai Capitalists and the Nationalist Government: 1927–37*, Parks M. Coble Jr described seeing him arrive at a nightclub in Shanghai:

> A carload of advance bodyguards came and 'cased' the cabaret from kitchen to cloak-rooms, then took up stations to wait for the boss. Du himself always traveled in a large, bullet-proof sedan . . . Behind the leader's limousine a second car-load of bodyguards traveled. Du never got out until these had surrounded him. Then, with one at each elbow, he ventured to cross the footpath and enter the cabaret, where his men were posted at every door and turn. Inside while he and his party sat at a front table, guards sat beside and behind, guns in plain view.

Those whom Du could not befriend through fraternal Triad relationships or common interests, he befriended by placing them under his obligation. An example of this is given in Frank Ching's family biography, *Ancestors*, in which the writer describes how Du ensnared his lawyer father. Ching's father, Qin Liankui, was a friend of a man called Zhu Rushan, who, from time to time, went gambling in one of the Green Gang casinos. One night, Qin went gambling with Zhu at Du Yueh-sheng's mansion, where he lost 4,000 silver Chinese dollars. At the end of the evening, he paid off his debt with a bank cheque and went home. After he had left, Du asked Zhu who his friend was. On being told he was a lawyer, Du handed the cheque to Zhu, demanding he give it back. Lawyers, Du said, earned too little for the amount of work they had to do. Zhu duly returned the cheque. At first, Qin refused it but Zhu persuaded him to take it: money sent by Du could not be refused. Too much face would be lost. He was not a man to have as an enemy. Qin took the cheque and was, thereafter, Du's attorney. They became close friends and often called each other brother, which probably only meant one thing. Du may have initiated his adviser into his secret society.

Moving in Shanghai's social whirl increased Du's standing in the community, as his entry in the Shanghai *Who's Who*, published in the 1930s, records. Listed as the Right Honourable Du Yueh-sheng, it reads in part:

At present most influential resident, French Concession, Shanghai. Well-known public welfare worker . . . councillor, French Municipal Council. Founder and Chairman, board of directors, Cheng Shih Middle School.

President of Shanghai Emergency Hospital. Member, supervisory committee, General Chamber of Commerce. Managing Director Hua Feng Paper Mill, Hangchow. Director, Great China University, Chinese Cotton Goods Exchange, and China Merchants Steam Navigation Co. Shanghai, etc. President, Jen Chi Hospital, Ningpo.

To further his credibility with foreign businessmen and investors, in 1936 Du was also baptized a Christian. At the time, Mei-ling Soong remarked that you could tell he had become a sincere Christian because, since his acceptance into the church, there had been a pronounced decrease in kidnappings in Shanghai.

Not all Du's friends came from Shanghai's high society, nor was he a visitor just to the salons of the rich. He frequently patronized brothels operated by the Green Gang, indulging his sexual peccadilloes not just for female prostitutes, with their thin waists and bound feet, but also for young boys. His favourite dive, like Chiang Kai-shek's, was the Maison Bleu and it was here that they came to know each other.

Sometime in 1912, Chiang Kai-shek, Ch'en Ch'i-mei and the Kuomintang chief of staff, Huang Fu, attended a special ceremony at which they swore blood allegiance to each other, a ritual usually performed only by men of the same family or clan. It was more than a spiritual alliance. It bound them together politically, morally, spiritually and criminally and meant that, as well as swearing to protect each other's kin, they promised, on pain of death, to protect, advance and ensure that they each prospered. At

138

the same time, Chiang also forged a deep friendship with another Green Gang senior official and confidant of Big-eared Du, a wealthy financier, banker and revolutionary sympathizer called Chang Ching-chang. A partial cripple, he was better known to Westerners as a dealer of international repute in Chinese antiques and antiquities, many of which he was fencing for his Triad associates through his art galleries in Paris and New York. On account of his work, he was nicknamed Curio Chang. In time, he was to become one of Chiang Kai-shek's most important political allies, arranging political patronage for him, laundering his money and, where it was felt necessary, acting as negotiator in his affairs with anyone with whom Chiang thought it best not to be seen dealing direct.

Inevitably, both Chiang and Ch'en were wanted by Yüan Shih-k'ai's police. In 1915, with Shanghai crawling with spies from all political camps, both came near to capture and had to flee. They went to Japan but returned to Shanghai on a number of occasions, slipping in to carry out some crime and then escaping. If anything, Ch'en was more sought than Chiang, for, as well as being a wanted criminal, he was also by now chairman of the Central Committee of the Kuomintang. Finally, in May 1916, a month after Yüan's deposing and a month before his death, the secret police caught up with Ch'en and he was murdered. Big-eared Du immediately offered Chiang his support and protection, ensuring that Chiang avoided arrest in the International Settlement.

The loss of his friend and mentor was a terrible shock to Chiang Kai-shek, but it paid him a considerable dividend. No sooner was Ch'en dead than there was a major realignment of power in the Kuomintang. Chiang became a senior political assistant to Sun Yat-sen and, in 1917, his military adviser in Guangzhou, where he was also appointed head of Sun's personal security. However, he did not allow political and military responsibilities to interfere with criminal or personal activities. He worked closely with Big-eared Du, with whom he set up a stock market and commodities exchange in Shanghai, enabling both to earn considerable sums of money, much of it derived from insider dealing. In the stock market, Chiang was listed as an accredited broker. A contemporary joke in Shanghai had him so named because he broke the limbs and fingers of those who crossed him. Big-eared Du made a contribution from his trading profits to the Kuomintang and was rewarded by being made a major-general in the Kuomintang army.

During the Warlord Period, internecine fighting de-stabilized much of China but it did not unduly affect the central government. Or the Triads. In fact, Big-eared Du profited from the unrest, for he was in touch with many of the warlords from whom he bought opium and to whom he either sold arms or directed foreign traders so to do, taking a commission for the introduction. When a warlord needed a bit of muscle, or military advice, the Green Gang provided it, for a price.

To anyone who cared to delve deeply, the government of China was by 1920 indistinguishable from the Triads and their criminality. The entire fabric of government was inextricably bound up with the intrigues and machinations of the criminal underworld. The country's finance was substantially underpinned by criminal money.

On several occasions Chiang made himself indispensable to Sun, but his motives were neither patriotic nor honourable. His Shanghai patrons – Du Yueh-sheng and the Soongs, with other wealthy industrialists, bankers and merchants – wanted him to ingratiate himself with Sun. They had plans for their boy Chiang. In 1923, he was sent on a diplomatic mission to Moscow to drum up Soviet support for Sun Yat-sen's government. Chiang and his patrons were not in favour of this socialist liaison, for they were right wing, but he put aside his political beliefs. The following year, he was rewarded at the Kuomintang national congress by being appointed chairman of the preparatory committee of the Whampoa Military Academy at Huangpu, near Guangzhou; within months, he was chief of staff of the Kuomintang army.

With Chiang in charge, the military academy opened its doors. The officer in charge of enrolment was Ch'en Kuo-fu, Ch'en Ch'i-mei's nephew. Since Ch'en's death, Chiang had kept his oath and was 'looking after' whomever of Ch'en's relatives needed help or advancement. Ch'en Kuo-fu recruited approximately 7,000 cadets into the academy, directly or mainly from the 49 and Red Pole ranks of the Green Gang; others who joined were relatives or clan members. They all became Chiang Kai-shek's personal staff.

When Sun Yat-sen died, a power struggle ensued for leadership of the Kuomintang. A number of candidates were put forward and it was generally believed by the public that the man who would step into the old republican's shoes was Liao Chung-k'ai, a left-of-centre politician who shared Sun's unattainable dreams of democracy and benevolent socialism. Yet it was secretly known in many political quarters that Liao stood little chance of promotion because he did not have the correct backing. Whoever did accept Sun's mantle would have to have the tacit, secret support of Du Yueh-sheng. Du would himself have liked to head the party, but that was out of the question: his criminal record was said to fill thirty-seven files in the Shanghai police vaults. Besides, Du knew he had no need to take over Sun's vacancy: he had instead his own man in position to act as his proxy if not his puppet.

In the months following Sun's death, China was bedevilled by unrest. The Communists, who controlled the General Federation of Labour in Shanghai, called over 500 strikes in 1925, but not just for the sake of their members. The walk-outs were also a political move. The Communists wanted to break the stranglehold the right-wing-biased Triads had over the labour market through Triad-affiliated workers' guilds, which were themselves in a state of chaos with Big-Eared Du and Pockmarked Huang at odds over who controlled whom in them.

To say Du was right wing is a considerable understatement. He was devoutly, methodically, almost pathologically anti-Communist and had kept a close watch on the developing Chinese Communist Party from, quite literally, the day it was founded in July 1921. At meetings convened at 106 rue Wautz and in the girls' school on rue Auguste Boppe (auspiciously called Joyous Undertaking Street by the Chinese), at which the Chinese Communist Party was born, Du had spies present. To him, Communism was not just an alien political concept thought up by Westerners. It was an ideology that could and, he believed, would undermine the entire basic framework of Chinese society. If it did that, he rightly feared, it would also undermine his extensive criminal empire. The justification of this fear had, in part, already shown itself. By organizing labour and trade unions, and developing the concept of working-class consciousness, the Communists were weakening the Triad societies' grip on the peasants. In some instances, the Communists had already shown their potential by masterminding major industrial unrest, such as the crippling seamen's strike in Hong Kong in 1922. It was, Du knew, time to act.

Curio Chang was despatched to Guangzhou to warn Chiang Kai-shek to be ready to make a concerted bid for power. Shortly afterwards, in August 1925, Liao Chung-k'ai was gunned down in Guangzhou, the assassination carried out by five Green Gang hit-men sent down from Shanghai. Liao's murder removed the left-wing candidate for Sun's seat. To further destabilize the situation, a rumour went around that the killing was planned by a right-wing moderate, Hu Han-min: that got rid of him. A power vacuum developed into which stepped Chiang Kai-shek, the middle-of-the-road candidate with a pro-ven pro-Kuomintang record and, seemingly, no real political axe to grind. In a sense, this was true: Chiang's axe was as much felonious as it was political. With him in charge, the Kuomintang was finally, thoroughly crim-inalized.

No sooner was Chiang in place than, in true Triad fashion, he appointed Chang Ching-chang to the chair-manship of the Kuomintang Central Committee. Further down the chain of command, everyone moved up one notch, especially if they were well connected. Between them, Chiang and Curio Chang controlled the entire party. Du Yueh-sheng had his proxies in place, but few knew of his shadow in the wings: even the Communists remained ignorant of his ghost-like presence.

Chiang Kai-shek's power seemed to come from his charismatic personality. He appeared to inspire loyalty from others. The army was staunchly behind him and party members looked as if they were fully in support. Yet his power was ephemeral. What kept him in place was his patron, Big-eared Du, to whom he was obliged, in the time-honoured way of Triad societies, to pay monthly tribute.

The Communists were not slow to try to take political advantage of Chiang Kai-shek's new position: they wanted to find his weaknesses. For eighteen months, they organized strikes and general public disorder across China, but primarily in or near the cities and main lines of communication. To counteract this insurgency, Chiang (with Du behind him) set out to crush the Communists, using the army and, in Shanghai especially, units of Green Gang 49s. It was hoped they would completely eradicate the socialists. Students with Communist leanings in Shanghai were murdered, frequently by decapitation, and their bodies dumped on street corners or at crossroads as a lesson to others.

Early in 1927, Chiang received assistance in his anti-Communist campaign from Western officials and businessmen. The police in the International Settlement began to turn a blind eye to Triad activity and arrest levels fell. No-one was apprehended – at least, not a single Triad was arrested or indicted – for the killing of a Communist supporter. The motivation behind this collaboration was the fear of what the Communists might do to trade were they to come to power. Most foreign businessmen had seen where the future lay just by looking at Russia and the substantial White Russian population in Shanghai, who had escaped from Soviet Russia at the time of the October Revolution in 1917. They were instrumental in spreading the fear of nationalization and the confiscation of business assets. Many of these refugees from Marxism actively supported the Triads by providing them with arms and information. At least one White Russian émigré acted as a spy, joining the Communists and betraying them to the Triads.

Actively or passively assisting the Triads was, as we have seen, widespread in the International Settlement. The French Concession was the centre of the illicit trade in opiates which stretched from Shanghai up the Yangtze River for at least 1,600 km and, from it, radiated into China like the legs of a vast, poisonous spider. The trade was entirely run by the Green Gang, Big-eared Du controlling it from production to consumption. He imported raw opium from Persia but he also owned thousands of acres of poppy fields in Yunnan and Szechuan, managing the transportation of raw opium down the Yangtze, overseeing its purification in Nanjing, Hangzhou and Shanghai. In Shanghai, he was ultimately in charge of the processing of raw opium into morphine and, later, heroin. In 1927, his estimated profits from narcotics alone stood at about US$2,800,000 at contemporary values, making him not only one of the richest men in Shanghai but also in the whole of China. His income made up a substantial percentage of the overall financial structure of the city, for much of it was ploughed back into legitimate businesses and the stock market he had set up with Chiang Kai-shek.

In order to keep his business running and the Green Gang unmolested, Du paid monthly backhanders of $150,000 to French government officials and police. Living in the French Concession, he was free from interference from the Chinese police, although it must be said, where they were concerned, he was virtually immune from harassment or prosecution in any case. He owned the head of the Kuomintang so it follows that he also owned the police; besides, many of the Chinese police were Triads.

The pervasiveness of the Green Gang in Shanghai was well summed up by an American journalist and China specialist, Harold Isaacs. Writing in 1932, he outlined the membership as consisting of:

> riff-raff of the slum proletariat, most of the detectives and policemen of the French Concession, International Settlement and Chinese municipality, military officers in the local garrison commander's headquarters, officers of the Bureau of Public Safety, minor politicians and jobholders, most factory foremen and labour contractors, KMT 'labour leaders' as well as many petty merchants.

The total membership numbered in excess of 100,000. In March 1927, Chiang started to move units of the army into or close to Shanghai. Foreign residents were perturbed at this: there was, they felt, trouble in the air. The French were not in the least bit concerned and said as much to their fellow expatriates. They knew there was no cause for alarm. Chiang's plans had been passed to them by way of Pockmarked Huang and Big-eared Du.

The troops were being stationed close by in response to

intelligence. It proved accurate. On 20 March, the Communists rose up in Shanghai and brought the city to a standstill with a strike which called out 800,000 workers. This was followed up, in accordance with training received from Soviet advisers, by the capture of key installations such as the electricity-generating stations, the telephone exchanges, the railway stations and the telegraph offices. In two days, the city was paralysed and in the hands of the Communists, the Triad hierarchy driven out of the Chinese sector of the city, losing Sun Chuanfang, lost a considerable amount of face.

Four days later, on 26 March, Chiang Kai-shek entered the city to hold discussions with the most senior Chinese members of the community. (The meetings were arranged by Curio Chang, to whom most of them owed money. As a financier, he had expediently made loans not only to gain himself the interest but also to ensure their loyalty should he or his masters have need of them.) Next, he held a council of war with the leaders of the main Triad factions in the city, Pockmarked Huang, Big-Eared Du and Chang Hsiao-lin. From the security of the French Concession, they prepared to take the city back.

At first, Chiang made public declarations of solidarity with the Communists, which confused and threw them off-guard. He told the working masses that their grievances would be addressed and he applauded them for their dignity and tenacity in standing up for themselves. Many of the strikers believed him and a good number of those who were armed surrendered their weapons in good faith, assuming he had come with the army to assist the Communists and liberate them from the grip of the Triads. He then criticized the Communists and the strikers for their unpatriotic behaviour. By the time he had finished, the Communists did not know which way the political wind was blowing, though they still believed Chiang would not go against them but would seek an amicable compromise.

Behind the scenes, Chiang and Du, whose initial incentive to join in was a 'gift' of 500 rifles and ammunition for his men, were wheeling and dealing with the main Shanghai traders and merchants, who were suffering major losses through the strike, upheaval and lack of future confidence. The Green Gang and Chiang, with his Kuomintang army at his back, held the entire Chinese part of the city to ransom. They were aided in this enterprise by the French authorities, who gave Du's men free passage through the French Concession.

At the same time that Chiang and Du were extorting the business community, the Communists set about driving out of Shanghai all vestiges of competition, especially forces loyal to local warlords and non-Du-affiliated gangsters. The Communists' leader was Zhou Enlai, later China's Communist Premier and arguably its greatest-ever statesman, formerly a Chiang supporter and one-time dean of the Whampoa Military Academy. Zhou, who had been a Triad member before his total conversion to Communism (and, possibly, after it), was utterly duped by the Chiang–Du alliance. He and the workers were ready to welcome them into the city.

It was a Triad protection racket like none ever seen before. Bankers, financiers, traders, merchants, dock-owners, shipbuilders and the Shanghai Chamber of Commerce paid over to Chiang and the Green Gang millions of Chinese dollars to have them drive the Communists out of town. Additionally, a loan of $30 million was made by them to Chiang, ostensibly to pay for the establishment of a moderate and liberal government at Nanjing. Another $20 million was publicly donated. How much Chiang personally pocketed on top of this will never be known.

With the money safely in the bank, Chiang acted. On 12 April, the Green Gang went on the offensive while the army held back: Chiang did not want the army to be seen to be fighting the people. Besides, this was more than a political matter. It was a settling of scores.

So began what is now known as the White Terror. Everywhere Communists who had even the slightest influence or presence were attacked. Union offices, party cells and 'safe' houses, the homes of Communist leaders and sympathizers were raided. The Communist leaders scattered, but only a few escaped. Mass executions were the order of the day. Units of Green Gang 49s roamed the streets, chasing anyone they knew to be – or thought might be – Communists. Corpses littered the main streets, hacked to death. Young girls caught by the Green Gang raiders were raped then disembowelled and tied up in their own entrails. Men were frequently castrated before being chopped to death, the traditional Triad death by a myriad of swords. How many were killed in Shanghai is unknown. Estimates range from 5,000 to 10,000.

With Shanghai purged of Communists, the Kuomintang army and the Triads moved out across China, to every city where there was even the least significant Communist cell. In a matter of months, Chiang Kai-shek and the Triads were in control of most of China, from Nanjing to Guangzhou.

3

THE GOVERNMENT GANG

When Chiang Kai-shek set up his government in Nanjing in 1928, local Triad leaders welcomed him and he was soon recognized by all the Western powers as heading the legitimate government of China. Many of the diplomats did not know, or chose to ignore, or failed to report to their political masters back home, Chiang's criminal involvement.

However, in Chiang's plan to unify China with himself as the military commander of a new dynasty, imperial or otherwise, the Triads had a major part to play – a Gestapo-like role which would allow the army to remain apparently non-partisan and popular. To pay for this accommodation, Chiang promised the secret societies an unlimited criminal free hand, so long as it did not interfere with the machinations of government or with his own profit margin. In addition, he guaranteed prominent government posts for key figures and committed himself to the annihilation of Communism in China, with all its trappings of trade unionist and labour reforms. The White Terror was allowed to run for several years. When a labour movement or similar organization was smashed –

a process which started with the infiltration of Triad spies in the body of the membership – its leaders were executed and the rank-and-file membership taken over by Red Poles, who became their new masters.

Outside the peasant and working-class environment, the more influence the Triads had in government, the more they came to control business. Soon they were attracting to their ranks merchants, businessmen, bankers, insurance brokers, shipping agents and the like. It became almost imperative for foreign traders, such as the managers of the leading British trading firms known as 'noble houses', to ensure they were in a position not to be hampered by the Triads. To overcome any hiccup in trade, they supported Chiang Kai-shek, loaned him money, sold him arms and made quite certain their compradors were – or were allowed to be – Triads.

The most senior Triads were appointed as government advisers. Big-eared Du, as well as being a major general, was one of these. Pockmarked Huang was another. Their henchmen were promoted generals, staff officers and senior civil servants. Under Chiang Kai-shek, anything in China was for sale at the right price or for the right favour. Corruption was no longer a subterfuge but an art. The legal process was devolved to crooks. The police and military, which in theory were supposed to combat underworld crime and corruption, were themselves thoroughly compromised and controlled by those they should have been arresting.

With help from the Green Gang, Chiang forced Shanghai's merchants and wealthy residents to donate large sums to the government, on top of their taxes. Most of this income went into either his own pocket or those of

Du, Huang and other senior Triad personnel. To raise money from the rest of the public, Chiang issued government bonds, using Green Gang thugs as salesmen to ensure the take-up was good. They sold the bond issues to everyone from coolies to corporate managers. When one Shanghai millionaire demurred, his eldest son and heir, in classic Triad fashion, was kidnapped; the son of another was arrested on the trumped-up charge of being a Communist counter-revolutionary, his release being secured by a generous donation. What had been Triad practice for decades was now tantamount to government policy.

Despite bond issues, donations and loans no-one rightly expected would ever be repaid, Chiang's government was still living beyond its means. T.V. Soong, Charlie Soong's son, was appointed finance minister but he refused to guarantee the extorted loans and he and Chiang fell out, until H. H. Kung and Ai-ling made him see sense and realize that he was no match for Chiang, who now took to styling himself Generalissimo. Thereafter, T.V. became Chiang's compliant yes-man.

Outside the realms of government and the underworld, Chiang and Du grew even closer, plotting and scheming. For years they had been almost like brothers, which in the Triad sense they were, utterly reliant upon each other. An indication of their closeness had been shown in November 1921 when Chiang dismissed his current concubine, divorced Mao Fu-mei and married a woman called Ch'en Chieh-ju. Prior to their courtship, she had been Du's property. This is no metaphor: Ch'en had been a sing-song girl in one of the Green Gang's whorehouses. Quite why they married is not fully understood. Possibly she was a tangible, physical expression of the bond between the two men, for it is certain they had both shared her favours. Within weeks of the marriage, however, Chiang transferred his loyalties and affection. Just as Sun Yat-sen had done, he fell in love with one of Charlie Soong's daughters, Mei-ling, the one who loved power. Big-eared Du assisted the courtship with the aid of his close friend Ai-ling and in December 1927 Chiang cast off Ch'en Chieh-ju and married Mei-ling.

Headstrong and self-confident, Mei-ling was now China's First Lady and wanted to stamp her authority. She suggested to Chiang that, now he was Generalissimo, he should no longer pay protection money to the Green Gang. This was a mistake. Word got out – it is certain Big-eared Du had a spy amongst Chiang's servants or personal staff. Shortly after the newly-weds returned from honeymoon, a car arrived at their house while Chiang was not at home, ostensibly to take Mei-ling to Ai-ling's house. The chauffeur did not drive her there, however, but to one of Big-eared Du's mansions in the French Concession. She was held there for a while as a guest but her whereabouts were let be known. When her brother, T.V., telephoned to enquire after her, he was told by Big-eared Du that she had been discovered driving round the city on her own. This was, he was told, a dangerous thing for the First Lady to be doing. Anything could happen. Du added that he was sorry Chiang had been so preoccupied with affairs of state as to neglect his wife's security and invited T.V. over to discuss the matter. T.V. obeyed. The protection money continued to be paid. These payments were not substantial sums: it was the principle that counted. The pennies were a drop in the ocean.

Big-eared Du's main source of dirty money stemmed from opiates. It was not just smoking opium with which he was involved. He also produced White Powder and Yellow Powder smoking heroin, which was mixed with tobacco in cigarettes; Sweet or Golden Pills for pipe-smoking; *k'uai shang k'uai* (literally 'quick up quick') which was extra-pure pipe-smoked heroin; impregnated paper rolls which were rubbed in the hands so that the opiate might be absorbed through the skin and keep craving down between fixes; Black Plaster (a block of opium from which shavings were cut and smoked with tobacco); morphine and cocaine.

Through his close relationship with Du, Chiang Kai-shek and his government became heavily dependent upon opium revenue, and Chiang knew the drug alone could fund the administration and keep him in power. One of the first moves he made after taking over the leadership of the country was, with T. V. Soong's assistance, to organize an official government opium monopoly. This was entitled the National Anti-Opium Bureau, Chiang putting out the word to foreign governments, which were beginning to demand action on the growing international drug problem, that he intended to reduce addiction in China through tight governmental control. It was, of course, hogwash: he wanted a share of the profits, for himself and his government.

The monopoly was a success, reaping substantial profits, until it reached Du's opium-growing regions in Zhejiang and Jiangsu. It then began to impinge upon his opium trading in Shanghai which was run by his opium-handling company, the Da Gong Si. Du complained. Chiang immediately disbanded the National Anti-Opium Bureau. The international outcry at this was so loud that Chiang was forced into a 'compromise'. He refounded the Bureau as the National Opium Suppression Committee, announcing: 'the National government will not attempt to get one cent from the opium tax. It would not be worthy of your confidence if it should be found to make an opium tax one of its chief sources of revenue.'

This was the truth. Not a cent was raised from opium tax. Dollars were raised from the profits instead, channelled through the Triads, or from what was hypocritically called opium-prohibition revenue: in 1929, this came to just over US$17 million. Not to miss the business opportunity, T. V. Soong took part in the trade as both minister of finance and as a private individual. In 1930, when there was a temporary shortage of home-grown opium, the poppy harvest having suffered due to unseasonable weather, he invested in 700 chests of Persian opium, imported by Du. Kuomintang soldiers off-loaded the cargo in the Shanghai docks and mounted guard over the godown in which it was stored. The government then sold the opium and T.V. earned a substantial commission.

The following year, eager to be seen to distance himself from the trade, Chiang forged an agreement with Du. The Green Gang would be completely unmolested in all aspects of the opium business, would possess a veto over the appointment of government opium officials and would be guaranteed a large percentage of the profits from opiates in exchange for a one-off advance payment of US$6 million. The agreement was never implemented, but its intentions were obvious. Chiang and Du were out to benefit from the addiction of 40 million of their fellow countrymen to a far greater extent than ever the foreign opium traders had benefited in the heyday of opium-clippers.

Du's opiate dealing did more than addict Chinese. At least half his heroin was exported to France, through the French colonial diplomatic-bag service. The captain of police in the French Concession, and Pockmarked Huang's immediate superior, Étienne Fiori, was a Corsican and a member of the Union Corse. With the French consul-general, Monsieur Koechlin, he was beholden to Du, who provided them with a constant supply of sing-song girls and kickbacks. In common with all his men, Fiori's salary was more than tripled by 'bonuses' paid by Du and Huang and it was Fiori who arranged the transportation of heroin to Paris via Hanoi, Saigon and Marseilles. Further kickbacks were paid through Fiori to customs officers along the route and to key French politicians and civil servants, the latter to ensure they kept their attention diverted from the French Concession. Although the bribes were substantial, and despite Du's sending as his secret envoy to Paris the wife of Wellington Koo, China's representative at the Treaty of Versailles negotiations and (inevitably) a senior Triad official, to speak on his behalf, the French government declared its intention to investigate what was going on in Shanghai. Big-eared Du interpreted this as a double-cross by Fiori and Koechlin. In 1933, they were poisoned at a banquet held in their honour before they retired to France. Koechlin and several other diners at his table died in agony. Fiori survived, but with his health broken.

In addition to the vast sums of money Chiang Kai-shek made out of opium, the issue of essentially valueless bonds and other nefarious activities, he also received considerable foreign aid, much of which vanished into his capacious pockets. So notoriously avaricious was he that foreign diplomats and the expatriate community in Shanghai nicknamed him Cash My-cheque.

In order to launder his money and keep tabs on it, he decided in 1933 to found his own bank. Ostensibly, it was intended to be a bank for the agricultural workers, tenant farmers and small landowners who made up the bulk of the nation's agricultural industry; consequently, it was called the Farmers' Bank of China. In the International Settlement it was mockingly referred to by foreigners as the Opium Farmers' Bank. The general manager was Y. C. Koo, a relative of Wellington Koo. Chiang Kai-shek personally approved the appointment of all board members, who were mostly either Triad members or businessmen over whom he held sway. Du and Pockmarked Huang banked there, as did many of Chiang's Triad cronies. Apart from laundering money, the bank issued its own currency notes. When Chiang started to run short of money, he simply ordered more from the printers, the American Bank Note Company. This greatly alarmed T. V. Soong and H. H. Kung, who struggled through the years to keep the government solvent in the face of Chiang's excesses or pilfering, but they could do nothing about it. Neither the reserves of the bank nor its books were ever audited. It was, for all intents and purposes, the Triad bank.

If the Farmers' Bank of China was a parody, it was nothing compared to the gift Chiang Kai-shek received from Du on his fiftieth birthday in 1936. Du had, for several years, been spending millions of dollars bolstering the Kuomintang armed forces: he and Chiang both knew China was poorly defended. Amongst his main purchases, made through H. H. Kung to disguise the source of finance, were 120 of the latest state-of-the-art American Curtiss Hawk II and III aircraft. Du's birthday present to Chiang was a Hawk XF11C-3, the upper surfaces painted in olive drab, the lower in light grey. The tailfin bore the white and blue stripes of the Kuomintang air force and the wings were emblazoned with the stylized white sun in a blue disc. On the side of the fuselage, just behind the engine, was painted the aircraft's name, *Opium Suppression of Shanghai*. The name prompted a humorous couplet amongst foreign residents: 'A way at last has now been found/To get opium suppression off the ground.' In addition to the Hawks, Du purchased Gloster Gladiator fighters from the British and other aircraft from Soviet Russia.

Seeing the success of Mussolini's extremist nationalist Black Shirts – especially against socialist and Communist factions in Italy – and of Hitler's SS, Chiang founded his own Blue Shirts. Their brief was to spy on, winkle out and liquidate Communists, deviant or corrupt (that is, non-compliant) bureaucrats and state enemies, in which last category was placed anyone the government or the Triads, or the hit-man, disliked and wanted eliminated. Over a span of four years from 1937 they were responsible for at least 150 murders, including the pro-Japanese

Mayor of Shanghai. In all, there were about 10,000 Blue Shirts, all of them instructed by Green Gang officers at the Whampoa Military Academy. Many were loyal Du supporters, who, when not doing the government's dirty work, moonlighted doing his.

He may have been the Generalissimo of China, but Chiang Kai-shek did not govern all of the vast nation. At the end of the Warlord Era, when Chiang set up his government in Nanjing, he was in command of little more than eastern central China. Over the next decade, he gradually increased the range, but against long odds. The national political scene grew more convoluted and complex by the year. The Communists, under the leadership of Mao Zedong, reasserted their presence. The Kuomintang divided, subdivided, rejoined and split up into factions like a vast multiplying amoeba. Chiang's presidency was weakened. He formed an alliance with Wang Ching-wei, a left-wing Kuomintang leader in Guangzhou and the government was influenced this way and that by such groups as the Military Clique, the CC Clique (led by Ch'en Kuo-fu and his brother, Li-fu), the Reorganization Clique and the Political Study Clique. It took all Chiang's skill to juggle his many political balls in the air at once. Of course, he had Triad assistance.

Triads, now completely criminal, flourished in the cities regardless of the political atmosphere. In the vast Chinese countryside, secret societies, including the Triads, retained much more of their traditional structure and purpose and continued to involve themselves with assorted peasant unrest, seeking to address grievances against the powers-that-be, whoever they were.

In Szechuan in 1924, the Shun Tian Jiao, or Will of Heaven sect, appeared. They were a sort of revisionist Boxer movement on a small scale. Bare to the waist, wearing scarlet *fu* trousers and believing they were invincible, their purpose was retribution against bandits and the local warlord's soldiers who were pillaging settlements. The following year, the Red Spears emerged in northern China, their purpose similarly to halt predatory bands of troops and outlaws. They were even more traditional in their appearance than the Will of Heaven followers, wearing red sashes and carrying red spears decorated with red silk tassels. Renowned as martial-arts fighters and reputed to be superb gymnasts who could leap 12 feet in the air, turn mid-air somersaults and jink from side to side to the confusion of their enemies, they must have looked like warrior extras from a kung-fu movie. Yet they were more than agile fighters, with a political as well as a vengeful motivation: they wanted regional self-government.

These peasant organizations were not long in coming to the attention of the Communists. The Red Spears in particular promised to be a very useful ally, for, being in the north, they provided a second force which could be used in pincer actions against the Kuomintang. With characteristic astuteness, Mao Zedong wooed the societies he believed would be of use to his cause. As Sun Yat-sen had done, he sought to harness their patriotism and demand for change. Yet there were those who were fearful of the move: Zhou Enlai warned of the pernicious character of secret societies.

His warning was not heeded. As the Communist gospel spread through central China, where the Kuomintang held little sway and the land was ruled by warlords, secret societies became even more relevant to the socialist struggle. They not only fought against Chiang Kai-shek's government but also against the rule of avaricious warlords and they influenced the thinking of the superstitious and simple-minded peasants. All through his Long March of 1934/5, which passed through eleven provinces, Mao actively encouraged relationships with rural secret societies. He needed to harness their potential just as Chiang Kai-shek did in the cities, and for some of the same reasons. They provided rank-and-file troops, were readily convinced by political arguments and were bound by their oaths to obey. Where Mao differed from Chiang was in not taking part in any criminality, although it must be said that the societies did bring finances into the Communist war-chest and these were invariably raised by extortion or coerced membership.

When, in the 1930s, Chiang Kai-shek's government started to build roads and railways, the Triads elbowed in on the contracts, running workers' 'unions' and taking protection money to prevent construction coolies from downing their tools. The national debts, already huge, mounted as the expansion programme got under way, but the Triads were not concerned: so long as they got their cut of the action, all was well with them.

For the vast majority of the Chinese population, little had materially changed from the last days of the Q'ing dynasty. The reforms, such as they were, hardly affected them. China was still a nation of subsistence farmers, buffaloes ploughing rice paddies, coolies working treadmills and women slaving long hours in the fields. Rent-reduction laws, curbs on landlords' greed, improvements in education and a whole gamut of promised reforms never materialized save in the cities which were the government's power-bases. And, for all the talk of suppression, opium remained a national scourge.

In Shanghai, opium was openly available at every level of society. Low-class dens catered for coolies, sumptuous dens catered for the better-off and, for the very wealthy, there was a home-delivery network. Opium-poppy growing was so common that corporation gardeners grew their own narcotics in the flowerbeds of Jessfield Park, one of the main public open places. Domestic production in Chekiang, Shansi, Yunnan and Szechuan went unchecked. Big-eared Du continued to reap enormous profits.

A detailed and far from flattering account of Du's appearance, by this time much ravaged by his own addiction to opium, was given by Ilona Ralf Sues, a League of Nations representative in Shanghai in the mid-1930s and an ardent anti-opium campaigner. She was summoned to a meeting with the now middle-aged Du after her mail had been intercepted by his 'postal censors' and her derogatory comments on his opium trading relayed back to him. In her autobiographical book, *Shark's Fin and Millet*, she wrote how she was

> struck and fascinated by every detail of the man's person: a gaunt, shoulderless figure with long aimlessly swinging arms, clad in a soiled, spotted blue cotton gown; flat feet shod in untidy old slippers; a long, egg-shaped head, short-cropped hair, receding forehead, no chin, huge, Baltic ears, cold cruel lips uncovering big, yellow decayed teeth, the sickly complexion of an addict . . . He came

shuffling along, listlessly turning his head right and left to look whether anyone was following him . . . I had never seen such eyes before. Eyes so dark that they seemed to have no pupils, blurred and dull – dead, impenetrable eyes . . . I shuddered. Childhood memories flashed back; Polish peasants had told us that witches could be recognized by their abysmal eyes which did not reflect your picture . . . he gave me his limp, cold hand. A huge, bony hand with two-inches long, brown, opium-stained claws.

Sues had the effrontery to address the problem of the opium trade directly with Du. At the time, he was Chiang Kai-shek's personally appointed director of the National Opium Suppression Committee: the lion in charge of the sheepfold. He claimed he was doing his best to eradicate opiates, confiscating every grain of heroin. Sues stated bluntly that this was untrue. Du slammed his fist on the table, terrifying Sues's Chinese companions and having his guards reach for their guns. She pressed the case and pointed out to Du that, if he really did drive opium from China, he would be internationally regarded as a hero, the man who had thrown off China's yoke of foreign imperialistic exploitation. This argument did not work. It could not. Du was making millions of dollars a month from opium.

He was not, however, trading alone. The Japanese were also importing a lot of opium and manufacturing their own heroin in Tientsin and other centres, often in Japanese embassy buildings. Their reason was simple and long-term. They were out to demoralize China, soften her up for invasion and occupation. Big-eared Du and the

163

Da Gong Si were also selling opium from their poppy farms in Yunnan to the Japanese. He can, therefore, be seen to have been aiding the enemy in the name of personal profit.

The Japanese made their first move in the spring of 1932, invading China's three most north-easterly states, which they amalgamated into a protectorate, Manchukuo, with the last Q'ing emperor, Henry Aisin-Gioro Pu Yi, as puppet-monarch. Chiang Kai-shek complained bitterly to the League of Nations but nothing came of it and he soon had other, more pressing, concerns.

In 1934, Chiang was facing an economic watershed. Inflation was high, the economy heading for a fall. He passed a law demanding that all banks invest a quarter of their fixed assets in government stock. The bankers howled in protest, to no avail. H. H. Kung set about a government takeover of non-compliant banks. Thorough and ruthless, it was known as the Great Shanghai Banking Coup. No-one was safe, not even Chang Kia-ngau, general manager of the Bank of China, virtual owner of the very powerful Bank of Communications and a long-standing Triad brother to Chiang Kai-shek. When it came to hard cash, fraternal honour went out the window. After being demoted to a position beneath H. H. Kung and losing much face, Chang Kia-ngau appealed for support to the Generalissimo. He received none and, not long after, retired to Los Angeles, where he taught economics at one of California's top universities.

The following year, Chiang decided to take his government off the silver standard in an attempt to stabilize the economy, which was at the mercy of price fluctuations in silver. In place of silver, it was mooted that the government would issue its own legal-tender notes known as *fa-pi*. Accordingly, the Central Bank of China, the Bank of China, the Bank of Communications and the Farmers' Bank of China were empowered to produce the new currency, supervised by the Currency Reserve Board. In theory, this was sound economic sense but the make-up of the board included T. V. and T. L. Soong and Big-eared Du, who was also a member of the Native Banking Supervisory Committee which controlled a massive mortgage and loan business. Indeed, the entire primary banking structure of the land was run by a virtual cartel of bankers who were either Triad members or sympathizers in their debt. H. H. Kung was on the board of the Central Bank of China and owned the Manufacturers' Bank; T. V., T. L. and Ai-ling Soong were between them on the boards of the Bank of Communications, the Central Bank of China, the Sun Hua Trust and Savings Bank, the Agricultural and Industrial Bank of China, the Kwangtung Provincial Bank, the Canton Municipal Bank and the Manufacturers' Bank; Big-eared Du was on the board of, amongst others, the Bank of China, the Tung Wai Bank, the Chung Wai Bank, the Kiangsu and Chekiang Bank and was chairman of the Commercial Bank. So prevalent was he in the world of finance that Du was often specifically referred to by the collective term, the Shanghai Bankers.

Du's presence in the financial world of Shanghai is not surprising. The Chung Wai Bank was his own highly profitable private banking business, its offices situated at 143 avenue Edward VII in the French Concession, where it was free of Chinese banking laws and coups. Du maintained a private office here on the second floor, reached only by a lift guarded by armed henchmen of whom one was famous for lacking an eye. In addition, his name was everywhere as a benefactor and man of considerable social conscience, as his entry in the social register showed. He was outwardly a respectable citizen and, to be fair to him, he did donate sizeable sums of money to charities and such establishments as hospitals and schools, mostly in and around Shanghai.

His prominence in the business world was not always welcomed, yet there was no alternative to his being allowed a place at any table at which he chose to sit. He was simply too powerful. This was well illustrated by an event which occurred late in 1935. Sir Frederick Leith-Ross, a British government economist sent to China to assist with the *fa-pi* reforms, complained to H. H. Kung about Du's inclusion on the Currency Reserve Board. His reservations concerned more than Du's criminal connections. When the *fa-pi* system came into force, it was alleged that Kung's wife tipped off Du about official policy towards foreign-currency dealing. Du misunderstood the information and lost £50,000. Blaming Kung, he requested the Central Bank reimburse him. Kung declined the demand. Shortly afterwards, according to Leith-Ross's memoirs, a traditional Chinese coffin accompanied by a cohort of pall-bearers arrived at Kung's home. The following day, at an extraordinary board meeting of the Central Bank directors, the motion was passed to make good Du's losses. Needless to say, Leith-Ross's objections were totally overruled.

In recent years, there have been attempts to rehabilitate Du's reputation, to point out what a nationalist patriot he was. This is not in dispute. He did much to further the Kuomintang cause, yet he also spectacularly lined his own pockets at the expense of the nation and must be judged first and foremost as a self-serving racketeer rather than as a dedicated patriot.

Gradually through the 1930s, the Communists increasingly posed a threat. Their propaganda appealed to the masses which had had enough of being exploited by the rich, the secret societies and the government. By 1937, with the Long March behind them, they were gaining ground, but suddenly the urgency of their rise was overshadowed by the Japanese.

On 7 July 1937, the Japanese engineered a military confrontation south-west of Beijing. It escalated over the coming weeks into a full-scale Sino-Japanese conflict which raged until Japan was defeated at the end of the Second World War. The Japanese military were better trained, armed and commanded than the Kuomintang. They were also not corrupt. The only way to be promoted in the Japanese military was by ability. In the Kuomintang army, appointment relied upon whom one knew, the level of one's bribe and to which secret society one belonged.

Japanese advances were quick and effective. Beijing and Tientsin fell in weeks. By the end of the year, after a three-month battle, Shanghai had fallen, to be followed by Nanjing. By March 1938, the Japanese had conquered most of northern China to the Yellow River, taken Hangzhou, and occupied Guangzhou and much of Kwangtung and coastal Guangxi, including Hainan Island.

In late 1937 Chiang moved his government, in effect now in internal exile, from Nanjing to Chongqing, leaving the former city undefended. His Triad associates and supporters fled with him. On 13 December, Japanese troops entered the city and, at the order of the Japanese Prince Asaka and in the face of no resistance, began the infamous Rape of Nanjing. Triad patriotism clearly did not extend to risking one's neck for 40,000 fellow Chinese, who were repeatedly raped, disembowelled, set alight with petrol or used as live bayonet and execution-by-sword practice.

Chiang was struggling to survive on two fronts, fighting both the invading Japanese and the Communists. The country was in turmoil. The Japanese set up a number of puppet-governments in Beijing and Nanjing. In doing this, they were tacitly assisted by local Triad elements who were prepared to back any horse if it meant they could stay in business.

Mao Zedong had approached Chiang in 1936 to suggest a temporary truce so that they might join forces to fight the Japanese, whom he was certain were spoiling for action. So serious did Mao deem the situation that he authorized the Central Committee of the Communist Party to publish an appeal inviting some Triad societies to unite with the party to counteract the Japanese invasion threat. Chiang resisted, advised by the stubbornly anti-Communist Du. However, Chiang's hand was forced by his being placed under house arrest by one of his generals and made to see sense, and after the Japanese invasion the Kuomintang and the Communists came to a compromise. Communist troops were taken into the Eighth Route Army of the National Revolutionary Army. Triad societies played a major part in the anti-Japanese campaign. The Red Spears joined in the fray and the Japanese, in a vain effort to counteract them, recruited their own 'Triad' society under the auspices of the Yakuza, Japan's indigenous equivalent of the Triads, which they called the Fish Spears. It was an utter failure.

Much to Du's annoyance, Chiang Kai-shek not only permitted the Communists to set up an embassy in Chongqing but he started to pay them a subsidy and allowed them to form the New Fourth Army from disparate Communist forces south of the Yangtze. This gave Mao Zedong a foothold in the heart of China upon which he was to build throughout the war, the Communists making great gains at the expense of the beleaguered Kuomintang government.

During the war, China was politically chaotic. At one stage, it contained five competing governments. The Kuomintang administration, recognized internationally, was centred on Chongqing. In addition, Mao Zedong had a Communist government established in Yenan, the Japanese had their current puppet-government in Nanjing, Wang Ching-wei had his own nationalist government in Mongolia and, in Xinjiang, there was a pro-Soviet autonomous mini-government. Chiang had competition which was too varied and widespread to be infiltrated or affected by his Green Gang comrades and it looked as if his political days might be numbered. What saved him was not the Triads but the Japanese themselves. They bombed Pearl Harbor, the Western powers entered the war and the Kuomintang, being the 'legitimate' Chinese government, was suddenly supported militarily, morally and monetarily by the British and the Americans, and, to a lesser extent, by the Russians. Like the Americans, they were looking to the long term and gave support to both Chiang and Mao.

As the war ground on, Communist cadres organized peasant guerrilla units in occupied territory. Secret societies were a seminal part of the resistance, many forging alliances with the Communists; but by no means all of them sided with the Chinese cause. A good many collaborated with the Japanese. The Way of Fundamental Unity in Shanghai, Nanjing and Beijing openly supported the invaders. When Wang Ching-wei established a pro-Japanese nationalist alternative government in Nanjing in 1940 he did so with Triad encouragement. The collaborating societies were mostly in the cities, where they were criminally motivated: as in any war, there was a profit to be made. In the countryside, most societies fought the occupation.

Chiang Kai-shek, as usual, made good use of the Triads. General Tai Li, the commander of the Kuomintang secret service, the innocuously named Military Bureau of Investigation and Statistics, and a very senior Triad, had been gradually drawing the Triads into the secret service for over a decade, partly in order to utilize their expertise and partly to keep an eye on them. He had achieved this in part through his links – fraternal, personal and criminal – with Du Yueh-sheng, to whom he also introduced Milton Miles, the Director of Operations for the American intelligence gathering organization, the Office of Strategic Services (OSS) in China, who was much taken with Du, whom he described as a 'mannerly and ostensibly amiable old gentleman'. The three of them were as thick as thieves. In 1943, Tai Li, by now nick-

170

named the 'Chinese Himmler', and Miles founded the Sino-American Co-operative Organization (SACO) with Tai Li as commander and Miles as his deputy. Probably partially funded but certainly politically supported by Du, it trained over 2,000 American personnel in guerrilla warfare at a training base near Chongqing; many of the instructors were ex-Whampoa Military Academy officers and Triads. When the Japanese surrendered in 1945, Tai Li, Du and Miles secretly prepared the smooth transition of power in occupied Shanghai in collaboration with the Japanese and the Chinese puppet governments.

Tai Li instructed all the societies, including the Blue Shirts of which he had overall control, to build up intelligence networks, plant agents in occupied territory and provide undercover sabotage operatives, forming an amalgamation of societies, with himself in charge, overseeing their intelligence operations but ensuring their continued autonomy. He had had plans to do as Du had partially done as a young man in Shanghai: unite all the societies under one roof with himself as supreme head, but he could not pull it off.

Besides the field of military intelligence, many Triads fought with the Kuomintang. Others operated escape routes for Chinese from occupied territory. In a few instances, they assisted escaping British prisoners-of-war from Hong Kong and operated an underground secret mail service in and out of the neutral enclave of Portuguese Macau, aiding the British secret service Special Operations Executive (SOE) in the assassination of the Japanese consul. For many more, however, the war was hardly an inconvenience. It was an opportunity to consolidate their wealth.

The Green Gang in Shanghai was not substantially affected and continued its racketeering, although it did come under strenuous competition in the narcotics trade from pro-Japanese Triad groups, the Japanese authorities themselves, Wang Ching-wei in person (who owned a number of opium dens) and privateer gangsters of both Chinese and non-Chinese ethnic origins. Amongst the latter were White Russian gangs, often Jewish, who came to accommodations with the Japanese and the Triads; it was not until late in the war that the competition started to make heavy inroads into Green Gang opiate profits.

Business was good for the Green Gang. It offered local businessmen protection from Japanese interference. Chinese police working for the Japanese were in on the game and took a cut. Gang-owned brothels thrived: so did gambling and lottery dens. As food shortages started to bite later in the war, the Triads ran a black market, some catering for Allied prisoners-of-war in the various prison camps around the city – especially in Pootung, into which they smuggled not only food but also medicines – yet at a price: payment was preferred in gold. By 1945, there was hardly a prisoner still in possession of his or her wedding ring. Even pen nibs were exchanged for black-market produce.

The trade in opium actually increased. Knowing the Triads could cause havoc if they wanted to, a pact was struck: the Japanese would not interfere with the Triads' business activities so long as the Triads in Shanghai did not involve themselves in the war. Consequently, they did not: they even ensured protection of the Japanese garrison in the city as part of the deal.

The Green Gang's and, therefore, Du's profits rose

accordingly. Du himself, with no friendly police chiefs in the French Concession to hide behind, and being a Kuomintang major-general, had astutely quit Shanghai. In part, he was losing face to Japanese-sponsored and protected gangsters who were trying to drive him out of business, but his real motivation was personal security. Several contracts had been put out on him and although he was well guarded the atmosphere in Shanghai at the time, redolent with the tart perfume of cross and double-cross, suggested caution be the better part of valour.

Just before Shanghai fell to the Japanese in late 1937, Du took a French passenger liner to Hong Kong, where he disembarked and booked himself into a suite in the Peninsula Hotel. One of the great colonial hotels, it was regarded as the best in the world outside New York and London. With him travelled one of his two favourite concubines; the other was currently in England where her sons by Du were being educated in private schools.

When it looked obvious that Shanghai was not going to be imminently liberated, and that the war was going to drag on, Du moved out of the hotel into a property on Kennedy Road in the Mid-Levels region on the Peak, the most prestigious place in Hong Kong in which a Chinese could live, being racially barred from occupying the heights of the mountain. He also kept a private suite in the Gloucester Hotel, only a notch or two down in standard and style from the Peninsula. With a quiet confidence, he moved in colonial society and took on a number of social causes to prove his bona fides as a respectable businessman.

From Hong Kong he made occasional forays into China, to tend to his business affairs and advise Chiang, and it was on one of these trips that he gave an interview to the English writers W. H. Auden and Christopher Isherwood, who wanted to know about his work as director of the Chinese Red Cross. Isherwood recalled the meeting in their co-authored book, *Journey to a War*.

> To visit Du's flat was to enter a strongly guarded fortress. At least a dozen attendants were posted in the hall, and, when we sat down to talk, there were others who stood in the background behind our chairs. Du himself was tall and thin, with a face that seemed hewn out of stone, a Chinese version of the Sphinx. Peculiarly and inexplicably terrifying were his feet, in their silk socks and smart pointed European boots, emerging from beneath the long silken gown.

When their meeting came to an end, Du thanked them for their interest in the Red Cross, in 'the name of humanity'.

Just ahead of the Japanese invasion of Hong Kong in mid-December 1941, Du moved to the safety of Chongqing. Here another side to this complex man came to the fore. At the same time as he was misappropriating foreign military aid with and for Chiang Kai-shek, he was also funding an anti-Japanese fifth column by rallying his Triad followers in Shanghai and organizing them into a force of saboteurs known as Blood and Steel. They blew up railway lines, murdered Japanese on the streets and smuggled essential supplies through the docks, right under Japanese noses. Du even suggested, and the SOE took a passing interest in the possibility, that they try to manipulate the labour markets in Shanghai, Canton and Hong Kong, a plan for which he certainly had both the contacts and the experience, but it came to nothing. And all the time that Blood and Steel was attacking the Japanese their ultimate commander-in-chief was operating whore houses in Shanghai catering for them, staffed with Chinese girls.

After the war, Du began at last to lose his power. He was now an old man, revered and respected but increasingly out of place, his health poor due to his narcotic addiction. New rivals, grown strong from war-profiteering, were rising up the Triad pack and the old tiger was being eased out, the Green Gang's supremacy starting to slip. An indication of how Du was now regarded can be seen in an event which occurred in 1946. During the war, Du's Shanghai stock exchange had been closed down. In its stead, Wang Ching-wei started up his own, in the same building on Hankow Road. After the war ended, the Wang exchange was shut down but the former one was not re-formed. Another, independent stock exchange was established by the triumvirate of the Bank of China, the Bank of Communications and the Central Bank. Big-eared Du was not included in the new set-up. He took legal advice and his old stock exchange, with its surviving assets, metamorphosed into a real-estate company. This, in turn, invested so much in the new stock exchange that Du was obliged to be named as a board member. He was not going to go down without fighting.

With the Japanese defeated, Chiang and Mao briefly attempted to negotiate a mutual settlement, but it failed and China slipped into civil war. In adversity, Chiang was still backed by Du, who continued to help him even after he fell from power. With the backing of the USA as well as the Triads, Chiang tried to smash the Chinese Communist Party. He appealed, as Sun Yat-sen had done, to Triads overseas to come to his aid. Just after the war, a secret meeting took place in Hong Kong of all the territory's *shan chu*s, called by an envoy from Chiang who told them that it was the Triads who had brought down the Q'ing dynasty and were now required to save China, not from a foreign ruler but from a foreign ideology. He asked that 300,000 49s and Red Poles be sent from Hong Kong societies. This was wildly ambitious, amounting to 10 per cent of the entire population of the colony. The Triad leaders voted their confidence in Chiang Kai-shek, sending him a telegram of support: but not one was going to cross into China for a merely political fight. Those days were over. Besides, they were doing too well in post-war Hong Kong.

Kuomintang Triad agents were used in a nationwide propaganda campaign to raise pro-Kuomintang support and halt the infiltration of Communist sympathizers into the army. To assure loyalty, mass oath-taking sessions were held to bind people to the Kuomintang cause. Tens of thousands were hurriedly initiated into Triad societies, the ritual reduced to one basic oath swearing obedience and determination to overthrow Mao Zedong and his army. Disloyalty meant death. In addition, the Triads attempted to mobilize the peasants but, as with the mass initiations, they were not successful. The Communist propaganda machine was powerful and the Kuomintang army was relentlessly driven south.

In 1949, as Communist forces moved in for the fall of Shanghai, Chiang asked Du to help him in one last, great and audacious enterprise – to rob the Bank of China.

Some time before, Chiang had tried to save the Chinese *yuan* by issuing gold coins and certificates at an exchange rate of four to the US dollar, but this was futile because there were insufficient gold reserves to support it. Half the reserve had 'disappeared' by way of the Soongs and the Kungs. The remainder was held in the bank's vaults in Shanghai. Du and his family had already benefited once from the gold *yuan* issue: on the day before Chiang announced it, one of Du's sons dumped 30 million shares, selling short. He was indicted, but only for selling shares outside the market, not for insider dealing. His sentence was a mere eight months in prison. Now there was a chance to make an even bigger killing.

At night, Chiang moored a cargo freighter alongside the Bund, Shanghai's waterfront, opposite the Cathay Hotel. It was crewed by hand-picked naval ratings dressed as ordinary seamen. Key bank personnel were paid off or threatened by Green Gang 49s working under Du's personal instruction. The bank staff unlocked the doors to the vaults and the entire gold reserve was passed hand-to-hand along a line of Green Gang 49s, stretching some hundreds of metres, from bank to boat. The vessel then sailed on the pre-dawn tide for Taiwan. Chiang Kai-shek went too.

As the Communists marked up victory after victory, Du began moving his assets to Hong Kong, where he was now resident. The colonial authorities knew all about him but decided not to act. In Hong Kong he had broken no laws, so it was thought best to let the old sleeping dog lie and treat him, along with the millions of others who swarmed into Hong Kong to escape Communism, as a refugee.

Despite his weakened position, Du was still considered a force to be reckoned with and Mao Zedong felt he might still be of use to China after the Communist victory in 1949. Mao believed that, if he had Du on his side, he would have control of the Triads across urban China. He sent an emissary, the scholar and lawyer Zhang Shixhao, to Hong Kong to ask Du to consider returning to China to help unite her. Du declined. He was cautious, even though an old friend, Shen Junru, was head of the Supreme People's Court and would most probably have ensured that no retribution would be exacted for the White Terror.

Du Yueh-sheng died on 16 August 1951. He was survived by seven sons and three daughters. Chiang Kai-shek, who became president of the free Republic of China in Taiwan in 1949, published a flattering tribute, praising his loyalty, patriotism and integrity. Du's body was refused burial in Hong Kong because he had not been resident there for the statutory period of eight years, so it was stored in a mausoleum, awaiting an auspicious opportunity to return him to China for burial in the land of his ancestors. This was not to be. In October the following year, his coffin was shipped to Taiwan for interment near Taipei.

Today, Du Yueh-sheng is regarded in Taiwan as a hero of the people, a patriot who fought the evil of Communism and upheld the basic tenet of the Triad societies of old: to restore China to her own, true citizens.

Before the 1949 establishment of the Communist People's Republic of China, Triads across the nation's cities used the chaos of civil war to reorganize after the upheavals of the Sino-Japanese War. Even after the Communist victory, well-connected Triad members still held positions of authority and were to do so for many years, forming an important but highly secretive set of cliques in the hierarchy of the Chinese government. Through them, Madame Chiang Kai-shek, Mei-ling Soong, was to stay in touch with the ruling class in China and, after her husband's death in 1975, continued to make her effect felt in her homeland from exile in New York. However, the Communist takeover changed things for Triad societies in general. They were clamped down upon. Opium, prostitution and extortion were banned as counter-revolutionary, anti-socialist and imperialist. The urban societies lost their income over a matter of months. Opium dealers and brothel-keepers were sent for political re-education or executed. The traditional secret societies in the countryside were regarded as socially unacceptable and anachronistic. Most disbanded. A few struggled on as little reactionary groups which the Communist government accused of being in collusion with Taiwan. One alleged counter-revolutionary group, the Tow Mu Tan, was accused in 1952 of seeking to bring to power an eight-year-old boy named Chu, said to be a direct descendant of the Ming dynasty.

Many of the Triad officials who remained in China, or could engineer no escape, were executed. Of those who fled, a large number followed their leader, Chiang Kai-shek, to Taiwan, where for the remainder of his life he relied upon them to keep him in power. Because they were from a number of separate societies, once they reached Taiwan they formed their own new society, the Chu Lien Pang, or United Bamboo Society. Others fled with the general refugee exodus to Hong Kong where they settled. Yet more spread around the world, travelling to the Malay peninsula, Europe, North America and Australia.

Not only individuals ran from Communism. So did entire societies. One of these has since become world famous — or infamous.

In 1945, the Kuomintang official responsible for enrolling Triads in southern China for the fight against Mao Zedong was a lieutenant-general named Kot Siu-wong. A longstanding Triad member personally appointed by Chiang Kai-shek, he was ordered, at Du's suggestion, to establish a league of all the Triad societies in Guangdong. Basing himself at 14 Po Wa Ching Chung Yeuk (Po Wah Road), Kot formed the Five Continents Overseas Chinese Hung League and was sworn in as its *shan chu*.

Kot was an able, patriotic man with no direct links to criminal societies. Indeed, he deplored their degeneration into crime, believing Triads should be patriotically honourable. He hoped his league would stem the Communist tide by adopting guerrilla tactics to match those of the Communists, although he received little support from orthodox nationalist generals for this approach.

By 1947, Kot had rallied all the Guangdong Triad groups into a single organization called the Hung Fat Shan Chung Yee Wui, or Hung Fat Shan Loyalty Association. The initiation ceremonies were organized by Kot and held in the Kwok Man University in Guangzhou. A large number of Kuomintang troops were initiated, in addition to thousands of civilians. As was happening with Triad recruitment across China, the ritual was simplified. At the ceremony, the Five Ancestors were replaced by a picture of Sun Yat-sen and the oaths pared down to obedience to the Kuomintang and dedication to the concept of a united, non-socialist nation. Only oath 35, reminding of the need for secrecy, was retained in full. Many of the initiates had never been associated with the Triads and, under normal circumstances, would never have joined. They did so now out of fear of the Communists or of being considered Communist sympathizers if they demurred.

Little known today, there was an ulterior, political motive behind the founding of the league. Chiang Kai-shek, despite receiving considerable assistance from the British during the Sino-Japanese and Second World Wars, hoped to use the league to cause mayhem in Hong Kong. The Kuomintang financed and passed military intelligence to the league to assist it in unifying the criminal Triad gangs in the colony, to have them organize strikes and social unrest, drive the British out and leave Hong Kong open for Chiang, and Du, and the others, to take it over. With all the Triads under one criminal roof, the potential for profit was huge. Hong Kong could be Chiang's new Shanghai. It was a dream which remained with him for the rest of his life.

For administrative purposes the various groups, of which there were forty-four, were given coded names each including the number 14, chosen because of the address of the headquarters. Gradually, however, the Hung Fat Shan Chung Yee Wui became known simply as the Sap Sze Wui, or Fourteen Association and, later, just 14. Later still, its name changed slightly with the addition of a single letter. Why it was added is lost in the mythology of the society. Some say it stood for the carat mark on Chinese gold, implying the society was good and true, like pure gold. Others maintain the reference to gold was for luck, that it might bring wealth to its members. Yet others say it was added in honour of Kot Siu-wong. Whichever was the case matters little.

The added letter was K. With its appearance, the 14K Triad society was born and the ancient patriotic and spiritual tradition of the Triads was finally laid to rest.

PART THREE

IN THE CITY OF WILLOWS

1

THE LEGEND OF THE MONKS OF SHAO LIN

Before looking further into the story of the Triads, and moving into the post-Second World War era, it is important to understand the traditional – the legendary and often apocryphal – history of the Triads, for no matter how far fetched or factually inaccurate it may seem, often at considerable variance with real events, this is central to the ethos of being a Triad member.

The traditions of the Triads might have started to erode after the Sino-Japanese and Chinese civil wars but they were nevertheless still important; legends and ritual were still to play an important part in their activities for several decades. Virtually unknown outside the milieu of the societies or the authorities combating them, they tell a fascinating if convoluted story of what a Triad believes his roots to be.

To the Western mind, history and legend are rarely more than tenuously connected: King Arthur may have a grave but this does not categorically prove his historical existence, nor the veracity of Sir Lancelot and the Knights of the Round Table. Yet, to the Chinese, fact and fiction are closely linked and frequently overlap. Into the grey area where they overrun falls what is best termed 'traditional history', which is often accepted as being literal truth.

The traditional history of the Triads is a fantastic amalgamation of real events and people, legend, magical parable and folklore. Like all legends, they indubitably have some roots in reality, but these have either been lost or reworked out of all recognition by passage through both written and oral traditions. The traditional history remains, however, as important to a Triad as any real history, for in it lies much of what he wishes to consider to be the truth about his background. It also establishes a powerful Confucian bond with his ancestors or forebears, giving him the sense of identity and continuity which is so important to Chinese culture. To the member of a Triad society, being part of a continually unfolding history is a vital justification for his actions. He is not an individual working for himself and of his own volition, but a cog in an ancient, cohesive – even honourable – association.

Triad history blends myth with truth, heroism with defeat and occult power with human failings. It has inspired some of the most famous stories in Chinese literature. This literary connection is useful as it gives a popular credibility to the Triads, placing them in the context of the greatness of China's past. There are also religious aspects to the traditional history which further strengthen plausibility: Taoist ancestor worship, shamanism, Buddhism and Confucianism mingle to provide a symbolic and ritualistic permanence. Furthermore, they lend a certain romanticism which has always been crucial in attracting recruits.

There are a number of versions of Triad traditional history, differing quite substantially depending upon where the story was heard, when it was recounted and by whom. The earliest, and more or less complete history, was given in *The Hung Society*, by J. S. M. Ward and W. G. Stirling, published in 1925. Although it specifically deals with the Hung Society at the turn of the nineteenth century, it reflects beliefs and symbols which have remained unchanged for hundreds of years and are closely related to Triad mythology and ritual. However, Ward and Stirling derived their information from colonial district and police officers' reports, and from material gleaned from missionaries, academics and academic journals. Hardly a Chinese was interviewed and direct contact with members of Chinese secret societies – Triad or otherwise – was all but totally absent.

The most intricate and probably the most accurate rendering of the traditional history was compiled in the early 1950s by a Hong Kong police officer, W. P. Morgan. Published in 1960, *Triad Societies in Hong Kong* is an astonishing piece of scholarship, much of its content being obtained directly from Triad informants and arrested society members. Considerably detailed, it recounts the epic narrative and complex political background to the Triad history and was the version broadly in use by Triads at the time. Since then, the story has become severely adulterated: in just fifty years, it has been corrupted by mis- or non-use so that, today, Triad members usually know only a truncated and often garbled rendition.

According to Morgan, the Triad traditional story begins towards the end of the reign of the Ming emperor Sung

Ching, at a time when the empire was threatened by internal unrest and outside attack. When exactly this was is unknown: there was no Ming emperor called Sung Ching. However, there was Lung-ch'ing (1567–73) so the legend may refer to his reign. On the other hand, many Triads believe their foundations lie rooted in the period 1644–1700, in the reigns of the last four Ming emperors, the first of whom was Ch'ung-chen (1628–45). The important fact for the veracity of the story is to imbue it with some historical context, no matter how tenuous.

The emperor was preoccupied with pleasures of the flesh, and imperial appointments and favours were bestowed upon everyone who pandered to his tastes. Gradually, as control of the kingdom passed into the hands of sycophants, the administration collapsed. The officials concentrated on self-enrichment and disregarded the needs of the people. Crops were devastated by drought, yet taxes were levied at increasing rates by rapacious officials. Millions were on the point of starvation and the air was full of rebellion. North of the Great Wall, the Manchurian armies were encamped, waiting to invade when the empire finally disintegrated into chaos.

Disgusted with the venality and corruption of the emperor's court, and convinced that the emperor had forfeited his mandate from the gods to rule by ignoring the rights and needs of the people, a group of honest officials, including Kam Shun, Sze Ho-fat, Ku Ting-lam, Hung Kai-shing and Wong Po-chau, formed a secret organization under the front of a money lender's shop. Their aim was to recruit patriots who would rid the court of corrupt officials, restoring the Ming dynasty to its previous levels of honesty and efficiency.

Sadly, their move was too late, for a peasant, Li Chi-shing (or Li Chong), had already started a revolt, his starving followers sweeping through the country, capturing Beijing and forcing the emperor to commit suicide. The Ming general, Ng Sam-kwai, who was holding the Great Wall against the Manchurians, could not tolerate the thought of a peasant on the Dragon Throne and, hoping to seat himself there instead, entered into a treaty with the Manchus to drive out Li Chi-shing. The rebels stood no chance and were quickly defeated. However, General Ng's forces suffered heavy casualties and, with the Ming army therefore greatly depleted by the time they entered Beijing, the wily and stronger Manchus seized the throne for themselves and in 1644 established their man, Shun Chi, as the first emperor of the Manchu Q'ing dynasty.

In the face of the Manchu expropriation of the throne, the organization set up by Kam Shun and the other honest Ming officials intensified its recruiting campaign. Ku Ting-lam outlined their aims in a book entitled *Ming Yee Fong Luk* (*The Record of the Enemies of the Ming*), in which he espoused nationalism and resistance to Q'ing rule. Knowing they had to act before the Manchus consolidated their grip on the country, the organization rose in rebellion but was resoundingly defeated in a battle near Yenchow, many of the leaders being killed. Of those who survived, Kam Shun managed to gain refuge in a monastery while another, Wong Sheung-shan, fled to Formosa (now Taiwan), where he too wrote a book, *Kam Toi Po Luk* (*The Kam Toi Precious Records*), naming it after a mountain on the island.

In time, a copy of *Kam Toi Po Luk* reached another

Ming exile in Formosa, Cheng Shing-kung, who had not previously been connected to the organization. He studied it and, following plans it contained, raised a small force to attack Nanjing. He was repulsed, returning to Formosa, where, upon his death, the book passed to his grandson, Cheng Hak-song. He took up where his grandfather had left off, leading an anti-Q'ing resistance in Formosa until imperial forces conquered the island, whereupon Cheng Hak-song locked the book in an iron chest and cast it into the sea before killing himself.

Some time after the Q'ing conquest of Formosa, a rebellion by Ming supporters broke out in Szechuan, led by Man Wan-lung, a monk who had changed his name from Wu Tai-hei and taken holy orders after committing a murder. While in the Ching Chung Shan monastery in Szechuan, he raised an army which marched on Chengtu, the provincial capital, but lost its way in the mountains and was obliged to employ a guide, Fong Pan-leung, to get them through the mountain passes. Unknown to them, Fong was a Q'ing agent. He got word to his masters, the Q'ing army ambushed the rebels and wiped them out in the Mo Shan mountains.

Man Wan-lung was killed in the skirmish, his commanders and officials scattering far and wide, many taking refuge in the Shao Lin monastery in the Kaolin mountains, Po Ting district, Fujian province. Here they carried on plotting and gathering supporters. One of Man's leading counsellors, Chan Kan-nam, fled to Pak Hok Tung, the White Stork Grotto, in Wukwong district near the borders of Hunan and Guangdong, where he independently started to make his own plans and raise an army.

Matters went on like this until, in the reign of the second Q'ing emperor, rebellious tribes from the state of the Silu rose up. The defending Q'ing military commanders were under pressure from local rebels and appealed to the emperor for reinforcements. The emperor, realizing his forces were ill-trained and under strength, commenced a nationwide recruiting campaign. To encourage enlistment, he decreed that all men who joined up to defeat the Silu rebellion would be granted high honours, favours and official employment.

News of the campaign reached Cheng Kwan-tat, a nephew of Cheng Shing-kung, at the Shao Lin monastery where he was living with his wife, Kwok Sau-ying, and his sister, Cheng Yuk-lin, who were undergoing instruction in the martial arts. With Chi Yuen, the abbot of the monastery, Cheng Kwan-tat called an assembly of the monks at which it was resolved they should offer their services to the emperor. Their resolution was influenced by many factors. First and foremost, they wanted to prevent any further foreign invasion. Second, the fighting would give them an opportunity to put into practice the methods of warfare for which they were training. In addition, they wished to gain confidence in their fighting abilities and, simultaneously, impress the population so that people would more readily join them when they called them to revolt in accordance with the precepts of *Kam Toi Po Luk*. Finally, they were keen to assuage the suspicions Q'ing officials had expressed regarding their martial activities at the monastery.

The abbot instructed his chief disciple, Tak Wan, to command an élite force of 128 monks, together with Cheng Kwan-tat, his wife and sister, and report for duty

191

to the emperor. They demanded no payment, just arms and provisions for their campaign, at the same time requesting no additional troops be sent with them into battle. Their terms met, the monks marched against the Silu rebels and, with superior military skill, defeated them in three months.

On returning to the imperial court, the monks were triumphantly acclaimed by the emperor, who, in keeping with his decree, offered them titles and senior posts in his government. The monks declined his offers, declaring that they had merely been doing their civic duty as patriots, their only desire being to return to their monastic existence. Cheng Kwan-tat, however, was not bound by monastic rules. He accepted the position of a commander of the Q'ing garrison in the Wuchow district. This was not him turning his coat: he intended to use his military posting to spy on Q'ing forces, sending intelligence to the monastery at Shao Lin.

With the monks back in their monastery, the grand secretary of the Q'ing Council, Wong Chun-mei, became jealous of the honours offered to them and the position bestowed on Cheng Kwan-tat. Fired by envy, Wong set about sowing doubts in the emperor's mind. If, Wong reasoned, this small band of monks had been so successful where the imperial forces had failed, surely they might just as readily turn against the emperor as defend him. He argued that the reason they had declined their honours was because their main intention was to raise an army against the throne. The emperor was persuaded by the logic of this argument and became so fearful that he ordered Cheung Kin-chau, the provincial high commissioner of Fujian province, and Chan Man-yiu, the magistrate of Po Ting district, to destroy the Shao Lin monastery and all its inhabitants. He further ordered Cheng Kwan-tat's execution.

The monastery was strategically situated on a tall hill. A surprise attack was impossible. Furthermore, the hill was reputed to be honeycombed with tunnels by which the monks would be able to escape were their monastery stormed. It was decided the best course of action was to drug the monks then kill them. However, in case the plan went awry, all exits from the monastery would have to be guarded: this meant the entrances to the tunnels would have to be located. Chan Man-yiu, disguised as a peasant, wandered the nearby villages to glean information.

Chan met and befriended a coolie and learned that he had been a monk in the Shao Lin monastery. On further investigation, he discovered that the coolie, Ma Yee-fuk (or Ma Ning-yee), had been ranked seventh among the monks in martial ability, but had been cast out because he had made advances to Cheng Kwan-tat's wife and sister and had broken the Man Nin Po Tang, a sacred lamp presented to the monastery by the Persian government. His shaven head marking him as a disgraced monk, he had been unable to obtain fitting work and was reduced to living as a common labourer. Embittered by his excommunication, Ma was ready for revenge and, when Chan Man-yiu admitted his identity, agreed to assist in the attack on the monastery. Chan promised him imperial honours and favours. Ma showed him the whereabouts of the tunnels and the paths leading from them. Finally, Chan requested that Ma swear his expulsion from the monastery had been caused by his refusal to join the monks' conspiracy against the emperor. Ma conceded.

With the traitor's inside knowledge, troops under the command of High Commissioner Cheung Kin-chau were placed at all the secret exits. Others hid near the main gates, to seal them when the signal was given. All were supplied with inflammable material. Chan Man-yiu, with a number of coolies carrying jars of drugged wine, openly approached the monastery. When the monks opened the gates, Chan announced that the wine was a personal gift from the emperor. He requested that the abbot and all the monks drink the emperor's health with it. The abbot, however, was suspicious and, testing the wine with a magic sword, found the blade changed colour. The monks, furious at the emperor's treachery, attacked Chan Man-yiu but he managed to escape. On seeing him flee, the troops advanced, igniting fires at the entrances to all the secret tunnels; they then set fire to the buildings.

One hundred and ten monks perished in the fire. The remaining eighteen sought refuge in the main hall of the temple and there, before the image of the Buddha, prayed for their deliverance. Their prayers were answered when a large yellow curtain hanging in the hall fell to cover them. It protected the monks from the flames but it and the smoke also smothered them so that they lost consciousness. When the Q'ing troops saw the walls of the buildings collapse, and could see no sign of life within them, they assumed their task was done and retreated.

When the eighteen survivors came to, they found themselves trapped in the ruins. One of their number, however, Tsoi Tak-chun, knocked a hole in the monastery wall, through which they managed to make their getaway. The entire hill was alight, but they ran over the burning grass, the smoke concealing them. Slipping through the military lines, they travelled to Ting Shan, near Sheung Yeung city, Hupei province. There, thirteen of them died from burns and wounds or from lack of food. They were cremated, their ashes wrapped in several bundles and retained for safekeeping by the five remaining survivors: Tsoi Tak-chung, Fong Tai-hung, Ma Chiu-hing, Wu Tak-tai and Lee Shik-hoi. These men became the First Five Ancestors.

Continuing their flight, the First Five Ancestors were much weakened. All they could find to drink was dew collected in the petals of lotus flowers. Of food, they could find nothing. Eventually they reached the Cheung Kong, Tai Hoi (the Long River and the Big Sea), where they threw themselves down on the shore and fainted from hunger. Whilst unconscious, they dreamed that spirits told them the sand was edible. When they awoke, they ate sand and their hunger was satisfied. Once fed and restored, they noticed something sparkling on the beach. Curious, they approached it.

The object was a three-legged incense burner. On the base were engraved the characters *fan q'ing – fuk ming*. On the side were more characters instructing them to act according to the Will of Heaven. In the burner was a sheet of paper upon which was written a prophecy of the destruction of the Q'ing dynasty and the return of the Ming.

When they had read this document, they worshipped the gods, thanking them for their deliverance and encouragement. They had no joss-sticks nor any other articles necessary for a service, making do with the branches of a small tree, which served as altar candlesticks, and burning grass for incense, which glowed brightly, sending fragrant smoke up to the gods.

Distracted by their act of worship, the Five Ancestors did not notice Q'ing soldiers approaching. Suddenly they were surrounded, with soldiers before them and the wide ocean at their backs. All seemed lost until a grass sandal, one of a pair they had brought from the monastery and which was said to have been worn by Mo Tat, the founder of their fraternity, turned into a boat. They boarded it and escaped.

On landing, they journeyed on to the Wu Lung (Black Dragon) River, where they encountered another Q'ing force which pinned them down on the banks. During the fighting, they lost their precious grass sandals. They managed to get away and searched for a place to cross the river: without the sandals they had no boat. At last, they came to a bridge called Yee Pan Kiu, the Two-planked Bridge, but it was guarded. Undeterred, the Five Ancestors succeeded in getting under the bridge unde-tected and found three large stones floating on the water, each carved with a character. They read *ting, hoi, pau* or calm, sea, floating. Stepping from stone to stone, they passed unnoticed.

Safely across the river, the Five Ancestors met a fruitseller, Tse Pong-hang, who gave them fruit to eat and water to drink, then took them to the hut of a woodcutter, Ng Ting-kwai. There they sheltered while the woodcutter went about his business. In the forest, cutting fuel, Ng Ting-kwai came upon Chan Man-yiu, the magistrate, who was out hunting the escapers. He asked the woodcutter if he had come across five monks. Ng Ting-kwai, sensing the magistrate to be an enemy of the men resting in his hut, felled him with his axe. He later found one of the lost grass sandals at a place called Chung Chau. For this, Ng Ting-kwai was afterwards recognized as being the first *cho hai* (Grass Sandal) official.

Tse Pong-hang, the fruitseller, took the Five Ancestors to Kwai Sin Shan, a hill on the border of Wai Yeung district in Guangdong, where they sheltered at the Po Tak monastery. The abbot, Kwok Yeun, introduced them to five of his friends, Ng Tin-shing, Hung Tai-shui, To Pit-tat, Lee Shik-tai and Lam Wing-chiu. Former Ming officials now living as rebels, they swore to join the monks and raise an avenging force. For this, they became known as the Second Five Ancestors.

Kwok Yeun sent the two sets of Ancestors to meet with Chan Kan-nam who was living in the White Stork Grotto, plotting and recruiting his own army. Fong Tai-hung went alone to the grotto, whilst his nine comrades travelled to the city of Sheung Yeung to pay homage at the grave of Cheng Kwan-tat, who had been executed. At Sheung Yeung, they met Cheng's widow and sister in the company of two of his close friends, Wong Cheong and Chung Man-kwan. Together, they worshipped at the graveside, but were discovered by Q'ing soldiers tipped off by the traitorous Ma Ning-yee. The worshippers fled in confusion, but Cheng's widow and sister were cut off by the soldiers on the bank of a nearby river. Rather than surrender, they jumped into the water and drowned. As if by magic, their bodies floated upriver against the current, to be found by Tse King-chim, Tse Pong-hang's son, who dragged them out of the river and buried them under a peach and a plum tree.

The nine Ancestors were on the run for many days,

197

until they came upon the graves of the two women. In anguish at what had befallen their sisters-in-arms, they knelt in their honour. As they did so, the two trees metamorphosed into a sword. With it, they turned and attacked the soldiers who were following them. The perfidious Ma Ning-yee was slain and the victorious Ancestors made their way to the White Stork Grotto.

In discussion with Chan Kan-nam, it was decided that they would all go to the town of Muk Yeung in Fujian to set up a headquarters and recruit patriots. Not being able to set up a base openly, they had to have a cover. Tse Pong-hang opened the Yee Hop Tim fruit shop in nearby Tai Ping Market. It was a clandestine recruiting office which signed up patriots, arranging for them to be housed and employed until it was time to raise the flag of revolt.

In the meantime, two fishermen plying their trade near Xiamen, Chan Sau-hang and his son, Chan Siu-kun, discovered Wong Shueng-Shan's missing book, *Kam Toi Po Luk*, in their nets and landed it along with a jade seal. Being loyal anti-Q'ing citizens, they delivered them to Chan Kan-nam, who immediately realized that the seal was that of the Ming emperors.

The recruiting campaign attracted thousands of patriots. Amongst them was a young boy, Chu Hung-chuk, who claimed descent from the Ming emperors, supporting his claim with his noble bearing and appropriate documentation. The Ancestors declared him their Crown Prince.

On the twenty-fifth day of the seventh moon in the Kap Yan year, Chan Kan-nam officiated at a mass ceremony. Officials of the rebel organization were elected and sworn in. The oath they took was *fan ch'ing – fuk ming*.

One of the officials appointed, Tin Yau-hung, was put in command of the rebel army, but it was not a fortuitous appointment, for he was the reincarnation of Wong Shing-yan, a faithful eunuch who had committed suicide with his emperor when the usurper, Li Chi-shing, entered Beijing. The eunuch's body had been left to rot without proper burial and his restless spirit had wandered the earth until one of Chan Kan-nam's leading fighters, So Hung-kwong, died. His corpse did not cool. Even several days after his death, it was still fresh and warm because Wong Shing-yan's ghost had acquired it. On the third day, the body came back to life as Tin Yau-hung.

At the mass ceremony, a bright red glow appeared in the eastern sky. It was considered a good omen because the character for red was pronounced *hung* and is similar to the phonetic sound of the family name of the Ming emperors. As a result of this fortunate coincidence, the Ancestors decided to refer to themselves as members of the Hung Ka, or Hung Family. The character *hung* was adopted, though it was the regal character rather than the colour character that was used. Chu Hung-chuk, as crown prince, changed his name to Chu Hung-ying in honour of his comrades: *ying* means heroes. The whole organization then took the name Ming Yeun Tong Kam Toi Shan – the Ming Eternal Society of Kam Toi Mountain.

The society embarked upon its military campaign, quickly conquering Fujian then marching north on Nanjing. It seemed nothing could stop them, but, because of poor communication, the force became disunited. The Q'ing forces selectively attacked rebel units and, predictably, the rebellion failed. Over 100,000 rebels were killed. Chu Hung-ying, the crown prince, vanished during the battles and was never heard of again. The rebel army retreated to Muk Yeung where it suffered another loss. Chan Kan-nam died. His successor was Sze Kam-ming, the son of Sze Ho-fat. Sze travelled to Ko Kai temple in Guangdong to raise a fresh army. Inside a year, he had a huge following and conquered seven southern provinces.

Once more, it looked as if the Q'ing dynasty was on the run but, near Pak Fu Kwan (White Tiger Pass) in Szechuan, Tin Yau-hung died. Without his leadership, the commanders fell to arguing over tactics and the Q'ing army seized the opportunity to defeat them again.

The First Five Ancestors now realized that the way to smash the Q'ing was not to have one rebellion but a number of simultaneous rebellions which would divide the emperor's army and stretch it to the limits. It was therefore decided that everyone should split up to raise independent forces nationwide. Before going their separate ways, the Ancestors devised a series of secret signs by which they and their supporters would be able to recognize each other when they met.

Tsoi Tak-chung and Ng Tin-shing went to Fujian and Gansu, where they set up the First Lodge of the Society, known as the Ching Lin Tong Fung Wong Kwan (Green Lotus Hall of the Phoenix District). Its troops marched under a black banner bearing the character *piu*, meaning glorious. It was also known as the Sap Kau Tai, (Nineteen Steps, or Ladder) and had a seal in the shape of a rhomboid. Tsoi Tak-chung changed his name to Chan Yeun; he also went under his Buddhist name, Fat Sam, and his society name, Ching Fong. He travelled as far north as Hangzhou, staying at the Ling Yan monastery where the abbot, Yat Chi, introduced him to another resident of the monastery, To Yuen, who was the Third Generation Ancestor of the Ching Mun (Green Family), a society established by Kam Shun to further the principles of Ku Ting-lam's book, *Ming Yee Toi Fong Luk*. (Kam Shun was known as the First Generation Ancestor, who, on his death, was succeeded by Lo Cho, the Second Generation Ancestor and, in turn, To Yeun.) The Ching Mun had successfully recruited almost every boatman and coolie in the ports of Hangzhou, Shanghai and Nanjing and on the waterways connecting the cities. Working for the Q'ing authorities, they reported on troop concentrations, movement of supplies, the whereabouts of storage depots and the strength and morale of garrisons. In a time of uprising, they could attack a wide number of targets and bring the canal system, upon which the military heavily relied, to a standstill.

To Yuen introduced Tsoi Tak-chung to the leaders of the three main branches of the Ching Mun – the Yung Ngan, Chin Kin and Pun Ching. Collaboration between the Ching Mun and the Hung Mun was considered and it was decided to alter the name of the Ching Mun to Ching Pang (Green Party Gang). This decision made, Tsoi continued northwards to Shanghai, where he stayed at the Hung Kwan Lo Cho temple, meeting with Shing Heung-shan, the notorious leader of the criminal gangs in the city. Shing might have been a criminal but he was also a patriot and, after listening to Tsoi Tak-chung's plans for a rebellion, became his disciple and formed his criminal followers into an association he called the Hung Pang (Hung Party, or Red Gang).

Fong Tai-hung and Hung Tai-shui went to Guang-dong and Guangxi, where they established the Second Lodge, the Hung Shun Tong Kam Lan Kwan (Hung Obedience Hall of the Golden Orchid District). Like the First Lodge, it had another name, Sap Yee (Twelve) Tai, a banner with the character *sau* (longevity) embroidered upon it and a triangular seal. Fong Tai-hung used the Buddhist name Fat Mo and the society name Ching Cho. His first concern was the raising of an army in the Guangdong area and he recruited Cheng Yat-so, a famous female pirate chief, to the cause. Members in the region of Heung Lo To and Wu Lo To named themselves the Sam Hop Wui, (Three United Association). Another famous pirate, Cheung Po-tsai, also founded a group in the Tam Shui/Kwai Chung area, which was known as the Yee Lung Shan Tong (Two Dragons Hill Society).

Accompanied by To Pit-tat, Ma Chiu-hing went to Yunnan and Szechuan provinces to found the Third Lodge, the Ka Hau Tong Fuk Po Kwan (Heavenly Queen Hall of the Happy Water Margin District) or Kau (Nine) Tai. The banner was scarlet with the character *hop* (united) upon it; the seal was square. Ma Chiu-hing went by his Buddhist name, Yan Wai, and his society name, Ching Kit. As well as the Third Lodge, he also established a society in Szechuan known as the Po Ko Wui (Robe of the Elder Brother Society).

Two other lodges, the Fourth and Fifth respectively, were established in Hunan and Hubei (by Wu Tak-tai and Lee Shik-tai) and Zhejiang, Jiangxi and Henan (by Lee Shik-hoi and Wing Chiu). The Fourth Lodge was called the Cham Tai Tong Lin Cheung Kwan (Great Blending Hall of the Beautiful Lotus District) or Yee Sap

Kau (Twenty-nine) Tai, with a parallelogram-shaped seal and the character *wo* (harmonious) on its white banner. Wu Tak-tai called himself Lun Hau or Ching Shing. In Sam Cho district, Hunan, he recruited Kwong Hon, who organized a branch society, the Ko Tai Wui (Elder and Younger Brothers Society), later known as Ko Lo Hui (Elder Brothers Society). The Fifth and final Lodge was the Wang Fa Tong Lung Sai Kwan (Extension Conversion Hall of the Western Dyke District), or the Sze Sap Ts'at (Forty-seven) Tai. The flag was green with the character *tung* (together, or mutual), the seal circular. Lee Shik-hoi, who was known as Chi Yau or Ching Kwan, also set up a branch in Chekiang called the Hung Cheong Wui (Red Spear, or Cannon Society).

With five lodges up and running, thousands of recruits were initiated. Yet, once again, the plan foundered. In some regions, a lodge went on the attack alone, in response to local Q'ing oppression, not waiting for a signal from the other society branches. These 'independent' uprisings predictably failed and those who survived them dispersed far and wide. Many went overseas, to the goldfields of America and Australia; others headed for the South Seas and the Malay peninsula. No matter where they went, they remained true to their society and set up new lodges so that they might continue, from afar, to work towards the liberation of China from the Q'ing yoke.

In 1903, Dr Sun Yat-sen, leader of the Republican Party, who had also been forced into exile, joined the Kwok On Wui (National Stability Society). Not long after his initiation, he formed a new branch of the society in Honolulu which he named Tai Luk Shan

203

(Main – or Big, or High – Land Mountain), with himself as leader.

Dr Sun was conscious that the combined efforts of the thousands of patriotic brothers in the society system as a whole could rid China of the Q'ing rulers, so he became anxious to co-ordinate all branches and extend their reach. As a result of his efforts, 140 branches of the Hung Mun and 128 branches of the Green Pang were established prior to 1911. One very important branch was the Hing Chung Wui (Prosperity for China Society), which later changed its name to the Kwok Man Tong (National People's Party).

Together with other well-known society leaders, such as Chiu Yuk, Wong Wan-so and Cheung Oi-wan, Sun Yat-sen went to America, where he obtained both moral and financial support from brothers living there. Other society officials visited Australia, Europe, Malaya and every country where a branch of the society existed, all for the purpose of raising funds and support. Having gained much support, Sun Yat-sen ordered the revolution to begin in 1911. Within a year, the Q'ing dynasty fell and the Republic of China was established.

So runs the Triad traditional history, as recounted by Triads to Morgan. Compared to earlier versions, Morgan's rendition was adapted to suit the times in which it was told, suitably embellished to have contemporary relevance. Certain 'local' factors were added to give the story more credence in Hong Kong, where Morgan recorded it. For example, Cheung Po-tsai was a real pirate who operated in Hong Kong waters, his base on the island of Cheung Chau and at the village of Stanley, on Hong

Kong island, which is still known to this day as Chek Chui, or Pirate Fortress.

Many of the places mentioned in the narrative are either imaginary or untraceable and correlating the many events of traditional history with actual history is well nigh impossible, except in more recent centuries when dates are given: indeed, the nearer the story moves towards the present, the more verifiable it becomes.

Despite the many vagaries and ambiguities, some identifiable historical links can be teased out of the narrative. Many of the place-names may be fictitious but some are, if not actual, then at least versions of real places. The monastery at Shao Lin, Muk Yeung and Tai Ping Market cannot be positively identified. On the other hand, Silu does appear in ancient annals: it was not a province of historical China but a region said to have lain between the Altai mountains and the Hwang Ho River. Today, it is the region of Sinkiang. Major centres are obvious and undisputed. Cheng-du, Beijing, Xiamen, Nanjing and Shanghai are of course genuine, as are provinces and, on occasion, districts within them. Even smaller places really exist. Kwai Chung, for example, was a tiny fishing village near Kowloon, in Hong Kong. Wuchow could well be modern-day Wuzhou in Guang-xi and Sheung Yeung could be Shenyang, long noted for its radical politics and at one time provincial capital under the Q'ing rulers. Sze Ho-fat was a real-life general, Cheng Shing-kung was a real character, as was Man Wan-lung. Playing such guessing games is all part of the Triad process: it adds to the mystique. For non-Triad members, it is rather like looking at medieval navigation maps, using one's imagination to fill in the areas marked *Here be*

205

dragons. The co-mingling of fact and fiction makes it impossible to discover the truth and the variety of versions complicates matters further: the tale as told in Shandong province has few similarities to the same story told in Guangdong, Fujian or Taiwan.

Yet all agree on one point. The thread which ties them is their common origin in an association established by pro-Ming, anti-Q'ing officials, bound together by the patriotic desire to restore China to the descendants of the Ming emperors. This patriotic motive has, of course, long been redundant. It has been many decades since a Triad society did anything other than look out for itself.

2

'THE CITY OF WILLOWS'

After the failure of the Taiping Rebellion, both Westerners and Chinese started to take an interest in China's secret societies. Until then, foreign expatriates had considered them to be just another facet of the impenetrable Orient – one that, whilst it occasionally impinged upon the business of selling Christ or trade goods to the natives, rarely affected them. For the Chinese themselves, they were part of a complex religious and cultural tapestry.

As early as the 1860s, Western orientalists were studying the secret-society phenomenon. One of the earliest in-depth studies was made by Gustave Schlegel, professor of Chinese at the University of Leyden. His book, *The Thian Ti Hwui, the Hung League or Heaven–Earth League*, published in 1866, was for many years the primary text for the study of Triads. Schlegel was unique in that he gained the majority of his knowledge first-hand from Chinese merchants and seamen in Batavia (now Jakarta), Hong Kong and Macau.

When anti-foreign sentiments began to increase, the Vegetarians and Boxers rising to prominence, so interest in secret societies swelled. One of the most important studies was written by a magistrate, Lao Nai-hsüan. Entitled *I Ho Ch'üan Chiao Men Yüan Liu K'ao* (*The Study of the Origins of the Boxer Sect*), it was published in 1899. Lao submitted it to the Q'ing authorities through a highly placed friend, but he was unsuccessful in promoting it as far as the throne. It is believed that the empress dowager suppressed it. Missionaries produced tracts about the societies, journalists wrote about them, often in the goriest tabloid terms, and scholars studied them. Suddenly, Triad societies were more than a subject of cultural interest: they had at last come to be regarded as an important part of the Chinese political and social landscape and, consequently, their actual and traditional histories were increasingly documented. Their inner workings are, understandably, less well known.

Although at some early stage Triad societies may have been administered by a central organization, for most of their history each society has operated as an autonomous unit, self-governing and answering to no authority but the collective dictates of its own officials. In some localities and regions they have had sub-groups or branches attached to them but, unlike most other secret or quasi-secret societies, they do not have a central administration or headquarters. Even individual societies rarely have a single place they can call their fraternity's base.

Only one specifically erected Triad society building has ever been identified. In the 1930s, police in Penang photographed its exterior. Few photographs exist of a meeting place prepared for a ceremony; those that do are held in police files, mostly in Hong Kong.

A semi-permanent Triad lodge actually existed in

Kowloon Walled City in Hong Kong. A singularly unimpressive room about 20 metres square, it had a tiled floor and bare, whitewashed walls and was usually half filled with piles of tables and chairs. At one end, there was an altar hung with dirty scarlet cloth, upon which stood an idol of Kwan Ti. Some joss-stick holders and candles, with a bowl of mouldy offering fruit, lay before the idol, which was surrounded by a number of rusting Triad fighting weapons, including an iron ball-and-chain with metal spikes protruding from it, another chain with a steel blade at one end and a wooden handle at the other, and several steel throwing-stars. These looked like large Christmas tree decoration stars with all but one of the spines sharpened.

This lack of a permanent meeting place is not surprising. Any organization with a head office can easily be traced, observed, investigated and ultimately infiltrated. This weakness undermined the American Mafia, which maintained favourite club houses and bars where members met, which were both observed and bugged. The Triads have rarely been so foolish; where they have centralized information, it has been their undoing.

Only members really know the true appearance and layout of a ceremonial hall. Descriptions are rare. There is, however, a detailed description in Morgan's study. His depiction, which avoids the usual bland policeman's style, is not only remarkable but of considerable historical importance, for since the 1950s ceremonial process has substantially deteriorated.

A lodge is a symbolic representation of the town of Muk Yeung, which is also known as the City of Willows, and, because it was the first place in which the Triad societies established themselves, is of great importance. Much in this representational city refers directly to the traditional history so that, in undergoing a ceremony in it, the member symbolically travels through the legend, sharing seminal events with the Ancestors.

Whenever possible, the lodge is oblong in shape and, if it is constructed in the open air, as early lodges often were, is surrounded by a high wall. Should it be in a building, the walls of the meeting room suffice. In each of the four walls, at the points of the compass, is a gate, each guarded by a legendary general, but only the East Gate, at one end of the lodge's long axis, is of any importance in the rituals. The North and South Gates are never used (and may be represented only by their attendant general) and the West Gate, behind the altar at the opposite end of the room from the East Gate, functions only as a common exit.

Recruits in initiation ceremonies or officers being promoted are assembled to the right of the East Gate, appropriate banners for the occasion suspended above them. On the other side of the gate is hung the scarlet banner of the society's most senior official, below which are paper effigies of the treacherous Ma Ning-yee, the magistrate Chan Man-yiu and the Q'ing emperor Hong Hei.

Down the centre of the lodge, before the East Gate, are three archways, each guarded by two generals. The first may be formed of swords, real or symbolic. Above each is a banner or inscription proclaiming the virtues to which each member must aspire in order to be a good society man.

These portals present a problem of interpretation. They

210

are in the lodge, yet a member does not enter the City of Willows until he has passed through them. This means that the City of Willows is not necessarily Muk Yeung but a building nearby, possibly a pavilion on an estate. The outer walls represent the estate perimeter, the portals gates in formal gardens, which often contain decorative archways, the city a pavilion at the far end. Most estates contained pavilions for concubines or loyal followers: perhaps long ago, in early Triad history, the Ancestors were given such a pavilion as a safe house by a sympathetic landowner. Another reason for thinking the City of Willows refers to a private pavilion is the fact that a pavilion in the Forbidden City in Beijing is called the City of Willows.

Beyond the third archway is a space referred to as the City of Willows, upon the floor of which are represented the Circle of Heaven and Earth, the Pit of Fire, the Stepping Stones and the Two-planked Bridge. The first is a hoop of cane with serrated pieces of paper glued to it, which stands for the hole in the wall of the Shao Lin monastery through which the monks escaped. The fire pit represents the burning hillside around the monastery, the stepping stones those used by the fleeing monks and the bridge under which they hid. All are made of paper. On either side are gathered all the society's officials, who stand or sit in front of two banks (one on either side of the lodge) of memorial tablets and banners. More of the same hang behind and to each side of the altar which is ahead, in front of and hiding the West Gate.

The memorials celebrate both the exploits of the Ancestors and those of individual members of the society. These are usually not commemorations of criminal successes but of fraternal achievement, which may include a record of victories over rival Triad societies.

One part of the City of Willows is usually not represented in the layout of the lodge. This is the Hung Fa Ting or Red Flower Pavilion and is used for just one part of the initiation ceremony which often takes place a few days after the main ceremony. However, the Red Flower Pavilion may be represented by a side room or area if the venue is sufficiently large. The Hung Fa Ting consists of a small altar in memory of the females in the traditional history, over which is a tablet in their honour with other tablets on either side, bearing poetic epigrams.

It must be explained that the banners and tablets are not necessarily permanent objects. In times past, society banners were made of embroidered cotton. They ranged in colour according to their meaning and were triangular with serrated edges, each bearing an appropriate Chinese character. The tablets were made of wood or flattened bamboo, painted red with black or white characters. Times, however, have changed. Most banners and tablets are nowadays made of paper, rewritten afresh for each occasion. They may, therefore, be destroyed so that police raids upon officials' homes do not unearth incriminating evidence.

The altar is an elaborate construction. Above it, a horizontal tablet proclaims '*Sham Tai Wang Fa*' ('Extensive Transformation and Uniting with Heaven'). Below this are hung or pasted four vertical tablets written in black on red paper, stating 'Faithful people join the society'; 'Disloyal people may not burn incense here'; 'The heroes are supreme'; and 'Brave men have no equals'. Between these four is a black tablet with white writing upon it

212

which reads 'The Spirit Seats of the Hung Family, Founders, Foundresses and Early Martyrs', followed by a roll-call of their names. To the right is another tablet naming the altar as the Hung Society temple, and two long tablets. These carry esoteric statements:

The lone effective turtle from the wide ocean promises success. Nine numbers by Ying and nine numbers by Yang. Nine times nine make eighty-one numbers. Every number goes back to the three main doctrines. Morality comes from the Principal Celestial Excellency. Complete single-heartedness is influential.

and

The two gay phoenixes on the lofty mountain signify prosperity. Six calls from the hen and six calls from the cock. Six times six makes thirty-six calls. Each call penetrates the nine divisions of Heaven. Heaven produced the holy emperor of the great Ming. May he live for ever.

On the left of the altar is a tablet to Man Wan-lung, outlining his personal history.

Upon the altar appear a variety of objects, according to the purpose of the ceremony. These include assorted documents; two brass single-stem candlesticks called the Ku Shu (Ancient Trees); a brass lamp called the Seven Stars Lamp, which represents what the Chinese consider to be the seven primary planets and the seven *mow* (a land-area measurement) of land contained within the City of Willows; a jug of wine and five wine cups for the five wells in the city; a pot of tea and three tea-bowls for the three ponds in the city; an incense bowl and a smaller incense pot for carrying around the city; eight dishes or bowls of offerings containing nuts, fruit, flowers and diluted wine; a society handbook (if one exists); a list of the particulars of initiates (if relevant); several small flags; a needle with a skein of red thread attached to it; and the *tau*.

The *tau* is the central object on the altar. It is a wooden tub like those used in Chinese stores to contain rice; indeed, the bulk of it is filled with raw rice, each grain representing a society member. It is painted red and bears the words *chung* (pine) and *pak* (cedar), both of which represent longevity, and *to* (peach) and *li* (plum), which signify loyalty. On the front is written Muk Yeung Shing, the City of Willows, and four other characters with esoteric connotations. In the rice stand a large number of significant society flags and banners, the red club (a symbol of punishment), a sword made of peach and plum wood, a sandal made of woven grass or straw, a yellow umbrella, a white paper fan, an abacus, a pair of Chinese scales and an assortment of lesser ritual items. Many of these may today be made of paper.

Hanging from the front of the altar is the *sha tsz pei* or yellow gauze quilt, representing the yellow curtain which fell and protected the monks in the monastery. Upon it are written a number of epigrams (including *fan q'ing – fuk ming*) and the 36 oaths taken by all members upon joining any Triad society.

One interesting footnote to the subject of the City of Willows and the lodge refers to the willow pattern plate, so popular in Victorian and Edwardian Europe and still a common crockery pattern.

The illustrative pattern tells a story of which most Westerners know at least the bare bones. It concerns two lovers in ancient China who are forcibly parted by the girl's father, who disapproves of their relationship. The girl is imprisoned by him and betrothed against her will to a man whom she does not love. She is rescued by her lover and, with him, flees by sampan to an island. There the two live together happily for a time until their whereabouts are discovered. The lover is murdered and the distraught girl sets fire to their house and perishes in the flames. The gods, however, take pity on the star-crossed pair and turn them into doves.

How this story came into being is not fully known. It was possibly invented by the Chinese exporter who first manufactured and sold the plates abroad: Europeans lapped up exotic romances of the mystic Orient. Yet the pattern was not, as is commonly believed, invented specifically for overseas trade. It certainly existed in China before being exported but, in many instances, was corrupted in the process. Plates made in Europe which copied the pattern often imitated the corrupted version. Only a few survive with the proper tale represented upon them.

In the light of traditional Triad history and the layout of the City of Willows, an alternative interpretation becomes evident. The willow tree which is central to the design stands behind a wall: this is the wall surrounding Muk Yeung, the City of Willows. On the island to which 'the lovers' flee, there is a building. It is clearly not a domestic house but a temple, which does not feature in the romance. Is this the memorial shrine to the Five Ancestors, or a pavilion? There is also a bridge of two arches, if not planks. The burning of the house in the tale may be a corruption of the torching of the monastery. Certainly, all the trees in the pattern other than the willow are recognizably peach trees. The whole willow pattern design, in fact, can be related to Triad traditional history.

3

PASSING THE MOUNTAIN OF KNIVES

Little is known of the ritual process of Triad societies. Members are loath to talk, even under duress, and the only reliable accounts either come from police records, especially those of the Hong Kong police, from sources like Morgan's seminal study, or from historical documents such as the writings of Gustave Schlegel.

Considering the disparate nature of Triad societies, the rituals are, with minor exceptions, surprisingly common to a wide number of groups, the structure almost identical due to the traditional roots from which all have sprung. It is this similarity which gives the Triads a sense of cultural and criminal identity. They may fight bitterly over territorial rights or criminal enterprise, but they share a common heritage which gives them a sense of outlaw solidarity. Enemies or competitors they may be, but they are simultaneously united against the powers-that-be — law-enforcement agencies or the government. This unity in disunity lingers from the days of *fan q'ing – fuk ming*.

In the past, each society conformed to a rigid ceremonial and hierarchical structure dictated by traditional history, but Triad groups today, especially those outside the Far East, often do without certain officers and functions, or amalgamate and redistribute their duties.

Originally, each society, or lodge of a large society, had an overseeing executive hierarchy, the members appointed for fixed periods and elected by fellow society members. Where this structure is retained, the ultimate leader is the *shan chu* or Master of the Mountain, sometimes colloquially referred to as the *lung tau* (or Dragon Head.) His responsibility is to exercise authority over every member and activity of his society. His word is law, although he may confer with a deputy, the *fu shan chu*, who acts as his proxy when he is absent. The next level is the *heung chu*, or Incense Master, who is on the same tier of the command structure as the *sin fung*, or Vanguard. These officials administer rituals, oversee promotions and elections for promotion, control initiation and, where necessary, order retribution against members who have fallen foul of their brothers. Beneath them comes the *sheung fa* (Double Flower), of whom there may be a number. Senior officials, sometimes retired from more exalted positions, they take charge of departments of their society's activities, usually control everyday business and, if there are sub-branches, may be in charge of these, each of which will have its own senior personnel but refer to the 'mother' lodge for the positions of Incense Master and Vanguard. These posts exist only in principal lodges, their presence indicating that the society has reached a certain advanced stage of organization. A *sheung fa* in charge of a sub-group – or its leader if he is not a senior mother-lodge officer – is called a *chu chi* with his deputy being a *fu chu chi*. Some societies also have a *cha so*, or treasurer, but this is not common. Finances are usually controlled by the *shan chu*.

Below the *sheung fa* level come three types of official who are all equal. The *hung kwan* – the infamous Red Pole official – is a fighting-unit commander controlling up to fifty men and is a real fighter, well versed in the martial arts. Most societies have a number of Red Poles, according to size and need. An 'enforcer', the Red Pole is the strong-arm man of a society, responsible for fighting with other societies, acting as a hit-man and making sure, where force is needed, that it is applied in the right measure.

Of equal rank to the *hung kwan* is the *pak tsz sin* (White Paper Fan). He is an administrative officer, a business manager who keeps the books and banks the money. Usually well educated, he frequently has commercial or legal expertise and is, in some respects, like the *consigliere* of a Mafia family – an adviser and strategist who is on the way to promotion to Incense Master. Additionally, he may be responsible for members' welfare as well as that of their families, looking after spouses and children should a brother be killed in action or imprisoned.

Also of equal status, and working alongside the White Paper Fan, is the *cho hai*, the Grass (or Straw) Sandal. In simple terms, he is a sort of membership-secretary-cum-go-between, who arranges meetings, liaises with other societies, ensures the collection of protection money, oversees business transactions and is the society's front man with the outside world. If Triad societies were to have a PR consultant, it would be the *cho hai*.

At the bottom of the Triad social ladder, and usually answering to the *hung kwan*, are the *sze kau* or 49s. In the past foot soldiers, these make up the bulk of the member-ships, the rank-and-file members who are the criminal workforce.

In addition to names, all members' ranks are given a numerical code, each of which begins with the number 4, referring to the ancient belief that the world was surrounded by four oceans. The system is based upon the ancient Oriental occult science of numerology in which numbers and combinations of numbers assume esoteric symbolic, even mystical, significance. The *shan chu* is also known as a 489, whilst the *fu shan chu, heung chu, sin fung* and *sheung fa* officers are all 438s, the *hung kwan* is a 426, the *pak tsz sin* is a 415 and the *cho hai* is a 432.

The *shan chu*, or 489, is also sometimes known as a 21 (4+8+9). When written in Chinese characters, 21 looks like part of the character for *hung*, as in Hung Society; 21 is also 3, the number of creation, multiplied by 7 which is a lucky number and the number of death, the numerological significance being that in the leader lies the life cycle of the society. The Incense Master (438) is also a 15 (4+3+8), being 3 (creation) multiplied by 5 (longevity or preservation), which is appropriate in connection with his responsibility for ritual. A sign of his position is to be found in the image of a tortoise, an animal symbolizing long life, often associated with Incense Masters. Additionally, 38 when written looks like the other half of the character *hung*. The *hung kwan* number, 426 ($4 \times 26 + 4$), refers to the 108 monks who fought in the Sung dynasty, whilst the *cho hai* number, 432 ($4 \times 32 + 4$), equals 132, the number of people from the Shao Lin monastery who assisted the treacherous Manchu against the Eleuths. The *pak tsz sin* number, 415, concerns the origins of Chinese calligraphy and the 49 responds to the 36 (4×9) oaths sworn in an initiation ritual. Of these numbers, 36 and 108 have a special significance and are often to be found in other contexts. Initiation fees, even sums gained by extortion, are often calculated by taking one of these base numbers and multiplying it by a factor of ten. For example, initiation fees into Hong Kong Triad societies in the 1970s stood at HK$3,600, whilst a Chinese takeaway in England might be required to pay £1,080 per month in protection money.

Triad societies today have mostly lost their traditional hierarchy. They have either retained the top four posts, with everyone below *heung chu/sin fung* level being equal, except for the 49s, or they have completely abandoned the traditional form and operate under a chairman and two senior assistants, with everyone else (save the 49s) being on a par. The individual officials in these 'modernized' societies share out responsibility according to expertise or vacancy, any official responsible for anything from finance, recruitment, membership and propaganda to internal discipline, inter-society liaison and even the education of members' children or the welfare of their families. This latter surprises observers, but it is in keeping with tradition. Although Triad societies today are primarily criminal, they retain some aspects of their historical role as semi-trade guilds. Particularly in Hong Kong and Singapore, there are a few societies which are self-help associations eschewing criminality.

However, no matter how modified or simplified a society has become, it usually still retains a *heung chu* for ceremonials. The reason for this is obvious. It is ceremony and ritual which unite the society.

The process of joining a Triad society is complicated. Initiates are required not only to pay a joining fee but also to obtain a sponsor to whom a further fee is payable, often far in excess of the initiation charge. The initiate-sponsor agreement is a private one, although it does not proceed until bona fides have been established by the Incense Master and the Vanguard. Initiates entering a society under duress must also have a sponsor. He is usually the person 'obliging' them to join, who may be recruiting them to swell society ranks or because he is seeking to increase his income from sponsorship fees; the joining fee is still charged. Whilst this preliminary outlay can be substantial, often beyond the immediate means of the initiate, he can recoup it many times over by sponsoring others. Of the official initiation fee, half goes into the society's coffers with the rest being shared between the senior officers. All money accrued, be it from fees or racketeering activities, is usually deposited in a central fund and is in theory inviolable. In fact, however, embezzlement by senior officers is common and the cause of rifts which lead either to retribution or the setting up of sub-groups by disaffected or disillusioned members.

The initiation ceremony symbolizes the forces and values which bind Triads together. The meeting is a coherence of past and present through which members become part of an evolving, potent continuum strengthened by the oaths of brotherhood. Here, past moral and religious precepts impress themselves upon the lives of all the members, who, outside the ceremony, rarely give them more than a passing thought. The honour, grandeur and rectitude of the Five Ancestors have long been divorced from everyday Triad existence. To the criminal brotherhoods that now constitute the vast majority of

Triad societies, the ritual is merely a means of imposing secrecy, discipline and loyalty.

Traditionally, meetings are held on the night of the twenty-fifth day of the Chinese month, notification being made on slips of red paper or thin strips of bamboo. A summons has to be obeyed unless there are extenuating circumstances of which the Incense Master has been made aware and of which he approves. Recruits are warned that divulging information about the meeting will be met with dire consequences.

At the ceremonial venue, a new candidate arrives barefoot with his hair tousled and his coat open. He is given five joss-sticks and recites four ritual poems, repeating them after a *sheung fa* who acts as a herald. Swearing to his identity, his name is announced to the assembly. He is then led to the first gate over which is hung a sheet of yellow paper. There he makes a salutation, is given a secret handshake and, after a small ritual dance, steps through to have his particulars entered in the membership records by the Vanguard. An archway of steel and copper, traditionally swords made of these metals, is formed and the recruit led beneath it. This is known as Passing the Mountain of Knives. Being handed three red stones, he then has to pay his initiation fee before being taken to the Hung Gate, which is guarded by two generals. Before them, he kneels three times while they demand his name, given by the Vanguard. This done, the generals go through the gate, obtaining the Incense Master's permission for the recruit to enter, then return and bring him through into the Hall of Fidelity and Loyalty. Two more generals demand his name and he kneels four times to them.

At this juncture, the recruit is given a brief lecture on the fraternal aims of the society and cautioned to be faithful. The concept of *fan q'ing – fuk ming* although no longer politically relevant, is explained and the need for members to be true not only to themselves and their brothers but also their clan and race is emphasized. The importance of being Chinese is, therefore, stressed. Assurances of fraternal agreement are made and dire warnings of what will happen to those who break their bond are given.

The lecture over, the recruit enters the Circle of Heaven and Earth, again guarded by two generals. Across this, and over an imaginary ditch, he is led to the East Gate of the City of Willows, where he kneels twice before the guard. Beyond the gate is the Hall of Universal Peace, sometimes referred to as the Tai Ping (Universal Peace) Market. If the ceremony is being held in a building, the East Gate is often a door leading into a separate room where senior officials are gathered. The Vanguard requests permission for Tse Pong-hang, the fruitseller, to enter: the recruit is the legendary character personified at this point. The Incense Master allows entry.

Once in the Hall of Universal Peace, ritual poems are recited. The recruit is joined by a member who stands by his side and answers for him 333 questions about the society, its objects, its history, its emblems and ceremonial. The Incense Master then asks if the recruit still wishes to join. He would be unwise to refuse, for by now he knows too much. Anyone imprudent enough to pull out now will not see the dawn.

The ceremony continues. In the last century, when Chinese men were obliged to wear their hair in plaited queues, it was cut off, sometimes being braided into a false pigtail that could be attached in public. To be without a queue was to admit to being a rebel. Today, a snip of hair is often taken as a token of this act of defiance. The recruit is then ceremonially shaved, his hair combed and his face washed as a sign of removing his past and wiping away any deceit lingering in his heart. Traditionally, this act of face-washing took place three days after the initiation ceremony, but in recent times it has been incorporated into the main ceremony. After being washed, the recruit's jacket and trousers are then removed and put aside; a century ago, they would have been cut up because they were tailored in the Q'ing fashion. Divested of his clothing, the recruit is then dressed in a long white robe with a red sash tied around his head and a pair of straw sandals on his feet. All the while, ritual poems, almost all of them quatrains, are recited. An example of one of the least esoteric is the Po (Treasure) poem which signifies a rite of passage in the ritual being completed:

> I passed a corner and then another corner.
> My family lives on the Five Fingers Mountain.
> I've come to look for the temple of the Sisters-in-law
> It's on the third of the row regardless of whether you count from
>   right or left.

The recruit is led to the altar whilst all members present hold nine blades of grass in their fingers. Two quatrains are spoken, then the oaths of fidelity and allegiance, written on large sheets of yellow paper which also bear the recruit's name and details, are next laid in a censer on the altar. Everyone present recites more poems and, with each verse, places a grass leaf in the censer. Two 'candles' (ideally splints of dried wood) are lit, more poems spoken and then a red candle is set up. A silver wine jug and three jade cups are produced and pledged to the worship of Heaven and Earth. After this offering, three lamps are lit, the last being red.

At this point the ceremony takes a religious turn. Having been largely concerned with Triad ritual, it now becomes a series of Buddhist and Taoist prayers and incantations to the earth gods and heroes of Triad traditional history. The list of oaths is taken from the censer and read to the kneeling recruit. This is the defining moment in the ceremony. To break the 36 oaths is to invite certain retribution.

The oaths are based upon three main concerns: the inviolability of the society and the importance of keeping its secrets; the demands of good fellowship; and the need to maintain internal order. All contain a definition of the specific punishment for infringement, which always involves the transgressor being killed.

In the first category are oaths such as *I shall not disclose the secrets of the Hung Society, not even to my parents, brothers or wife; I shall never disclose the secrets for money; I will be killed by a myriad of swords if I do so* (oath 5); and *I must never reveal Hung Society secrets or signs when speaking to outsiders; if I do so I will be killed by a myriad of swords* (oath 35). Fraternal relationships are covered by, for example, oaths 11 and 16, *I will take good care of the wives and children of sworn brothers when entrusted to my keeping; if I do not do so I will be killed by five thunderbolts;* and *If I consciously make use of my sworn brother's money or property for my own use I shall be killed by five thunderbolts.* Oaths concerning internal order include *I shall not be the cause of disharmony amongst my sworn brothers by spreading false rumours about them; if I do I shall be killed by a myriad of swords* (oath 23); *I must not conspire with outsiders to cheat my sworn brothers whilst gambling: if I do I will be killed by a myriad of swords* (oath 22); and *I shall not appoint myself as Incense Master without authority; after entering the Hung gates for three years the loyal and faithful ones may be promoted by the Incense Master with the support of the sworn brothers; I shall be killed by five thunderbolts if I make unauthorized promotions myself* (oath 24). At face value, the oaths seem reasonable, yet they illustrate how fragile Triad fraternal relationships can be. If a Triad member, after a solemn induction process, actually needs such oaths as *I must not take to myself the wives and concubines of sworn brothers nor commit adultery with them; if I do so I will be killed by a myriad of swords* (oath 34) to keep him on the fraternal path, then the moral core of the whole organization is brought into question. This morality is further questioned by oath 31, which states *I must not take advantage of the Hung fraternity so that I may oppress or take violent or unreasonable advantage of others; I must be content and honest; if I break this oath I will be killed by five thunderbolts.* Every landowner and merchant throughout Chinese history and, in the present day, Chinese takeaway owner who is paying protection money, must have frequently viewed this oath with a considerable degree of scepticism.

The oaths sworn, the recruit seals his allegiance with blood. After swilling his mouth out with cleansing tea, a bowl is filled with wine. The recruit (sometimes everyone present) pricks his middle finger and drips the blood into the wine. An alternative, much more common in modern times, is to drip the blood of a cockerel into the wine instead. The yellow paper hanging at the entrance of the hall is burned, the ash added to the wine. The mixture is then tasted by dipping the pricked finger in and sucking it dry, the cockerel is slaughtered and a curse spoken to the effect that should anyone, having now partaken of the drinking of the bloody wine, break his vows, he will share the cockerel's fate. Often the empty bowl is broken to signify the death of traitors.

The recruit now passes to the West Gate of the City of Willows, beyond which the oath list is burned, the smoke rising to the heavens where the gods acknowledge and become witnesses to it.

The recruit is now a fully fledged Triad with the rank of a 49. The *shan chu* presents him with his membership certificate – if he has paid for it – on the reverse of which his name is written in code. In times past, he would also be given a book, rather like a freemason's handbook, containing the oaths, regulations, secret recognition signs and the like, but this is rarely done today for fear of detection. He might also be given a knife or dagger and three 'Taiping coins': today, where these are given, ancient Chinese cash are used, easily bought in the Far East, even in tourist shops.

Although the ceremony is ended, the recruit is not dismissed. He is shown the society banners, kow-towing and making a libation of wine. Triad weapons are symbolically dipped in the blood of a white horse and a black ox: tea, wine or brandy may be used in lieu of blood. Once, this was really done, the animals providing the post-ceremonial feast. Nowadays, the feast usually takes place in a restaurant or with food brought in.

All presiding officials wear ceremonial dress similar to

that worn by Buddhist monks. The *shan chu* wears a full-length red robe, the Incense Master a white one. The former's robe may be embroidered but not the latter's; however, only the Incense Master may carry prayer beads. All other ranking officials wear black. These used to be black robes but, nowadays, black suits are worn. All the robes are made of cotton because Buddhism forbids the taking of life: silk, wool and leather are therefore prohibited. Loose headbands are also worn. If the ends are long, they hang over the front of the shoulders. Officials may also roll their trouser legs up over three folds, the left folding outwards in the Western freemasonic manner but the right inwards. They remove their shoes and put a grass sandal on their left foot: this may sometimes be replaced by a plastic sandal made to look as if woven of grass. The Vanguard may hold a whip and an umbrella, signifying that he has been on a journey; he may additionally carry a small knapsack or parcel which symbolically contains the ashes of the monks who died at the Shao Lin monastery.

In all, the traditional ceremony lasts about six hours, but nowadays societies can no longer afford the luxury of elaborate initiation sessions. Rituals have to be shortened to avoid discovery and the old, complex ceremonies, which have in any case become irrelevant to the sophisticated new generation of Triads who dress in Pierre Cardin shirts and drive expensive cars, have finally been abandoned. Fraternal bonds have been suborned by the ever-present threat of painful revenge or death by chopping. A shortened ceremony, referred to as 'Hanging the Blue Lantern', has become the norm. It lasts less than fifteen minutes and requires no real regalia. The 333 questions are trimmed to 33, many of the ritual poems are omitted, religious prayers are kept to a minimum or excised completely and the recounting of the traditional history is shortened to just a brief outline of the Shao Lin episode and the overthrow of the Q'ing dynasty. The name of this truncated ceremony comes from the ancient Chinese custom of hanging a blue light outside the house of a recently deceased person. To the initiate, it stands for the end of his former life and resurrection as a Triad.

On rare occasions, longer ceremonies do take place, to celebrate an important event such as the installation of a new Incense Master or other senior figure, yet even these are mere shadows of what they were. When they do take place, the ritual procedures are often inaccurate for there are too few Triads alive now who know how to pass on the traditions.

Apart from the initiation ceremony, which is the most commonly held, there are other ritual meetings. The most important is known as Burning the Yellow Paper. It is conducted when the members of two societies come together for a specific common purpose. It is also held when a new sub-group is founded or to combine weaker societies with a stronger. It frequently forges a bond between Triads from different societies who operate in the same area. For example, members of one society running brothels in a city may 'burn the yellow paper' with members of another society who operate the street narcotics trade, thereby ensuring neither poaches on the other's business. The arrangement might go so far as to stretch to the latter not selling drugs to the former's 'employees', thus not ruining their 'girls' in the process.

The ceremony of Burning the Yellow Paper is based

on an ancient Chinese legal custom: each party to a contract would write their name and address on a piece of yellow paper to which was added a brief summary of their agreement and a statement of their intention to honour it. The two papers were then burned to make them inviolate. The practice was common well into the twentieth century in law courts in Hong Kong, the burning of the paper before a trial, by the accused or by a witness, being regarded with the same gravity as taking the oath on the Bible. To Triads, the yellow paper has an added significance as it relates to the yellow paper sheet hung over the lodge entrance and to the paper on which the names of the initiates and the oaths are written.

Triad society documents, where they exist, are traditionally certified with the application of 'chops'. These are seals, usually carved of ivory, jade, jadeite or soapstone and stamped on the certificate with red indelible ink; documents are very rarely marked with a seal pressed in wax. The chops are divided into primary seals (used only by the *shan chu* or *fu shan chu*), secondary seals and individual seals specific to certain types of document. The system of seal usage is exceedingly complex and few Triads – if any – now appreciate its structure or symbolic significance.

Members recognize each other by hand signs. Within the confines of a secret meeting these are manifestly overt, appearing in the ritual dance during the opening of a ceremony and whenever objects are given or received. The *pak tsz sin* accepts small objects, such as a wine bowl, with his thumb, third and fourth fingers extended into a stiff tripod, whilst the *cho hai* makes his tripod with his index, middle and third fingers. Other hand signs are used

231

to denote rank or represent the characters found on society banners and flags. An example is the character *sh'e*, meaning snake, which relates to the Ancestor Wu Tak-tai. The index and middle finger form a fang-like shape but the hand too is a rough approximation of the calligraphy of the character.

In public, hand signs are muted yet widely used. Just as a freemason can inform an acquaintance of his membership by a handshake or the way he stands, so do Triads let others know who and what they are. Hand signs, which seem incongruous to an ignorant onlooker, can instruct another in the signaller's society and rank. The manner in which a cigarette is offered and accepted, the way in which chopsticks are held, the method of offering money in payment, the style of holding a pen and writing with it can all indicate membership and status.

In everyday conversation, coded phrases serve as introduction. Much as a freemason may ask, 'Are you on the square?' so a Triad may enquire, more ambiguously, 'Where were you born?' To a Chinese, this is not an unusual question, for men often enquire into another's patrimony or clan: it is all part of establishing ordinary social contact. If the innocuous answer is a little village just outside Guangzhou or not far from Taipei, the Triad enquirer will back off. If the reply is, 'Under a peach tree', 'In an orchard of peach trees' or a similar phrase referring to a peach, then he will know he is in the company of a brother, albeit of another society. He may then seek to learn more by asking other questions, receiving coded answers. 'Have you a mother?' would elicit the reply, 'I have five.' This is rather blatant. Another common exchange is: 'Don't you owe me money?' 'I paid you, I recall.' 'I do not recall that. Where did you pay me?' 'In the market.' This is not, of course, the local market but the Tai Ping Market.

It is a shame that the complexity and symbolism of Triad ritual have been lost, not because this deprives criminal fraternities of a heritage but because it removes an integral part of the rich corpus of Chinese culture. To see Triad ritual fading is akin to seeing Cantonese opera being replaced with Canto-pop music, or traditional teahouses with karaoke bars.

PART FOUR

SNAKE-HEADS AND SYNDICATES

1

ON THE SHORES OF THE FRAGRANT HARBOUR

Whatever Mao Zedong had hoped to achieve by inviting Du Yueh-sheng to return to China – the old gangster's help in setting up the country or the opportunity to execute him for the White Terror – his attitude towards the Triads in general was made plain. Almost from the foundation of the Communist state, Mao proscribed them with a vigour to which his imperial predecessors had never aspired.

The Triads were considered a very significant threat. History had shown they could create political mayhem and they drew support from the peasant masses which placed them in competition with the Communists for the hearts of the people. They were also uncontrollable: the Kuomintang had used them and, ultimately, they had virtually run the country for their own ends. What was more, the hated Kuomintang was by now in effect the political arm of the Triads. Mao was not going to risk the Communist Party's being similarly compromised. That being said, he still hankered after using them to his advantage if he could.

In 1963, in a re-run of his abortive approach to Du,

Mao revitalized his dream of a united China and a bringing of the Triads into the Communist sphere, despite his hatred for Chiang Kai-shek. The nation was at the time, and unbeknownst to the rest of the world, reaching the end of a terrible famine: between 1959 and 1963, 30 million Chinese starved to death. After the disaster of 1958's Great Leap Forward – the failed rejuvenation of China, and the collapse of the country's industry and agriculture – Mao needed a new drive, a new direction and all the help he could get to build China up again. The Triads' wealth and power could serve him well. A secret meeting was brokered between the Communist Chinese premier Zhou Enlai and Chiang Kai-shek, with Zhang Zhizhong, a former Kuomintang supporter who had gone over to the Communists, acting as intermediary; also present was Chiang Ching-kuo, Chiang's son and political heir. The meeting is thought to have taken place at Dongshan, south of Xiamen, the subject of discussion being the unification of China. Yet Zhou was ultra-cautious. Chiang's Triad affiliations were high in his thoughts and the only agreement reached was a mutual understanding not to infiltrate each other's territories.

Mao may have made overtures to and even befriended a few Triad powerbrokers, but he was not going to give them a position from which he could be threatened. As for the gangs and societies, they were out of the question: he no doubt remembered the old Chinese dictum, loosely translated, that one finch sings a pretty song but a thousand make a disharmonious cacophony over which no other bird can be heard. To form any society was forbidden as counter-revolutionary. Labour associations were disbanded and everyone worked for the good of society – not for the Red Pole who collected weekly 'membership dues' but for the Red Flag which promised a brighter future.

Above all, what Mao Zedong feared and abhorred was Triad criminality. They had plundered China for decades and it had to stop, but, as a pragmatist, Mao knew he would never erase the Triad underculture of graft, the concept of *guanxi* and the allegiance to clan or family, upon which, in any case, he himself heavily relied. Yet he had to do something, so he hit at Triad business, clamping down on prostitution and extortion. The root of the Triad problem, however, was not vice and corruption. It was opium. Until that was eradicated, the nation was weak and could neither achieve its potential nor realize the socialist dream.

Within three years of the Communist victory, opium had been completely removed from Chinese society, the nation 'clean' once more after several centuries and the Triads bereft of their most lucrative business. It was an astonishing feat. Addicts were treated sympathetically, farmers ordered to grow food crops instead of poppies. Opium-den owners were publicly humiliated then sent for political re-education in labour camps from which many never returned. Dealers and traffickers were deemed beyond re-education. They were shot by firing squads after brief trials. Most executions were public spectacles.

The vast majority of those executed were Triads: a membership certificate was a ticket to the labour camps. For the first time ever, it was illegal to be a Triad throughout China and the law was enforceable for, also for the first time, the nation was truly united under one, albeit totalitarian, government.

China was not, however, the first country to outlaw the Triads. That had already been done in the tiny colony of Hong Kong which had experienced Triad crime for a century before Mao swept into power. Nowhere on earth have the Triads been studied in greater depth than in Hong Kong, where they have been so transparently active, and nowhere has law enforcement against them been so determined and successful.

In Hong Kong, the Triad societies had evolved as a purely criminal sub-culture, which, save on a few isolated occasions, was never politically inspired. It was to their advantage to maintain the colonial status quo. The British governed the place and made it run smoothly, whilst the Chinese got on with doing what they were best at – entrepreneurship. As every criminal knows, the more affluent a society becomes, the more worthwhile crime becomes. As Hong Kong prospered and grew, the colony became a proving ground, a training school and an opportunity like no other for the Triads to hone their criminal and entrepreneurial skills and master the arts of criminal survival.

The foundation of the Triad international crime network began in Hong Kong and has resulted in its unjustly gaining the reputation of being the 'Triad World Headquarters'. This is nonsense. It is not and never has been. The Triads do not have a headquarters any more than the Russian crime gangs or the Mafia have. If anything, Hong Kong is to the Triads what Palermo is to the Sicilian Mafia – a spiritual home but by no means an operational base.

Hong Kong had been a refuge for pirates and malcontents from all over China south of the Yangtze long before the British arrived. Both geographically and symbolically isolated from the centres of imperial rule, it was beyond effective control. In addition, it offered an all-weather harbour for pirate vessels, hundreds of islands in which to hide and scattered settlements in which it was easy to disappear, or which were easy to pillage. The nearby Pearl River estuary was the entrance to the only major river system of southern China, and this was the regional highway. Cargo travelling up the rivers was ready prey. As international trade arrived, the pirates' income increased and they took to raiding foreign ships as well as coastal junks. With the ceding of Hong Kong to Britain by the Treaty of Nanjing in 1842, the pirates received more than a safe harbour. They were presented with a new jurisdiction unaffected by the imperial authorities: and, just as the pirates suddenly had a judicial haven, so did the Triads.

Coolies, fishermen, merchants and others, attracted to the new colony and the chance of trade, arrived, immediately establishing trade associations and guilds to protect their interests under a foreign government. With them the Triads came in droves. They recruited large numbers of coolies and quickly took control of many of the guilds. Within a year of the British landing, there were four Triad societies operating in the colony. In 1844, Captain William Caine, the man charged with establishing the police force, raided a Triad lodge, founded in 1842 in the Taiping Shan area of the town, arresting seventeen members.

Even the name of the urban district had Triad connotations. Taiping Shan means Peace Mountain and it was claimed to be the original name for the Peak, the summit which towers over the modern skyscraper district now known as Central, at that time called Victoria. This claim, however, is false. The mountain was most likely referred to as Hung Heung Lo Shan (Red Incense Burner Mountain); it is now known as Che Kei Shan (Raise the Flag Mountain). The Taiping Shan district is now called Western District but was, in the early days, styled the 'native quarter', where coolies and the working-class predominantly lived. It was there that they had their market, which was, therefore, both literally and symbolically the Taiping Market.

The report on Caine's raid mentioned the 'Secret association of the Triads', which, it stated, 'exercised an evil influence over the Chinese'. They did more than that. They extorted money and thieved. On 26 April 1843, they actually burgled the residence of Sir Henry Pottinger, the first governor. On 28 April, they broke into and looted the godowns of the three biggest foreign traders.

By 1845, Triads were so prevalent, and their activities considered so harmful, that an ordinance was passed for their suppression. Under it, it was illegal to be a Triad member, or even to impersonate one. The law stands to this day. Known as the Societies Ordinance, it has gone through many changes, keeping abreast of developments. At the time of its ratification, Hong Kong effectively had two governing authorities: the British ran the colony and the Triads ran the workers. What worried the British was not the fact that there were secret societies in their colony: what concerned them was the efficiency of the societies' organization and the number of members. Being merchants first and foremost, the British were afraid such power could disrupt trade through coolie strikes, for it was reckoned that 70 per cent of the 'native population' was under the thrall of Triads. This was probably a conservative estimate.

The punishment for Triad membership was three months' imprisonment and 100 lashes with a bamboo cane. It was hardly a disincentive. In China, a Triad found guilty of a crime could be caned to death, strangulated, decapitated or suspended in a cage by the neck until dead. The British punishment was a mere inconvenience and the prison, when it was built, was a criminal five-star hotel. Good food was plentiful, the cells cool in summer and warm in winter, the warders comparatively humane and the roof rainproof. Later, in addition to imprisonment, Triads were branded with a hot iron on the left cheek, but this was considered excessive and might prevent rehabilitation so the brand was moved to the upper left arm. Deportation to China after the completion of a sentence was discretional, but, if a defendant could prove he had been forced into Triad membership, all charges were dropped. The British were out of their depth, the laughing-stock of the Triad community. The Chinese police constables were colloquially known as *luk yee* (green jackets, on account of their uniforms), which quickly became a general term of derision. It is still used by Triads in Hong Kong and overseas.

By 1847, Hong Kong was considered the nerve centre for Triad activity all over southern China. The Triads grew so bold they even massed to attack the garrison when it was temporarily under strength due to illness. The police, however, got wind of the plan and, with a small unit of soldiers, rounded up 200 men who had gathered in the hills. A number of these had Triad certificates on them; the remainder were temporary conscripts.

The Triads had the local labour market in their grip. They extorted protection money from coolies, charged commission to arrange work and organized strikes. The colonial government grew increasingly alarmed, their concern exacerbated by the Taiping Rebellion, which was reducing neighbouring China to anarchy. A force of Taiping rebels even gathered in Hong Kong, in the Taiping Shan native quarter, in readiness to attack the *yamen* in the walled city on Kowloon, at that time not in British territory. The police and army confronted the rebels and ordered them to leave: Hong Kong was neutral and intended to stay that way.

With this declaration of neutrality, the Triads realized they were safe in Hong Kong and began to avoid confrontation with the British. Constrained from political opposition to the Q'ing dynasty, they directed their energies into crime. Not content with extorting coolies and labourers, they moved in on legitimate businesses, charging protection money and levying 'taxes' on trade. No fish could be landed without a Triad landing fee being paid. No meat reached market without the payment of a toll. Rice, flour and vegetables were similarly controlled. Nothing was moved, sold or traded without a kickback. By the 1880s, Triad criminality was deeply rooted in Hong Kong. Related crimes began to occur. In 1886, three police informers were murdered, stabbed then hacked to death. A Chinese Legislative Council appointee, who was therefore responsible for law-making, received death threats.

The Triads were now powerful. People feared them. They paid up when demands were made. The *shan chu*s were wealthy men and their societies rich. When one of their number was arrested, they put up bail – which was usually skipped, the arrested man fleeing overseas, making for Portuguese Macau or returning to China. It was at this time that the Triads began to infiltrate the Hong Kong police. Although the colonial police force officers were all Europeans, with some Sikhs in senior NCO positions, the bulk of the force consisted of local Chinese. By 1885, every police station had at least one Triad constable and, the next year, the first case of a policeman being a Triad was discovered. That same year, the first serious outbreak of inter-society warfare erupted.

Hong Kong was a major embarkation point for the hundreds of thousands of coolies heading for America and the Triads were well in on this human trade, running coolie travel agencies in every southern Chinese port. They charged the clients for finding lodgings before departure and often advanced loans for fares at usurious rates, collected commission from shipping lines for finding passengers and commission from the passengers for finding them a berth, levied boarding fees on emigrants and docking fees on vessels, and offered protection to every doss-house in which coolies lodged whilst awaiting departure. This last was the cause of a dispute. One society increased its protection charge. The doss-house owners rebelled. Their coolie customers, fed up with being ripped off, joined in. To gain extra protection and a street-fighting force, the doss-house owners employed some 49s from another Triad society. A riot broke out in Western District, close to where most of the emigrant vessels moored.

In the government inquiries that followed, it was discovered that the Triads had men placed not only in the police but in every government department. The Man On Society, it was discovered, had a Chinese police detective as its *shan chu*. He was arrested and given bail, which he promptly jumped and fled to China, where he was killed fighting the Q'ing authorities. In his absence, the society changed its name and faded from sight, but reappeared in 1949 as the Man Shing Tong, a small narcotics gang. The other society involved in the doss-house uprising, the Fuk Yee Hing, is still functioning in Hong Kong.

In the years after the Taiping Rebellion, thousands fled from China to Hong Kong, amongst them Triad criminals on the run, opportunists and political agitators. When the republicans set up the Chung Wo Tong, it liaised with and received funding earned by extortion from the criminal fraternity. Once the Republic of China was established in 1911, the Chung Wo Tong split up and metamorphosed into the Wo group of societies. These are today one of the most powerful groups in the world.

With the Republic founded, another wave of immigrants from China arrived in the increasingly affluent British colony. They were not refugees but Triad entrepreneurs moving to avoid the ubiquitous presence of Big-eared Du and Pockmarked Huang in Shanghai. They quickly joined existing societies, established branches of their 'mother' societies back in China or started their own. They were, with hardly an exception, all criminal. Carving Hong Kong up between them, their activities covered extortion, labour racketeering, blackmail and kidnapping, prostitution, gambling and even slavery. They ripped off Chinese businesses, operated brothels, ran illegal gambling dens and provided child concubines known as *mui tsai* for wealthy Chinese merchants.

The *mui tsai* business was traditional. Chinese families want sons to carry on the family name. When a mother bore a daughter, she was often unwanted and the infanticide of girls was commonplace. Those mothers too soft-hearted to kill their offspring frequently dumped them outside temples or on the doorsteps of Christian missions or wealthy Chinese families in the hope that they might be taken in. Alternatively, the girls were brought up by their parents until they were five or six then sold, or, in the case of peasant children, exchanged for food. Girls were bartered directly with purchasers, but from the 1840s the Triads moved in on the trade, buying peasant children and then, at a mark-up, selling them on. The *mui tsai* were frequently treated as minor members of their owner's family (*mui tsai* means little sister) but were in effect servants and not unusually their master's bed-warmer. In theory, a *mui tsai* was supposed to be married off by her owner at the age of eighteen, but many were not. They were repurchased by Triads who turned them into whores.

By 1920, the Triads were thoroughly institutionalized, senior officials well integrated into the fabric of the colony's social life. Many lived behind a façade of respectability. They owned legitimate businesses and registered their societies behind charitable fronts, listing them as sports organizations, social clubs and *kai fong* associations.

To avert the authorities' attention and avoid internecine

gang disputes such as the Man On vs. Fuk Yee Hing riot, they agreed to subdivide Hong Kong into criminal territories, each society holding sway over a particular ethnic group or a specific geographical area. Such demarcations exist even today: for example, in the 1980s the Wo Hop To society controlled Jaffe Road in the Wanchai district of Hong Kong, which locals actually called Wo Hop To Gai (Wo Hop To Street).

By 1931, there were eight primary Triad groups in Hong Kong: the Wo, the T'ung, the Tung, the Chuen, the Shing, the Fuk Yee Hing, the Yee On and the Luen. Each maintained its own integrity and ran its own branch societies. To cover their activities, they sought different guises. The Fuk Yee Hing became a registered society known as the Fuk Yee Industrial and Commercial General Association, a sort of trade union which also went under the name of the Kiu Kong Hoi Lok Fung Workers' and Merchants' Benevolent Association. It openly operated twelve regional offices with a membership of 10,000. The membership subscription was HK$1 per month. The legitimate subscription income alone, therefore, was about HK$120,000 per annum: at 1998 rates, this was equal to US$4.25 million. How much criminal activity earned is inestimable. Of the membership, approximately a third were oath-bound Triads.

Although they were criminal syndicates, many societies provided a genuine beneficial service. In hard times, they educated members' children, paid medical bills, found jobs for the unemployed and subsidized families in temporary dire straits. On the surface, this seemed positive and the colonial government ignored such activity as it took pressure off the official social services provision. Yet it had a negative effect, for it forced real trade unions and guilds to become more like Triad societies, recruiting members with rituals and oaths to assure their loyalty. Inevitably some, such as the Tung Society, became Triad societies. Originally founded as a charity running a hospital for coolies, it had to go to the Wo group for protection. In association with it, the Tung Society expanded its activities and degenerated into a full Triad society itself. One section, however, did not become criminal. Breaking away and re-forming, it eventually became the Tung Wah group of hospitals, Hong Kong's biggest hospital organization today, operating some of South-east Asia's most up-to-date hospitals, training medical staff and conducting research at the cutting edge of international medical science.

Other societies followed the Fuk Yee Hing trail. The Yee On legally registered themselves at various times as the To Shui Boxing Club, the Tai Ping Shan Sports Association and the Yee On Commercial and Industrial Guild. The Chuen established associations of street hawkers and traders. The Luen founded several ironworkers' associations in Hong Kong's commercial shipyards and held sway over shipworkers in HMS *Tamar*, Hong Kong's Royal Naval base and one of its biggest establishments east of Suez. The Wo operated 'death-gratuity associations', which were funeral-cost insurance companies: funerals are very important to the Chinese.

Many of the sports clubs behind which the Triads hid were dedicated to the martial arts. Numerous throughout Hong Kong and expatriate Chinese communities the world over, they are still more often than not Triad affiliated if not directly run by them. They provided –

and still do – not only a sports and social venue but also a 49 and Red Pole training ground. So important are they to Triad enforcement that, on more than one occasion, a non-Triad association has founded a martial-arts club to defend itself against Triad fighters. This was the case in the 1930s, when Hong Kong government sanitary department coolies formed a kick-boxing and kung-fu club to defend themselves. Over time, it developed into a Triad society called the Ching Nin Kwok Ki Sh'e.

One non-criminal activity the Triads moved in on was peculiarly Chinese. It was the takeover of the curiously named 'bomb associations'. Every year, the Goddess of Mercy and the God of the Earth were honoured by a major festival which drew large crowds. The climax of the festival was the detonation of a large bomb, a powerful firework containing a bamboo plaque engraved with the name of the deity and its temple. Officials representing local guilds and associations lined up to try to catch the plaque as it fell to earth. The association whose representative caught it kept the talisman for a year and had to maintain the relevant shrine. Both deities were traditionally worshipped by Triads, so their involvement in the festival was more or less obligatory. Yet there was more to it than religious reverence. Whoever maintained the temple had access to the alms-box, which could bring in a sum in excess of the capital required to keep the temple going. In time, the possession of the plaque and the income it bestowed caused such gang fights that, from 1948, the bomb was banned.

As the eight main Hong Kong groups fragmented and the number of autonomous societies grew, they became increasingly disunited. From the mid-1930s, inter-society rivalries, often very complex and requiring considerable police intelligence effort to unravel and understand, broke out. Corpses killed by a myriad of swords were regularly discovered. People disappeared. Others were maimed or crippled, their scalps sliced off or their calf and biceps muscles slashed, the tendons of their knees and elbows severed. The police attempted to intervene but they were powerless. No-one came to them for help. Victim or witness anonymity was not guaranteed with so many Chinese policemen being Triads.

Despite being infiltrated, the police did keep a lid on Triad crime, which never achieved the same level of government corruption or social dominance as it had done in China, especially in Shanghai. Colonial government and an impartial legal system were beyond in-depth corruption. Street hawkers bribed their way to a trading permit and learner drivers bought their driving licences, but high-level graft was mostly absent.

This situation changed in December 1941 when the Japanese invaded and conquered Hong Kong. They had been preparing for this since the late 1920s, when they placed a number of covert agents in the colony. One was Mr Yamashita, a well-known barber in the Hong Kong Hotel. A key intelligence-gatherer, he obtained much of his information from his customers, for he cut the hair of most of the colony's top civil servants and forces personnel. In 1937, at his instigation, the Japanese sent a Chinese collaborator to Hong Kong to obtain Triad support: the barber knew, should the Japanese occupy the colony, they would need the Triads on their side. By lavishly entertaining and bribing Triad leaders, the collaborator

251

obtained an assurance of co-operation from several so-cieties. The most obliging were the Wo Shing Wo and Yee On. In fact the police observed the collaborator and apprehended over 100 Triads, many employed in pro-minent positions in the civil service and as locally enlisted military personnel. Yet the damage was done: many Triads were ready to form a fifth column when war broke out.

By early 1941, with the Japanese occupying much of coastal China north of Hong Kong, an invasion seemed inevitable, although the colonial authorities pretended there was no real threat. The Triads were ambiguous and divided. Some were anti-Japanese and threw in their lot with the Kuomintang, to which they were closely af-filiated in any case. Others played safe and took no side, preferring to see what might transpire. The remainder supported Japanese aggression, sabotaged British military equipment and supplied valuable intelligence to Japanese field commanders. During the invasion, as British troops were beaten back to become besieged on Hong Kong island, Wo Shing Wo 49s operated as fifth columnists, sniping at retreating soldiers from rooftops. The first thing they did upon the British surrender was to release all their incarcerated brothers from Victoria prison. Ordinary criminals remained locked up; many were subsequently murdered by the Japanese.

Other Triads supported the British, as if the invasion by their old enemy, Japan, rekindled their patriotic zeal. The pro-British Triads and Kuomintang were led by the nationalist admiral Chan Chak, who was a senior Triad. As soon as the Japanese attacked, he ordered his men to patrol the streets wearing Triad armbands. They prevented widespread sabotage and furtively murdered every collaborator they discovered; they also used this as an excuse to eradicate rivals. In addition, they aided many prominent nationalists to escape ahead of the Japanese victory. Once the colony fell, however, they either took a more pragmatic stand or went underground. As partisans, they aided British intelligence, assisted prisoner-of-war escapers, teamed up with the Communist East River Brigade guerrillas to sabotage Japanese military sites, smuggled messages and medicines into and out of prisoner-of-war camps and murdered Japanese at every opportunity. Many were caught, tortured and executed.

Those Triads ambivalent to Japanese rule were in as bad a position. Neither the occupying force nor the Kuomintang trusted them and they, too, were rounded up, tortured, executed or transported to Taiwan or Japan to work alongside Allied prisoners-of-war in slave-labour camps attached to deep-shaft coal and manganese mines.

No sooner were the Japanese in control of Hong Kong than they set about organizing the Triad societies into the Hing Ah Kee Kwan or Asian Flourishing Organization. The force behind the Hing Ah Kee Kwan was the Wo Shing Wo, which established itself under the Japanese Kempetai, equivalent to the Nazi Gestapo, moving through Hong Kong informing on anti-Japanese activity and turning in spies, Kuomintang sympathizers and, of course, rivals. Devoid of traditional Triad patriotism, they were recruited into Japanese military intelligence and into the civilian police, where they already had brothers *in situ*.

The Japanese administration encouraged Triad activity. Collaborators were well paid by the Japanese, who took a share of the income earned from prostitution, gambling and narcotics. Triads also provided brothels catering exclusively for Japanese with young Chinese girls, not only in Hong Kong but elsewhere in China. The notorious Japanese 'comfort houses', in which Chinese women were raped over and over again in conditions of virtual enslavement, and which are still a bone of considerable contention between China and Japan, were frequently operated with Triad connivance. On Stonecutters' Island, a British military base in Hong Kong's western harbour, the Japanese set up an officers' mess in a house at the top of a small cliff. Triads rounded up Chinese women in Kowloon, abducting them in the street at dusk and shipping them to the island. Once there, they were repeatedly raped and tortured before being bayoneted off the balcony of the house into the sea below.

As the war progressed, food came into short supply throughout southern China. The Triads cornered the black market. By the winter of 1944–5, people in Hong Kong were resorting to cannibalism, eating corpses. No-one could afford a funeral and the hospitals took to tipping cadavers into the street, where they were butchered. The Triads even controlled this market, selling the right to gather what was euphemistically termed 'white meat' in specified streets, one of which was Dundas Street, in Kowloon, behind the Kwong Wa hospital. There was nothing to which they would not stoop to turn a dollar. Yet the food and corpse markets were as nothing to their stock-in-trade, opium.

In pre-war Hong Kong, opium could be purchased and smoked legally, provided it was obtained through an official distribution agency known as an opium 'farm'. Once acquired, it could be smoked only in the privacy of the addict's home, a measure intended to discourage dens, divans and street peddlers, therefore keeping the drug taxed and also reducing its becoming a source of criminal income. Supplies were plentiful. Consequently, criminal involvement in narcotics was minimal and restricted to contraband, which was smuggled only to avoid excise duty. Needless to say, smuggled opium was trafficked by Triads, who sold it mainly to coolies, rickshaw-pullers, stevedores and others on the poorer social levels. During the Japanese occupation, the sale and distribution of opium was completely taken over by the Triads, who set up opium dens, the opium supplied by the Japanese in an attempt to keep the population docile and demoralized. The trade gave the Triads a stranglehold on the Chinese community from which they recruited extensively; for many, the only way to survive the Kempetai and fill one's rice bowl was to be a Triad.

When Japan capitulated in 1945, the Hong Kong Triads were in the strongest position they had ever been. Not only had they profited from the war and been given four years to tighten their grip on the underworld without police intervention, but they were also virtually anonymous because, as part of their mutual co-operation pact, the Japanese had destroyed most police Triad society records. It took some weeks for the British to re-establish civil order. The Triads made the most of that time, looting empty buildings, robbing and burgling with impunity. Pro-Kuomintang Triads spent their time getting even with those who had collaborated.

For the remainder of the 1940s, the Triads concentrated on building their power-base, regained control of dock labourers, and exerted considerable influence over construction and transportation labour, as well as consolidating their presence amongst government workers. The police were largely ineffective. Most officers, being Europeans, had been incarcerated by the Japanese and took time to regain their health; the force was still infiltrated, undermanned and disadvantaged by having to reconstruct their Triad society records. Furthermore, the Triads received a tremendous boost by a British blunder of unconscionable proportions.

Hong Kong was relieved by a British military force, which put in place a temporary military administration. This, with good intentions but from a position of considerable ignorance, proscribed narcotics. The prohibition gave the Triads, with decades of contraband opium-smuggling experience, an opportunity to reap vast profits, for they were suddenly in sole control of a massive market. The world still pays for this grave error of judgement.

The monopoly they had operated under the Japanese went underground. Within months, business was back to normal and promising to increase as war refugees returned home. The opium dens set up during the occupation thrived and became operational hubs of criminal activity running the post-war black market.

Almost every commodity was in short supply. Ever ready for the main chance, the Triads soon controlled the black market in everything from herbal medicines to clothing, timber and building materials. Another chance also presented itself which they used to their full advantage. The understaffed police mounted a major recruitment campaign. Triad members queued to sign up.

Others forged ongoing relationships with previously honest policemen who were finding it hard to survive on low salaries. Lacking their criminal records, the police also had to rely upon Triad co-operation to make arrests, and Triads used this to undermine competitors or get rid of enemies. Senior Triads not infrequently shopped expendable 49s in order to ingratiate themselves with the police and government officials. The colonial administration was virtually emasculated, described at the time by one senior civil servant as being like a piece of Gruyère – more holes than cheese.

Although no longer motivated by patriotism, the Triads made some efforts in the post-war years to assist the Kuomintang. In 1946, at the top-secret conference convened in the heart of rural Hong Kong at which the senior officers of every main Hong Kong Triad society were present, the keynote speech was made by a high-ranking Kuomintang officer. He reminded them that it was Sun Yat-sen's republicans, the forerunners of the Kuomintang, who had brought down the Q'ing empire with Triad assistance and he revealed that there were underground Triad cells operating in Communist-held territory in China. He then requested that the Hong Kong societies unite their members to fight with the Kuomintang. For good measure, he added a piece of propaganda that was to echo down the years: he declared that the Communists were the new imperialists, the new Q'ing, admittedly not foreign but motivated by foreign ideology and therefore not truly Chinese. The proposed alliance was to be called the Kuomintang New Society Affairs Establishment Federation, Hong Kong Division.

The senior Triads agreed in principle, but junior

officials did not. No-one wanted to go off and risk a Communist bullet when crime in Hong Kong was beginning to boom. The idea grew less appealing as the Kuomintang suffered defeat after defeat at the hands of the Communists, and it was eventually dropped.

Around the same time, the American government began to involve itself increasingly in Chinese politics. They had substantially backed Chiang Kai-shek during the Sino-Japanese and Second World Wars and were now giving him considerable aid to fight the Communists. Indeed, their support had been so strong that it had been their secret intention to allow the Kuomintang to relieve Hong Kong when Japan fell, thus ousting the British and giving the Americans the balance of influence in the tiny, but strategically and politically vital, colony. The plan collapsed only because the Royal Navy under Admiral Harcourt arrived ahead of the US Navy.

Thwarted, the Americans put another plan into operation. They financed the Third Force. It was, on all counts, a Triad-orientated secret society, which, ironically, was registered as a charity in Hong Kong, calling itself the Man Chi Tong or Overseas Chinese Democratic Party. Its long-term objective was to overthrow both the Kuomintang and the Communists to establish a Western-style democratic Chinese government. The leader of the Man Chi Tong, chosen by the American secret service in which he was an operative, was an experienced Triad called Chiu Yuk, a member of several Triad societies in the USA. Through their secret service, therefore, the Americans were knowingly funding an illegal Triad society in the territory of a friendly power. Their action was akin to the Italian government's deliberately funding a Mafia family in Brooklyn.

By December 1947, the Man Chi Tong was in close alliance with the Wo Shing Wo. As the Communists became increasingly victorious, the Third Force went the way of the Kuomintang's attempted federation, American involvement dropped off, the Man Chi Tong being absorbed into the Wo Shing Wo, Chinese patriotism further diluted by criminality.

The scale of Triad criminal income accelerated sharply in the late 1940s. Opium reaped profits never before anticipated in the colony. The Hong Kong Triads' new-found wealth brought about an irreversible shift in their criminal status. Once little more than extortionists, they were now elevated to the level of the pre-war Shanghai societies, making huge sums and investing it in both legal and illegal enterprises. They continued to rip off their fellow countrymen, just as they always had, but their criminality also began to adapt.

Prostitution was one area which noticeably changed. Sex became a big money-spinner with the post-war influx of expatriate Europeans and the presence of a large British garrison, temporarily much increased in the early 1950s by American and Australian troops *en route* to the Korean War. Once the Triads realized the potential, they organized prostitution, moving it off the streets and into bars, each controlled if not owned outright by Triads, the Yee On being the dominant society engaged in vice.

Large numbers of young women were needed as the vice trade grew. Many were imported by Triads from China, where they were either enticed away by a promise of employment in prosperous Hong Kong or purchased.

259

The *mui tsai* system had been banned in the colony before the war, but there were still many families willing to sell an unwanted daughter: the only difference now was that only girls over sixteen were being bought and they had no chance of being married off. In addition, as Mao Zedong's Communist forces advanced through China, increasingly large numbers of refugees fled to Hong Kong where, jobs being scarce, young women were obliged to turn to vice to support themselves and their families. When the prostitutes became too old or diseased, they were thrown out to fend for themselves. Many turned to opium, thereby contributing even more to Triad profits.

Manipulating the post-war labour market was almost as lucrative as opium. Hong Kong suffered greatly during the war and massive rebuilding programmes were instigated. As the colony expanded, so investment, industry and trade increased, coolies being in great demand. Manual labour was hired through firms specializing in specific forms of work: one handled stevedores, another bricklayers, a third quarry workers and so on. Most hiring firms were Triad managed. Every morning an overseer, usually a Red Pole or similar-ranking Triad official, would allocate work for the day. To ensure employment, the coolies had to stay on the right side of the overseer: the only way to do this was to pay him squeeze or tea-money. The overseer withheld 50 per cent of a coolie's wages at source, handing this to the firm's Triad management. To make up lost income, coolies stole from their workplace, fencing their loot through Triad channels often run by their overseer.

When their long working day was over, the coolies were still not clear of the Triads. Many smoked opium.

The tenement doss-houses in which they lived, often sleeping in the beds on a rota system, were Triad owned. Meals were provided by Triad landlords at inflated prices. The only way a coolie could escape this vicious cycle of exploitation was by joining a Triad society, as had long been the case. The doss-houses were, therefore, primary recruiting centres. Some were so full of 49s they were little short of Triad barracks.

Not only manual labour was Triad controlled: so were office clerical staff, hotel servants and low-paid government workers. Employers were 'squeezed' for commission to look for workers – this in a colony where there were more workers than vacancies. The workers paid a further commission. Companies paid protection money to keep their workers working and their premises open. Even street hawkers had to pay protection to avoid beatings, having their stalls destroyed or their goods confiscated by a Triad-sympathetic policeman or urban services inspector.

Triad business operated as it had before 1941, but now it was much more lucrative. A vast labyrinth of corruption and exploitation fuelled a criminal underground which steadily grew richer, more powerful and more ruthless. Honest policemen were ineffectual and the corrupt did well. Even when arrests were made, witnesses were rare and prosecutions failed with sickening regularity. The cases that did lead to a successful prosecution often did so because the defendant was a fall guy, sold down the river by his brothers to mollify the authorities.

By 1949, it looked as if Hong Kong was set to become the biggest criminal city on earth, a sort of Chinese Palermo. However, there was a threat on the horizon which was to affect not only the colonial government and the local Chinese population but also the local Triads.

After four years of civil war, Chiang Kai-shek's Kuomintang forces were beaten and Mao Zedong's Communists ruled China. Over 600,000 refugees flooded into Hong Kong, encouraged by the British policy of refusing haven to no-one. Amongst their number were landlords and factory-owners, military officers and their troops, Buddhist priests and traders. The factory-owners often arrived with their entire workforce, each family member – even children – carrying a piece of vital machinery; they set up in Hong Kong and formed the backbone of its subsequent industrial might, especially in the field of textiles.

Included in the influx were Chinese criminals and Triad society members from the north, many of them ex-Kuomintang officers and other ranks recruited and militarily trained at the Whampoa Military Academy. In an attempt to segregate them from the local community and keep them where they could be monitored, the government housed them in a massive deserted hilltop military artillery emplacement at Mount Davis, on Hong Kong island. It was hoped they would emigrate to Taiwan. Before long, however, they started fighting both Communist sympathizers and local Triads, who stormed the hilltop. In the ensuing battle, a number were killed on both sides. On 26 June 1950, the government moved the whole 7,800-strong Kuomintang contingent to an isolated spot at Junk Bay in the New Territories where there was a derelict flour-processing plant called Rennie's Mill: it was to be their home for the next fifty years, a tiny corner of Kuomintang Free China on the edge of the Communist bloc.

Most of the other refugees set up home in communities of squatter shacks on mountainsides, which became shanty towns of houses, shops, restaurants, even factories, constructed out of scrap timber, sheets of corrugated iron, packing cases and sacking. Periodically, these areas burned down, were washed away by typhoons or destroyed by landslides. It was some years before the government began to erect permanent housing in purpose-built blocks of flats.

The squatters were a lucrative target for the Triads, who sold them building materials, charged them to level house-platforms on the steep slopes, erected illegal power and water supplies (for which they levied a fee), sold them their food at a mark-up, extorted protection money from squatter businesses and added duty to postal deliveries or provided a 'post office box' system to which the postmen, being bribed and reluctant to clamber over the hillsides seeking for an address, would drop off the squatter area's mail.

They did not have it all their own way. The squatters brought with them their own secret societies, which presented the local Triads with a unique problem: competition. What was more, they found it hard to associate or ally themselves with the interlopers, who came from different ethnic groups, had unfamiliar customs, spoke unintelligible dialects and were both insular and suspicious. Once a squatter area was established, fights took place for the control of utilities. The squatters' societies usually won. Emboldened by their victories, they organized their own prostitution, protection and gambling rackets in the squatter areas, handled their own narcotics trade and, through this, introduced a new scourge to the world. It was heroin.

Heroin was known of well before 1950. A comparatively easily produced derivative of morphine, the main narcotic ingredient of opium, it had significant financial potential. It was far more addictive than opium and, being highly concentrated, far easier to traffic. Its use was common in northern China and it had appeared in Europe, especially France, thanks to the corrupt officials in Shanghai's French Concession, but it was not internationally widespread.

The first Hong Kong heroin laboratories were financed by Big-eared Du and went into production in 1950 to supply addicted refugees. It was not long before refugee former Green Gang members extended heroin sales outside the squatter areas. With an orchestrated, vicious ruthlessness, they started their own extortion rackets and staged armed robberies on Chinese jewellers' and gold shops. Well organized and financed, they were soon challenging the local societies on a broad front, coordinating vice with the efficiency of corporate managers. They opened dance halls full of 'taxi-dancers', who, charging clients by the dance, in turn paid the Green Gang operators for the right to work in their establishments. They ran brothels and massage-parlours, and administered opium and gambling dens. Not content with this, they bribed immigration officials then preyed upon wealthy criminal exiles, offering protection to prevent deportation or extradition back to China. Wealthy non-criminals were forced to invest in Green Gang-controlled legitimate businesses.

Things did not entirely go to the Green Gang's advantage. In 1952, a well-known wealthy immigrant, Li Choi-fat, was arrested and deported when it was discovered he was a senior Green Gang office-bearer. This was a significant coup for the police and a serious setback to Big-eared Du's followers. They lost a lot of face and much ground to the local Triads.

The coup was not due to effective policing. Li had, in fact, tried to out-bribe the local Triads and buy his own policemen, but had failed, and it was through a tip-off that he was caught by a squad, staffed in part by Hong Kong Triad policemen, especially constituted to bust his society. With Li out of the country, the Green Gang were hit over and over, their men arrested and deported. Much weakened, they abandoned many of their rackets and turned to the burgeoning tourist industry, owning or extorting hotels, operating tourist bars and forcing many famous 24-hour-suit tailors to pay protection. They continued to produce heroin but this business was soon to slip from their grasp. Local Triads moved in on their supply of – and became their only source of – morphine base and took over street distribution. In a decade, the Green Gang was extinct.

The Green Gang was not the only Triad society to escape to Hong Kong. The colony was awash with ethnic societies: police intelligence listed Hakka, Cantonese, Teochiu, Hoklo, Shanghainese and Fujianese groups all operating at various levels and all criminal. Many were small, consisting of less than 100 members and, as time passed, they broke up, amalgamated, changed their names, faded away, were resurrected, busted by the police, wiped out by rivals, joined local groupings or simply died out. The stronger became dominant and set the pattern for the future, not only in Hong Kong but around the world. Three Triad societies in particular survived: the Wo Shing Wo and its allied Wo group societies, the Yee On and the 14K.

The Wo Shing Wo was the longest established in Hong Kong. From the home territory in Western District, formerly Taiping Shan, and the Yau Ma Tei district of Kowloon, they controlled labour markets and dosshouses and engaged in all the criminal activities of Triads. In the 1950s they began to diversify and divide, three Wo societies competing for dominance. A police report at the time revealed that several Wo group members were earning a conservatively estimated HK$15 million (US$1.75 million) per annum from initiation fees and the control of street hawkers, rickshaw-pullers, shoe-shine boys, illegal gambling, dance-hall hostesses, prostitutes, illegal taxis, black-market theatre and cinema tickets, restaurant protection rackets, pickpockets and narcotics.

By the end of the 1950s, the Wo group comprised forty-one affiliated societies, more than any other grouping. Some were small and some lacked criminal intentions, being more self-help societies than gangs. Amongst them were the Wo On Lok, specializing in loan-sharking, the Wo Shing Tong with about 5,000 members and the Wo Shing Yee, which controlled dockworkers. Yet a number were massive. The main Wo Shing Wo had a membership of about 10,000, including not only civil servants and police officers but even locally enlisted British army personnel. They were based in Kowloon Walled City and Macau, in both of which they were safe from police interference.

Kowloon Walled City was a famous criminal bolt-hole. Originally a small, walled village containing a mandarin's *yamen* surrounded by paddyfields and vegetable plots, it covered about $6\frac{1}{2}$ acres. Built around 1850 on the site of a settlement dating back to 1668, it contained a small garrison of Q'ing troops and a customs post. A jetty ran from the main gate across the paddyfields to the sea. By 1950, it was a misnomer for an anachronism. The castellated walls had been demolished by the Japanese, using British prisoners-of-war slave labour and coolies dragooned into the work by Yee On collaborators. The stone served as hardcore for the apron of nearby Kai Tak international airport. When the New Territories were ceded to the British in 1898, an ambiguous wording in the convention caused the walled city to be a disputed territory until 1984, both sides claiming sovereignty. Within its precinct, Hong Kong police jurisdiction was doubtful and it developed into one of the world's most notorious criminal ghettos.

The Yee On, originally a society for Hong Kong Chinese of Teochiu origin, traced its roots back to the Man On and Fuk Yee Hing societies involved in the dosshouse disturbance of 1886. After registering as the Yee On Commercial and Industrial Guild in 1921, it 'disappeared' during the Japanese occupation but re-registered in 1946. The registration was cancelled three years later. With the 1950s' rush of refugees, it assimilated a number of prominent Red Gang members. Based in urban Kowloon, it had about the same number of members as the Wo Shing Wo. As with the Green Gang, enemies informed on it and, in 1953, its senior figures were arrested and deported, whereupon the society split into two, the Chiu Kwong and the Chung Yee, which

267

themselves subsequently fragmented, to re-form some years later as the San Yee On – *san* means new in Cantonese. It grew in strength and fought other societies, particularly the Wo Hop To, for the protection rackets of Wanchai. Today, the San Yee On is one of Hong Kong's most important societies with international ramifications.

The third of the great societies was the 14K. After the defeat of the Kuomintang in 1949, Kot Siu-wong – who at Chiang Kai-shek's instigation had united the Triad societies of southern China into the Hung Fat Shan Yee Wui, and who with the Communist takeover now had a price on his head in Guangzhou – escaped to Hong Kong with a large entourage. Neither the colonial authorities nor the Hong Kong Triads were best pleased, but whilst the former had to accept him as an ally, for Chiang Kai-shek and the Kuomintang were the internationally re-cognized Chinese government-in-exile, the latter did not. They took every opportunity to attack the new-comers: part of the motivation behind the battle of Mount Davis was an attempt to oust them.

Very soon after arriving, the 14K tried to gain a criminal foothold in Kowloon, fighting a gangland battle in the Mong Kok district with the Yuet Tung Society. The 14K grew apace, assimilating members of weaker societies and recruiting disparate refugee Triads. Within two years, it had a membership of about 10,000.

Kot was deported in 1950. The authorities were fearful that he would be a rallying point for patriots and crim-inals, and Hong Kong had to avoid being regarded by Communist China as an iniquitous den of political in-trigue. In 1951, Kot surreptitiously returned to organize the Triads into a political force, but he was unsuccessful and, upon his death in 1953, destructive internal power struggles erupted between the 14K and the societies it had enveloped, only brought to an end by the societies' *sheung fa* burning the yellow paper.

Once comparative peace was made, the 14K expanded again. It was already the strongest society in Hong Kong, for it had stepped back from conflict with the Green Gang which had weakened the other antagonists. By 1955, it boasted a membership of around 80,000, both in Hong Kong and elsewhere in South-east Asia, although a fair proportion of those in Hong Kong were not necessarily continuously criminally active: some had been press-ganged into the society or were members of convenience.

With the increase in membership came an augmentation of influence. The 14K's methods of extortion were so ruthless that even the *shan chu* of other societies were shocked. Hong Kong had never seen anything like it. It became almost a daily occurrence to see a man staggering in the streets of Kowloon, dripping blood and missing a finger or two.

Ambitious and skilful, the 14K senior echelons not only cornered much of Hong Kong's criminal enterprises but started to spread their wings. Capturing a large share of the narcotics trade, they started purchasing raw opium direct from the producers, Teochiu gangsters and displaced Kuomintang soldiers operating in the Golden Triangle, the mountainous and impenetrable poppy-growing area straddling Laos, Thailand and Burma. The opium was shipped to Hong Kong, processed into heroin and not only sold locally but exported to 14K members in other South-east Asian countries.

So blatant was the 14K that questions were raised about it in Parliament in London and, despite being thoroughly penetrated, the Hong Kong police were, in the mid-1950s, ordered by the British government to suppress them. In a well co-ordinated raid in 1955, 148 members, including Kot Siu-wong's son, were apprehended. The arrests made no impact upon the society's strength, but they did make it lose face before the other societies. To regain this, the 14K leadership decided to attempt the impossible, to amalgamate every criminal in Hong Kong under one umbrella society.

Chiang Kai-shek, now president of the Republic of China in Taiwan – and a supposed ally of the British, who were giving more foreign aid to his country than to any other apart from India – saw the possibilities. Here was a second stab at the idea of a Kuomintang federation. Additionally, he knew that if he could take over Hong Kong and kick the British out he would have a toehold in China. This would be a powerful propaganda tool against Mao Zedong and could even provide a platform from which to launch an attack on Communist China. The whole concept was a typical Chiang Kai-shek pipedream, with no chance of success, but he had to be seen to harry Communist China in order to retain his credibility in Taiwan and reap foreign, particularly American, aid.

The Taiwanese government therefore sent the 14K funding siphoned off from American aid, passing on intelligence about the British forces in both Hong Kong and Malaya. To co-ordinate action against the Hong Kong administration, a summit meeting between the 14K and top Taiwanese government representatives (including Chiang Kai-shek himself) was set for late October 1956. Before it was held, however, the 14K was subjected to a fierce police campaign, organized not as a result of the impending summit, of which the Hong Kong government was ignorant, but because of a series of events which occurred earlier that month.

The Double Tenth (10 October) is an important date for nationalist Chinese. It celebrates the Wuchang insurrection of 1911 – the first act of the revolution which established Sun Yat-sen's Republic. For hundreds of thousands of Hong Kong Chinese it was a day of parties, political rallies and nationalist flag-waving. Nowhere were the celebrations more lively than in the newly-built refugee resettlement estates. On the sixth floor of Block G of the Lei Cheng Uk estate in the north-western Kowloon suburb of Sham Shui Po, the residents had pasted nationalist flag posters on doors and in hallways. This was against housing rules, which forbade the posting of handbills, but the authorities usually ignored any infringement on the Double Tenth. However, one officious resettlement officer decided to stick to the letter of the law and, on the morning of 9 October, set about tearing them down. An argument ensued and a crowd gathered. The argument grew more heated. It was suggested that the official make an apology and light a string of firecrackers to announce it. He, loathe to lose face, refused, retreating to his nearby office. The crowd thronged outside, he barricaded himself in and called the police. When a patrol arrived, it found a crowd several thousand strong smashing the office windows, hauling out the furniture and burning it. They got the resettlement officer out, but in the process were stoned by the mob which then torched the office.

By the afternoon, 2,000 rioters faced 300 riot police. They were dispersed by tear gas. As dusk fell, the rioters regrouped, looting shops, pulling drivers out of their cars, beating them up and setting light to their vehicles. A fire engine rushing to a burning car was hit by a small bomb: it veered into the mob and killed two people. A police post at nearby Tai Hang Tung was set alight. Riot police were stoned from the rooftops, but made several hundred arrests. It was then that they discovered a nasty twist. Several rioters admitted to being 14K members who had been incited to riot.

The next day, 10 October, passed more or less peacefully, but that night rioting flared up again. Throughout the 11th, Kowloon was in chaos. Looting, arson and extortion were the order of the hour. All shops selling Communist goods were ransacked and burned. Members of the 14K set up road blocks and charged tolls. Any driver not displaying a Kuomintang flag or sticker in his vehicle was forced to buy one: 50-cent flags cost $10.

Foreigners were special targets. A European couple were pulled out of a taxi on the Tai Po Road and badly beaten up. The taxi was overturned and set on fire: the driver, outside the vehicle but trapped by his arm, roasted to death. Later, the Swiss consul and his wife were attacked and, whilst locked in their vehicle, it too was set alight. They were dragged free, but the consul's wife died.

The police reacted to every riot with appropriate violence, using baton charges, tear gas and Greener guns which fired heavy rubber or wooden bullets the size of a salami; the latter, when aimed at the ground in front of a mob, broke into a hail of flying splinters. A curfew was imposed and the government announced that anyone breaking it would be shot on sight.

Triad elements continued to make hay. They unsuccessfully stormed a bank. In the industrial town of Tsuen Wan, a mob overpowered the police and set fire to a textile factory. The Triads then visited every other factory, selling flags to be hung from windows to show 'solidarity with the Kuomintang'; each flag cost $500. Then came a further twist. The mob, driven by the 14K, began rounding up Communist sympathizers. Over 200 genuine Communists took refuge in Tsuen Wan police station. Those who did not reach it, or were caught unawares, were savagely beaten and made to kow-tow to the Kuomintang flag. Then the killing started.

The army was called out. When the Tsuen Wan mob dispersed, over thirty bodies were discovered on the street, twenty-seven of them young women textile-factory workers. Most had been innocent bystanders. However, before they could be gathered up, most of the corpses vanished, whisked away by order of senior 14K officials aghast at the killing and fearful of a police backlash. The official death toll for the riot was six.

On 13 October, six senior Triad officials were arrested in a Kowloon hotel room from which they had been strategically planning the troubles. Simultaneous raids netted 1,700 others: in total, over the four days, 6,000 were arrested. The colonial government blamed the 14K and other Triads for the riots. As Communist Chinese premier, Zhou Enlai blamed the nationalists. Chiang Kai-shek, in Taiwan, blamed Communist agents. In all, the cost of the riots was sixty-two dead, hundreds wounded and shops and factories destroyed at a financial loss exceeding US$20 million.

The 14K had made a ludicrous error of judgement. They had thought they could overthrow the British. Now the British were furious. The Triads' arrogance made them start to address the acknowledged problem of police infiltration, and a specialist task force, the Triad Society Bureau, was empowered to investigate secret societies.

Many Triads, especially traditionalists of the old school, were disgusted by the excesses of the rioting. As never before, a number co-operated with the police, partly to pour oil on rough waters, partly to save their own skins and partly to eradicate opponents. Their informing resulted in many senior officials, including an Incense Master with power over societies across South-east Asia, being apprehended. More importantly, these highly placed stool-pigeons gave the Hong Kong police valuable insights into Triad structure, activity, initiation ceremonies and rituals.

Over the next eighteen months, more than 10,000 Triads were arrested, of whom over 500 were deported. It was an impressive figure, but still accounted for not much more than 3 per cent of the official estimate of the criminal population.

Deportation to Communist China was not allowed: to send a Triad back to China was tantamount to executing him and the British authorities balked at the thought. Instead, most were shipped off to Taiwan. It was a big mistake. With Chiang Kai-shek's government consisting almost exclusively of Triads, the deportees were able, with hardly a missed stride, to continue in their life of crime. They joined the new now government-sponsored society, the United Bamboo Society, which in time helped other Taiwanese Triads gain a foothold in Hong Kong. They also formed an effective branch of Chiang Kai-shek's secret service.

The 1956 riots did more than teach the Hong Kong police about Triads. It taught the Triads that amalgamation was impossible: the only way to progress was to be autonomous and collaborative. Lower unit profits but higher turnover was their new aim and, with Hong Kong embarking upon its boom years, the climate was just right. Financial growth meant an affluent society with more cash available for spending on vice and gambling, and more successful businesses to squeeze for protection money. At the same time, the Triads also appreciated that they had to draw in their horns, lie low and consolidate their position whilst keeping a look-out for new opportunities. One of these was not long in coming.

In searching for new criminal business, they increasingly turned to the staple which had made Du Yueh-sheng so wealthy – narcotics. Within four years of the riots, they were in a position to internationalize the narcotics trade. A new Triad era was dawning.

2

IN THE SHADOW OF THE NINE DRAGONS

The Hong Kong riots of 1956 left the Triads, with their lack of political motivation, regarded as solely criminal and a major threat to law and order. For the next ten years, they were constantly under police surveillance. Arrest rates rose. Considerable intelligence was gathered about their activities and organization, some of it, as had happened in the past, coming from one Triad society seeking to undermine another. In 1967, when China's Cultural Revolution spilled over into Hong Kong in pro-Communist riots and a street-bombing campaign, the Triads acted as anti–Communist informers, letting the police know the whereabouts of Communist activists, their meeting places and the location of bomb-makers who occasionally operated out of left-wing trade-union offices. Of course, the Triad spies had a vested interest: the left-wing unions were their main competitors in the control of the labour market. There was yet another side to this informing: the police force was still riddled with Triads and the passing of sound information was not only easy but a ready source of pocket money for the informers, who were often paid for their knowledge, as well as for corrupt police officers who took a cut and used their 'contacts' to advance their reputations and career prospects.

Triad corruption in all branches of government was serious. Senior civil servants knew it had to be addressed, but were often stonewalled when the subject was broached. Triad sympathizers in the administration simply sidetracked the issue and others believed it was best let well alone. After all, corruption was part of Chinese life, as traditional as moon-cakes and joss-sticks, and had been endemic in Hong Kong from the start. No matter what it was called – 'squeeze', 'tea-money' or 'kumshaw' – bribery was a traditional way of doing business and dealing with the authorities.

Corruption in the police was considered worse than in the general administration. Not only were police officers on the take, but many were criminals themselves, either by association or by being senior Triad office-bearers. The government tended to overlook the problem: it was too big a can of Oriental worms. Furthermore, it was not as if Hong Kong suffered an outwardly obvious crime wave because of them: it was still amongst the safest cities on earth. The murder rate was the lowest of any major city, the incidence of sexual assaults was comparatively insignificant, street mugging was unheard of and burglary was not rife. With Triad activity being directed more towards extortion, vice and gambling, there was little of the kind of crime which bedevilled other countries. Even narcotics did not spawn widespread crime: addicts maintained their income by holding down menial or unskilled jobs and trading in the narcotics market. With full employment, there was no need for an addict to thieve or rob.

The general public hardly ever encountered a Triad. The nearest most came to them would be having a pocket picked. As with the government, the attitude was one of letting the sleeping dragon lie. Triads were an acceptable evil. Shopkeepers built their protection costs into their prices and property companies accounted for extorted labour costs in their budgets. The Triads were little more than an unofficial added tax, inconvenient but acceptable. What finally did for this system of criminal *laissez-faire* was narcotics trafficking.

By the mid-1960s, heroin was becoming a powerful international criminal and political tool of subversion. Attention was brought to this by a seminal study published in 1972 by an American university professor, Alfred W. McCoy, *The Politics of Heroin*. The book was a bombshell. It showed how US covert operations used heroin to undermine governments: the Vietnam War, McCoy claimed, was dirty for many reasons besides the use of napalm and the massacres of innocent peasants. It was a war in which heroin was as much a weapon as high explosives.

The Hong Kong police force, McCoy declared, was corrupt to the core. There were, he stated, non-commissioned officers who were narcotics millionaires. He was right. When, in the summer of 1969, an anti-corruption drive had been announced, a number of middle-ranking police officers resigned. One of these, a sergeant called Lai Man-yau with thirty-three years' service behind him, was thought to hold real-estate and business assets worth nearly US$6 million.

Revelations of police corruption could not be ignored:

the Hong Kong government was obliged to act. An internal report reckoned that 35 per cent of all Chinese police officers were Triad associates. A lower but still significant figure stood for Chinese civil servants in every other government department.

It was soon discovered that not only Triad corruption but also intimidation was rife in the police. Officers who maintained their morals were threatened. Triads holding key positions could stall promotions, smear good-conduct records, even have their non-compliant comrades assaulted on patrol; the coercion of family members was not unknown. Those who were not prepared to toe the line had to shut up or get out. Most shut up, ignoring the brown envelopes found in desk drawers on Fridays containing bundles of Hong Kong dollar bills, each officer's cut of the week's pay-offs.

The corruption was thought not to reach above inspector level and never to filter through to the European officers (mostly British) who held the vast majority of senior ranks. This was a misconception. A number of senior European officers were corrupt, but they were hard to unearth, for, being in positions of power, they were able to act as a firewall between the corruption below and the government above.

Matters came to a head in June 1973 with the issue of an arrest warrant for a very senior police officer. His name was Peter Fitzroy Godber. He was discovered by pure chance. A routine bank check in April that year in Canada, run by the Royal Canadian Mounted Police (RCMP) to catch money launderers, noted substantial deposits coming from Hong Kong. Over C$200,000 had been deposited in March alone to an account in Godber's name. They alerted the Hong Kong government. On 4 June, the Hong Kong acting attorney general wrote to Godber asking him to account for his wealth. He was given a week to comply. Later the same day, his apartment was searched and a mass of incriminating documentation unearthed. Godber, who was to have retired at the end of the month after twenty-one years' service, was a millionaire: his Canadian deposits were his nest-egg being moved overseas in readiness for his departure. On 7 June, Godber's wife flew out of Hong Kong; the following day Godber followed her, avoiding immigration controls at Kai Tak airport by using a police security pass. He left without withdrawing HK$250,000 from a local bank or taking a bundle of traveller's cheques hidden in the icebox of his refrigerator. Godber and his wife met up at his retirement home near Rye, in the south of England. It took until January 1975 to extradite him from Britain to Hong Kong, where he was sentenced to four years' imprisonment. Upon his release, he faded into anonymity. His assets were never seized.

How long Godber had been accepting bribes from Triads or their associates was never assessed. The amount he earned overall was also never known, but another expatriate police officer, who was apprehended at about the same time, did shed light on the matter of Triad infiltration and corruption.

Ernest 'Taffy' Hunt, a close friend of Godber, had been charged under anti-bribery legislation for maintaining 'a standard of living above that commensurate with present or past official emoluments'. He was sentenced to one year in prison on a plea bargain. At Godber's trial, he talked. A one-time officer in charge of Triad investigations, he was alleged to have received vast sums from criminal syndicates. He admitted receiving kickbacks for eighteen years and said it was not unreasonable for a divisional officer such as Godber to earn between HK$700,000 and 1.2 million per annum. Although it was never proved, it seems likely that Hunt had not only received massive bribes but had also perverted the course of justice by diverting criminal investigations away from Triad societies and individuals.

The Godber scandal rocked Hong Kong. The government was no longer able to ignore Triad infiltration. With commendable alacrity, it set up a special commission to investigate police corruption. Known as the Independent Commission Against Corruption (or ICAC), it had a staff of 600 handpicked investigators. Within a year, they were handling 500 cases, living beyond one's means was made an indictable offence and ICAC officers were given swingeing powers. They could raid the homes of individuals and their close relatives, waive banking confidentiality to receive account statements without recourse to account holders and demand proof of finance for every purchase from a chair to a car. The police were incensed. There were mass resignations and many arrests. Hundreds of policemen staged a near mutiny, rioting outside their own headquarters, but to no avail. The ICAC and the government were not for turning.

What they discovered shocked the population. The Triads not only paid sweeteners to general divisional officers. In the Triad Society Bureau, it was found that five key personnel, all of them sergeants, were senior Triads. The gamekeepers and the poachers were hand in hand.

The kingpin was Sergeant Lui Lok, holder of several police medals with a high arrest rate. He turned out to be a senior 14K member, receiving massive kickbacks from gambling, vice and narcotics. To junior officers, he was respectfully referred to as Tai Lo, or Big Boss, but the press was to nickname him '$600 Million Man'. They were not far wrong: he and the other four sergeants were estimated to have illegally earned over HK$1,500 million during their period of service. Having been tipped off by corrupt colleagues, Lui Lok retired from the police and fled Hong Kong in November 1974. Another forty police officers took to their heels at about the same time, running for Taiwan, Canada or the USA, the clean-up in Hong Kong thus leading to a further expansion of international Triad criminality.

Lui Lok and the other four sergeants, Choi Bing-lung, Chen Cheung-you, Nam Kong and Hon Kwing-shum, were collectively known as the Five Dragons. When they quit Hong Kong, they flew to Vancouver, where there was already a substantial Chinese immigrant population which had been under police surveillance for some time; it had been this vigilance which had, by chance, rumbled Godber. Vancouver was known to be a Hong Kong Chinese money-laundering centre and a channel for smuggling heroin into North America.

In Canada, they founded the Five Dragons Corporation, a general trading and property company. One of its purchases was a prestigious downtown office block for which they paid C$60 million in cash. This blatant purchase was too much for the Canadian authorities. They pressured the corporation. It closed and the Five Dragons discreetly left for Taiwan, where they joined a growing band of ex-Hong Kong policemen, including one, a much-respected career officer called Tang Sang, who was so wealthy that he arrived having skipped bail of HK$330,000.

Once in Taiwan, they were home and dry. No extradition treaty existed between Taiwan and Hong Kong and the country was still under the sway of Chiang Kai-shek, who died in 1975, and his son, Chiang Ching-kuo, who was the country's premier and became president in 1978. Chiang Ching-kuo was instrumental in organizing the Taiwanese armed forces and its intelligence service. The Kuomintang, being the only party of government, was in his pocket, which meant the Triads were also in his grasp: the United Bamboo Society was an integral part of state security. In time, he brought about widespread change, introduced democracy and was the architect of Taiwan's transformation into an Asian 'tiger' economy, yet he was in debt to the Triads until his death in 1988.

After arriving in Taiwan, the Five Dragons started to live ostentatiously. Not needing to disguise their wealth, they painted Taipei red in the company of Chinese film stars and models. They invested in local industry, purchased nightclubs, set up brothels and opened restaurants; in a high-profile act of criminal showmanship they forfeited a million-dollar deposit on a restaurant site rather than become embroiled in a lawsuit over the ownership of the land. Eventually the Taiwan government, fearing that such high living might draw attention to their lax attitudes towards Triads, requested they lower their profiles. They obeyed, conscious that sanctuary in Taiwan was too valuable to risk.

No longer conspicuous, the many outlaw refugees

from Hong Kong did not desist from criminal activity. They invested heavily in the narcotics trade and substantially increased its international reach. Any other international criminality which came their way was also investigated and financed. With their millions, they exercised a considerable international criminal influence and were vital to the funding of the global expansion of Triad activity in the mid-1970s.

Back in Hong Kong, the ICAC purged the police of most of its Triads. After the mass resignations and near mutiny, the force was developing into a very fine law-enforcement service: no longer would it be referred to as the best police force in the world that money could buy. Yet the police were up against enormous odds. Years of corruption had weakened their position and, although public confidence now increased, they were still unable to uncover and arrest top Triad officials.

In part, these failures were due to a secret government report published in 1976 which formed the basis for police policy regarding the Triads. Drawn up by a senior police superintendent, Teddy U Tat-ming, it stated that the Triads existed largely in name only and were little more than loose-knit associations of criminals. The report was accepted as gospel, resulting in the police closing its admittedly corrupt Triad Society Bureau and playing down the Triad problem. Triad investigation was delegated to regional forces. For ten years, there was to be no centralized or dedicated police unit fighting the Triads.

Needless to say, the Triads were not slow to take advantage of the situation. They expanded their membership, developed their infrastructure and increased their grip on Hong Kong. In particular, they turned their attention to heroin trafficking, the narcotics trade being particularly attractive to Teochiu groups.

There were three principal Teochiu Triad heroin dealers in the 1970s: Ma Sik-yu (White Powder Ma), his younger brother Ma Sik-chun (Golden Ma) and Ng Sik-ho (Limpy Ho).

The Ma brothers began their criminal careers in the traditional way, as street-gang members. With little formal education, they worked in menial jobs and as runners for a numbers racket; from this, they graduated to operating their own numbers game, which was exceedingly lucrative and provided them with the seed capital to break into narcotics.

Ma Sik-yu started trafficking narcotics in 1967. He knew the way to succeed was not to be a middle-man but to get in on the trade at source and control it from production to distribution. He travelled to the Golden Triangle to set up a purchasing agreement with Kuomintang general Li Wen-huan, who was hiding out in the jungle, ready to strike at Communist China and paying his troops by selling heroin. Li took to Ma and agreed to supply him, smuggling the heroin to Hong Kong on his behalf. But Li also had designs on Ma. He considered him of considerable use to the Kuomintang cause and introduced him to Taiwanese intelligence agents who were also United Bamboo Society men. They recruited Ma into the Kuomintang secret service. Three years later, Ma was trafficking in heroin and operating a sophisticated spy ring throughout South-east Asia, his agents predominantly Teochiu Triads who infiltrated pro-Chinese Communist organizations and reported on their activities. A three-way exchange was set up. The Mas toed the Taiwanese line and spied, Li gave them their heroin at a discount by way of payment and the government in Taipei made up Li's shortfall by sending him cash and arms.

Brother Sik-chun remained in Hong Kong, where he received the heroin, laundered the income and invested the proceeds in general and commodity trading companies, commercial property, cinemas, restaurants and bars. In addition, in 1969, he founded the Oriental Press Group, the flagship publication of which was the blatantly pro-Taiwanese *Oriental Daily News*, one of Hong Kong's most popular daily newspapers. He moved in society circles as a respectable businessman and took part in a number of high-profile philanthropic activities. Sik-yu, an inveterate gambler often to be seen at the casinos in Macau or on the Hong Kong racecourse, was so well regarded he was elected a member of the Royal Hong Kong Jockey Club, an accolade afforded to very few in the colony and considered the very top rung of the social ladder. Like his younger brother, he gave generously to charity and lived flamboyantly, noted for his expensive cars, gold jewellery and spectacularly luxurious mansion in suburban Kowloon, where, in 1970, a 25-metre-square building plot would cost upwards of US$4,600 a square metre. Police surveillance reports show him entertaining top Chinese movie stars, Taiwanese politicians, the European *taipans* (literally Big Boss) of the noble trading houses, international industrialists and an assortment of Triad leaders.

In the early 1970s, the Mas took on a nephew, Ma Woon-yin, as a partner. His particular responsibility was money laundering. In this role, he allegedly flew frequently to Taiwan and Singapore with suitcases full of cash, otherwise disposing of it through shell companies in Hong Kong and Macau. By the time he joined them, the Mas had turned the heroin trade on its head. With entrepreneurial skill, they controlled the entire business. The opium was produced in the Golden Triangle and turned there into No. 3 heroin, suitable for smoking but still comparatively impure. The No. 3 was then taken to Ma-owned refineries in Thailand, or smuggled to Hong Kong, where it was refined into No. 4 heroin, the purest, injectable variety. From Hong Kong, it was shipped to Taiwan or Malaysia and, in due course, to the whole world. A fair amount was sent to Vietnam, where it entrapped thousands of US army personnel fighting the war there.

The Mas did not rely just upon General Li. Like all good businessmen, they spread their risk. In Thailand, they were in league with other Teochiu Triads, who purchased opium from insurgent armies fighting for independence from the Burmese, transporting it to refining centres at such places as Chiang Mai or Ban Houei Sai, there turning it into No. 4 heroin. Corruption in Thailand reached the highest levels of government and made the country a heroin dealer's dream. Senior military officers engaged in the trade until 1973 when a civilian government was sworn in. The demobilized officers carried on trading, regaining control in a military coup in 1977 under General Kriangsak, who was heavily involved with narcotics. The Triads were unhindered.

Yet it was in Laos that the Mas made one of their most valuable alliances, striking a supply agreement with

General Ouane Rattikone, head of the Laotian army from 1965–71 and mastermind of a narcotics ring with agents in Bangkok, Saigon and Hong Kong. His product was famously trademarked '999', the numbers impressed into blocks of morphine base, implying the 99.9 per cent purity of 24-carat gold; in fact, his morphine base was about 50 per cent pure. His heroin was the equally famous Double UO Globe brand, which is still produced. Rattikone shipped his narcotics in Laotian air-force cargo planes or on Air America flights.

Air America was an airline operated by the Central Intelligence Agency (CIA), which had been covertly working with Hmong guerrillas in Laos since 1959, monitoring the Laotian Communist Party and fighting Communist Pathet Lao forces. In order to retain Hmong loyalty and keep their leader, General Vang Pao, on side, the CIA transported Hmong opium, which was used by the guerrillas to raise finance. Air America, Continental Air Service (CAS) and Lao Development Air Service flew narcotics from jungle airstrips to Long Tieng and Vientiane, from where it was freighted to Saigon in Vietnamese or American military aircraft, thence to Hong Kong on commercial or American government flights for distribution into the international marketplace by way of Hong Kong traffickers. The hypocrisy of the CIA's political utilization of narcotics played right into the hands of the Triads, who obtained a substantial percentage of their supplies with the tacit, if clandestine, assistance of the US government.

Vietnam was central to the Mas' operation. As in Thailand, the Vietnamese military was corrupt to the core, the most notorious heroin ring being operated by

Vietnamese Air Vice-Marshal Ky. Heroin was purchased in Vientiane from a Chinese, Hu Tim-heng, who was a business partner of Rattikone. In collaboration with the son of the Laotian prime minister, Souvanna Phouma, Hu and two other Chinese diverted finance from a US government grant to erect a Pepsi-Cola bottling works in Vientiane, the money used to purchase heroin-refining chemicals in the name of the non-existent Pepsi plant. Hu's heroin was shipped to Phnom Penh in Cambodia, flown in Vietnamese military transports to the Vietnamese air-force base at Tan Son Nhut, then sold to Teochiu Triads who diverted a percentage of it into the local market before sending the balance to Hong Kong. When Ky's star was in the descendant, General Dang Van Quang, Vietnamese President Nguyen Van Thieu's military intelligence adviser and commander of the navy, used naval vessels to ship heroin from Cambodia into South Vietnam then on to coasters sailing for Hong Kong. The American government knew of this trade, even accusing President Thieu of complicity in it, but they took no steps to curtail it. Hypocrisy ruled once more and, by 1973, the South Vietnamese armed forces were a primary link in the Mas' chain of supply.

It is hardly surprising that the Mas' heroin business thrived, yet there was a problem looming on the horizon. In January 1973, the Americans announced their intended withdrawal from Vietnam. The Mas were taken by surprise. Suddenly, a large part of their market ceased and moved back home across the Pacific. Their reaction was predictable. They would have to follow the market to the USA and go global. Knowing they could not do this alone, Ma Sik-yu sent envoys to North America and

Europe with orders to contact organized-crime syndicates to see if they could all co-operate in this lucrative business.

It has long been assumed that, until the American forces pulled out of Vietnam in the early months of 1973, the Mas had made no attempt to contact foreign criminal syndicates, but this is incorrect. They were almost certainly in touch with American mobsters before 1973.

Frank Carmen Furci was a *mafioso* from Tampa, Florida, where his father, Dominick, was a lieutenant in the Mafia family run by Santo Trafficante Jr, controller of organized crime in Florida and much of the Caribbean. In 1965, Frank Furci went to Saigon, where he and others, including a cabal of seven US army sergeants, ran a series of multi-million-dollar scams on supplies to servicemen's clubs; he was also a successful black-market currency dealer. In July 1967, Furci left Saigon, forced out by one of his competitors, and moved to Hong Kong, where he opened a restaurant, the San Francisco Steak House, and founded a trading company called Maradem Ltd.

With connections to French Corsican crime syndicates in Saigon, Furci was well placed to become an important fulcrum in the heroin trade he saw burgeoning around him. So important was he that Santo Trafficante Jr visited him in 1968, with Furci's father. From Hong Kong, Trafficante travelled on to Saigon where he met the Corsicans. The network of international heroin routes was being set up.

Whether or not the Mas met Trafficante or John Pullman, a top financial adviser to Meyer Lansky (one-time associate of the infamous American mob bosses Lucky Luciano and Bugsy Seigal, and a criminal mastermind almost without equal in the West) who stopped off in Hong Kong in 1965, is unknown. However, Hong Kong police sources believe, with hindsight, that they probably did for, shortly afterwards, a courier network of Filipino drug runners started trafficking heroin from Hong Kong to the USA via Chile, Paraguay and the Caribbean. Other connections were also likely, if unproved: they may have met with Anthony Turano, a New York Mafia boss who was assassinated by Triads when they believed he had double-crossed them, or Auguste Joseph Ricord, a French gangster from Marseilles who had been a Nazi collaborator in the Second World War and was responsible, between 1968 and 1973, for smuggling Golden Triangle heroin worth over US$2 billion into the USA.

Certainly, the Mas were not in touch with Americans only. According to the American Drug Enforcement Administration (DEA), an attempt was made by one of them to form a partnership with the Japanese criminal syndicates, the Yakuza, who proved to be uninterested. In 1971, they approached a Singaporean criminal syndicate and went into business with a Teochiu Triad-affiliated group in Saigon, known as the Saigon Cowboys, which sold heroin from ice-cream stalls along the road from Saigon to the US army base at Long Binh. They also operated resident dealers amongst locally enlisted domestic servants in the base itself.

By mid-1973, with the Americans finally pulled out of Vietnam, the Mas were ready to go international. With consummate skill, they ensured that the criminal climate remained favourable by brokering agreements with the other Triad societies in their patch, allowing them a piece of the action. This not only pacified rivals but distanced them from sections of the trade: the more complex it was, the less easily it could be penetrated by law-enforcement organizations. The Wo Shing Wo was put in charge of importation by sea, running narcotics into Hong Kong from deep-sea trawlers lying offshore; the 14K organized the refining laboratories; and the San Yee On looked after the bribery of police and customs officers. Everyone profited in the short term, but there was also a longer-term pay-off: the Mas showed the Triads how, with organization and diversification, they could become major international players.

As the 1970s progressed, heroin-addiction rates in Hong Kong rose sharply. In America and Europe, the rate similarly escalated, partly due to the influx of addicted forces personnel from Vietnam and partly to a concerted effort by the Mafia to make heroin the drug of choice over cocaine. With Vietnam in the hands of the Communists, the supply lines shifted: instead of heroin coming out of Saigon, it came by way of Bangkok, where the Teochiu Triads were in league with the military.

Interest in the Mas grew until, in 1976, the Hong Kong police had no alternative but to target them specifically. A task force was set up with sixty officers dedicated to nothing else. They were assisted by the DEA, Interpol and, ironically, the CIA, which had now changed direction somewhat in its attitude towards Asian narcotics trafficking. They were ready to pounce when, in February 1977, Ma Sik-yu was tipped off and fled, predictably, to Taiwan. The warrant for his arrest was lodged at Interpol's headquarters in France, since Taiwan was a member country. Nevertheless, the Kuomintang government refused to arrest him.

Ma Sik-chun and Woon-yin were not so fleet. They were arrested with seven lesser fry and charged with operating the largest narcotics syndicate ever known in the colony, but, inexplicably, they were released on bail. Their bail was considered high, at HK$1.5 million (US$200,000), but it was petty cash to them. In July 1978, three of the nine escaped from Hong Kong despite having had their passports confiscated and being under continual police surveillance. They headed for Thailand. Two months later, just before the case came to court, the two Mas slipped out of their houses at dead of night, avoided the watching police, reached the harbour, boarded a Panamanian freighter and followed Sik-yu to Taipei, where, shortly after their arrival, they were 'arrested' for illegally entering Taiwan and sentenced to a year in prison for possession of forged documents. This was a formality. The *Far Eastern Economic Review* reported on 6 October that the Ma brothers had been spotted on 18 September in a Taipei restaurant, dining with two former Hong Kong police officers. One of these was Lui Lok.

The Hong Kong authorities were embarrassed. The remaining defendants were tried but the mainly Chinese jury acquitted one, who had been the Mas' financial adviser, whilst the rest, although convicted, were subsequently released on appeal. The whole business had barely affected the Mas, who simply shifted their operation to Taiwan. In 1979, one of the Thailand-bound fugitives, Cheng Ah-kai, was arrested in Bangkok whilst organizing a huge shipment of heroin to Hong Kong by way of a Panamanian freighter which was said to have been registered to one of the Ma brothers' front companies. He was acquitted.

From 1978, the Ma brothers lived in Taiwan, building up a number of legal companies using laundered criminal proceeds. Ma Sik-yu died in 1992 but the legitimate businesses he and Ma Sik-chun set up continue to flourish in Hong Kong and around the world. They include commercial properties in Europe, North America and Australia; according to investigative journalists working for the *Sunday Times*, the companies own a valuable property portfolio in Britain, which includes an office block in Aldermanbury Square in the centre of the City of London's financial 'square mile', and in Westminster. The Oriental Press Group is the most obvious of their successful companies. Now the biggest newspaper publisher in the Far East, the company is headed by Ma Ching-kwan, Ma Sik-chun's son. One of the wealthiest men in Hong Kong, where multimillionaires are 10 cents a pair, Ma Ching-kwan wields considerable influence which reaches well outside the former British territory.

For some years, Ma Sik-chun has been gravely ill. A diabetic, he harbours the dream common amongst expatriate Chinese: to return to live out his last years, and be buried in his ancestral country. Ma Ching-kwan, in an attempt to expedite his father's wish, has gone to considerable lengths. Knowing that the only way his father could return to Hong Kong would be for him to be granted either a pardon or bail on grounds of ill-health, he sought throughout the 1990s to enlist the support of the British government. According to a *Sunday Times* report, the Oriental Press Group has donated considerable sums to Conservative Party funds: in the party's headquarters, Ma Ching-kwan was allegedly referred to as the Golden Boy, an ironic nickname in the light of that of his father. Christopher Patten, the last governor of

Hong Kong, attended functions at the Oriental Press Group headquarters and gave his blessing to the founding of a new English-language daily newspaper, the *Eastern Express*. John Major, as party leader as well as prime minister, entertained Ma to tea at Downing Street to thank him for his generosity. It was mooted that Ma might be given an honour for financial services rendered, but this was not forthcoming. Other generous benefactors from Hong Kong to Tory Party coffers have been honoured by the Queen, but Ma's pedigree was considered just too grey, although it must be stressed that he is not involved in any criminality whatsoever.

Individual Tory Members of Parliament have also been recruited to the drive to bolster Ma Sik-chun's reputation. They have been wined and dined in the grandest style in Hong Kong – but to no avail. Right up until the last day of the colonial administration of Hong Kong, no pardon was forthcoming although the British government did concede to Ma's body being interred in Hong Kong when he died. In the meantime, the Conservative Party continued to take Ma Ching-kwan's money. When his attempt to give his father respectability and allow him to die in Hong Kong failed, Ma Ching-kwan demanded his political donations be repaid. News of these contributions hit the headlines in January 1998. William Hague, John Major's successor as Conservative Party leader, tried hard to play down the matter, but the damage was done. Ma Ching-kwan, whilst promising further details, had his revenge.

The Mas were major narcotics traffickers but they were not alone, nor were they without competition. Their main rival was Ng Sik-ho.

Ng's life began in poverty. He was born in 1929 in a village near Shantou, 300 km up the China coast from Hong Kong. His parents were agricultural peasants. Uneducated but quick-witted, he joined a gang of youths collecting protection money for a local Triad society in which he aspired to become a 49. When China fell to Communism, he joined the flood of refugees heading for Hong Kong. He was twenty-one years old. Arriving in the colony, he was very much a fish out of water, having no money, no contacts and unable to speak the local Cantonese dialect. As did many in his condition, he searched for and found a community of people from his region. Within this was a Shantounese Triad society called the Sam Shing Sheh. Because he was Triad-affiliated back home, he was enrolled as a 49. *Guanxi* saved the day.

Within a year, he had been promoted to Red Pole. This was rapid promotion, but Ng had earned it: his income from protection rackets exceeded his peers' and he was far better organized. They were just street toughs: he was shrewd, intelligent, cunning and ambitious. Branching into vice, he increased his society's income further and was elevated to *pak tsz sin*. In this capacity, he was in charge of the day-to-day activities of the Sam Shing Sheh. Additionally, he was now Burning the Yellow Paper with other societies and extending his power-base. Untypically, he was made an honorary member of the 14K and the Wo Shing Wo.

In 1958, Ng Sik-ho diversified further, into street narcotics. He owned a fruit-and-vegetable stall in Shek Kip Mei, Kowloon, from which he sold No. 3 smoking heroin to coolies and local residents from a nearby resettlement estate and the shanty town on the hillside behind it. He was soon earning over HK$2,000 a day.

Such rapid advancement and success had a drawback. Ng made enemies. Others grew jealous and he made the seminal mistake of selling heroin just over the border of another society's territory. He was ambushed and his right leg savagely beaten with a heavy teak pole. This was the Triad equivalent of a warning: if he had not had such powerful connections he would almost certainly have been killed. There were onlookers to this assault, but no one was foolish enough to get involved or come to his assistance. Bleeding profusely, his leg shattered, he did not dare go to a hospital as then the police would have become involved. He succeeded in reaching a traditional Chinese medicine shop where a bone-setter did his best. However, Ng's leg was broken in a number of places, the bone not just fractured but actually shattered. For the rest of his life, Ng was partially crippled and walked with a limp, hence his nickname, Limpy Ho.

The attack did not diminish his ambition. He continued to deal in heroin, extending his retailing and going into partnership with a fellow Triad, Lo Shing and Lo Shing's wife, Cheng Yuet-ying, who took charge of couriering their merchandise around Hong Kong.

The police, tipped off by a rival, raided the fruit stall in June 1960. Ng was arrested and sentenced to twelve months' imprisonment – a low penalty as this was his first offence. Lo Shing, who had a previous record, got three years. Ng's lameness and the fact that many of the warders in Stanley prison – Hong Kong's maximum-security jail where he was held – were on Triad society payrolls made his sentence easy. He was given only light work duties and kept his head down. In late 1961, after serving nine months, he was released on parole and moved in with Cheng Yuet-ying, who became his common-law wife: so much for Triad oath 34.

Cheng Yuet-ying, aged twenty-seven, was also of uneducated peasant stock but, like Ng, she was intelligent and ambitious. As Ng's business grew, she became increasingly important to him, her tact, diplomacy and cunning complementing his organizational skills. Although she had been in Hong Kong only since 1957, she already had three children by Lo, who was now impotent due to his heroin addiction. Under Lo's tuition, she had learned the finer points of narcotic dealing, but this did not save her. She was apprehended in the apartment she shared with Ng in Hung Hom, a crowded tenement area of Kowloon, packing heroin into single fixes. Like Lo, she was sentenced to three years. The police tried hard to get her to implicate Limpy Ho, but she remained steadfast and he kept his liberty.

Whilst Cheng was in jail, Ng carried on trading, expanding further. He purchased a small teahouse and, close by, a rice shop. Narcotics sales were made over a bowl of tea and the heroin collected from the rice shop, where it was hidden in barrels of rice, the customer buying a packet of rice containing the purchased heroin. It took the police a long time to work out how this clever scam was operating: it is thought Cheng devised it. In 1965 they were both arrested again, but the charge did not stick. Ng was bound over for two years under the Societies' Ordinance on the charge of being a Triad.

By 1966, Ng was getting itchy feet, tired of small-time street dealing and keen to move up in the criminal world.

The only way to do this was to control not only resale but also supply and manufacture. To achieve such an empire required sufficient capital and the right timing. In 1967, Ng found both. Taking advantage of the 1967 anti-British riots keeping the police preoccupied, he quickly founded a number of heroin partnerships, financing them from Triad associates and legitimate businessmen who had spare cash to risk on such a potentially profitable venture.

Ng's plan was to purchase morphine base in Thailand, ship it to Hong Kong in his own vessels and refine it in his own heroin laboratories tucked away in the crowded tenements of Kowloon or the secluded hills of the New Territories. The refining would produce as much No. 3 heroin as the local market needed, the remainder being refined further into No. 4 heroin for export. To aid in this enterprise, he teamed up with another Shantounese, Ng Chun-kwan, whom he had known for some years and who had links to Teochiu Triads in Bangkok. A deal was struck whereby the Thai Triads would send a consignment of morphine base once every four months by both sea and overland routes.

The transhipment was superbly organized. Thai-registered cargo vessels sailed from Bangkok to hove to in international waters off Hong Kong. The morphine base was transferred to Hong Kong-registered deep-sea fishing junks, which carried it into territorial waters where, at night, it was off-loaded into a flotilla of inshore fishing junks. The one shipment was by now split into up to 100 packages, making detection virtually impossible. Deliveries overland, using the chaos of the Cultural Revolution as cover, were conducted by couriers, between each few of which was a cut-off so no-one could betray the whole system. Once the morphine base arrived in Hong Kong, it was dealt with by two separate operational groups. One received it, the other took it into storage for access by the refineries. Each group was headed by a different Triad, neither of whom knew or met the other. The whole operation was aided by Ng Chun-kwan, who 'owned' a number of Hong Kong marine police officers, thus ensuring the unhindered landing of cargoes. By 1970, Ng Sik-ho's annual profit was estimated to be over US$22 million.

To outside observers, Limpy Ho was a prosperous businessman. He dressed in well-cut, expensive suits and drove or was driven in a top range Mercedes-Benz saloon. His non-criminal associates assumed he was yet another successful entrepreneur who had invested wisely. With Cheng Yuet-ying, in whose name many of the investments were made, he sank money into property, owning blocks of apartments, houses and commercial buildings, and retaining three private houses for himself. The most impressive was 20 Kent Road, Kowloon Tong, a garden suburb where, in the 1970s, many wealthy Chinese and Indian businessmen lived. A mile away, he maintained a luxury apartment in Waterloo Road for his mistress, Chan Mui-lan. His third home was in the New Territories.

Amongst Ng's legitimate businesses was a chain of restaurants, two in Kowloon and two on Hong Kong island; all were managed by Sam Shing Sheh officers. In industrial Ma Tau Kok and in Tsuen Wan, famous for its textile mills and dyeing works, he owned a number of factory units. He also founded the Hong Kong Precious Stone Company, which imported gemstones from Thailand and Burma and was very useful for sending money to Thailand to pay for morphine base and as a money-laundering facility. All the businesses were run from a suite of offices in the Tung Ying Building in Granville Road, Kowloon.

Not all Ng's investments were legal. He possessed four casinos, the biggest of which was above his Pak Lee Restaurant in Prat Avenue, Tsim Sha Tsui. To distance himself from it and maintain his air of respectability, it was managed by his wife. The casino was run on American club lines, offering both Western and Oriental games. It never closed, served food and drink and one had to be a keyholder to enter. Although Ng bought off corrupt police officers not to raid it, his clientele was as much a security as his bribery, for the membership list included a number of well-connected tycoons, senior civil servants, lawyers and bankers.

Curiously, as if he could not let go of his criminal origins, Ng still maintained a number of street stalls, some unlicensed, which sold fruit, clothing, household utensils and heroin. The police and street-hawker trading inspectors ignored them. Ng 'owned' nearly 200 police, including a British senior officer, and employed in his businesses (legitimate or otherwise) over 1,500 people. His gemstone cutters were said to be amongst the best in the Far East.

Ng Sik-ho was extremely clever. He never personally involved himself with any narcotics delivery or trading, did not gamble, drank only moderately and never used drugs. Apart from his concubine in Waterloo Road – of whom his wife was aware and approved – he did not womanize. He also paid tribute to the most senior 14K

301

and Wo Shing Wo men. They, in turn, provided him with 49s when he needed a hit carried out.

Now one of the Far East's primary narcotics dealers, Ng was in a position of considerable power. He crossed the boundaries of several societies, his various allegiances keeping him safe from too much reprisal or envy. The Triads respected him and his main problems came from rival Teochiu Triads in Thailand, who periodically executed his couriers in a futile attempt to gain back some of the narcotics market they had lost to his superior organizational skills. Yet Ng, like the Ma brothers, was not satisfied with being a big fish in a small pond. In 1971, he believed he was ready to advance. Like the Mas, he knew the way ahead was to go international, which meant dealing with the Mafia. He had competition. The Thai Teochiu were already dealing with American *mafiosi* through Vietnam and could gain a better return on their product than Ng could guarantee, but this did not deter him. The so-called French Connection, the running of heroin through Marseilles to the USA and Canada, had been broken and the time was ripe. Ng planned to buy opium direct from the Golden Triangle, refine it into morphine base in his own laboratories in Thailand, ship this in his own vessels to Hong Kong and refine his heroin there in existing laboratories. The Thai Triads were against this, as they would be cut out of the profits made from morphine-base production, and they put a stop to the plan, but they sold Ng morphine base nevertheless. When this reached Hong Kong, it was passed to an elderly heroin chemist from Shanghai who had worked for Big-eared Du. A master heroin 'chef', he was soon producing No.

4 heroin of 92 per cent purity, the highest level ever attained at that time.

Over the winter of 1970–71, Ng met on a number of occasions in Japan with *mafiosi*, several of them Santo Trafficante Jr's representatives, who were keen to find a new trade route now France was closed. An agreement was reached and, for about six months, Ng sent heroin to the USA by way of Japan, South America and the Caribbean, but then the deal was terminated, the *mafiosi* claiming that Ng was too arrogant and untrustworthy. This could hardly have been the case. He was far too shrewd a businessman to jeopardize the operation, the height of his ambitions. What really happened was that the Thai Triads pressurized the Mafia not to deal with Ng; the Ma brothers, who were already dealing with the Mafia, also used their influence to try to get rid or reduce the influence of their rival.

This rebuff cost Ng a lot of face, but his brush with the Mafia brought more than a bruising to his pride. The DEA had the mobsters under close scrutiny around the world: now Ng was in their files. His details were circulated, the DEA sharing its information with the Hong Kong police, who had not fully appreciated the scale of his operation. Ng remained blissfully unaware of this attention for, although the Hong Kong police Narcotics Bureau contained Triads, it was not as corrupt as some divisions and the British officers played their cards close to their chests. A new dossier was opened on Ng Sik-ho.

Slighted by the Mafia, Ng turned his attention away from North America. Another market was developing into which he could move more or less unhampered. It

303

was Europe and it had an Achilles heel – The Netherlands. Dutch attitudes towards drug-taking were extremely liberal and Ng knew he could move into Europe through Amsterdam. Malaysian and Singaporean Triads were already importing heroin through The Netherlands, but they were disorganized, underfinanced and did not own their own chemists.

Ng went on a mission to Singapore, where he was welcomed by the local Triads. Purchasing a coastal freighter, he had it refitted with a powerful engine and started running morphine base from Bangkok to Singapore where a laboratory was established at nearby Johor Baharu. Singaporean couriers then flew the resulting heroin to Amsterdam, where Dutch-based Triads trafficked it. It was a good plan, but it did not last long. The Thai Triads tipped off the DEA in Bangkok, who in turn alerted the Singaporean police. The freighter was boarded. No narcotics were discovered but Ng knew he was vulnerable. The vessel was sold and he retrenched to Hong Kong, thereafter using trusted Hong Kong couriers. The Malaysian Triads, displeased at being used, carried on running heroin for the Thais into Amsterdam in direct competition with Ng.

His extraterritorial venture over, Ng consolidated his business in Hong Kong by employing a fishing-junk captain, Leung Fat-hei, to oversee importation by sea. Leung was a vicious, mendacious character who made a living running illegal Chinese immigrants on to isolated Hong Kong beaches for US$2,000 a head, then tipping off the immigration authorities and collecting an informer's reward. Annoyed by the Thais, Ng and Leung planned a sting against them. Leung dressed his junk crew

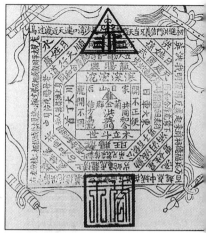

ABOVE LEFT: A somewhat faded but unique seventeenth-century illustration of a Triad lodge depicted as a courtyard.

ABOVE RIGHT: A nineteenth-century Triad membership certificate. Printed in black on silk, the heavy characters are vermilion 'chop' (or seal) marks.

The Tai Ping Shan district of Hong Kong, photographed in the 1860s by William Pryor Floyd. It was here, free of imperial interference, that the Triads flourished under the unwilling protection of early British colonial rule.

ABOVE LEFT: Kwan Ti, the Triads' deity. This idol stands in the Man Mo Temple, Hong Kong, a popular destination for parties of tourists, who do not realize its significance.

MIDDLE: A non-criminal Triad society ceremonial parade, photographed in Hong Kong in the early twentieth century. Note the turbaned Sikh policeman accompanying the marchers.

(*Hong Kong Police*)

ABOVE RIGHT: A rare photograph of a Boxer.

OPPOSITE: Shanghai, April 1927: Communist 'sympathizers' killed by Green Gang thugs in the White Terror.

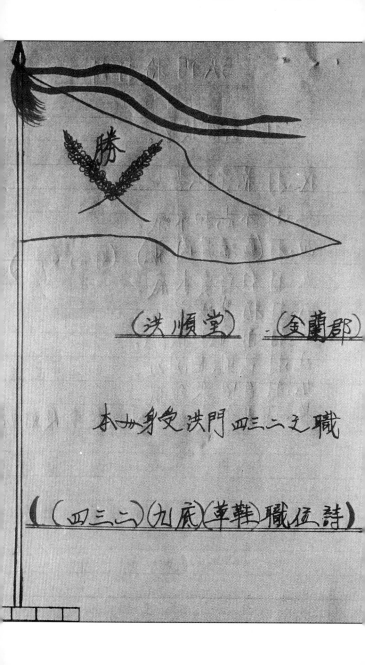

（洪順堂）　（金蘭郡）

本身身黨洪門四三二之職

（（四三二）（九底）（華華）職位詩）

ABOVE LEFT: A traditional Triad altar. (*Hong Kong Police*)

ABOVE RIGHT: A modern-day Triad altar. Discovered in Hong Kong, it is a shabby imitation of the real thing. (*Hong Kong Police*)

LEFT: A traditional Triad ceremonial banner made of silk.

OPPOSITE: A modern-day Wo Shing Wo ceremonial banner crudely drawn on a sheet of file paper. As such, it is easily destroyed in the event of a police raid, but it is also indicative of the deterioration of ritual observance. (*Hong Kong Police*)

INSET: Detail of a Wo Shing Wo member's T-shirt bearing the usual insignia of the society.

TOP: A very rare sight of a Triad-style tattoo. Photographed in 1998, this worker has taken off his T-shirt on a hot day, exposing a magnificent dragon which covers his entire back.

ABOVE: A unique surveillance photograph taken by a hidden miniature camera at the New York Chinatown funeral of Benny Ong Kai-sui, showing mourners giving traditional Triad hand signs. No other photograph of this sort exists.

OPPOSITE: An Incense Master in full regalia. This is a posed photograph taken by the Hong Kong Police. The 'turban' (which is that of a *shan chu*) and stole are red, the gown and sash white. Note the grass sandal on the left foot. (*Hong Kong Police*)

Triad street-fighting weapons, including throwing-stars. These examples were confiscated by the Hong Kong Police in the 1980s.

A meat-chopper, the traditional weapon of Triad retribution. The blade is 20cm long; the characters impressed into the steel are the name of the manufacturer.

A Triad street-fighting weapon as used in London. Made from a penny cut and twisted to form several sharp points, it is thrown into the face of opponents or used knuckle-duster fashion.

The result of a chopping. (*Metropolitan Police*)

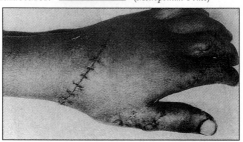

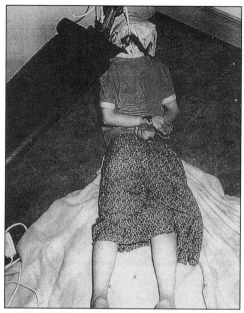

A Triad kidnap victim, raped and strangled in New York. Note that the little finger of the victim's right hand has been severed as proof to relatives of her kidnap. (*Mark Craig/NYPD*)

The final, sordid destination of a Triad-smuggled illegal immigrant, this is a cellar corridor dormitory behind a kitchen in New York. (*Mark Craig*)

Sun Yat-sen and his wife, *née* Ching-ling Soong.

BELOW LEFT: Du Yueh-sheng, alias Big-eared Du (*right*), with Huang Chih-jung, or Pockmarked Huang (*centre*), and an unidentified man. (*University of Nanjing*)

ABOVE: Lim Bo-seng, the Singaporean merchant and senior Triad official who fought with the SOE against the Japanese in occupied Malaya. He is photographed with the British SOE agent, John Davis. (*Faith Spencer-Chapman*)

Kot Siu-wong, founder of the 14K Triad society.

Chung Mon, or '5% Man', head of the 14K in Amsterdam, who was gunned down outside his office in Prins Hendrikkade in March 1975.
(*Hong Kong Police*)

Ng Sik-ho, known as Limpy Ho.
(*South China Morning Post Publishers Limited*)

An early mug-shot of Yau Lap-yuen, alias George Pai.
(*Hong Kong Police*)

Heung Wah-yim.
(*South China Morning Post Publishers Limited*)

Wan Kuok-koi, or Broken-tooth Kui, the most powerful Triad leader in Macau and, arguably, in South-east Asia.
(*David Paul Morris*)

LEFT: The China City nightclub, Kowloon, which, according to the Hong Kong Police, was a venue in 1995 for San Yee On initiation ceremonies.

ABOVE: The former luxury home of Ng Sik-ho, at 20 Kent Road, Kowloon Tong. Financed by his multimillion-dollar international heroin dealing, it is today a quick-time 'house of assignation'.

OPPOSITE LEFT: The Lisboa Hotel, Macau.

OPPOSITE RIGHT: The Golden Shopping Arcade, Kowloon, for a decade until 1998 the centre of the illegal pirated computer-software trade.

OPPOSITE BELOW: The lodge of the Che Kung Tong in San Antonio, Texas, c.1930. Note the freemasonic insignia above the door proclaiming it to be a masonic charity.

ABOVE LEFT: The Golden Dragon restaurant in San Francisco. It was here, in September 1977, that a ferocious gun battle took place between the Cheung Ching Yee and the Wah Ching societies in which five died and eleven were wounded. (*Mark Craig*)

ABOVE RIGHT: Gerrard Street, Soho, in London. The statues, a gathering point for illegal immigrants, are referred to by the local Chinese as the 'Unemployment Exchange'.

LEFT: A Triad narcotics dealer on the streets of Hong Kong. Note that he has two mobile phones, to act as a 'cut-out' to protect his supply sources.

OPPOSITE: Triad recruits, apprehended in a Hong Kong Police raid in the late 1980s. (*Hong Kong Police*)

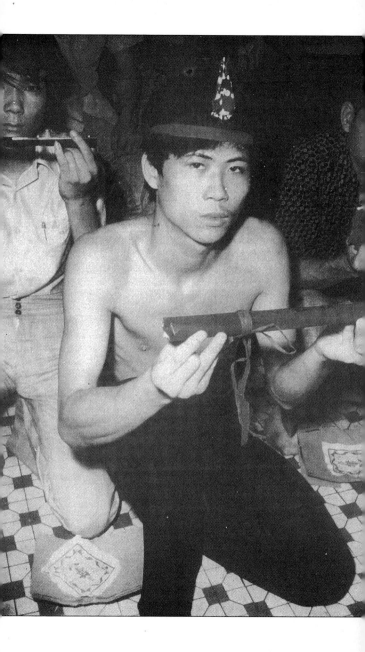

The cover from the pirate video CD-ROM of the film
Casino, based on the life of Broken-tooth Kui. The pirate
edition was manufactured and put on sale by a rival Triad
society within hours of the film's release.

A Hong Kong government anti–Triad information poster: a
Chinese version was also published.
(Hong Kong Government Information Services)

as Chinese soldiers, sailed under a Communist Chinese flag and intercepted a Thai-owned trawler running morphine base to Hong Kong for, it is thought, the Ma brothers. The Thai crew were held at gunpoint while the Chinese 'soldiers' confiscated the heroin and threw it overboard. What actually went overboard were sacks of either concrete dust or flour. The heroin was transferred to Leung's vessel and taken to Hong Kong. At this point, the plan unravelled. Ng paid Leung but Leung shortchanged his men, who began to talk. The police did not hear the tale, but the Thais did. Ng's morphine supply was suddenly cut off and Cheng had to go to Bangkok to smooth things over. She convinced the Thais that Ng had had nothing to do with such piracy and they believed her.

Meanwhile, the DEA was closing in. They had traced the Singapore–Amsterdam courier route by targeting Singaporean Triads, whose trafficking was amateur and transparent. In Amsterdam, they trailed US servicemen from bases in West Germany who were both ex-Vietnam addicts and dealers to other servicemen and German civilians. Backtracking from these, they discovered Ng's operation. The Hong Kong police were kept abreast of developments.

With Ng under continuous surveillance, his police file grew fat until, in 1972, two locations in the New Territories were raided. In a tunnel on Pearl Island near Tuen Mun, where Ng rented apartments, and on a duck farm he owned, they discovered over 700 kg of raw opium and 80 kg of morphine base. Arrests were made but no-one talked. Ng Sik-ho was safe. Even when his casinos were busted that same year, the police found nothing they could pin on him.

Business continued. By 1973, Ng was the biggest exporter of heroin to Europe, fuelling a soaring addict population across the continent. Any surplus travelled on to the USA, carried by US military personnel or posted in the military mail system. Yet the police were no nearer to implicating him. Talk on the streets was not proof in the courts.

However, matters were coming to a head and were accelerated by Ng himself. Early in 1974, Leung Fat-hei double-crossed him and was murdered, supposedly at Ng's behest. The police investigated the murder and Ng's name came up when three of his men were marked in connection with the assassination. The Narcotics Bureau was informed. Ng panicked and, in March, fled to Taiwan, followed by two of the alleged murderers. However, the murder case could not be proved, the charges were dropped and for the time being the dust settled.

With the heat off, Ng returned to Hong Kong on 25 October, but the climate was changing fast. The ICAC was shaking up the police. No longer were their officers for the buying. The Narcotics Bureau, under a very experienced and utterly incorruptible British superintendent, John Rumbelow, made Ng its prime target. Constant surveillance paid off. Three narcotics deliveries were apprehended, a fourth being lost at sea. Ng re-started his gambling business: it was promptly raided and forced to close.

All this police attention was not Ng's only problem. Fellow Triads were growing to dislike him. He was getting too bold, living too flamboyantly and flaunting his wealth, something which jarred with the usually conservative Triad bosses. Many were afraid that if Ng went down he might take them with him. His domineering manner also annoyed some of his own men. A key importer, a Shantounese called Ng Ping, walked out on him. Another departed after surviving three murder contracts which he found Ng had commissioned, believing him to be a police informer, which is just what he became by way of retaliation.

The police, however, had far more valuable informers in the Ma brothers. They passed information to the Narcotics Bureau through police officers they had – or had had before the ICAC clampdown – on their payroll. At last a handpicked team of clean narcotics officers was assembled and Ng Sik-ho was arrested late in 1974.

He was taken straight to police headquarters in Arsenal Street, Wanchai; here he was beyond the reach of any corrupt officers not yet weeded out of regional police stations. He was questioned for hours but denied everything. Meanwhile, a 200-strong police squad, chosen for their untouchable qualities from several different divisions, raided a number of his premises. As an added precaution, only the senior officers knew the purpose and locations of the raids: the teams were informed of their targets only once they were *en route*.

The apartment in Waterloo Road was empty: Chan Mui-lan, Ng's mistress, had flown. At 20 Kent Road, the police found Cheng Yuet-ying gone. It was later rumoured that both had been tipped off by a very senior police officer, who pocketed HK$200,000 for his pains. The police were still elated. In the house they discovered documents referring to Thai morphine-base shipments and to Ng's partnership with Ng Chun-kwan, now a narcotics syndicate boss in his own right. At other raided venues, a number of wanted criminals were apprehended.

It was obvious that Ng Sik-ho was done for. As his henchmen and employees were rounded up they one by one struck bargains with the police and, when the case came to court the following spring, there was a string of men willing to testify. Ng Ping was a star prosecution witness. In May 1975, Ng Sik-ho and eight others were sentenced. Those who testified were treated leniently. Ng was sentenced to thirty years' imprisonment in Stanley prison, from which there has never been a successful break-out: only two prisoners have ever made it over the wall and both badly injured themselves in the drop.

The case was a milestone. It was the first time the Hong Kong police had successfully indicted such a major criminal and it was a considerable morale booster after the years of corruption and the upheaval caused by the ICAC. It also highlighted the difficulties in bringing an international crime boss to book. The complexities of sorting out Ng's businesses posed a serious problem, for his empire was discovered to cover most of South-east Asia, Switzerland (where he had bank accounts), Paris, Amsterdam and New York. The revelations were to lead, over the coming years, to the emergence of a new profession: the forensic accountant.

No sooner was he incarcerated than the word on the streets was that Ng was offering HK$10 million to anyone who would spring him. He also put out a HK$1 million contract on Ng Ping. Policemen who had given evidence and their families were protected round the clock; several British officers involved in the case sent their families to the United Kingdom on leave. Yet no hits were made and no-one arrived outside Stanley prison with a ladder. The Triads were not going to get involved with a hit on a police officer and it is fair to assume that the Mas made it known that anyone who got Ng out of jail would not live long enough to spend $10, let alone $10 million.

Cheng Yuet-ying escaped immediate arrest, moving from one safe house to another around Hong Kong, but she was unable to leave the colony. The airport was alerted and undercover officers from the immigration services and the police kept an eye on likely ship departures. A reward of HK$50,000 was put on her head. It worked. She was arrested in an apartment in North Point, on Hong Kong island, as a result of a tip-off. The reward was collected. Held on remand, she tried to kill herself but was eventually brought to trial and sentenced to sixteen years. She was released in the late 1980s and, it is said, became a common street pusher.

In Stanley prison, Ng Sik-ho was at first segregated from the other prisoners and kept in a cage cell on death row for his own safety, but was later moved to a cell in the main prison to spend his time working with the rest of the prison population: prisoners in Hong Kong jails have to work making hospital sheets, government office furniture and, by a sharp twist of irony, prison officers' uniforms and policemen's boots. Seven years after he began his sentence, Ng offered to become a witness in a court case against Lui Lok *in absentia*, to try to seize his assets. The case came before the court in 1984 and Ng testified. On the witness stand, he stated that Lui Lok took massive payments to prevent heroin traffickers and casino operators from being raided; he claimed that Lui Lok boasted he could make or break them all. This led to Lui Lok's lawyers trying to broker a plea bargain with the Hong Kong government, which came to a head on 1 May 1986. On that day, Lui Lok's lawyers surrendered title in eight properties valued at HK$14 million. They also suggested that their client was prepared to detail everything he knew about corruption in Hong Kong in exchange for immunity from prosecution. The properties were accepted but the offer was not and an ICAC warrant for Lui Lok's arrest remained active.

By 1990, Ng Sik-ho was a frail, elderly man with close-cropped grey hair who still walked with a pronounced limp. Although he was still only halfway through his sentence he was not to complete it, for he was found to be suffering from cancer of the liver and was released on bail for compassionate reasons. He died in 1991.

With Ng behind bars, the authorities continued to address the Triad problem, coming to comprehend the fallibility of Senior Superintendent Teddy U's secret report of 1976 and taking measures to nullify its influence. Their ranks rid of Triad influence and the ICAC well established, the police were in a strong position to respond to every opportunity. Various drives were made against Triad operations, most of them successful to a certain degree, but it was not until 1987 that the police really hit the headlines.

On 13 December 1987, the *Sunday Morning Post*, Hong Kong's leading English-language Sunday paper, carried a feature article which began:

Police are locked in a protracted war against Triads where the battle lines rarely move. Advances and retreats are sometimes barely noticeable in this war of attrition, as each time an enemy pocket is overcome another trouble spot flares on the front. But a recent all-out assault on one gang has driven a salient deep into Triad territory.

The gang was the Ngai faction of the 14K and the police operation was to dispel, once and for all, the commonly held myth that the Triads were somehow unconquerable.

The story began two years earlier, in August 1985, when a secret police team was assembled under Superintendent Steve Vickers to go after the Ngai (Resolute) group, which had come to their attention through an outbreak of vicious reciprocal killings between the Ngai and other Triad gangs over the proprietorship of illegal gambling rackets. Vickers's select team consisted of Chief Inspector Roger Booth, two Chinese inspectors, Michael Yu Shi-cheung and Henry Chan Tai-ling, and four other policemen. They started from a position of considerable tactical strength because, since 1980, the 14K had been infiltrated by two exceedingly courageous police undercover agents codenamed Sandy and Rodney. Their real names were police constables Yu Kam-cheung and Ma Chi-man.

The infiltration of a Triad gang is highly dangerous. Discovery means certain, often lingering and very painful, death. It is also very difficult, for Triad societies are extremely cautious about whom they enrol. Every candidate is screened, his family background and past gone into, his associates noted and studied. One slip, one anomaly, one fact ringing not quite true and the would-be 49 is rejected or worse.

To establish their bona fides, the two agents began in

1979 setting themselves up as street hawkers in Mongkok, in the heart of 14K territory. Once they were known, they joined the Ying Fat Sports Association, a martial-arts club affiliated to the 14K and used as a recruiting station. Ma succeeded in being enrolled as a 49 and was taken under the wing of a senior 14K official. The intelligence the two agents compiled from within the 14K was utterly invaluable.

Vickers's strategy was brilliant. First, his team publicly and obviously investigated the gambling-racket murders, arresting and successfully prosecuting a number of the Ngai faction's members. From the accused, they built up a picture of the structure of the Ngai group and the 14K illegal gambling enterprise.

The main business centred upon bookmaking on Hong Kong horse races. The system was sophisticated, with over fifty bookies' offices located on race days throughout the colony, connected to banks of telephones run off legal subscribers' lines. The offices took heavy bets from wealthy punters seeking to avoid betting through the official Royal Hong Kong Jockey Club computers: in this way, they avoided affecting the tote odds which were assessed by the computers. It is possible that race-fixing was going on as well, but that was less likely, as the structure of racing in Hong Kong makes such activities very difficult.

The team identified the locations of most of the Ngai betting centres but raided only a small number, arranging to have these busted by units of ordinary local officers. The idea was not to close down the network but to test Ngai reaction. A massive simultaneous raid was then planned. A race day in March 1986 was to be zero hour. Two hundred officers from four different specialized units gathered during the morning. As racing began in the early afternoon, they were issued with their orders: until then, no-one knew why they had been assembled. Vickers was playing it as safe as he could. In mid-afternoon, forty-three Ngai bookies' centres were simultaneously raided. Not one had received a tip-off. Furthermore, the police were prepared for the Triads' tricks, having learned of them from the previous small raids. The tricks were clever. Many telephone bets were recorded on cassette recorders, by each of which were powerful magnets ready to erase the evidence. All betting slips were made of soluble rice paper: by each table stood a bucket of water ready to receive them. Some evidence was lost but most was retained.

Thirty-three arrests were made, the Ngai gambling system smashed. Intelligence gathered from the raids and from subsequent interviews indicated that the Ngai faction was cross-betting with other Triad societies' gambling networks, but the police ignored these connections. They had a bigger quarry to hunt down.

It was learned that the nominal *shan chu* of the Ngai group was a man known as Tai Bei Tang, or Big-nose Tang, but he was elderly and terminally ill. The person really in command had to be someone else. The police gradually succeeded in piecing together much of the puzzle of the Ngai personnel because those arrested did not appreciate the magnitude of the police operation – they thought they had been picked up in an anti-gambling drive and were therefore not on their guard when asked the occasional oblique question. The society leaders erroneously shared this opinion. By July the police were ready to strike.

At midnight on 13 July, police headquarters were sealed off for security reasons. There was no chance of a leak. Even the telephone switchboard was monitored. Search warrants were issued. An area of the headquarters car park and main building was organized as a holding pen; a caterer was brought in and mobile toilets positioned on the periphery. The police officers who had taken part in the bookie raids were joined by hundreds of others, some from the élite tactical unit. At 3 a.m. the raids began, continuing for forty-eight hours. Fifty-three suspects were rounded up. The repercussions reverberated throughout not only the Ngai faction but the entire criminal community. Never before had the police mounted such a concerted, determined and all-encompassing raid without any lapse in security.

The police missed one important office-bearer who had left Hong Kong for Taiwan just before the raids began, but it is likely his departure was due to coincidence rather than corruption. Of the fifty-three apprehended, seven were accused of serious crimes, two of them women. Four of the seven, Lam Wing-kei, Tai Chi-kwong, Sung Hueng-lan and Leung Hung, were major catches and charged with the management of an unlawful society, conspiracy to traffic in narcotics and a variety of assaults or incitement to cause assault. Not believing the police to have sufficient evidence against them, they all pleaded not guilty. Yet the police had an ace up their sleeve in the form of police constable Ma Chi-man, codenamed Rodney. On the stand, he told a fascinating story.

In 1981, he had fallen in with one Chui Shun-kwok, a 14K member under the command of a man called Ng

Wah-hei, whom the prosecution believed was a senior Ngai official. Chui put Rodney up for membership and he joined the 14K on 25 November that year as a 49. Lam Wing-kei was his proposer and the man to whom he owed allegiance. Before this, however, on 4 July, Lam had introduced him to Ng Wah-hei over a meal: it was evident to Rodney that Ng was an important man. A fortnight later, Rodney, Tai Chi-kwong and Leung Hung met with others to plan an attack on a rival society's mahjong school. Other attacks were later planned against another society and, in December, Rodney was taken to see a man known as Hak Chai who declared the others to be his 'cousins'. A strategy was made at the meeting to divide up a criminal territory.

Not all Rodney's time was spent in discussion. He reported to the court how he had been present at the revenge beating of a young woman who had testified against a Triad-affiliated female and he had himself taken part in an attack upon a sauna-cum-massage parlour belonging to a rival society. His role was to smash fittings with an iron pipe and, it was alleged, kill anyone who opposed him.

After a seventeen-day trial, all the accused were found guilty. On appeal, the narcotics charges were overruled. The defence lawyers wanted them quashed as they were liable to increase the overall sentence quite considerably. The sentences were reduced accordingly.

The 14K was by no means defeated, but the operation had been highly successful beyond just the seven convictions. The public now saw the police as determined and effective Triad busters. The police received a massive boost to morale. Conversely, Triads' morale slumped. It was to suffer another blow in the shape of Operation Amesbury.

In the spring of 1987, a large operation was mounted by the Organized and Serious Crimes Group, based upon intelligence received. The target was the leadership of the San Yee On, thought to be one of the biggest and best-run Triad societies in Hong Kong. It was certainly the most traditional. It followed a set ritual, although this did not take the standard form, and every recruit was given a membership number indicating his position in the hierarchy. His particulars were entered on a society identity card, which included a contact telephone number, the date of the holder's initiation and details of his protector or sponsor, and were recorded in a membership list. By 1987, the membership numbers reached more than 33,000, of which 1,400 were office-bearers.

For the previous two years, a police research team had studied the San Yee On with the ambitious intention of identifying senior officials and obtaining a list of members. Other objectives were to discover if the society had a central funding mechanism and to obtain intelligence on it. Ultimately, it was hoped to accrue sufficient knowledge to arrest and prosecute the leaders.

As work progressed, the true power of the San Yee On was discovered and assessed, the reasons for its success understood. First, the San Yee On was united, the *shan chu* uniquely able to command the loyalty of a large number of officials. This was virtually unknown in Hong Kong's Triad societies in which rivalries were forever fomenting. Second, it had an ongoing recruitment campaign which had trebled membership between 1978 and

1987, some recruits teenaged school pupils. Third, the structure of the society was organized as effectively as that of a corporation. The Dragon Head was reckoned to have been in office for about thirty years. A truly well-established figure, he sat as chairman of a small central committee with eight advisers. They did not control criminal activity but society management as a whole in which the Dragon Head was very active. Everyday control was maintained by lesser officials, referred to as Responsible People. Even minor infringements of behaviour, which in other societies would be ignored or dealt with by a Red Pole, were put before the committee. They commanded respect, gained loyalty and were feared.

It was not long before the police investigators discovered the identity of the Dragon Head. His name was Heung Wah-yim.

Heung was born in Hong Kong in 1932. According to police intelligence, he had two wives and, according to Chinese custom, kept a concubine. By his first wife, Lui Hang-wah, with whom he lived, he had four children, the eldest being a daughter, Anita Heung Wing-yee. The second wife, Fong Chu, whom he visited daily, bore him a son, whilst the concubine, Li Hsiu-mei, whom he visited three or four times a week, gave him two more children, a daughter and a son, who were, in 1987, both small children. He had no criminal record of any sort and worked as a senior clerk with Samuel Soo and Company, a well-known firm of solicitors with offices on the sixteenth floor of the Car Po Commercial Building in Pottinger Street, in the skyscraper heart of multinational, corporate Central District. Heung, who was not an articled or accredited law clerk, maintained his own office

317

within the law firm and had a number of junior clerks working for him.

His business interests were wide ranging. He was a shareholding director of Fair Finance Company, a legal savings and loans firm with offices in the Golden Hill Commercial Building in Argyle Street, Kowloon. Heung's son was the manager. It was thought that most of the company's transactions were with San Yee On members, for the police discovered that members were allowed to borrow up to HK$10,000 without collateral and at low interest rates. In addition, Heung owned the Yee Hing Lok Kee mahjong school in Kowloon City, which his father had founded in 1951. The accounts were maintained by his daughter, Anita, who also worked for Fair Finance. The annual profit from the mahjong school was estimated to be around HK$2.5 million but only about $60,000 was declared for tax purposes.

Like many Triad officers, Heung moved in society circles in which he was seen as a benevolent philanthropist. In 1978, he was made a full member of the Royal Hong Kong Jockey Club, was elected chairman of the Lions' Club in the New Territories in 1986, was president of the Ten Districts of Wai Chow Association (a benevolent clan organization) and honourable chairman of the Association of Hoi Fung Residents in Hong Kong. The estimate that he had been the Dragon Head for thirty years proved to be conservative, for he had succeeded to the position in 1953 when his father, Heung Chin, the post-war reviver of the Yee On guild, was one of those deported. When that society disintegrated on Heung Chin's departure, it was Heung Wah-yim who reunited it with the San prefix.

Intelligence suggested that a list of members was kept by Heung Wah-yim, another list being maintained by a son-in-law, Cheung Leung-sing. It was reasonably suspected that Heung's list would be stored in his office at the law firm, so his office hours were carefully monitored. Any raid had to take place whilst he was at work. It was discovered that he could be counted on being at his desk between 3.30 p.m. and 5.30 p.m. every weekday.

The operation was timed to start at 4 p.m. on 1 April 1987: the date was specifically chosen for its irony by the officer in charge, Senior Superintendent Michael Horner. Eighteen teams were assembled, to hit thirty-five target premises. All those arrested were to be taken not to local police stations but to two centres: those captured on Hong Kong island would go to May House, in the police headquarters complex in Wanchai, whilst those apprehended in Kowloon would be sent to Wong Tai Sin police station. In both locations, specifically briefed officers of the Criminal Intelligence Bureau would be in charge. To maintain security, no-one was informed of their target until zero hour because it was known that, although the police were not nearly as corrupt as in the past, there was still a small number of Triad officers on the force, several of these San Yee On members.

When the raids began, seemingly innocuous but incongruous items were unearthed in a Kowloon apartment owned by one Chan Kai, a member since 1947. He already had several convictions for being a Triad, dating from 1980 when he was arrested for officiating at a ceremony. One of Heung's central committee, he was a former Incense Master, now in semi-retirement yet still very much involved. He was the teacher of ritual to office-bearers going overseas to set up branch societies, issued membership numbers and acted as an inter-society arbitrator. Discovered in Chan's home were sheets of red paper, scarlet cloth, vermilion ribbon, goldleaf, two cassette tapes and a hula hoop. These all looked innocent enough. It was claimed the hula hoop belonged to his granddaughter, but it was wrapped in red and white tape and, with the other items, could have been part of a Triad ritual kit. The cassettes contained, amongst other tracks, a number of Hung League poems recited by Chan and another San Yee On official, Lam King, and his wife.

Another target individual was Kong Kwai-wing, known to San Yee On members as Kong Chun-hung. He, like Heung, had no criminal record but was the current Incense Master. He was arrested that evening outside 322 Ma Tau Wai Road in Kowloon, where he owned an apartment on the second floor. A search of the flat produced some objects of use in ceremonies and three booklets of Triad poems. It also produced a bank deposit-box key. The next day, the police took Kong to the Liu Chong Hing Bank in Kowloon City: deposit box 7697 contained thirteen Triad poetry books.

The main target was, of course, Heung Wah-yim. Horner led a team of eight officers to the premises of Samuel Soo and Company. Heung was seated at his desk as Horner presented a search warrant and Detective Inspector Peter Ip Pau-fuk cautioned him, declaring he was going to effect his arrest as a San Yee On official. The search produced a large number of relevant documents. A metal seal, engraved with the word Heung and five characters for the word On, was also found with some red packets upon which the seal had been impressed. A supposed membership list was discovered, but it was not a proven list. The police had to be able to show incontrovertibly that it was a San Yee On membership roster; there was no way of telling until a police informer, Chung Kin-ling, was contacted.

Chung had joined the Hong Kong police in 1977 but had been dismissed in 1981 for disobeying an order. Through a contact he had made whilst in police service, he was introduced to Tam Wai-ming, a San Yee On official and manager of the Fuk Wah Kok Fraternal Association and Sweden Association, which operated a massage parlour in Kimberley Road, just off Nathan Road, Kowloon's main street and famous tourist shopping drag. Tam employed him as a door usher. Through this connection, he came to know a large number of San Yee On members and their business in Tsim Sha Tsui, running protection rackets and vice. Late in 1981, he was initiated into the San Yee On and told that the Dragon Head was Heung Wah-yim, nicknamed Sze Ngan Lo, or Four-eyes Man. Now a 49, Chung took part in gang fights and, when the massage parlour lost its trading licence, joined the San Yee On illegal gambling network.

Early in 1983, Chung was taken to the offices of Samuel Soo and Company and introduced to Heung Wah-yim, who often interviewed new members there. Afterwards, Chung attended a number of initiation ceremonies and seemed set for a solid Triad career. Yet it was not to be. All the while he was working for the Triads, Chung held down a string of legal jobs as an office clerk. He also started gambling in San Yee On gaming establishments, which led to a quarrel with another San Yee On member, Ma Tak, who started to threaten him. Chung

321

grew frightened, quit his job and went into hiding. Ma put it about that if he was seen, he'd be chopped. Fearing for his life, Chung went to the police and turned informer in January 1986. It was he who confirmed the membership list.

Another valuable arrest was that of Heung's son-in-law, Edmund Cheung Leung-sing. Born in 1950, he was the son of the Hon. Cheung Yan-lung, OBE, a justice of the peace and member of the Legislative Council, Hong Kong's 'parliament'. Cheung Leung-sing, a director of one of his father's businesses, the Lica Property Management Company, had a criminal record, for he had been arrested in 1975 in Vancouver and sentenced to twelve years' imprisonment for conspiracy to traffic in narcotics. He served six years, was released on parole and deported.

Cheung was apprehended in the coffee shop of the five-star Shangri-La Hotel in Tsim Sha Tsui East, Kowloon, an area 'owned' by the San Yee On. He was taken to the property management firm's offices in the Bank Centre at 636 Nathan Road. A search of the office safe, to which Cheung held the only key, produced San Yee On membership lists. He was charged with assisting the management of a Triad society and brought before Senior Superintendent Horner, who asked him if he remembered their previous meeting. Cheung made no response until Horner reminded him. He had testified against him in Vancouver. On asking him how much time he thought he'd serve on this occasion, Cheung broke down.

Others were arrested, including David Heung Chin-sing, Heung Wah-yim's son and manager of Fair Finance. He denied everything, but three teenage San Yee On recruits made statements to the effect that David Heung had admitted to them that he was a Red Pole and helped arrange their initiation.

In all, eleven defendants were charged under the Societies Ordinance. On 24 June they were committed for trial.

Heung stolidly maintained that he was not a member of a Triad society but admitted knowing a number of San Yee On men because his solicitor employer represented them. He denied that most of the seized papers were his and discounted the information on those proved to belong to him. A Triad expert claimed the seal was a San Yee On Dragon Head's chop with Heung's name on it. Additionally, Heung's fingerprints were found not only on the membership lists in his office but also on those found in Cheung's safe. When the informer, Chung Kin-ling, took the stand, he more or less sealed the defendants' fate. The teenagers added their evidence and the police produced surveillance photographs to prove association.

At the end of the trial, in January 1988, a large number of the charges were successful. Heung Wah-yim was sentenced to seven years' imprisonment. Along with the other defendants, he appealed. The appeal judge, Sir Yang Ti-liang, ruled the membership list inadmissible because the eye-witnesses were unqualified to authenticate it, this despite the fact that one of them was a police officer with over thirty years' Triad crime experience. He further dismissed the testimony of two of the accused, stating that they could not substantiate each other's statements as they were accomplices in the same crime. To the extreme fury of the police, Heung and his fellow accused were released after serving about two years of their sentences.

Heung may have won on appeal, and the Triads certainly learned the lesson that the keeping of uncoded records was foolish, but the police won the day. Once again, they had successfully brought to book the senior members of a Triad society, causing it to lose considerable face.

Within three months of Heung's starting his sentence, another Triad crackdown was organized. In March 1988, police raided nightclubs and vice establishments, questioning 17,000 people. In the early hours of 3 July, 750 premises were raided with 13,000 people taken in for questioning. The eight-hour operation, personally commanded by the acting assistant commissioner of police, John Shepars, concentrated on the specific Triad domains of Mong Kok and Yau Mai Tei in Kowloon, a stronghold of the 14K, and Wanchai, where the San Yee On operated. Seventy arrests were made, including eleven men on the wanted list. Intelligence identified eleven Triad groups at work in Wanchai, the San Yee On the largest with the Wo Hop To in second place, extorting over 200 businesses. The police closed down a large number of vice and other illegal enterprises, disrupting but only temporarily denting Triad business. These successes were however instrumental in forcing Triads to abandon their traditional elaborate ceremonies in order to avoid detection.

Anti-Triad police campaigns in Hong Kong have continued through the 1990s, for Triad crime remains prevalent and successful, impinging itself upon every level of society, from the extortion of street traders to the employment of law clerks in solicitors' offices. It is not

324

unreasonably believed that virtually every single law firm in Hong Kong has a Triad member on its staff who is frequently responsible for bringing business to the firm. He is often a senior clerk. However, unlike in Britain, for example, where barristers seek briefs through solicitors' clerks, in Hong Kong the brief must be acquired from and signed by the solicitor himself, not merely his clerk. It still follows of course that Triads are instrumental in acquiring legal representation, often to the benefit of their society brethren, simply because of the close relationship between a solicitor and his senior staff. It is also not unknown for some solicitors themselves to have close Triad connections and a number are non-criminal members of various societies.

There remains, nevertheless, still much controversy over the Triads. Membership numbers are, for instance, the subject of debate. The DEA claims there are between 150,000 and 250,000 active members in the territory, but Hong Kong police estimates do not run as high.

The make-up of Triad societies is also subject to wide interpretation, with some observers claiming they are as tightly knit as Mafia 'families' whilst others declare they consist of up to 100 disparate gangs. The truth is that the Triads still consist of three main groups. These are the 14K, with twenty sub-groups such as the infamous Ngai; the Wo group, with twelve factions including the Wo Shing Wo and Wo On Lok; and the Teochiu societies, with six subdivisions of which the San Yee On is the biggest and best known. In addition, there are four other distinct society groups totalling thirteen societies, with three other small societies which are unaffiliated. All are criminal.

Attacks on individuals are, as they have long been, common. In May 1996, retribution was taken out on Leung Tin-wai, the proprietor of a new magazine, *Surprise Weekly*, which published an article on Triads. Leung was accosted by two men and dragged into his editorial office where one of them severed his left forearm with a meat cleaver; it was subsequently sewn back on in a seventeen-hour operation. Despite Leung and his staff being able to give an adequate description of the main attacker, and a reward of HK$3.8 million being offered by fellow senior journalists, no arrests have been made. Another attack, in the summer of 1998, was made upon the well known and outspokenly anti-Triad radio chat show host, Albert Cheng King-hon, who suffered severe injuries which have left him permanently partially crippled.

As a result of such attacks, accusations of Hong Kong police complacency are not uncommon. Whatever the truth, there is a very significant Triad presence and, unlike any other place on earth, membership is virtually essential for anyone seeking to engage in a career in organized criminal activity.

3

TIGERS, TIN MINES AND TRIADS

Although over the last 150 years Hong Kong has without doubt given the Triads a secure base, it has by no means been their headquarters; for, as the Chinese diaspora expanded around the world from the middle of the nineteenth century, the Triads inevitably travelled with it.

The first region of expansion was South-east Asia. As Chinese merchants spread across the islands of Indonesia, Borneo, the Philippines, Irian Jaya and Papua New Guinea, into the Malay peninsula and Indochina throughout the nineteenth century, they took with them coolies, for wherever they went the merchants preferred to have their own countrymen working for them. When Western colonialism reached the Far East, the number of coolie migrants increased, tens of thousands working the plantations and mines, docks and railways. They dug ditches and paved roads, served as crew on colonial shipping lines and as domestic servants, and whatever work the locals would not do they did.

With the coolies came the Triads. At first, they were not criminal syndicates but societies which saw to the coolies' needs, bailed them out of trouble, loaned them

327

money and gave them a sense of identity and a link to their past. Some even arranged for the bones of the dead to be transported back to China for burial. Their influence became considerable. In the Dutch settlements of Indonesia, Thailand and Vietnam they were at the centre of Chinese social life. By 1900, for example, there were over 200 societies in Saigon alone, where they were known as Nghia Hoa, Thien-dia-hoi, or Nhon-hoa-duong, Vietnamese for Righteous Harmony, Heaven and Earth Society and Virtue and Equity Association respectively. They were similar to the Triad societies of China, with similar religious beliefs and rituals, but with a political agenda, to drive out the oppressive French colonialists who, unlike the paternalistic British or trade-hungry Dutch, were cruel colonial masters.

It was not long before the Triads started to become criminal, preying upon their own race, selling them opium, lending them money at usurious rates, providing them with women and controlling their employment. They helped Chinese escape from the law and offered protection not just to Chinese but to colonial businesses as well. This pattern was repeated wherever they went.

The Malay peninsula was the first heavily settled destination for the Chinese, who were not new to it, having traded there for centuries. Their first permanent settlement had been at Palembang on Sumatra in 1349. At about the same time, they set up a trading post in what is now Singapore and, by the time the Portuguese arrived in 1511, were trading in Malacca, which they had colonized by 1641 when the Dutch arrived.

The main influx of Chinese began in the 1820s, when thousands went to Assam to work and die in the tea plantations. Mainly male, they had two reasons to migrate. Conditions in China were appalling, landlords charging exorbitant rents, taxation crippling and starvation common. Twenty-five years later, with forests across South-east Asia being felled for timber and cleared for agricultural use, hundreds of thousands more arrived to slave in the rubber plantations and tin mines. By 1900, there were 60,000 Chinese living in Rangoon, 120,000 in Saigon and 200,000 in Bangkok, whilst in Singapore they were the racial majority. Triad societies looked after them and exploited them.

Most migrants came from Fujian and Guangdong, especially the Sam Yap or Sze Yap. From the start, they were exploited by Triad-controlled coolie travel agents and foreign ships' captains, of whom more than a third were Americans, many experienced Negro slavers; the immigrant business was colloquially called the Pig Trade. The migrants, crammed into corrals like animals, were regarded as a commodity. The British consul in Guangzhou reported in 1852 how they were frequently painted with letters like cattle, according to their destinations: P, C or S meant Peru, California or the Sandwich Islands. Over 95 per cent were indentured workers who had paid for their passage with money advanced against their salary by their eventual employers or by Triad moneylenders. The remaining 5 per cent consisted of criminals, deportees or kidnap victims, hence the derivation of the verb 'to shanghai' meaning to kidnap. The coolie ships were grim but not illegal, for the coolies, having paid their fares, were not technically slaves under international law. Many died in transit. The *John Calvin*, a British transport, lost 50 per cent of its passengers on one trip; 40 per cent mortality rates were common. Some ships carried women, although, under Chinese law, females were forbidden to emigrate; the Triads, however, supplied some to foreign employers as whores to entice the coolies to stay in their destination countries. It was thought that if they had female companionship, they would not yearn to return to China. Most of the women were either *mu tsai* or kidnapped, some little more than children. Another British vessel, *Inglewood*, hove to off Xiamen in 1855 with a cargo of girls under eight years old: the crew refused to sail with them. The British government in Hong Kong tried to control the trade with the Chinese Passengers Act of 1855, but it was ineffectual, the coolie agents and Triads simply moving away from the colony.

Once abroad, Chinese emigrants lived miserable existences. They were worked for long hours, often until they dropped dead; they pined for China, missed Chinese female company and culture. The Triad societies addressed these longings, importing not only whores but also opium, which relieved the pain of physical labour, counteracted malaria, suppressed sexual desire and reduced homesickness with its knack of making strange places seem familiar. Employers made no effort to stamp out the Triads for they kept their workers going.

The early Portuguese administrators in Malaya did not seek to rule over the Chinese but governed them through what was called the Kapitan system, begun in Malacca in the 1580s, whereby the Chinese ran their own social affairs under a *kapitan*, a Portuguese-appointed community headman. He was more an administrator than a ruler, although the Chinese regarded him as they would have done a mandarin in China. His word was law and he was a conduit of communication between the Chinese and the colonial powers. The system was extended by the British when they took over Malaya, the 'captain' becoming a magistrate who arbitrated over social disputes, oversaw the settlement of debts and acted as a lower court to the British magistracy. His word was considered final, as the Chinese were reluctant to go to European court officers: it was deemed better to sort out their problems with their own kind. The system ran until 1825, when it was replaced by the *t'ing chu* system. A *t'ing chu*, or Temple Master, was an elected leader chosen by prominent Chinese centred upon a local temple.

In theory, the *kapitan*s were Chinese sub-rulers, but in fact they were not, for they had problems that the foreign colonials did not appreciate. The Chinese communities were disparate groups from different clans and regions of China, each with individual customs and languages. There needed to be a mechanism of unity which over-rode these differences. The Triad societies provided it. Although some were clan- or place-based, many were not, being brotherhoods open to any Chinese except those barred by profession. Sedan-chair and rickshaw coolies, gravediggers, undertakers and, ironically, brothel-owners were excluded. The *kapitan*s and the *t'ing chu*s delegated responsibility for ruling to the societies, the *shan chu*s becoming their proxies. Only where Chinese communities were homogeneous, such as in northern Burma, were the Triads unimportant. Elsewhere, indirect rule was responsible for their emergence.

The influential *kapitan*s, known as *liutenant*s, *kapitein*s or *majoor*s in the Dutch East Indies and as *nai am phoe jek* in

Thailand, were frequently wealthy, for they were in a position to control government contracts which they 'sold' for favours in exchange for kickbacks, usually to Triads. Many were senior Triad officials and, in time, the differentiation between *kapitan* and *shan chu* was indistinguishable.

At first, the Triad societies operated openly, only their rituals secret. They were publicly registered as charitable societies, looking after new arrivals and often arranging their passage from China in tandem with societies back home. Membership was little short of obligatory. In 1795, the British authorities in Malacca found every Chinese in the settlement was a Triad. When Stamford Raffles founded Singapore in 1819, Chinese coolies flocked there to work, all of them Triad members. Within ten years, the embryonic city state was the Triad centre for the entire Malay peninsula.

As Malaya opened up, demand for labour escalated. The mine-owners and rubber planters relied upon Triad Chinese coolie importers to supply their workforce. By 1865, the Triads had the monopoly. One coolie importer, Cho Kim-siang, was head of the Ghee Hin, a Cantonese Triad society with branches all over Malaya and centred on Singapore. He represented a dozen European companies, his followers incarcerating the coolies in lodging houses until they were sold on and subsequently policing them to ensure they did not abscond. If they went to a Chinese employer, they were required to speak his dialect and were obliged to join his Triad society as a condition of employment. To Europeans, they were sold at random. Few could change jobs, for they were indentured and in debt, sometimes for years on end.

The first Triad society in Singapore was recorded in 1830, its members mostly political malcontents in self-imposed exile. They called themselves the Thian-ti-hui. Europeans called them 'hueys' or 'hooeys', the name becoming the generic term for Triads in Malaya. Needing income, they extorted Chinese and foreign businesses, some Europeans reportedly joining them to avoid trouble. Living on remote plantations or tin mines, it was the only way a foreigner could ensure his personal security and the welfare of his business.

In 1841, the first study of Triad societies in Malaya appeared. Written by Lieutenant Newbold and Major Wilson and published in London, it was a paper entitled, 'The Chinese Secret Triad Societies of the Tien-Ti Hui'. It raised little more than academic interest in Britain, but in the Far East it was more closely read, for by now the Triads were causing trouble. In 1843, Singaporean Triads were so powerful that Chinese merchants convened a public meeting at which two resolutions were agreed. The first stated quite bluntly:

> it is an understood fact that many of the Chinese shop-keepers and traders in the town, particularly the native-born subjects of China, pay regular sums to the Hueys or Brotherhoods (organised associations of Chinese, often for unlawful purposes) as protection money for their own property, or as a contribution in the nature of blackmail, and that it rarely or never happens that the Chinese are themselves sufferers from the depredations complained of . . . it is highly expedient a law should be passed having for its object the suppression of these brotherhoods . . .

Legislation was passed, but it was futile and for years Singapore was intermittently plagued by riots, some anti-British, complaining at the lack of efficient Triad policing, but most of them either anti-Triad or provoked by inter-society rivalries.

One cause of rioting was the Triads' animosity towards Roman Catholicism, which had gained many converts in Singapore and the hinterland of Malaya. They objected to Christianity partly on semi-patriotic grounds, because it was the underlying force in the Taiping Rebellion which was currently tearing China asunder, and partly because it undermined their authority exercised through the *t'ing chu*. At first they attacked Chinese Christians, but when the Europeans came to their defence, the Triads consequently pitted themselves against the colonial powers. Rioting broke out in 1851. An eyewitness recorded the fate of a Christian Chinese called Tan Ah Choon, who received warning that his plantation had been targeted by the mob.

[He] took all the money he could collect, amounting to more than $80, and two piculs of white pepper, and departed for the town with two or three coolies, but was stopped near Amokiah by some Chinese, who seized and carried him into the jungle with the decided intention to murder him after having robbed him. The coolies escaped and reported the fact; on which Mr. Dunman with a number of peons went himself in search. On the road a man informed him that Tan Ah Choon had been carried to Loh Siah's plantation. The chase was continued, some bangsals were passed, where Chinese were gambling to their hearts' content; and Mr. Dunman finally succeeded in delivering Tan Ah Choon, who was in the custody of three of his captors in Loh Siah's premises, who himself was secured. The other criminals escaped, having been informed by the calls and cries of the nearest neighbours of the approach of the police. Here is a most visible proof of the effects of the power of the Hoe [Triads]. A man is kidnapped, carried through some crowds of Chinese, without any person interfering to prevent the crime, and these same men save the criminals by their calls and signals. Tan Ah Choon's plantation has since been robbed of nearly all its contents.

The 1851 riots were suppressed, the Triads losing face and forced to compensate every Chinese Christian they had attacked with M$1,500. Yet, despite their defeat, they did not lose members: indeed, their numbers grew as the Taiping Rebellion drove thousands of Chinese overseas. Well over 10,000 arrived legally each year from 1852 to 1860 in Singapore alone. How many arrived illegally is inestimable.

Three years later, rioting broke out again over a disagreement in the rice trade and escalated into internecine warfare. The Royal Marines reinforced the police and the riots were put down, only to flare up spasmodically until October 1863, when a gang war developed over the control of prostitutes in Singapore. This confrontation was cleverly defeated by a British magistrate called Read, who swore in several dozen Triad leaders as special constables. After thirty-six hours on patrol with regular forces, the special constables were exhausted and asked leave to return to tend to their businesses for the safety of which they feared in their absence. Read stated that they could be stood down when the rioting ended. It promptly did. Before disbanding his criminal cops, he declared that, if rioting occurred again, every Triad member would be sentenced to two dozen lashes on the buttocks: the stinging pain, Read knew, would be as nothing to the loss of face. Shortly afterwards, the Singaporean press announced that Tan Wee Kow, one of the special constables, had been banished from the Triads.

That same year, gang warfare erupted in Penang between the Ghee Hin and the Toh Peh Kong, with two non-Chinese Malay societies, the Red Flag Society and the White Flag Society, joining in the fray. After ten days, the fighting subsided when the governor of the Straits Settlements, Colonel Archibald Anson, acting as ombudsman, brokered a peace then fined each society M$5,000, simultaneously building fortified police posts in the native quarters of the settlement. He added insult to injury by making the societies pay reparations to merchants whose property had been damaged.

The Penang riots caused the instigation of a commission which outlined Triad activities, looked into their history, assessed their numbers (it was reckoned the Ghee Hin was the largest with 125,000 members), studied society interaction and drew the conclusion that the riots had started as a conflict between the two Malay societies, which were Muslim, and subsequently stirred up by the Triads, whose organization and discipline were reported to be as complete as 'any disciplined force of the Government'. The commission suggested the suppression or registration of Triad societies, the prohibition of oath-taking, the banning of processions and the obligation of legal liability for criminal damage. Registration was the chosen path, the published listings giving not only office-bearers' names but also their addresses and occupations; they included a gambling-den owner, opium-divan operator, doctor, theatre manager, geomancer, gunsmith and coffin-maker.

Registration publicized the societies, making them marginally less secret, but it did nothing to weaken them. The Larut Wars of 1872–4 showed just how powerful they remained.

As Malaya's tin-mining industry grew, large numbers of migrants arrived, until, by 1871, over 40,000 worked for predominantly Chinese mine-owners, who were extremely affluent. Triads put the squeeze on these wealthy mine-owners, organizing occasional worker unrest, 'protecting' payroll deliveries and 'guarding' tin-ore shipments. In this rich environment, one society was forever trying to muscle in on another's business, the situation exacerbated by inter-mine rivalries: the owners of some of the biggest mines were also senior Triads, most exercising influence in high places.

Malaya was under British colonial rule, but consisted not of a single colony but a confederation of sultanates known collectively as the Straits Settlements. The rulers collected royalties from the mines in their kingdoms and the Triads allied themselves to sultans for protection, often paying them kickbacks and maintaining a status quo. Two such alliances were held by the Ghee Hin and Hokkienese Hai San societies.

The status quo was preserved until in 1872 the succession to the throne of Perak came in doubt. Each society sided with a different pretender and war broke out, fuelled by a longstanding battle of wills between the societies over which owned water rights, essential for driving ore-crushing machinery, and rights of way over jungle paths. What tipped the balance was the importation of strong-arm thugs from Penang by the Hai San in an attempt to oust the competition.

The Ghee Hin erected stockades on the Larut River, blockading it and boarding passing vessels, robbing them or charging them a toll. The Hai San attacked. The war was bloody and could have dragged on for years were it not for Captain Speedy of the Strait Settlements police, who resigned his commission to be employed by the Hai San-backed pretender. With his finance, Speedy sailed for India, raising a mercenary army of Pathans and Sikhs renowned for their fighting skills. On his return, he destroyed the Ghee Hin river stockades. Worried at this turn of events, the colonial government realized it had to act before the war spilled over into the neighbouring British settlement of Penang and ordered several gunboats up the Larut. The Ghee Hin sent to China for reinforcements. The war raged until the British called a council in January 1874 on an island off the coast. Present were local rulers, the Hai San and Ghee Hin leaders and a newly appointed British Resident for the area, whose assistant was none other than Captain Speedy. Peace was brokered, the Triads taking an active part in governmental decision-making and gaining much face.

By the 1870s, the population of Malaya was over a quarter Chinese: in some places, they outnumbered Malays. This potentially explosive situation was highlighted in 1876 by a British colonial civil servant who wrote a long article on the subject in the influential

338

Fraser's Magazine. W. A. Pickering, an Oriental scholar, understood the Chinese and was the first person to really study the Triad threat. He wrote:

> We cannot shut our eyes to the fact that peace in the Malay states means a large influx of Chinese; this involves our interference to keep the peace. The men who find the capital for mining or agricultural purposes are, for the most part, born or naturalized British subjects, and the labourers are all connected with our colonies by the secret societies, so that any disturbance in the Native States injures the trade of our people, and endangers the good order and tranquillity of our settlements. Furthermore, we have a moral duty to protect the Malays from majorities of Chinese, and to protect the turbulent Chinese from massacring each other.

Pickering was subsequently appointed protector of the Chinese and set about trying to stop coolie exploitation by both employers and Triads. He arbitrated in inter-Triad society arguments, acted as a go-between in conflicts between different clan groupings, and came to be considered by all Chinese as a fair, unbiased and highly regarded ombudsman to whom they could turn instead of Triad leaders and the *t'ing chu*.

Within weeks of the publication of Pickering's article, a British official, Captain Lloyd, was found chopped to death with an axe in Perak. It was a Triad murder, organized by a society called the Ho Seng, for which a Chinese was hanged. He was almost certainly a scapegoat put up by the society to appease the authorities. Hugh Low, the British Resident in Perak, reported that the whole coast of Perak is in possession of the Ho Seng Society, from the Krian to the mouth of the Bernam River, and they have an idea that having established themselves, as they allege, without the assistance of Government, the Government had no right to tax them or impose regulations for their guidance. The Government of Perak was defied by two of these communities in 1877, but successfully vindicated its authority, and the belief is current in Larut that discontent at the dues charged at Pangkor had engendered a feeling of resentment which has encouraged the perpetration of crime.

Lloyd's assassination, unusual in that the Triads rarely risked killing a European for fear of a backlash, was intended to teach the British a lesson not to interfere in Triad affairs.

In 1884, Perak was given its own specific Protector of the Chinese, Captain Schultz, who liaised with the Triads but had little effect upon the local murder rate amongst the Chinese, which was, as he put it, due to

> the pernicious influence of secret societies which through their perfect organization for evil have caused petty quarrels and jealousy between individual members of rival societies to develop into serious breaches of the peace resulting in murder, arson, and destruction of valuable property.

Schultz's failure was hardly of his own doing. He was at a disadvantage from the start. The Triads did not want him interfering, the ordinary Chinese were afraid to approach him and, besides that, there were Triad societies in his domain of which he was quite unaware. Perak consisting mostly of jungle, there was little way the authorities could keep track of society activities. The Hok Beng Society from Malacca initiated 2,000 members in Selangor before the police had even heard of them. Schultz realized that society registration was pointless. He wanted the Triads outlawed, the carrying of a membership certificate to be indictable.

> These secret societies [he wrote] consider the Native States, especially Perak, as a happy hunting ground from which they derive a very considerable portion of their exceedingly large income: so tempting is this to them that notwithstanding the considerable risk to their emissaries and agents in carrying on their work here, any number of these latter over-run the State secretly inducing their countrymen to join their societies. Not content with doing this, in order to increase their numbers and their revenue, they have lately, I understand, relaxed their own rules with this object in view, by not making it a condition any more that the candidates from the Native States who are willing to enter the Societies must come over to Penang to be initiated. Their travelling agents or Secret Masters have power to hold lodges in the State and there to make the candidates acquainted with the necessary signs and take the oath from them.

Schultz's suggestions came into force in August 1889. Triad membership, the conducting of rituals and the ownership of Triad paraphernalia and documents resulted in fines, imprisonment, caning, deportation and the seizure of assets. The new laws achieved nothing. In Perak,

9,447 miners were found to be Ghee Hin members, 5,394 Hai San men. Fewer than 100 were unaffiliated.

As British-administered Malaya thrived, so there was an increase in opportunity for criminal activity. The Triads added armed and highway robbery, kidnapping and piracy to their usual businesses of extortion, prostitution, illegal gambling, labour control and opium. Although the British gave them an affluent colonial climate in which to operate, many societies were distinctly anti-British, a stance they maintained until independence in 1957. It was to their advantage to be seen as anti-imperialist because they were – making up one third of the Malayan population – on shifting political sands.

Malaya was racially diverse, religiously divergent and politically divided. The Chinese were considered by the Malays to be as much intruders as the Europeans. The Chinese were Buddhist or Taoist whilst the Malays were mostly Muslim. They had different customs, different languages and were opportunist, the Malays regarding them as many Europeans regarded Jews: pushy, money-conscious upstarts who kept to themselves, looked after their own and had a secret agenda which included taking over business to the exclusion of the indigenous people.

Lumped together with the British, the Chinese had to do something to gain face and establish themselves. They therefore sided with the Malays in regarding the British as colonial despots. The Chinese considered themselves exploited by the British, the Malays believing they were being oppressed. Whenever nationalism came to the fore, the Triads supported the Chinese community to do all they could to destabilize the British.

342

The Chinese were not the only ones to have secret societies. The Malays had their own religious *jema'ah*, known in English as 'flag societies' because they assembled under religious banners. Although proscribed, they were never as much trouble as the Triads and, by 1900, had coalesced into just two exclusively non-Chinese groups in Penang, the Red Flag with headquarters in Acheen Street and the White Flag.

During the First World War, the Triad societies in Malaya did little other than carry on their criminal activities. The war did not affect the Far Eastern colonies, although the British did have a number of Malay and Hong Kong Chinese coolie battalions in the mud of Flanders. They were not used as combatants but as construction workers, building bridges, repairing salients, excavating trenches, digging graves, collecting corpses and making duck-boards. Each unit was comprised of Chinese from a similar background and many if not all were Triad members. They served with stoicism, occasionally gallantry, and were utterly reliable, many never returning to be buried, as they would have wished, in the land of their ancestors.

By 1920, the main Chinese societies in Malaya and Singapore were the Tsung Fak, Hai San, Tsung Sun Kongsi and San (new) Ghee Hin. This last was the largest and most powerful, having been formed in 1905 out of the Ghee Hin. The societies were criminally very active, but they were beginning to lose their roots and traditions, trimming rituals, shortening and disguising membership documents and reducing meetings to avoid detection.

A new development occurred in the 1920s, when the Muslim flag societies began to come together with the

343

Triads. A society with Malay and Chinese membership was found operating in 1923 in Johor Baharu, concentrating on robbery in nearby Singapore. The White Flag Society, originally a benevolent institution for Tamils and Muslims from Madras who had come to Malaya as labourers and traders, and primarily concerned with conducting religious ceremonies, funerals and circumcisions, reached a secret agreement with the San Ghee Hin in Singapore. Thereafter, the White Flag Society gradually divested itself of its social and religious *raisons d'être* and became criminal, the Chinese taking it over to corrupt the mainly non-Chinese Malay police. The Red Flag Society was similarly absorbed by the Ghee Hok, rivals of the Ghee Hin.

The flag societies had a lot in common with the Triads, which made some observers believe they had been founded by Chinese for Muslims. Both conducted semi-religious initiation rituals and members knew each other by a set of seemingly innocuous questions. Whereas a Triad might ask of an acquaintance, 'Have you a mother?' and expect to be told, 'I have five', so a Red Flag Society member might enquire, 'Has your mother old iron?' The flag societies had special handshakes, as freemasons do: a Red Flag greeting pressed a knuckle with the thumb, the common recognition for craft freemasons. When the societies became multi-racial, the Chinese members, who did not customarily shake hands, recognized each other and Muslim brothers by Triad-style hand signs. Even though Chinese dominated the amalgamated societies, allowances were made for Muslims. A Muslim initiate had a copy of the Koran placed upon his head during the oath-taking and pork, a favourite Chinese meat, was excluded from any meals. Much was made of the red and white flags because they were symbolic to the Chinese. Red was the colour of the Hung League, whilst white signified both fealty and mourning, suggestive of the Triad rite whereby an initiate died from his old life to be reborn when entering a society.

By the 1930s, the situation in Malaya was serious, with secret societies under every stone. The Malays, seeing the leverage secret societies could exert, formed their own, partly to make a stand against Chinese power and partly to infiltrate colonial circles in the cause of independence. Autonomous they may have been, but these usually exclusively Muslim societies 'borrowed' Triad ritual: ceremonies took place at night, in the jungle, before an altar upon which a cockerel was sacrificed and its blood drunk from bowls which were subsequently broken. Triad ranks were adopted. The Incense Master was called the *tembaga*, the Malay for copper, the metal from which incense burners were made. The Paper Fan was simply called a *kipas* (Malay for fan), the Grass Sandal was a *kasut* (shoe) and a Red Pole was a *tongkata* (staff). As with the Triads, some societies started out as social organizations but changed. The Darul Ma'amur Football Club, founded in Penang in 1920, became a fully fledged secret society within five years.

Unlike Triad societies in most expatriate Chinese communities, the Malayan Chinese Triads had a political as well as a criminal agenda, which began in July 1905, when Sun Yat-sen arrived in Singapore to raise republican funds. The Chinese community rallied to him with a large sum of money, a good percentage raised by Triad crime. In the spring of 1906, Sun returned to set up a Malayan branch of his Tung-men Hui and, to raise further funds, sold mining rights in China, which he did not own, to Chinese tin-mine owners and republican 'passports', costing S$2 each, which would allow entry to China after the revolution. Both were scams. When the revolution failed to materialize, Sun started to lose support in Singapore, so he decamped to Penang in 1909. Nevertheless, republican feelings were kept alive in Singapore by the Chung Wo, a group of Triad societies which met secretly in, amongst other places, a committee room of the Chinese YMCA: and, when the Wuchang Uprising occurred, thousands joined the Tung-men Hui in a rush of patriotic solidarity.

Although the Triads were proscribed from the turn of the century, little real effort was put into policing them and they were only hit hard when they caused obvious trouble. The result of this *laissez-faire* attitude was that the societies gained an iron grip on almost every aspect of Chinese life in Malaya. Only restrictions on Chinese immigration, which were enforced in 1939 to halt the flow of refugees from the Sino-Japanese War, had any impact upon Triad recruitment figures.

During the Japanese occupation of South-east Asia in the Second World War, the Triads fought the invaders. Whereas in Hong Kong some Triads collaborated, in Malaya, Singapore and Sumatra they became an underground movement aiding any enemy of the occupying Japanese. During the Japanese invasion, they attacked a police post at Selangor, liberating Australian prisoners; eleven Chinese were caught and executed. They blew up bridges on the Kuala Lumpur–Seremban railway: the destruction of the bridge at Bangi led to the revenge massacre of 300 Chinese. With the Japanese victorious,

Triads joined SOE 'left-behind' parties of Chinese and aided Allied agents in the field. Most were recruited through a Chinese in Chongqing called Lim Bo-seng, a Singaporean merchant codenamed Gustavus, who had rallied the Chinese as Singapore was besieged. He was a senior Triad office-bearer. Escaping to India as Singapore fell, he made his way to China to be employed by the Kuomintang General Tai Li. His Gustavus ring of agents, known as Dragons and fluent in Malay, included Wu Chye-sin (a Hokkienese codenamed Ah Ng), who worked under the cover of being a black marketeer in Ipoh and was rumoured to have operated a forge for the Japanese, melting down scrap metal for shipment to Japan. In this occupation, he is believed to have assisted in the smelting of gold looted by the Japanese which was subsequently to form a part of the legendary Yamashita's treasure hoard which was later hidden in the Phillipines. Amongst the other Gustavus members were Lee Han-Kwong (Ah Tsing), who was a fish merchant in Pangkor, Yee Tien-song (Sek Fu), who was a storekeeper in Tapah, Lung Chiu-ying, who ran a coffee shop-cum-tea house in Sigari, Tan Sieng-yang (Ah Lim) and Lim Bo-seng himself, who often went 'into the field'. These men were the most reliable of all SOE agents in Malaya: they were also all Triad members or close affiliates. Many were arrested by the Kempetai: Wu, Tan and Yee survived, but Lim died in Batu Gajah prison in late 1944.

Another important Triad member – or Triad-connected operator: no-one is sure of his allegiances – was Chang Hung, a senior official in the Malayan Communist Party (MCP) and the Anti-Japanese Union and Forces movement (AJUF), which controlled many guerrilla bands throughout Malaya and Sumatra. It was armed and trained by the SOE at the personal request of Lord Mountbatten, the Allied commander-in-chief stationed in Ceylon. After the war, it was discovered that Chang Hung had been backing both horses by passing information to the Japanese: he had over a dozen aliases including, curiously, Mr Wright. It was he who betrayed a large number of guerrilla leaders at a secret conference for which he arrived late, and he tipped off the Japanese about the activities of the SOE's South-east Asian Force 136. After the war, his past was denounced by the MCP. In September 1945, he absconded with most of the MCP funds, never to be heard of again.

After the liberation of Malaya, the Triads started to reorganize and, by 1948, were regarded as a major criminal threat. In the aftermath of the war, they were well armed and dangerous. New firearms laws were quickly ratified to curb them, but shoot-outs between the police and Singaporean Triads became almost weekly occurrences. As the MCP started their anti-British guerrilla war, and the Malayan Emergency was declared, the Triads set up in business selling arms to the Communists and acting as *agents provocateurs* on their behalf, despite the fact that their comrades in China were busy fighting Mao Zedong's Communists. They also spied for them. Most British military establishments employed Chinese domestic servants, of whom a substantial number were Triads, some of whom stole maps or reported overheard conversations. In the isolated rubber plantations, Triads intimidated Chinese workers into reporting the movements of their European employers, many of whom were consequently ambushed and killed.

In Singapore, the British authorities set up Operation Dagger to combat the Triads and, where they came across it, the MCP. The operation ran through to Malaysian independence in 1963. By October 1959, Triad crime was so prevalent that the government proclaimed an amnesty for the estimated 10,000 Triads living in Singapore. The Triad response was an acceleration of kidnappings, assassinations and robberies. Their arrogance was astounding. One Singaporean Triad leader, Oh Kim-kee, even named his gang after himself and was much feared by wealthy Chinese for his ruthlessness, kidnappings and extortion. Oh started out as a petty criminal in the early 1950s and was arrested for robbery in 1953, for which he was sentenced to eight years in Changi prison. On gaining his freedom, he and a fellow inmate called Ko founded the Oh Kim Kee Triad society and, in October 1959, robbed a store. The next February, they held up a European paymaster for the British army called Wetherburn, who was transporting a payroll to a barracks. Wetherburn put up a fight, so Oh shot him in the back, killing him and getting away with S$35,000. With a price on his head, Oh embarked on a kidnapping spree, abducting a rich Chinese merchant called Tan Ling-hung, whose family met the ransom demand. Fired by success, he then kidnapped three more Chinese tycoons. Every crime was planned to the smallest detail. The Singaporean population was outraged, the police under pressure to catch him. Eventually, they tailed him to 134 Sims Avenue, one of the main roads through Singapore, where he was killed, it was reported, with a hot, smoking revolver in either hand. Others followed in his mobster-style footsteps, however, and Malaysian Triads were regarded at that time as the most violent, merciless Chinese gangsters on earth.

Operation Dagger and successive drives did not eradicate the Triads, but they severely weakened them and their criminality altered. By the 1970s, there were only three main societies in Singapore: the Ang Soo Tong, the Guat San Sih and the Sio Gi Ho, the last a unique all-female society engaged in forcing young girls into vice, robbery and blackmail, which was conducted mostly on high-rise urban middle-class housing estates.

In July 1975, the Singaporean police staged a massive anti-Triad operation in which more than 200 suspects were rounded up, many of whom, including the Ang Soo Tong hierarchy, were indicted for a wide range of crimes. The same year, Malaysian police moved against the Triads, capturing a number of senior officials who were sentenced to the penal colony on the island of Palau Jerejak. This concerted drive altered the demography of the Triads in the Malay peninsula. By 1980, the Wah Kee was the dominant society in Kuala Lumpur whilst the Ang Boon Huey held sway in Singapore, Penang, Malacca and Kuantan. Still involved in traditional Triad crimes, they were also major players in the international narcotics trade.

Today, the Triads still operate in Malaysia and are of great concern to both the Malaysian and Singaporean authorities. Nowadays almost exclusively Chinese, they are a source of racial contention. Racial tension between the Malays and the Chinese is subdued but omnipresent, the business acumen of the Chinese resented just as it has

350

been for years. Occasionally, this resentment boils over, as it did in 1969 when a moderate political party won the national elections but were considered by the Chinese to favour Malays. Rioting broke out in Kuala Lumpur. The army was called in and ran roughshod over the Chinese community, the leaders of which called on the Triads for assistance. Unrest continued for several years, eventually petering out as the Chinese gained political concessions. Since the mid-1980s, the Malaysian Triads have become politically active again, supporting Chinese candidates in national elections, much to the chagrin of the Malays.

Elsewhere in South-east Asia, anti-Chinese feeling also occasionally runs high. In Indonesia, the Triads have sided with the outlawed Indonesian Communist Party (PKI) in the hope that they might bring about a swing against the pro-Muslim administration, thus making life easier for the substantial Chinese ethnic minority, and they have aided anti-government causes by supplying weapons, such as to the rebels fighting for autonomy in East Timor. When the Suharto government was overthrown in 1998, there was much civil unrest of which a fair proportion was aimed at the Chinese community. Posters appeared calling them Asian Jews and a number were murdered. Many Chinese-owned businesses were looted or destroyed and a report-edly large number of Chinese women raped by Indonesian rioters. Triad 49s are said to have defended Chinese businesses on occasion but, generally, they kept a low profile, not wishing to draw the attention of the Indonesian security forces.

Stringent laws are now aimed at the Triads, some of them so draconian that they draw complaints from human rights campaigners. In Singapore, where narcotics dealing is countered by a mandatory death sentence, Triads and similar racketeers can be detained without trial. Many languish in jail without having been through a judicial process. This saves the police the effort of finding relevant evidence and risking a case collapsing due to the sudden amnesia or assassination of witnesses. An example of witness execution, intended to discourage others from coming forward, was the killing of Tommy Chui To-yan, an ICAC witness from Hong Kong who was to have testified in a case involving a billion-dollar international cigarette-smuggling ring. His body was found in April 1995 in the sea off Clifford Harbour in Singapore. He had been strangled and facially mutilated, the keys of his Porsche sports car, from which he was abducted, laid out in a certain way to represent a symbol for the Wo On Lok society. A Hong Kong Chinese, Cheung Wai-man, was eventually arrested and prosecuted for conspiracy to murder and sentenced in November, 1998 in Hong Kong to twenty-seven years' imprisonment.

Whilst the Malaysian Triads still run illegal gambling, prostitution and protection rackets, it is on a much smaller scale and they have moved into areas of white-collar crime such as embezzlement and fraud and, more recently, the trade in wildlife products – particularly the big cat parts so sought after by practitioners of traditional Chinese medicine. They import tiger bones, flesh and fat from India and Indonesia and have, according to conservation agencies, been instrumental in bringing the Sumatran tiger to the brink of extinction. Of course, they continue to be important heroin traders. Even the hangman's noose is insufficient deterrent where the Triads are concerned.

4

THE TURNING OF THE TRIAD BUCK

Triad societies today exist to make money for their members. Whatever motivations they had in the past – patriotism, fraternity, religious conviction, political agitation or social conscience – always ran concurrently with turning a dollar. In the last fifty years, the financial incentive has eradicated any other purpose.

Criminal activity breaks down into three more or less distinct varieties: the common street-crime business, larger criminal enterprises and others that are, for want of a better term, corporate. The first is usually conducted by Red Poles and 49s, the second by middle-rank officials backed up by Red Poles and 49s, while the third is the domain of the most senior officials, supported by underlings with specific skills and business associates who are not necessarily Triads. It must be added that not all Red Poles and 49s are, these days, uncouth street thugs carrying weapons. They may be far more adept with a computer than with a meat cleaver.

Triad basic rice-bowl businesses are extensions of the outlawed activities with which they have been engaged for centuries. The most common of these are extortion and protection rackets. No matter where a Triad society exists, it will prey upon Chinese businesses. The *modus operandi* follows an almost textbook routine. A Red Pole, perhaps accompanied by one or two 49s, visits a Chinese business. This may be a restaurant or shop, or it might be a more established company such as an accountancy firm. At first, the Red Pole makes himself known as a customer. For example, he may enter a restaurant, sit down and order a meal. When the bill comes, he will settle it but suggest to the owner that he might like to take out insurance against unseen contingencies. The owner, if he is wise, will agree and thereafter have no choice but to pay a certain sum every week or month to the Red Pole or his representative. If the restaurant starts to do better business, this sum will increase. It may, from the start, be a percentage of the gross income.

Should the owner decide against insurance, the Red Pole will probably just smile and leave. The situation will then escalate. A few nights later, he will return with some 49s. They will take a table and, during the course of their meal, cause trouble. They may be rowdy, start a fight, insult other customers, 'accidentally' drop a serving dish of food upon the carpet, choosing one with a lot of soy or black-bean sauce in it which will stain. Customers will leave, their meals unfinished. The restaurateur will lose face and the reputation of his restaurant will be damaged. Alternatively, the Red Pole may arrange for a Saturday-morning delivery of supplies to be delayed or not turn up at all, thus ruining Saturday-night business. Finally, he may simply send in a dozen 49s one night to smash up, but not destroy, the kitchens. Like all parasites, the Triad makes quite certain he does not kill his host. By the end of a fortnight, the restaurateur has no choice but to pay. If he does not, and continues to hold out or goes to the police, he will be chopped or forced out of business. Or both.

As Triads often control, or are involved in, many Chinese businesses, they are able to twist arms to great effect. In some places, they deliberately control key areas of a trade in order to be able to flex muscle through it. An example exists in the catering trade. Chinese restaurants obtain their supplies from companies specializing in Oriental foodstuffs. One such is bean sprouts, a common ingredient of many dishes. Being fresh, they are not imported but grown in a number of bean-sprout 'farms', usually buildings in which the beans are soaked in water, spread on trays and forced into germination under lights. They are harvested at two days and sold within twenty-four hours, after which they rapidly deteriorate. Triads become involved with the farms, either owning them or, more usually, acting as or controlling the distribution agents. In this way, they command the transportation of bean sprouts, straw mushrooms and other fresh vegetables, glass noodles, steamed bread, fish balls and other specific fresh produce, and can therefore omit certain deliveries to non-compliant restaurateurs.

Restaurants are comparatively easy targets and have been so for decades; so today are Chinese video stores. Wherever there is an expatriate Chinese community, there are video-rental stores providing Chinese entertainment on video cassette or laser disc – usually Chinese television soaps, opera and Hong Kong action movies. These shops are specifically sought by Triads and are not only ripe for protection but also ideal for the distribution of pirated videos and music CDs. Triads approach a store

355

and demand compliance. If they do not get it, they discreetly run a powerful magnet over the shelves. Random videos are 'snowed' and customers become annoyed. The Triads return: comply or the whole stock will be either magnetized or burned. When the proprietor caves in, the Triads not only take a cut of his earnings but also force him to buy or retail counterfeit material. In this way, black money is earned by extortion and dirty money laundered through copied films.

Even supposedly safe companies are not beyond extortion. A Chinese accountancy firm in London was targeted in the 1980s by Triads. The approach was direct: pay a protection fee or have your business ruined. The Chinese partners, believing a professional firm beyond common extortion, refused. The extortionists broke into the offices. They did not destroy computer records or dossiers, nor did they smash the furniture and fittings; instead they stole information which was then leaked back to the accountants' clients. The confidentiality of the accounting firm was compromised, its clients moved to other, non-Chinese firms and the business was forced to close.

In some places, the running of labour markets continues, just as it did in nineteenth-century Hong Kong. However, Triads are now more likely to control services than labour. In Hong Kong, they maintain a high if hidden profile in a wide range of service industries, including the provision of illegal taxis and it was over this that there occurred one of the rare instances of the Triads facing a European other than a police officer. Elsie Tu was born in Newcastle upon Tyne and endowed with native Geordie bull-dog determination. Married to a Chinese, she served for many years as an urban councillor and became famous for championing working-class Chinese. Coming across Triads was unavoidable, and she clashed with them on a number of occasions. Her account of the intimidation of taxi drivers, published in her autobiography, demonstrates how the Triads impose their authority on the streets.

Hong Kong now has the most highly developed public-transport system on earth, but for a long time it was inadequate and led to the appearance of scores of illegal taxis and *pak pai*s, or minibuses. In the late 1960s, illegal transport services were ripe for exploitation and the Triads moved in. Some vehicles were operated by Triads, others through a joint ownership of Triads and police officers. The trade burgeoned and licensed legal taxi drivers began to lose business. Barred from picking up in certain streets, they were frequently harassed or beaten. They were at a further disadvantage as in many locations they were permitted to operate only from ranks, whereas corrupt policemen allowed illegal taxis to pick up fares anywhere. Elsie Tu, armed with photographic proof of police collusion, approached senior police traffic officers but met a stone wall. The traffic division was riddled with corruption to the very top. That nothing was done is hardly surprising, for one of those senior officers to whom Elsie Tu went for action was Peter Godber, who was already taking massive backhanders to ignore the situation. The rackets merely went underground, and continue to prosper. Elsie Tu continued to fight for social injustice and against the Triads and, in 1997, was one of the very few non-Chinese to be included in the post-colonial legislature.

Some labour markets are still Triad-dominated. The Hong Kong construction industry is probably the Triads' richest domain in the world. For forty years Hong Kong has undergone a building boom and the 1997 change of sovereignty seems not yet to have dented it. Skyscrapers go up in record time, land is reclaimed from the sea at the rate of an acre a week, demolition is speedy and effective. However, because of the high cost of land and the need not to tie up investment for any longer than is necessary, most property companies operate as quickly as possible. Time is of the essence – and time is what the Triads own. They charge high premiums to ensure scaffolders arrive on time, cement lorries are not delayed, workers do not fall sick, building materials are not in short supply and concrete is not adulterated with salt to weaken the structure. Until the 1988 economic slowdown, Triads imported labour, especially from China, smuggling illegal immigrants to fill any manpower shortages. It is estimated that up to 12 per cent of the cost of building a Hong Kong skyscraper is written off in kickbacks. With an average skyscraper costing HK$4 billion, the extortion is astronomical. Few property firms will admit to it, but it has been rumoured that some contractors building the new Hong Kong international airport at Chek Lap Kok, the biggest civil-engineering project ever, regularly paid millions of dollars in protection. This does not seem to have protected the project completely: some months before it was completed, it was admitted that about 20 miles of wiring had been stolen from the buildings.

Triad income from construction-industry extortion in Hong Kong cannot be imagined. When it is extended to buildings in Singapore, Jakarta, Bangkok, Manila, Hanoi,

Ho Chi Min City, Shenzhen, Guangzhou, Zhuhai and Macau, the total is beyond estimation.

Another labour market on which the Triads retain a firm grip is that of Hong Kong's substantial, highly successful film industry. With film-making being labour intensive, the merest threat to disrupt a tight filming schedule is usually sufficient to force a producer to pay protection. Location shoots are controlled by 49s, exposed film is 'protected' on its way to the processing laboratories, stars are 'minded' and props are 'insured' by Triads. Studio scene-shifters, carpenters and electricians are subject to Triad-inspired walkouts. Despite all this protection, film shoots are still interrupted because they become targets for one society trying to move in on the lucrative racket of another. It is not unusual for a producer to have to pay off more than one set of protectors.

Not only Chinese film-makers have problems. So do foreign companies using Hong Kong as an exotic location. In 1996, a British Granada television crew came up against the San Yee On while shooting a two-hour special in the highly successful drama series *Cracker*, starring Robbie Coltrane as a maverick forensic psychologist. The location production manager was Neil MacDonald, a former Hong Kong police officer. Whilst filming in Wanchai, MacDonald was abducted in full view of the crew and driven to a restaurant in Kennedy Town, the western end of what had once been Tai Ping Shan. There he was robbed of a Rolex watch and gold chain and ordered to pay HK$4,000 for a round of drinks. When it was discovered that he did not carry sufficient cash – his kidnappers having mistakenly assumed he was a wealthy director or producer rather than the manager – he was divested of some of his clothing, which was sent back to the film crew with the message that if the money was not forthcoming, MacDonald would have his legs broken. The film company paid the 'ransom' and MacDonald was set free.

Throughout the filming, San Yee On 49s periodically demanded 'rent' on the street in which filming was taking place. Cameramen setting up shots were deliberately knocked by passersby. The police were not well pleased: there are codes of practice laid down to prevent the intimidation of film crews, involving the police being informed of locations, police officers attending the shoot to discourage Triads and, in some instances, advance notification being given to Triads so that, although they are not bribed, they are informed of the film company's intention and given the opportunity to 'waive their fee', thus saving face. Yet the Granada team seemingly ignored these provisions and the San Yee On gained much face and pecuniary reward.

Other forms of extortion are more minor but still widespread. Triads, especially in Hong Kong but also in many Chinatowns, often charge parking or delivery fees in streets they control. It is a simple scam. A van arrives in a street to unload at a store. There are no parking spaces. The driver double-parks and a 49 approaches him. Double parking is illegal but, for a fee, the 49 will 'watch out' for a traffic warden. Or there may be a parking space, in which case the 49 will say it is 'reserved' but he can let the van use it for 20 minutes for a charge. Other street-level activities include 'protecting' a parked vehicle from vandalism and charging pavement tax to street hawkers.

In most Far Eastern cities, this is a good money-spinner. Where street stalls are licensed and allocated a regular spot, Triads offer ordinary protection to legal hawkers and enhanced protection for the unlicensed. For a 'service charge', they will watch out for official hawker patrols. If the service is refused, the Triads beat the hawker up, smash his stall then anonymously report him.

Another highly profitable street-level crime is narcotics retailing. In Hong Kong this is a slick operation run by teams of trained 49s using a variety of methods. One is the street-corner pusher, easily spotted by the trained eye but less easily apprehended. Heroin is usually sold in a single dose known as a straw, contained in a 2 cm section of plastic drinking straw, heat-sealed at the ends. It is concealed in the mouth or in the hand, held between thumb and middle finger. At the first sign of danger, it is flicked away and either lost or later retrieved. Skilled pushers can shoot a straw up to 10 metres, in through a tenement window above to a waiting accomplice. Another method of dealing is by telephone order. The addict rings a mobile phone, usually in the possession of a 49 on the move. He takes the order then passes it on over another phone. (Alternatively, the order is placed to a mobile phone in an empty apartment, switched untraceably to call forwarding.) The heroin is then delivered by straw or in plastic envelopes of between 1 and 28 g, in powder or rock form, or in 2 g *po chai* (Chinese traditional medicine) bottles. These methods, or variants of them, are now found the world over.

Nothing is sacrosanct. Even religious festivals, a crucial part of Chinese cultural life, are usurped for profit. At festival time, Triads organize 'donations' from shopkeepers and passersby and take part in temple celebrations. The famous Bun Festival on the Hong Kong island of Cheung Chau was presided over by Teochiu Triads for decades; they still show up today but are more restrained in their donation-gathering. In 1982, at the Tin Hau Festival in Hong Kong's Junk Bay, one of the largest religious festivals on the calendar, two groups of 14K and Wo Shing Wo members turned up, brazenly flaunting specially printed society T-shirts. In the thousands-strong throng, with a minimal police presence, they got away with it.

Triad societies have, of course, long been associated with vice. In the nineteenth and early twentieth century they operated sing-song houses and brothels in all the major Chinese cities, as well as overseas, although it was in Shanghai and, even more so, in Hong Kong that their most famous establishments existed. Today Triad-controlled vice splits into two main categories: the running of brothels or prostitutes, and the production and retailing of pornography.

Until the late 1940s, most prostitution in Hong Kong was based upon either common streetwalkers or 'cat-houses', a euphemism for a bordello which still lingers in Hong Kong, where Upper Lascar Row, now famous for its antique shops, is still locally referred to as Cat Street. Upmarket brothels were run by and catered exclusively for Europeans. Next down the vice ladder were the sing-song girls, who mainly entertained Chinese men with some expatriate European clients. Some brothels for poor Chinese existed, staffed by low-class whores or by those demoted through age or disease from the better establish-

362

ments. The streetwalkers were the most common prostitutes, run by pimps who 'protected' them, found them customers, provided premises and paid off the police to leave them alone. Prostitutes for servicemen and the like were traditional streetwalkers who hung around the gates to HMS *Tamar*, the British naval base, lurked in the shadows of the arcaded buildings in the red-light district of Wanchai or lingered in Tsim Sha Tsui, where there was a large army base known as Whitfield Barracks. Without exception, their pimps were 49s. Different streets were owned by different societies or sub-groups and, generally, no one group poached another's territory. Prostitution was regarded, unofficially, as a 'necessary' crime, so the police did not hinder them.

Not all Chinese prostitutes were Triad run, however. Some young women attached themselves to just one customer, usually a serviceman, for whom they provided a 'home' off the military bases which the customer visited when on leave. It was usually a small tenement room or flatlet for which he paid the rent. There, his lady would be a surrogate wife, doing his laundry and sewing, cooking for him as well as providing sex. To visit one was referred to as 'Going Down Home' and the women were called Dahnomers ('down-homers'). Some married their customers or, having been trained to look after them, became respectable domestic servants to expatriate European families. A good number were members of their own spinster societies, sometimes secret or quasi-secret, but never Triad related. One such was the Kit Paai Chi Mui, or Sworn Sisters Society.

The girlie bars, romanticized by Richard Mason's famous novel, *The World of Suzie Wong*, were insalubrious places, usually just one large room with a small bar, a minuscule wooden-planked dance floor, cubicles with tables and leatherette bench seats, and a jukebox, although several, slightly larger, could accommodate a small combo or, in later years, a rock-and-roll band. On the pavement beside the main entrance, hung with a bead-curtain door, was invariably a tiny shrine dedicated to Ts'oi Pak Shing Kwan, a god of wealth, whilst behind the bar would be a larger shrine to Kwan Ti, to encourage wealth and proclaim Triad affiliation.

The bar-girls, invariably Chinese, wore figure-hugging *cheong sam*s, the traditional dress with slits up to mid-thigh which could be extended even higher by a zip. All were 'owned' by Triads and the bar-operator was usually a 49 or Red Pole. Brothels as such were uncommon, the whores usually plying their trade in one-room tenement apartments nearby, also Triad owned, operated or protected. The method of employing a bar-girl was simple and easily monitored by the Triads. A sailor would be attracted to a whore and express his desire for her. She would inform him of her charge, this ranging from a quick blow-job to an all-night session. Once the deal was struck, the sailor had to 'buy her out' of the bar – that is, he paid the barman a fee to walk out with her. This sum all went to the 49 running her, who subsequently split it with the bar-owner and possibly his superiors. The girl was then allowed, in theory, to keep the fee for sex. In fact, she often had to pay protection money, a 'utilities fee' not to have her electricity cut off or rent hiked and various other petty extortions. It was more than likely that she rented her tenement apartment from a Triad landlord. In this way, the Triads took a cut at several levels.

Bar clients' drinks were charged at not unreasonable rates and food, if it was served, was also often cheap and of good quality, but bar-girls' drinks were a form of blatant, yet seldom realized, extortion. All bar-girls requested a drink from a client as soon as he settled in a cubicle. When he acquiesced, the bar-girl was served what was variously known as 'fuck wine', 'Hong Kong tea' or 'tart's tonic'. Consisting of cold tea, flat Coca-Cola or coloured mineral water, it cost approximately twice as much as an ordinary drink. For each glass sold, the bar-girl received about 25 per cent of the charge, the barman took 30 per cent and the remainder went to the Triads or, if the bar had one, to a *mama-san* who was employed by the Triads as a girl-minder. Everyone, save the punter, was a winner. The bar-girl could also continue to earn without providing sexual services and, tart's tonic being non-alcoholic, stay sober. In some upmarket bars, the whores were paid a small percentage of the bar take above a certain ceiling, which encouraged them to encourage clients to drink more.

Drunk servicemen were also prey to Triads. They were seldom physically harmed, unless face had been lost or damage done to Triad property in, for example, a bar fight, but they were rolled, robbed and cheated by them. It was not unknown for Triads, operating through prostitutes, to blackmail servicemen. Innocent servicemen, preferably just two comrades out on the town together, would be wooed by girls in a bar and permitted to charge their drinks and a whore to a tab. At the end of the evening, payment would be demanded. The suckers, having been encouraged to overspend, would find themselves short of funds. At this juncture, the barman would call in a few 49s to menace the hapless pair. The barman would then seem to relent and offer a deal: if they agreed to steal from their comrades, vessel or barracks, or smuggle drugs (which they had to purchase) into their bases or on to their ships, the debt would be overlooked. To ensure compliance, one of the pair would be sent off on his clandestine mission whilst his comrade was kept by way of assurance. A double scam was often involved: the drugs, purchased as heroin, might turn out to be talc, fine sugar or rice flour.

The girlie bars survived until the mid-1970s, most under the wing of the San Yee On, but the end of the Vietnam War and withdrawal of American forces from the Far East, coupled with a gradual reduction in the strength of the British garrison, forced many out of business. None now exists. The very last, the Red Lips Bar in Tsim Sha Tsui, became a discotheque in 1995. The New Tonnochy Night Club in Tonnochy Road, Wanchai, continues the tradition but is a large, very plush club with multi-racial hostesses, a live and usually quality dance band, valet parking and prices to match. Whether or not these are directly or indirectly owned by Triad societies is indeterminable.

The shape of Hong Kong prostitution has shifted. The girlie bars have been replaced by karaoke bars, where clients go to drink, sing, have a good time and pick up prostitutes who come to the tables to sing to or with the customers. In a way, the karaoke bar is a hi-tech extension of the sing-song houses of old. The prostitutes may not be Triad run, but shop-girls and office clerks out to make money on the side to keep up with the affluent lifestyle of Hong Kong. Nevertheless, a majority of karaoke bars are

Triad operated or owned and are good earners, which makes them liable to inter-society wrangling. On 25 January 1997, thirteen revellers were seriously injured and seventeen burned to death when the Top One karaoke club in Prat Avenue, Kowloon, was set alight with a fire-bomb by a Triad society seeking retribution against the one which owned it. In early March 1998, the Flower City karaoke club in nearby Granville Road was the target for a bomb containing sufficient industrial explosive to demolish the building in which the club was situated. It was intended as an attack on the San Yee On, which controls entertainment businesses in the Tsim Sha Tsui area of Kowloon. By chance, it failed to explode.

Triad-operated vice rings are international. The size of the trade may be assessed when one considers that just one of five Teochiu Chinese families in Bangkok involved in the global vice market operates at least 700 women in Australia alone. Brothels exist in every country where there is a Chinese presence. The practice dates back 150 years, when expatriate Chinese communities were pre-dominantly male. Triads imported girls for Chinese men who either did not wish to mix with local women or were barred from doing so. The girls, usually teenagers and sometimes as young as twelve, were often purchased from families who sold them to avoid loss of face at their inability to provide a dowry. Although prostitutes to Western eyes, to the Chinese they were concubines and it was not frowned upon to be one: some of the longest-established and richest Chinese families in Hawaii and California can trace their roots back to a concubine who subsequently married one of her clients.

Prostitutes today are not usually sold, but are enticed

abroad with promises of a better life working as a waitress, domestic servant or shop-girl. Some have run away from home or come from families which have split up. The reality of the promise is bitter: they arrive in a foreign land, often illegally, unable to speak the local language and virtually trapped. Their Triad owners tell them they are illegal and spin them stories of a terrible fate if they run to the local police. Most, especially those from China, have an inbuilt dread of coming across a law-enforcement officer: a police officer in Beijing is not as amenable as one in Birmingham or Boston.

To ensure that they do as they are told, they have their travel documents confiscated, are kept under virtual house arrest in the brothel and provided with food, drink and make-up. Some are given no clothing other than 'whores' rags' – the negligees and split-crotch knickers of their trade – to ensure they do not escape. If they are ever allowed out, they go only in ones or twos with a minder, usually a Chinese woman. Sometimes they are let out to ply their trade in hotel lobbies, casinos or on resort beaches, but they are never out of sight of the minder. Any infringement of the rules does not lead to a beating, because a bruised tart attracts no custom, but it may lead to death. Non-compliant whores are expendable. Their earnings are theoretically reasonably high, but in practice are meagre because the Triads charge them for their imprisonment. Board, lodging and travel costs are deducted. The girls are worked hard and it is not unusual in successful brothels for a prostitute to have a dozen clients during an eight-hour shift. When she is unable to work, perhaps because she has a cold or is menstruating, she is set aside to do domestic tasks around the brothel.

Triad prostitutes need not be Chinese. They also entrap Filipinas, Thais, Cambodians, Vietnamese and, to a lesser extent, Malaysians and Indonesians. They no longer cater exclusively for Chinese men, although these do still make up a fair percentage of their clientele. The bulk are Westerners on the lookout for a submissive 'Asian babe' who is always petite, accommodating and (so legend has it) sexually dextrous. The myth that all Oriental women are sex goddesses is, of course, bunkum. Many of those trapped into vice are taught their trade by their Triad controllers, who 'break them in' like docile mustangs. Gang rape is a common means of subduing and establishing ownership over a prostitute, some of whom are also used for sex by Triad members or 'boyfriends'. The better-looking girls star in pornographic movies.

Many Triads operate prostitutes on a circuit, keeping them for a certain time in one brothel before moving them on. The success of a vice establishment lies not only in the beauty of its women but also in the turnover of faces and flesh. In Europe, prostitutes are moved from brothel to brothel on a roughly three-month rotation. Those who retain their innocent looks are often re-sold as virgins and command a higher price for a short while after their arrival in a new location. They are often traded between societies, sold or bartered as a commodity, and may even be exported to North America after a run in Europe. They are given periodic health checks by their owners, for a whore with an obvious venereal disease is hardly an asset, but there is no screening for 'unseen' disease such as HIV: international prostitutes are, therefore, a channel for the spread of AIDS.

When a Triad prostitute reaches the end of her

working life, usually by the age of thirty, several courses of action lie ahead. She may be sold as a domestic servant, often in the Middle East where she will disappear into an Arab household never to be seen again and where, after a harsh life of servile abuse, she may well be killed. Alternatively, she may become a Triad employee, a *mama-san* in a brothel or a whore-minder, narcotics courier or dealer. Yet again, if she is lucky, she may be given her freedom. After a decade or more of sexual slavery, she might be trained for release, much as captive animals are released back into the wild. Some Triads ensure their better whores are educated, providing them with language lessons, buying them a fashionable wardrobe and setting them up in a small business which is Triad controlled. The majority, however, are just turfed out on to the streets.

Other forms of prostitution, easily seen in Hong Kong, are also run by Triads. They organize cheap whores for working-class workers, especially in the Sham Shui Po area of Kowloon, where, around Un Chau Street, nocturnal prostitution is flagrant. Gay liaisons and massage parlours, much patronized by Japanese sex tourists, are common Triad operations. The Temple Street area of Kowloon has been well known for a particularly perverted sex trade using physically or mentally handicapped prostitutes. Sex with minors is also offered by Triads, but this is not considered paedophilia as girls as young as twelve have been concubines in China for centuries and marriages between minors were once common. In the 1970s and 1980s, establishments where young girls were available were known as 'fishball stalls' because the girls' breasts were tiny, soft and white like the dumplings in fish soup. These have now closed down, but sex with minors is available through establishments advertised as *hong lok chung sum* (health or recreation clubs). Where paedophilic tourism exists, in Thailand in particular, it is often run by Triads on their own or in alliance with the Yakuza; in the Philippines, gangs with Triad affiliation are frequently involved. Not all the Triad sex trade, however, is seedy. They run Western-style nightclubs and escort agencies employing foreign hookers, the very highest class of whom not infrequently become mistresses of very wealthy businessmen, especially in the Far East.

Alongside prostitution, the Triads have also had a virtual monopoly over pornography in South-east Asia since the early 1950s. They started with the publication of pornographic books, then graduated to 8 mm ciné film and, as technology changed, to videotape. Initially, sex films were made using 49s and Triad prostitutes as cast, but in time they took to employing backpackers travelling the world, foreign servicemen who were willing to star in sex movies and local teenagers looking to make a bit of money. Today, whilst videotapes are still being made, the sex-film trade is increasingly switching to CD-ROM with its high technical standards.

With Hong Kong's position as a world leader in electronics and plastics manufacturing, it is not surprising that the Triads have also cornered the market in sex-toy production. Dildoes, vibrators, inflatable sex dolls, fetishist equipment and Spanish Fly-type drugs are made in abundance. In the 1980s, Kowloon Walled City contained one of the biggest manufacturers of rubber penises in the world: to visit the factory was like entering a bizarre, Salvador Dali-esque subterranean world, with racks of latex male organs hanging up to dry like sausages in a butcher's shop. This trade has now moved into China, where production costs are lower, but it is still Triad dominated.

Like all criminal gangs, Triads engage in ordinary robbery, although this is not one of their main activities: it is too high profile to be worth the risk. Unlike the Mafia in America, which used to steal wholesale from the warehouses of New York's Kennedy Airport, the Triads prefer to be more discreet. That being said, it is not unknown for them, in some circumstances, to engage in armed robbery. This is most common in Hong Kong, where gold-dealers and upmarket jewellers' shops are ready targets. When a premises is hit, the attack can be devastating, the stuff of a blockbuster action movie. The gangsters go in with automatic weapons – even light machine-guns – blazing, tossing grenades with abandon. A spate of such robberies took place in the first half of the 1990s, the gangsters on these occasions not local Triads but syndicate gangsters from China armed with weapons borrowed or stolen from the military: many were ex-soldiers who had access to armouries and some acted upon the orders of their officers, who were themselves secret-society affiliates if not actual members.

The main perpetrator of the armed robberies was a man called Yip Kai-foon. Born in 1965 at Hai Feng in Guangdong, he moved in the early 1980s to Hong Kong, where he was arrested in 1985 for a HK$1 million armed robbery on a jeweller's. Sentenced to sixteen years' imprisonment, he faked appendicitis and escaped from a secure hospital ward at Queen Mary Hospital on Hong

Kong island in August 1989, kidnapping a car driver and a child in the process. On his return to China, he lived in his native town under the protection of a relative who was an important local government official. In 1991 and 1992 he led a gang of Chinese criminals, some of them ex-Chinese army soldiers, on three raids into Hong Kong, netting HK$10 million. He spent most of his share on gambling and a decadent lifestyle. A reward of HK$1 million was put on him, the highest ever placed on a single individual in the territory. At 4.30 a.m. on 13 May 1996, having grown a moustache as a disguise, he was encountered on the street by two constables on the beat and opened fire on them with a Polish-made Black Star automatic pistol. The police returned fire and hit Yip three times. Five accomplices who were with him fled, dropping a bag containing a Russian 7.62 mm automatic and 1.8 kg of Chinese army-issued explosives. The policemen were lucky: when it was picked up, Yip's gun was found to have jammed. The police did not at first realize whom they had caught, for Yip was carrying a forged identity card and Chinese re-entry permit in the name of Lau Chi-cheung. It was only when they fingerprinted him that they appreciated they had arrested the most brazen and dangerous armed robber and Chinese gangster of the last twenty years. Now wheelchair-bound, he is kept in solitary confinement in Stanley prison.

Usually, however, if Triads are involved in robbery, it is likely to be conducted with stealth. In the 1950s and 1960s they operated gangs of pickpockets throughout the areas of Hong Kong frequented by tourists. Today they still run pickpockets, but these are usually either Vietnamese employed for the job or freelances whom the Triads protect; and they are not out to steal wristwatches or wallets for the cash, as in the past, but for credit cards and passports which have a far greater value than hard currency. Most common robberies nowadays are from warehouses or factories, with little or no violence. Triads have long since learned that the less they resort to violence the less effort the police will put into their apprehension.

One crime to which Triads are particularly inclined is kidnapping, which since the nineteenth century has been a regular feature of Triad activity throughout South-east Asia. In Hong Kong, businessmen have periodically disappeared, some to reappear, others gone for ever.

Amongst recent cases are those of Walter Kwok Ping-sheung, chief executive and chairman of Sung Hung Kai, one of Hong Kong's biggest property conglomerates and Victor Li Tzar-kuoi, the son and heir of no less a person than the multibillionaire Li Ka-shing: both have been kidnapped in the last three years. Kwok, who has since hired a regiment of bodyguards and goes everywhere in customized bullet-proof BMW saloons, was released on a reputed pay-off of HK$600 million whilst Victor Li's freedom was only achieved after the payment of a rumoured HK$1 billion ransom.

Outside Asia, kidnapping is not uncommon either. A Chinese entrepreneur and impresario based in London, Terry Tam, was abducted in 1986 by members of the Wo Shing Wo as the result of a debt. Lured to the Metropole Casino in Manchester, Tam was kidnapped and driven to Birmingham. For several days, as he was driven around England, he tried to raise a £4,000 ransom by telephoning friends and relatives. A cousin tipped off the police and Tam was eventually rescued in a police ambush in London's Leicester Square.

The kidnapping of Chinese in Britain came to the fore in 1996 when a Fujianese called Cao was mistakenly abducted in Hendon, north London: his kidnappers thought he was a man called Cheng. He was held captive and, even though he was not the originally intended victim, it was decided to hold him to ransom in lieu. Forced to divulge the number of the communal telephone in his family village in China, his kidnappers rang his wife and demanded a ransom of 500,000 *renminbi* (approximately £45,000) – a sum well beyond the means of the entire village population. For twelve days, Cao was kept handcuffed to a radiator and repeatedly beaten whilst calls were made to China. The ransom was reduced to 150,000 *renminbi*, but there was a twist: it was to be paid in China. (This settlement arrangement, beyond the reach of overseas law-enforcement agencies, has in recent years increasingly become the norm worldwide.) At this point, the British police and the Chinese national police force, the Public Security Bureau (PSB), liaised: it was the first time they had ever worked together. As a result of their co-operation, codenamed 'Operation Jupiter', the house where Cao was being held was identified and raided. He was released and his captors sentenced to fifteen years' imprisonment. That the co-operation worked so well was surprising, for it was fraught with difficulties: the eight-hour time difference between London and Fujian raised logistical problems; there were no Fujianese interpreters available in Europe; and the PSB were all for paying the ransom whilst the British method was to stall for time. Yet important lessons were learned and a definite link established between nations fighting a common criminal enemy. Since then a number of kidnappings using the same modus operandi have been similarly solved.

Another longstanding Triad activity is loan-sharking which has existed in China for at least two centuries. With banks non-existent in China until well into the twentieth century, the Triads have always been well placed to offer loans, earnings from other criminal activities providing them with an asset base. Farmers could apply for loans to tide them over till harvest, coolies in the cities could turn to them when unemployed and poor families could borrow to pay for the wedding of a son or the funeral of a revered elder.

Today, people still turn to Triad moneylenders to borrow sums they cannot obtain from a bank, either because the money is required for dubious reasons, such as the settlement of a gambling debt, or because the borrower has no collateral to offer. Loans are always made in cash with interest charged at a very high rate indeed: it is not unknown for a loan to accrue compound interest at a rate of 20 per cent per week. Failure to repay at the agreed schedule leads to the interest rate increasing, the borrower trapped in a spiral of inexorably mounting debt which has been known to go on for years. Continued failure to settle invariably leads to a maiming or the killing of a victim's family member, and eventually himself. In Hong Kong, loan-sharking has been substantially reduced by the establishment of Deposit Taking Companies (DTCs), which lend money against a lower collateral than the banks demand. Yet these companies have not eradicated loan-sharking: even such detrimental and usurious traditions die hard.

Loan-sharking has a darker side than the simple loaning of money. It can be connected to kidnapping. When repayments fall behind, or the loan-shark considers his debtor to be a poor risk, it is not unknown for him – or her – to be abducted and held until the family settles the debt. Whilst held captive, the victim may well be beaten or raped, and possibly further humiliated either by way of punishment or for future extortion. Typically, the victim is photographed naked in sexually compromising situations. Women may be photographed or videotaped having sex with several men, sometimes simultaneously. Men are photographed in homosexual union in order to exact the most shame possible should the photos be made public, sent to family or business associates. To obtain the negatives, the victim is either charged an additional sum of money on top of his loan or, as is becoming prevalent in the Far East, is forced to open a bank account then hand to the loan-shark or blackmailers all the debit and credit cards issued with it.

Gambling has of course always been a major source of Triad revenue and is conducted in Chinese communities worldwide, the Chinese being a nation of gamblers. The range of what they will risk their money upon is vast. Cock- and dog-fighting were popular until the Second World War; cricket-fighting remains popular. In one far-flung area of China, horse-fighting was carried out as recently as 1988 and may still continue. Games of chance are numerous, the most popular being mahjong, *fan tan* and *tien k'au*. Mahjong is played socially in much the same way bridge is played in the West, between friends or families; in Hong Kong it is also played in clubs known as mahjong schools. These, practically all operated by Triads, are generally free of police intervention, as mahjong is considered a national cultural pastime. The schools are usually simple establishments furnished with tables and chairs for players, a tea urn or two for refreshment and waiters who provide the tea and light food such as *dim sum*, brought in from outside. The Triads make their money from charging membership fees, table fees and in some instances taking a cut of high-rolling tables. *Fan tan*, in which the gambler has to guess the number of counters remaining after a pile has been sorted in groups of four, is played predominantly in casinos, whilst *tien k'au*, vaguely similar to dominoes, is played in the street, on trains and ferries, wherever there is space and time to play. Illegal gambling dens are common where gaming is proscribed.

Numbers rackets, known as *chi fa* (pronounced 'gee far'), are common in Chinese communities. These are simple lottery games. In Hong Kong, they provided a steady income for decades until an official lottery, the Mark Six, was founded by the government. *Chi fa* then lost ground and is no longer widespread. Similarly, in the Chinese community in Britain, the numbers game was popular until 1994, when the National Lottery killed it off.

In the Far East, gambling nets profits counted in billions of dollars. The two main sources of highly lucrative gambling are horse racing and casinos, the latter primarily in Macau.

Hong Kong is one of the main horse-racing centres of the world, the sport governed by the Hong Kong Jockey Club, the richest racing association in the world and a non-profit-making organization, all profits being ploughed back into the local community in the form of educational, health and recreational facilities. Complete universities, schools, hospitals and even Ocean Park, Asia's biggest seaquarium, have all been funded entirely from racing profits. Races are held on two courses, the most modern anywhere. All betting is controlled by a massive, highly sophisticated and hacker-proof computer network which assesses the form in a complex betting system. Punters do not just bet on a win or a place but on a combination of placings, accumulated consecutive race results and the order of finishing. All racing is on the flat, all betting legally conducted only on the course or at Jockey Club-owned and controlled off-course betting centres.

Needless to say, the Triads have found ways to circumvent the system, but not to a very great extent. The ideal key to breaking the Jockey Club betting monopoly would be to use mobile phones on the course, but these are rigorously banned and all spectators are scrutinized for them. Both racecourses are overlooked by high-rise apartment blocks, but the huge tote boards which give the running odds are positioned in front of the main grandstand and are not readily visible outside the course. The only way the Triads can get a piece of the betting action is by observing the race through binoculars, relaying the information by mobile telephone to illegal bookies' shops in Macau or Guangzhou. It is not a satisfactory arrangement for them.

More easily infiltrated are the casinos of Macau, where gambling is actively encouraged to such an extent that Macau is now the Monte Carlo or Las Vegas of Asia. To understand Triad involvement in legalized gambling, one has to look at the history behind gaming in Macau and the major players concerned with it.

The casinos have been in existence for many years, but since the early 1960s the kingpin in the Macanese gaming industry has been the redoubtable Stanley Ho Hung-sun, who is in some respects the Howard Hughes of Asia. Rarely seen in public, he lives in a luxurious house in Hong Kong and is said to be worth US$800 million, though this is a guestimate. His family history is vague, but what is known or surmised is the stuff of fiction. His grand-uncle was Sir Robert Ho Tung, the primary comprador for Jardine Matheson; his father was comprador to the Indian-born Iraqi–Jewish Sassoon family which controlled three quarters of the opium in China in the 1870s. This position made him very wealthy but he lost his fortune and good name through insider trading. To escape the scandal, he went to Saigon in the late 1930s, abandoning his wife and son in Hong Kong where they were consequently ostracized. When the Japanese invaded Hong Kong in 1941, Stanley Ho and his mother took shelter in neutral Macau where he spent the war years, having had to give up his formal education. Poor in material terms, he was rich in another sense. Through his forebears, he had accrued a vast amount of *guanxi*, which led to a Chinese employing him as a junior executive in a company trading between the Japanese and the Macanese. He learned Japanese and embarked upon his business career. By 1945, he was reputed to be a millionaire in a society brought to its knees by war.

With peace, Ho started his own trading company in Hong Kong and Macau, investing the profits in property in the former: by 1959, he was one of the wealthiest men in the colony. A substantial part of his success lay in the fact that in Macau he could deal in gold, for Portugal was not a signatory to the international Bretton Woods Agreement governing the post-war gold market. In Macau, gold could be bought and sold like any other commodity.

For all this, Macau was a sleepy backwater. The tiny enclave had no industry. It was a quaint historical city state which looked like a cross between Oporto and Guangzhou. The buildings were ancient and much of the place looked like the film set for a historical drama. Tourists were few and those who did go there came through Hong Kong, making the 72-km voyage in a coastal passenger steamer. By the early 1960s, however, it was set to change, with Ho its new architect.

Macau permitted gambling. There was even a casino in the decaying Central Hotel on the Avenida Almeida Ribero. The gaming concession was held by the Fu family, but it was up for renewal, being issued on a 25-year licence. Ho decided to strip them of it. To do this, he struck a deal with the Macanese authorities and the Portuguese government. Ho promised to build new casinos and hotels and to revitalize the tourist industry if the Portuguese dredged the silted harbour and permitted ships and ferries from Hong Kong into its waters. They agreed and, after an acrimonious tussle with the Fus, the deal was closed.

With the gaming monopoly in his pocket, Ho founded a company, the Sociedade de Turismo e Diversoes de Macau (the Macao Tourism and Entertainment Company), known as STDM. Ho's stake is said to be 25 per cent of the whole, for he has partners, one of which is the

Hong Kong property conglomerate New World Group. He controls the monopoly to this day, paying a surcharge on betting income which accounts for over 50 per cent of Macau's gross domestic product, even taking into account tourism and manufacturing, which have increased dramatically since 1960. In 1990, STDM was estimated to be worth US$1 billion.

The main casino in Macau is the Lisboa Hotel. Architecturally bizarre, built in a style described as Asian kitsch, it looks like a gaudy perforated barrel with a Disney World crown on top. Inside are nearly 100 gaming tables, one-armed bandits and slot machines, blackjack and baccarat and Oriental games such as *fan tan*, a dice game called *dai siu* and mahjong. Gambling goes on twenty-four hours a day with no floor shows or distractions. Elsewhere in the Lisboa – and in other hotels in Macau such as the prestigious Mandarin – private rooms are rented out to small gambling syndicates who operate them for high rollers. These syndicates are frequently Triad controlled and often cause inter-society friction, but they are very important to the Triads for they provide a foothold in the legitimate gambling world.

Ho's enterprises transformed sleepy Macao. Hotels are now plentiful, the restaurants of international standard. Visitors arrive by air to a new international airport, overland from China or by high-speed ferries plying to Hong Kong every fifteen minutes for twenty hours a day and half-hourly for the other four. The jet-foil service is owned by STDM: it is the biggest jet-foil fleet in the world.

Over time, Ho has expanded his empire of hotels and casinos (where legal) to Pakistan, Australia, Malaysia,

Spain and Portugal, Indonesia and the Philippines. In the Philippines he received the gambling concession from Ferdinand Marcos, who forced himself into the business. It has been said that Marcos, with characteristic arrogance, systematically cheated Ho out of gambling receipts. Ho also has substantial business holdings in North America, including a second home in Toronto and extensive industrial investments.

One of Ho's partners, and his right-hand man for twenty years, was Yip Hon, who started his career as a croupier for the Fus. A professional gambler, he was said once to have paid off an evening's losses in Caesar's Palace, Las Vegas, with a certified cheque for US$800,000. He was the centre of attention in the casino in 1988 when he won over US$1 million playing baccarat and again in 1992 when his evening's winnings, US$200,000, were mistakenly paid to another Hong Kong Chinese gambler, Yip Hon-fat. Yet there was allegedly a seamier side to his life. In 1980, it was claimed by the San Francisco police that Yip was a Triad and heroin trafficker and that he co-owned a building on Mott Street, in New York City's Chinatown, which the DEA declared was a major narcotics and illegal gambling establishment. Yip was also said to be an associate of a wealthy Hong Kong businessman, Lee Wai-man, whom the US authorities believed was laundering money for Triad narcotics syndicates. Despite these allegations, no charges or indictments were made and at no time was Stanley Ho implicated in the American authorities' investigations or suspicions.

In the 1980s, Ho and Yip Hon began to fall out, Ho finally buying out Yip Hon's gambling interests for an undisclosed sum. A rumour circulated that Yip Hon had been so aggrieved and lost so much face that he had a contract put out on Ho, which was unfulfilled only because of the intervention of senior Hong Kong Triad officials. Yip Hon used his buy-out earnings to start a horse-trotting racetrack in Macau, but it failed. He died in May 1997, aged ninety-three, of a heart attack at his luxury home on Magazine Gap Road in Hong Kong.

Ho may have survived, but some of his employees have not been so fortunate. In July 1987 his personal secretary and a manager of STDM, Thomas Chung, was chopped to death. Ho put up a reward of HK$1 million for information, but no-one claimed it. Theories were rife. The Macanese police said the hit concerned Triad-operated loan-sharks who maintained an 'office' in the Lisboa. This is feasible: rooms on the eighth floor of the casino are frequently occupied by loan-sharks. Hong Kong police suggested the hit was to do with a Hong Kong Triad group muscling in on a Macanese Triad's loan-sharking business. Neither hypothesis made complete sense. Why Chung was hit when neither he nor Ho was involved in loan-sharking was never explained. A link between Chung's murder and that, three months previously, of a rich Chinese gambler, Wong Ti-ho, was also mooted but not proven. Neither death has been solved and it is now generally believed that Chung died because a Macanese gambling syndicate wanted to put the squeeze on Ho, though why is not known.

That Ho's casinos are used to launder money goes without saying: casinos the world over are highly efficient laundromats and there is little proprietors can do about it, even if they want to. Triad money is washed through the

Lisboa. Top Triads from all over South-east Asia play there and 49s are sometimes paid in chips rather than cash, thus hiding the source of their income. Over the years Macau has become the convention centre for Triad societies. They go for the gambling, but they meet to forge deals, broker peace, burn the yellow paper and liaise with top-flight businessmen seeking to invest in shady business. As a sideline, they operate vice businesses catering for high rollers and those on a winning streak.

There has long been speculation over Ho's relationship with the Triads. Opinions vary. Some sources claim he is a very high-ranking official indeed; others emphatically maintain that he is not but has close dealings with them. A third school of thought is that he has certainly had to come to more than one accommodation with them in order to stay in the gambling business. Whichever might be the case, Ho has never been proven to be a Triad or shown to have had dealings with Triad criminality. Ho denies involvement with criminals. A cool, imperturbable man who rarely shows his emotions, he is, if anything, a consummate politician, running a business empire which, by its very nature, attracts criminals, and maintaining a status quo which, by and large, keeps a lid on Triad societies.

All the crimes mentioned so far are in essence traditional, in that they are up-to-date versions of the sort of criminal activities that have been Triad stocks-in-trade for, in some instances, centuries. The next level of crime is more modern and tends to be international.

The Triad crime which is most apparent, although many do not realize it, is the counterfeit-goods trade. This is blatant in the Far East, but in fact reaches around the world and is an ideal Triad crime, for it serves as a very efficient money laundry.

The Triads have been engaged in counterfeiting for decades. As far back as the 1880s they were known to be counterfeiting Malaysian, Thai and Hong Kong currency, turning out poor replicas of low-denomination coins and higher-denomination Chinese cash. In the early 1960s, they produced a large number of fake Hong Kong 50-cent coins stamped out of aluminium: they looked exactly like the real thing, albeit dulled by usage, but when they were dropped they thumped rather than rang. For many years, until the late 1960s, they counterfeited books, especially expensive textbooks such as the Concise Oxford and Funk & Wagnell dictionaries. Bought by impoverished students across South-east Asia, they were offset-litho copies in paperback form, printed on flimsy paper, yet they served their purpose, bringing the texts within the reach of those who could not afford the genuine article.

Today, the emphasis has moved to other, often luxury, goods which find a wider market. The most famous, most advertised, prevalent and conspicuous of these is the counterfeit wristwatch. Tsim Sha Tsui, the tourist shopping mecca of Hong Kong at the tip of the Kowloon peninsula, is world renowned for its fake-watch sellers, most of them 14K 49s. Peking Road is a favoured haunt. The modus operandi is simple and time honoured. Like the dirty-postcard vendors of old, they mix with the crowds, pick out the all-too-obvious tourists and approach them with a small brochure of their wares. The sales pitch is usually blunt: 'You wan' fake Rolex?' Accept this invitation and the customer is taken to the nearest fake-watch dealer. One well-established dealer operates out of a small room behind a shop unit in the upmarket shopping arcade beneath a 5-star hotel, sandwiched between stores belonging to top international couturiers. Once in the shop, the customer is shown a folder of enlarged pictures and details of the watches on offer, which include Rolex, Gucci, Dunhill, Cartier, Hermes, TAG Heuer, Brietling, Vacheron et Constantin and Audemars Piguet. Prices vary from item to item but rarely exceed HK$1,000 (US$175). When the customer has made a selection, or requests to see one or two samples, these are produced from a back room or corridor where they are stored in suitcases in readiness for a quick getaway should the shop be raided. The imitations are exceedingly good, although the straps and metal bracelets often give the game away by being less well made than the original: the gold rubs off after a few months. The casing and the faces, however, are often indistinguishable from the genuine article, even viewed under a magnifying glass. The mechanisms are usually of good quality and frequently taken from Casio, Citizen, Seiko or other branded but cheaper watches. All keep good time.

Other goods are also faked. The counterfeiting of designer clothing is widespread and covers all the leading consumer brands: Ralph Lauren Polo shirts and Calvin Klein T-shirts and jeans are readily obtainable throughout the world. These are so well made they even contain fake labels. They are even more difficult to identify as non-genuine and, South-east Asia being a major international textile-manufacturing centre, some are actually made in the same factories as the real articles. In this respect they

387

might be classed not as fakes but as over-run rip-offs. Ladies accessories, such as handbags, are also copied, the favourite brands being Gucci, Louis Vuitton and Chanel. In 1995, the Far East sales managers of some major brand-name-accessory companies appeared on television in Hong Kong, confronted with fakes and genuine items: they could not tell their own brands from the copies. Even the stitching of the leather was identical. One manager even declared his own brand handbag to be a fake because it was not as well made as the illegal copy.

In recent years, the Triads' most ingenious counterfeiting enterprise has been that of computer software. It is a multi-billion-dollar business. The Business Software Alliance and the Software Publishers' Association reckon that, of the 523 million new business-software applications in use worldwide in 1996, 225 million were counterfeit, at an estimated loss of US$11.2 billion to software producers. Some law-enforcement and copyright-protection experts believe this will, in time, take over from narcotics as the most lucrative global crime.

Computer-software piracy, as the counterfeiting is officially termed, is comparatively easy. The Triads buy a legal software package at the market rate then reproduce it *ad infinitum*. Their only costs are of reproduction and distribution. Software protection, in the form of codes, registration serial numbers and the like, is skilfully by-passed by Triad hackers, who are among the cleverest in the world. Any commercially viable software programme is duplicated, from zap-'em-up games to complex computer languages. When this market began, in the mid-1980s, most software was reproduced on to floppy disk, easily run off from one PC to another across a cable link. Today, with software programmes running to many hundreds of megabytes in length, the manufacturers sell these in CD-ROM form. The Triads have moved with the times and now own or operate entire CD-ROM factories in southern China, the Philippines and Thailand.

The 'world trade centre' for this illegal business was, for over a decade, one city block in Hong Kong. Every computer nerd the world over knew of it even if they had not visited it. The main entrance was on the corner of Fuk Wah and Pei Ho Streets in the Kowloon suburb of Sham Shui Po, opposite a well-known snake restaurant. It was even officially signposted in the nearby MTR subway station. It was innocuously called the Golden Shopping Arcade.

The bottom three storeys of a commercial–residential tenement block, the arcade had been taken over by more than 200 computer-software shops selling pirated material. All were owned, operated or protected by Triads. Product was sold not according to its face value but to the cost per CD-ROM: the average cost in 1997 was HK$30 (US$4.50). Each CD was crammed with as many programmes as might be fitted upon it. One single CD-ROM purchased there by the author in May 1997 contained thirty-four complete programmes, including the entire range of Microsoft applications (including Windows 95), the full Norton Utilities suite and the Visual Basic programming language, amongst others. The total legitimate retail price of the contents of the CD in London exceeded £1,100 (US$1,800). Everything on sale existed in the very latest version: sometimes serious computer nerds could buy α or β versions ahead of official release. Not only software was sold here. So too were movies on CD-ROM. Some were Triad hard core porno-movies or Japanese Yakuza skin-flixs (with, for some curious reason, the genitalia delicately blocked out) but many were current cinema releases: the *Star Wars* trilogy was available on six CD-ROMs in 1996 for a total cost of HK$300 (US$40). From time to time, the police or customs authorities raided the arcade but this does not bring an end to trade. The purveyors simply moved to a different location such as the 328 Arcade in Wanchai Road on Hong Kong island, setting up their stalls again. Today, with copyright laws being more rigorously applied, the pirates are kept on the hop: yet their business is still vibrant.

To visit the Golden Shopping Arcade was to experience organized crime at its most conspicuous. Little effort was made to disguise what is going on. Customers ranged from Chinese youths addicted to arcade games to Armani-suited jet-setting corporate bosses carrying Saatchi briefcases who were calling in whilst in transit through Hong Kong on business. The latter often bought counterfeit software not to rip off the copyright-holders but in order to obtain the latest programmes to assess before legitimate purchasing.

Another Triad activity is the counterfeiting of music CDs. These are usually copies of big-selling bands and pop-music singers, again copied from the purchase of a single legitimate original. Not only Western bands are copied: Chinese Canto-pop music and rock bands are also ripped off, for sale in overseas Chinese communities. Movies on video are copied but, not surprisingly, movies on laser disc are rarely counterfeited: the laser-disc market,

390

being mostly restricted to Hong Kong and Singapore, is too small to make it worthwhile. However, with recent international expansion in DVD (Digital Video Disk) technology, a new channel of counterfeiting is opening up.

Triad counterfeiting is not limited to the manufacture of items for sale. They also fake bond or share certificates, passports and other travel documents, and excel at counterfeiting credit cards.

Credit-card crime takes two forms involving predominantly gold or platinum credit cards, with high credit levels used. There are two approaches to the crime. The first is the simple theft of a credit card and its fraudulent use either in a shop where an assistant is corrupt or by opportunist thieves in other retail establishments, the card being used until the lawful holder finds it missing and the issuing authority puts an electronic stop on it. Such basic theft is usually the province of street gangs, pickpockets and 49s who conduct it for petty personal gain.

The second method is far more sophisticated. A counterfeit card is made up in a card-making press. With templates and a high degree of technological skill, the resulting laminated card looks and feels just like the original. This is due to some cards being formed on redundant real card-making equipment either discarded by a bank or obtained from the machine manufacturer. However, there is still a problem to surmount before the fake card can be employed. No matter how good it looks – and it will pass close scrutiny, even incorporating a hologram security mark – what has to be 'genuine' is the information encoded on the magnetic strip. There are three ways to obtain this code: to have a corrupt accomplice in an issuing bank, to obtain a random number from a credit card number generator to be found on the Internet (if one knows where to look), or to borrow a genuine card. The chances of the former, whilst not unknown, are very slim; the latter is far more easily achieved and the most common method.

In the Far East, from where the majority of fake cards emanate, 'plastic' is the universal currency. Even street-market stalls and cubicles in alleys selling ballpoint pens and cheap digital watches have a telephone swipe-box. The acquisition of a code strip usually happens in a shop or restaurant which is either Triad owned or protected and forced into compliance. A card-owner presents his card for legitimate payment and the card is taken away to be swiped. Out of sight, it is passed through the telephone terminal to extract the payment but also run through a scanning device which records the details. The card is returned to its owner, the legitimate transaction completed. In the meantime, the coded information has been copied on to a fake card, which will now run through a swipe-machine. Such counterfeit cards are used to purchase high-value luxury goods which are sold at a marked-down price, providing an ideal channel for laundering money.

The fake card is good for up to a month, until the owner of the real card finds transactions appearing on his statement which he did not make, or the issuing authority realizes the code is being fraudulently used. Banks are cautious of giving details on how they detect fake code numbers, but will admit to using 'dynamic systems' of sampling by computer to check for irregular patterns. For example, if a card-holder usually purchases nothing more expensive than £200 and his card is suddenly used to buy four items of £500 each, then the computer double checks. A code suddenly being used overseas also alerts a computer, especially if transactions occur in two distant localities within a very short time. This certainly catches a large number of fraudsters, as Triad fake-card operators frequently visit Europe to make high-value purchases for retail back in the Far East. That said, Triad counterfeiting rings still account for about 40 per cent of worldwide counterfeit-card losses, totalling US$350 million in 1996.

Counterfeiting of all kinds is financed in two ways: either from dirty money obtained through narcotics and other illegal activity, or from legitimate businessmen investing in Triad enterprise. These crimes being deemed 'victimless' – in that no-one dies of a fake Rolex or MasterCard as they might from a heroin fix – lowers the risk of involvement in them, for the police naturally put narcotics and vice higher up their list of priorities. But, of course, no crime is without victims and counterfeiting profits are readily invested in other organized crimes.

One area of Triad investment is an offshoot of a labour-market protection racket. It is the film industry in which, by the 1980s, Triad interest had changed direction. No longer satisfied with taking a protection fee, many groups actively sought to be involved in production and distribution.

Chinese films make big money. *Hard-Boiled*, directed by John Woo, who has been dubbed the Martin Scorsese of Asia, and starring the famous Hong Kong Chinese actor Chow Yun-fat, grossed over HK$11 million in the first three weeks of its run in 1992. Any successful Chinese film can expect to make at worst a 300 per cent profit and, in the long run, including overseas and video sales, will probably net a 1,500 per cent profit. It is no wonder that Triads want a piece of the action. Yet there is another reason for their keenness to promote Hong Kong movies, especially kung-fu films, for these highlight and often glamorize the Triads. *To Be Number One* (1991) was a highly successful film based upon the life of Ng Sik-ho, whilst *The Prince of Temple Street* (1992), starring heart-throb actor Andy Lau Tak-wah, was the story of a Kowloon gang leader. The former grossed HK$38.7 million and the latter HK$12.6 million in the first three weeks of release in Hong Kong cinemas alone.

By 1990, the Hong Kong film industry was the biggest in the world after those of Hollywood and Bombay. It was then that the Triads started to muscle in on the business, trying to corral top stars such as Anita Mui, Jackie Chan, Leslie Cheung or Chow Yun-fat, as well as the sex goddess Amy Yip. Any film starring one of these was sure of box-office success in Hong Kong, with high residual earnings in Taiwan, Korea and across South-east Asia. At first, Triad producers and directors offered parts to the big stars, who turned them down, usually because the scripts were weak and the narratives facile or deriva-tive. The Triads resorted to violence. Amy Yip, who had retained her allure by never taking off all her clothes on screen, was threatened that if she did not agree to star in a film in which she bared all she would pay the price: the Triad producer knew that such a film would have grossed massive box-office receipts. She sought police protection. An actress who pulled out of a Triad film had her HK$150,000 fee burned in front of her. Another unnamed star was said to have been gang-raped for refusing to accept a contract, whilst Andy Lau's office was smashed up and a gun put to his manager's head to force him to comply. One famous film star who refused to play ball was reputedly kidnapped, taken to a secluded house in the New Territories and forced at gunpoint to eat his own shit. The extortion is not restricted to Hong Kong. Jackie Chan, the most famous kung-fu movie star since Bruce Lee and now an international star, was ordered to take the leading role in a movie financed by the Wah Ching, an American Chinese organized crime syndicate. Chan, under contract to the Golden Harvest production company (makers of the *Teenage Mutant Ninja Turtle* films), refused. Whilst he was filming *Cannonball Run II* with Burt Reynolds, the film company's office in San Francisco was shot up. Chan was reputedly ordered to pay US$4 million for damages and loss of face to the Wah Ching leader. Back in Hong Kong, a 14K representative tried to collect part of the debt. Whether or not the debt was paid is unknown.

By 1992, Triad pressure on the Hong Kong film industry reached bursting point. In January, a public demonstration was mounted by leading film-makers and stars, protesting at the Triad infiltration of their business. It was a brave thing to do and aroused public awareness, yet it did little to stop the problem. One of the marchers, the handsome sex idol Tony Leung Kar-fai, was so threatened that he and his family moved to a secret address; yet he lodged no complaint with the police. Three months later, a film producer called Jimmy Choi Chi-ming was murdered, although this may have been unrelated to his film work for he was also involved in narcotics. Not long after that, another producer with Triad connections, Wong Long-wai, was stabbed in Wanchai. He was rushed to hospital, only to be murdered in his bed in the early hours of the morning.

Wong's murder was said to have been commissioned or carried out by a senior San Yee On office-bearer called Andely Chan Yiu-hing in revenge for Wong's slapping Anita Mui's face when she refused to sing at a party. Andely Chan, known as the Tiger of Wanchai because he ran the San Yee On protection rackets in the Wanchai district, was a ruthless streetfighter with a love of fast cars. His prowess as a racing driver even had him enter the Macau Grand Prix in November 1993. He did not, however, make it to the starting grid: he and his racing mechanic, Tse Chun-fung, were gunned down in a hail of sub-machine-gun fire outside Macau's New World Emperor Hotel. It was his punishment for ordering the killing of Wong Long-wai.

By the start of 1994, the Hong Kong film industry was in decline. The all-action movie was becoming stale, the narrative possibilities played out. Western-made films were staging a comeback in Hong Kong, especially multi-million-dollar blockbusters like *Terminator 2: Judgment Day* and *True Lies*, against which local product could not compete for special effects and set action scenes. Taiwanese investors withdrew and began backing their own embryonic film industry. In China, film-makers started to produce international product, although many of the directors were Hong Kong Chinese, some having turned their attentions to China to avoid or lessen the Triad impingement. By the summer of 1995, the Triads were taking less interest in film production, although they did not abandon it altogether.

With the market depressed, it was a good time to restructure, buy in or expand existing holdings. Two entrepreneurs did just that: their names were Charles and Jimmy Heung, brothers of Heung Wah-yim. They had originally entered the film business in 1991, forming Win's Movie Production Ltd, although Charles Heung had dabbled in the film game as a young man, acting in kung-fu action features. Together, they made mediocre films which would have flopped had they not been vehicles for top stars such as Jet Li, the most celebrated martial-arts actor of the decade, who began working solely for the Heungs in 1992 upon the murder of his manager in the spring of that year. At the time, it was not uncommon in the Hong Kong film industry for violence to be levelled at actors and actresses, to coerce them into accepting specific parts, although no police complaints were ever made. This violence was not restricted to film stars: it was also aimed at the Heungs, and Jimmy Heung was attacked by three armed men in the Win offices.

By 1995, the Heungs were established film-makers with a successful production house, a string of allied cinemas and a folio of good movies under their belts. With Hong Kong and Chinese financial backing, they even built a state-of-the-art, 18,500-square-metre studio complex in Shenzhen, in the Special Economic Zone in China close to Hong Kong, from which they produce about twelve high-quality films a year under the sub- sidiary companies Win's Entertainment and China Star.

Jimmy Heung is no longer actively working in the movies, leaving the running of the companies to Charles, who has returned, on occasion, to acting: he took the part of an honest policeman in the 1992 cops-and-robbers film *Arrest the Restless*. Whilst Win's Entertainment has become one of Asia's foremost production companies, matters have not gone so smoothly for Charles Heung. The United States Senate Permanent Sub-committee on Investigations listed him that same year as a top San Yee On official, their allegations given further substance in 1994 when a San Yee On 49, testifying in a Brooklyn court, fingered him as one of the society's major figures. In 1995, the Canadian authorities refused him an entry visa on the grounds that he was, in their opinion, a San Yee On top official.

Criminal influences have continued in the Hong Kong film business. Others have seen the Heungs' success and joined in. A noted figure amongst these is a Taiwanese called Wu Tuan, who was convicted in the USA of the murder of the distinguished historian and biographer, Chan Nan. In October 1995, the famous film producer Steven Lo Kit-shing, who had sponsored Andely Chan's racing car and who had been with him less than a minute before he was shot, was badly chopped. Since then, however, the violence has abated, commentators putting this down to the influence of the Heung brothers, whom some industry observers have dubbed the Samuel Goldwyn and Louis B. Mayer of Asia. The Hong Kong film industry has come of age, but not without considerable Triad involvement.

Smuggling has been a Triad crime for centuries: they have always been consummate buccaneers. Before the Second World War, Triads and pirates operated throughout

South-east Asia, trading whatever made a profit. During the war, pro-Allied Triads ran guns and food to partisans, transported refugees and worked with the SOE; pro-Japanese Triads fought them. When the war ended, they used the networks built up to smuggle contraband. One of the most successful networks ran cigarettes into the Philippine Islands where there has long been a substantial Chinese population. This trade lasted from 1945 until at least the mid-1970s, the cigarettes smuggled from Taiwan across the Luzon Strait to the Babayun Islands, then landed in the province of Ilocos Norte in northern Luzon where indigenous Chinese took over distribution.

The main clan in the province was the Fujianese Chua family (pronounced 'Tsai' in Putonghua), which claimed descent from a famous pirate explorer, Li Ma-hong. The clan leader was a judge and, it seems reasonable to assume from studies made into Ferdinand Marcos's patrimony, the Philippine president's father. Marcos, whose presidency ran from 1965 to 1986, was well connected to the cigarette-smuggling world through Triad contacts; he made a fortune from it even after he became president. He also collaborated with Lino Bocalan, a smuggler with close ties to the Kuomintang and the CIA, for whom he ran armaments to anti-Communist groups around South-east Asia, but who also smuggled cigarettes, perfumes and other luxury goods back home to the Philippine province of Cavite. Marcos ensured that members of the Chua clan held senior posts in the Bank of Communications in Manila, a branch of the Taiwanese bank of the same name.

Marcos was not the first Philippine head of state to be Triad connected. Elpidio Quirino, who became president in 1948, was married into a Chinese clan, the Syquia, who were in alliance with Triad societies in Taiwan, Fuzhou and Xiamen. President Macapagal, Marcos's immediate presidential forebear, had another Chua family member, Santos Chua Haw-ko, as his main political fixer. The Philippine administration could not – and still cannot – operate without the co-operation of the Chinese community and, through it, the Triads.

In recent years, Triad smuggling has become more ambitious. With Deng Xiaoping's liberalization of the Chinese economy in the late 1980s, there was suddenly a market in China for Western luxury goods and Hong Kong Triads went into the provision of TVs, hi-fis, VCRs, microwaves and CD-players on a large scale. These were legally purchased from wholesalers in Hong Kong, then loaded aboard custom-built vessels called *dai fei* (big wings). Grey-painted, fibreglass-hulled speedboats, they were like international racing power-boats in appearance but stripped to the barest essentials, driven by four immensely powerful, synchronized outboard motors giving a top speed of over 60 knots. Filled to the gunwales with consumer goods, and showing no running lights, they set out by night from Hong Kong territorial waters, heading along the Chinese coast to deserted rendezvous points where the cargo was off-loaded – often with the assistance of corrupt Chinese soldiers or police – for sale on the black market.

They also had another lucrative smuggling operation which was illegal in both Hong Kong and China. Hong Kong's having the highest density of luxury vehicles in the world made it a virtual supermarket for car thieves. Stolen to order, the *dai fei*s ran top-range Mercedes-Benz,

BMW, Lexus, Audi and even Porsche cars into China, one to three per boat, each vehicle padded with foam and old tyres to prevent damage. At the height of the trade in the early 1990s, twenty to thirty a day were being stolen. The Hong Kong police frequently pursued *dai fei*s in high-speed chases, capturing a number which were then converted into police chase craft. The trade was hit hard when the Hong Kong police, in collaboration with the Chinese PSB, saw a way to stop it. In Hong Kong, all cars are right-hand drive, whilst China drives on the right. A law was therefore passed forbidding the licensing of right-hand-drive vehicles in China. None the less, cars are still stolen in Hong Kong and smuggled overseas. Africa is a boom market, especially the former British colonies which have retained left-hand driving. Vehicles originating in Hong Kong have been discovered in South Africa, Zambia, Zimbabwe, Tanzania and Kenya; a few have even been found as far afield as the Caribbean and a number have turned up in Canada or the USA, their steering altered from right to left.

The smuggling of illegal immigrants, especially Chinese, is also very big business. Ever since the Triads moved in on the coolie trade in the nineteenth century, they have had an interest in immigrant transportation. This is now an inhuman international business run in association with gangsters in China, many of their clients coming from the southern Chinese provinces of Guangxi, Guangdong and Fujian, the same catchment area as in the 1860s.

Unemployment in China is endemic. Figures vary according to source, but it is estimated that up to 300 million people in Communist China are either unemployed or live on the threshold of extreme poverty. It is no wonder there are those who seek a better life overseas, where they can earn enough to feed themselves and send valuable foreign currency back to their families. Reaping a crop from this harvest of human misery is an occupation at which the Triads are well skilled.

Fuzhou is the main departure point for illegal immigrants from China and the business is a major part of the local economy. Would-be migrants are charged a journey fee, which for a passage to the USA in 1995 averaged US$31,000. Some families scratch and save the required sum to send a son abroad, their insurance for their future. Others borrow from Triad loan-sharks or go abroad having made only a small percentage down-payment, naïvely promising to pay off the balance once they are earning at their destination. Those going to Europe are sent by air and overland, whilst those heading for the Americas travel by sea or, less commonly, by air. The overland route to Europe goes from central China through Xinjiang province (north of Tibet) to Tadjĭkistan across to the Caspian Sea, into Turkey, on to Bulgaria and thence by a number of routes into Western Europe. With hardly a secure national border to cross, it is a fairly safe, if very arduous, route and those who take it are said to be 'looking for the full moon'. One well-tried route is through Albania, Italian *mafiosi* running aliens from the ports of Durrës and Vlorë, which resulted in Italy having an illegal Chinese population of over 100,000 by 1991. Since the fall of Communism in Albania in the early 1990s fewer come that way; instead they are often sent via the Czech Republic and St Petersburg into Germany. A staging-post *en route* is Bucharest, where a Triad society known as the Red Dragon (or Snake) Society handles the human cargo. Immigrants travelling by air, usually on false Taiwanese or Thai passports, fly from China to Bucharest, Prague, Moscow or St Petersburg before transferring to local European flights.

The immigrants end up all over Europe, even insular Britain into which they are smuggled in container lorries; air travel into the United Kingdom is rare, as British airport immigration officers are especially astute. In November 1997, the Metropolitan police raided a council flat on the Croxteth Estate in Clapham, south London, detaining thirteen Chinese aliens (one of them a woman) who were virtual prisoners, only let out to work long hours for very low wages. Five minders were arrested with them. In the flat was found approximately £10,000 in currency and a number of Triad-style weapons. Although neighbours had noticed well-dressed Chinese men visiting the flat, arriving in conspicuous BMW and convertible Saab saloons, no-one had realized it was a holding centre for illegal immigrants. In 1998 it was estimated that 400 Chinese were arriving illegally in Britain every month.

Those destined for America are transported in small cargo ships little better than eighteenth-century slave galleys, living in the holds and allowed on deck only for exercise. A well-known example was the decrepit freighter *Golden Venture*, which in January 1993 ran aground 200 metres off a public beach in the New York borough of Queens with 281 illegal immigrants aboard, six of whom drowned trying to swim to the shore. Many of these vessels are barely seaworthy, the human cargo frequently disembarked by launch or rowing boat off a lonely stretch of coast rather than at a dock and the launches running the risk of capsizing. Several instances of ships foundering at sea with the loss of all on board are on record.

The majority of ships are owned by Indonesian or Taiwanese companies with Triad directors. Each vessel is commissioned by a Triad or Communist Chinese gang and crewed by ordinary seamen, but on each there are a number of 49s known as *ma zhai* (horseman): these are essentially minders who make sure there is no trouble. Some are paid for the job, others are immigrants who accept the responsibility for a reduction in their fare. In charge of them is a Red Pole referred to as a *sh'e tau* (snake-head). The immigrants are referred to as *tou du ju jia* (little smuggled pigs): little has changed in a century and a half. The alien smuggling business is known as *jue sh'e*, or digging snakes.

Accounts gathered over the last fifteen years from immigrants to the USA make up a catalogue of horrific tales which has been compiled by Ko-lin Chin, a professor at the School of Criminal Justice at Rutgers University, New Jersey. He quotes a young man from Guangdong province:

The hours I spent on board a smuggling ship were the most tragic hours of my life. On the ship, everybody cried at least once. We ate bad rice, drank water that was stained. We had to live a life of humiliation. That old run-down ship broke down often. The passengers were all nervous and scared. Once in a while, we would have to endure an uncalled-for beating. When the ship was in the Atlantic Ocean, two groups of passengers got into a bloody fight over food. The sailors had to stop it by wielding guns. The females were abused by the sailors, who used food to persuade them to have sex. The *ma zhais* also took the opportunity to rape the women, who ranged from 18 to 30 years old.

Stories of hetero- and homosexual rape, starvation, extortion, beatings and execution are legion. Some raped women have committed suicide by jumping overboard. Disease and sea-sickness are widespread.

Once ashore, the immigrants are still far from safe. Those landed in the USA or Canada are bussed to major cities like San Diego, Los Angeles or Vancouver, where they vanish into the Chinese community and criminal underground. For those who arrive in Mexico, it is a long, difficult and dangerous journey northwards. Chin recounts one story:

When our ship arrived in Mexico, the local people brought us ashore on small boats. They drove us to some foothills and dropped us there. We lived in the heavy forest and ate like primitive people. Once in a while, they brought us some food, but not enough. People often fought over a piece of bread or a mouthful of water. There were wild fruits, but we were afraid to eat them. Seven days later, two guides came at night to lead us on a rugged hike to the border.

Crossing into the USA is achieved by bribing Mexican and American border guards to allow a minibus or camper of illegal aliens to pass unchecked. Where guards are uncorrupted, border fences are breached. Another of

Chin's interviewees, a middle-aged Chinese, told of his journey in 1988 with two men, a woman and her child. They were fortunate in travelling to Mexico by air from Hong Kong, via Thailand and Japan, but once in Mexico their ordeal really began:

. . . a guide who spoke English and some Mandarin came to meet us at the airport. He put the two males in a car trunk. The woman and her son were asked to sit in the front seat of another car. We could not move inside the trunk, and there was not enough air. The driver drove very fast, and the heat was unbearable inside the trunk. The engine was right underneath my back . . . We almost passed out; we were exhausted . . . After they [the driver and the guide] opened the trunk, they moved us out . . . like we were baggage. We were extremely hungry . . . [They continued their journey on foot through the hills. . .] When the boy could not walk, his mother started to cry. The guide said she might have to pay a local Mexican to carry her son. [The interviewee and a companion carried the boy.] After we walked for a few days, there was little water left, but we kept most of it for the boy. The mother was very appreciative. Her husband was already in the United States, and that's why she came with her son . . . After we arrived at the border, we crossed the fence at night. I helped the boy over the fence. His mother crossed the fence with trembling feet. At the US side, we checked into a hotel with the aid of a guide waiting for us there. At midnight, someone came to tell us to flee. The two of us jumped down from a window. The woman and her son stood at the front of the window and dared not jump.

The interviewee and another man then caught the boy and mother and they hid in bushes until the danger passed. They were later flown to New York.

Not all those led over the border on foot fare so well. Those crossing into Arizona often die of heatstroke and dehydration in the desert. Some freeze to death – but not from the weather: it is not unknown for illegal immigrants to be smuggled inside refrigerated meat trucks.

Worldwide, it is estimated that the illegal Chinese immigrant trade is worth in excess of US$3.5 billion annually and, as the employment situation in China deteriorates, the figure is rising. In 1994, the PSB reckoned there were approximately half a million Chinese in illegal transit somewhere in the world. This assessment, however, was thought by Western observers to be conservative, for in some countries, such as Germany, over 1,000 were leaking in per month – and those were only the ones about whom the authorities knew.

For all the inhumanity of this appalling trade, one tiny fraction of it has been humanitarian and almost patriotic. After the Tienanmen Square massacre of 1989, an illegal immigration organization was established to smuggle dissidents out of China. Codenamed Operation Yellow Bird, it was funded by wealthy, anonymous Hong Kong Chinese, several of them show-business personalities, working with Western diplomats and Triad narcotics dealers. Dissidents were sent down the smuggling routes, provided with false documentation by alien smugglers, then spirited into Hong Kong or Taiwan. A large number of important dissidents escaped from China with the organization, which continued to operate until mid-1997. Indeed it may still be operating: its activities are highly secret, few of its participants having ever been identified.

By far the most lucrative Triad enterprise is the international trafficking of narcotics, particularly heroin.

Prior to the Second World War, opiates were commonplace in China but drug-taking was comparatively rare in Western society. Bohemians, intellectuals, artists, writers, actors and film stars indulged, usually taking hashish or cocaine, but the public was largely unaffected. Their addiction was to alcohol. When this was made illegal in the USA in 1919, organized crime moved in and the bootlegger era was born. Vast profits were made out of booze. Upon the repeal of Prohibition in 1933, gangsters wanted a replacement for moonshine and contraband whisky and when, after 1945, opiates were internationally declared illegal, organized criminals were presented with their new money-spinner. It was inevitable that the Triads, who had traditionally supplied opium or heroin to Chinese all over the world, should become suppliers outside the Chinese milieu. By the late 1950s, they had realized that it was comparatively easy to set up trafficking networks and just what potential for profit existed. Raw opium, which cost US$100 at source, could be refined into heroin with a street value of US$5,000.

Most Triad opium comes from the Golden Triangle: at least 60 per cent of the world's heroin originated there in 1995. Populated by around half a million tribal people of Tibetan–Burmese and Chinese ethnicity, the economy of the area is agricultural. Over the last forty years, this has meant opium. In the 1930s, annual production was about

40 tons, most of it smuggled by Triads to China to evade excise duty. In 1950, after the Communist takeover of China and Mao Zedong's drive against drugs, a Kuomintang general and colleague of Kot Siu-wong, Li Mi, escaped to the Golden Triangle with the 93rd Division. Hiding in the mountains, he realized the commercial and political potential of the tribal farmers' poppy crops. Systematically corrupting Thai officials, he came to rule his own Kuomintang mini-state and, as an anti-Communist agitator on China's western flank, obtained US government aid. Re-armed with American weapons, he was primed by the CIA to attack China and 'halt the spread of Communist aggression into South-east Asia', as a US government release put it. In April 1951, Li's 15,000-strong 93rd Division, renamed the Yunnan Province Anti-Communist National Salvation Army, invaded China. It was easily repulsed. Li retreated to the Golden Triangle and metamorphosed into an opium warlord.

As a Kuomintang general, Li had contact with Triads in Thailand, Taiwan and Hong Kong. Working alongside the commander of the Thai military police, General Phao Sriyanonda, he evolved a distribution network, transporting opium by caravans of mules and coolies, escorted by his soldiers, to Chiang Mai, from where it was sent on to Bangkok to be handled by Triads.

When Li died, his empire was taken over by a second Kuomintang officer, Tuan Shih-wen. In the 1960s, another Kuomintang soldier, Li Wen-huan, set up in business: he was to become the Ma brothers' supplier. Then a fourth, Lo Hsing-han, came to prominence. In addition to these three, another half-Chinese, half-Shan, one-time

Kuomintang soldier, Chan Chi-fu, better known as Khun Sa, also entered the business. The narcotics market was now so huge that the trade could accommodate four rival drugs barons, but this did nothing to halt a long-term feud between Chan and Lo. By 1995, the Golden Triangle was producing over 1,500 tons of opium a year but of the generals only Lo Hsing-han was still alive whilst Khun Sa was said to be 'in retirement' after surrendering to the Burmese authorities in January 1996.

The main distributors of Golden Triangle heroin are, as we have seen, Teochiu Triads. They have been in the opiate business since 1875 when a cartel of Teochiu merchants in Siam won the official licence to retail opium in the French Concession in Shanghai: the first opium-retailing company in Shanghai, the Hongtai opium store, was theirs. They infiltrated the modern trade in the 1950s in Bangkok and, by 1965, held a virtual monopoly over heroin manufacture and supplies going through Hong Kong. Since 1972, they have been primarily responsible for sourcing the international trade.

As the world's largest ethnic grouping of Chinese expatriates, they are well placed. They have their own global underground banking system, based upon *guanxi*, their money launderers are the most skilled, their business managers the best organized. They own lawyers and politicians across South-east Asia. An indication of their influence was seen in 1971 when the Laotian ambassador to France, Prince Sopsaisana, was discovered stepping off his flight from Vientiane with 60 kg of heroin in his baggage. The prince, who was not only ambassador but vice-president of the National Assembly of Laos, president of the Alliance Française, and chairman of the Laos

410

Bar Association, was forbidden to present his credentials and was obliged to return home. The Teochiu are very close to the Taiwanese government, often working for or with the Taiwanese secret service, have links with the American and Italian Mafia and Russian organized-crime syndicates and are establishing a money-laundering presence in the Caribbean. They are the most international of all criminal organizations.

The Triad profit from international narcotics dealing is inestimable. When one considers the World Bank assessment that more money exchanged hands in the world in 1994 for drugs than for food, the level of Triad income can be assumed to outstrip the gross domestic product of many nations. Another indication of the amounts involved may be gauged by the fact that it is believed one Teochiu Triad heroin boss has a reputed HK$980 million deposited with a Chinese bank in Hong Kong. It cannot be touched by the authorities, for they know that, were they to seize it, there would be a run on the bank forcing many small legitimate investors and account-holders into ruin. The gravity of the situation is highlighted by the report of the ninth United Nations Congress on the Prevention of Crime and the Treatment of Offenders, published in 1994, which bluntly states that organized crime now threatens the political and economic structure of many UN member states, placing their national economies at risk from becoming financially dependent upon organized-crime receipts.

The proceeds from narcotics are partially invested in other illegal operations, but the bulk is laundered into legitimate businesses. Many legal businesses are therefore either entirely funded by Triad crime or have

411

a percentage of dirty money in their infrastructure. The type of legal business into which Triads sink their laundered money has no boundaries. They traditionally invest in entertainment businesses – hotels, restaurants, nightclubs, cinemas and casinos – but they also put money into construction, finance, transportation, the media, sports promotion and real estate. Off the record, it is admitted that there is not a single business in Hong Kong with an annual turnover exceeding HK$10 million (US$1.3 million) that does not, usually unwittingly, have Triad investment somewhere on its books. This assumption may be applied to every Chinese community the world over – and many that are not Chinese.

5

FROM FEI JAI TO FINANCIER

Fei jai is Cantonese slang for a spiv, a wide boy, a smart alec. He is a common sight on the streets of any Chinese community from Hong Kong to Toronto to London. Aged between eighteen and twenty-five, he dresses in the latest fashion, his shirt clear and crisp, his jeans tailored and pressed. His watch is expensive, his shoes polished and his hair slightly long, even ponytailed in the classical Chinese warrior style. Yet he stands out for another reason. People show him respect, either obviously and obsequiously or by giving him a wide berth. The chances are good that he is a Triad gangster, probably a 49 or, if not, on his way to becoming one.

Today, a Triad member's advancement through the ceremonial or official ranks of his society, from 49 to *shan chu*, is mirrored in his progress through the criminal structure of his society, which — regardless of where he joins — is generally similar to that of any syndicated criminal the world over, though it has its individual differences from, say, a New York *mafioso* or a Jamaican Yardie. For the sake of definition, the Hong Kong police force has divided the progression of a Triad through his

413

criminal career into four distinct phases, which, if he survives them, can lead to considerable wealth and power.

The key to any successful society lies in its gaining recruits to phase 1. Triads do their recruiting, if they can, amongst the young. Teenage males between the ages of fifteen and eighteen are primary targets, although on occasion youngsters of twelve may be approached. School playgrounds and the streets are the usual recruitment venues, with, in Hong Kong, tenement blocks or sports associations. The recruiting Triad offers brotherhood, solidarity and a sense of belonging to a group, which often seems attractive in a rootless urban environment.

Once a youth is recruited, he is not automatically initiated as a 49 but is more likely to enter a sort of probationary period, during which time he has to prove himself. His first Triad affiliation is with a youth gang in which he learns loyalty, joining comrades in recruiting peers and the bullying of non-gang youths. An illustration of how extreme this aspect of Triad youth behaviour can be was shown by a court case in Hong Kong in March 1996. Li Man-kit was a seventeen-year-old youth-gang member and drug addict who had already been put on probation at the age of fifteen for robbery and having sex with an under-age girl. During two years of intimidation, extortion and petty crime on a Hong Kong housing estate, he had forced others to join his Triad society, demanded money with menaces, viciously assaulted youths younger than himself and, ultimately, forced a fourteen-year-old boy to swallow white powder on the pretext that it was a lethal dose of heroin, then set his victim's pubic hair alight. When sentenced to a youth-detention centre, Li requested that the judge send him to an adult prison. The former sentence clearly constituted a loss of face.

A Triad youth hangs out with his 'brothers', of whom some may be 49s, wears similar clothing and shares in the sense of power and identity the gang affords. Gangs often have names, though these bear no relationship to the Triad society to which they are attached. The name may be based upon the gang 'uniform', brand of cigarettes smoked or favourite hang-out. In this way, a gang could be called the Nike Boys, the Lucky Strikes or the Cheung Wongs because they hang out in Cheung Wong Road. In the 1960s in Hong Kong, gangs often took the names of current pop singers or songs: there were youth gangs in Kowloon in 1962 called the Everly Brothers, the Buddy Hollies and the Runaways, after Del Shannon's hit song, 'Runaway'. Another group identity is established by tattoos. These are usually on a part of the body that is not readily visible but may briefly become so by, say, a quick flick of a sleeve to show a design high up on a bicep. Some tattoos can be elaborate and even artistically accomplished, consisting of entwined dragons and phoenixes drawn by a professional tattoo artist while others can just as readily be crude scratchings done by a comrade, or self-inflicted. On occasion, the tattoo is avoided and substituted by a geometrical pattern of scars branded upon the abdomen or inner arm with red-hot coins.

Not all youth-gang members progress into fully fledged Triads. They may well quit the gang on leaving school, going into employment or simply moving house, and are not criticized. Those who do not drift away take part in various acts of delinquency and will most probably join a Triad-owned or affiliated martial-arts club, taking

415

instruction in readiness for moving on to phase 2: membership of a street gang.

Once in a street gang, the youth is most likely to be initiated as a 49. Most street-gang members, aged between sixteen and twenty-five, are Triads. He will come to know his brothers and start to pick up Triad slang, such as *yeung ku* (a castrated lamb = sucker), *tan pat chau* (fiddling eight claws = being fingerprinted) and refer to himself as a *san ting*, a new soldier, who does not want to *sat fung* (lose wind = be arrested) for being caught in the act of *tong si ngau* (slaughtering an ox = robbing). Now involved in criminal activity, he may be either legally or criminally employed or live off the earnings of a girlfriend for whom he pimps, she being a willing prostitute. If she decides to leave him, either to go 'off the game' or transfer her allegiance, he will charge her a disconnection fee, which will be paid either by her or her new boyfriend. No hard feelings arise: this is business.

The street gang's main concern is muscle and intimidation, protection rackets, loan-sharking, debt collecting, low-level illegal gambling, vice and drug peddling. The streetwise youth member is now a criminal apprentice. He determines how far to push an extortion victim: if he is too demanding, the victim may turn police informer, but if he is not sufficiently rapacious he loses face and credibility. Should he be engaged in illegal gambling, it is now that he discovers how to operate a numbers game or a gambling joint. If involved in vice, he is taught how to pimp, manage whores and blackmail clients. Throughout this period, he is on a steep learning curve. At this time, he may form his own small gang under the wing of an experienced Red Pole who calls the shots.

Being a soldier, he also has to fight. This invariably involves conflicts with other gangs, usually instigated by a clash of interest or territory, which might be very specific. In Hong Kong, demarcation between one society's patch and another's is very clear cut, a certain street being as well defined as an international border. Transit through another society's territory is allowed: doing business in it is unacceptable.

At this stage in a Triad's career, he may well be called upon to act as a hit-man. In this capacity, he will be sent out to 'chop' someone.

Traditionally, Triads do not use guns, although nowadays firearms are increasingly being employed. The real Triad weapon is a chopper and hits – termed 'choppings' – are conducted with a Chinese-style meat cleaver. Chinese butchers do not sever meat into specific joints as Western butchers do: all meat is chopped through the bone into appropriately sized lumps then cooked; it is for this reason Chinese meat dishes frequently contain pieces of bone. The cleaver – which is also used as a slicer and, in the Chinese kitchen, is a universal cooking implement – is a flat, razor-sharp blade about 25 cm long and 12 cm wide with a wooden handle. When a victim is chopped, unless it is intended to kill him, the cleaver is used on his arms. It is not uncommon for a victim to lose several fingers and suffer forearm lacerations but otherwise not be wounded. Many choppings act as a lesson rather than as a terminal execution. If the victim is to be murdered, the whole body is lacerated, the victim bleeding to death. This is the traditional death by a myriad of swords.

Other traditional weapons are more subtle and highly developed. One is the throwing-star, made of thin steel and rather like the Jewish star of David, all its points except one sharpened on both surfaces. The star, usually about 10 centimetres in diameter, is thrown frisbee-fashion. Spinning at high speed in the air, it slices deeply into anything it hits; at close range, it can penetrate a car-door panel although it is not likely to pass through it. The throwing-star can be substituted with a coin, the rim of which has been cut into with a pair of metal pliers, each tine produced being twisted to form a rising point. Although not as effective as a throwing-star, it can make a nasty superficial wound. Other weapons, the design of which goes back at least 1,000 years, include a heavy iron chain with a handle at one end and either a spear point or a spiked iron sphere at the other. The former is used to slash or, with the chain flicked forward, to stab. The latter merely acts as a bludgeon or bolus.

As well as fighting, a 49 also takes part in settlement conferences. When one society crosses another, there follows a period of fighting, ultimately resolved by a meeting. This is an important aspect of a Triad's educa-tion, enabling him to learn the boundaries of criminal propriety and diplomacy, and the importance of com-promise.

Until now, a 49's salary will have been paid according to his success, most of his earnings, less a possible com-mission, going to his superiors. However, if he is lucky and has done well, he may now graduate to phase 3 of his Triad career. Comparatively few 49s graduate to this point: they remain in phase 2 for their entire working life, grafting and obeying, making ends meet. Just as in any other business, only a few make it from the shop floor through middle management to the board of directors.

At stage 3, the opportunity to become an official arises. The 49 becomes a White Paper Fan, a Grass Sandal or Red Pole. The most likely promotion is to Red Pole, for there can be any number of these in a society, depending upon its size and the strength of its fighting units of 49s, each of which require a Red Pole overseer. Promotion is not automatic and depends upon expertise, ability and the resignation, retirement or death of more senior officers. The only alternative way for a 49 to rise up is to found his own society.

Once he is an official, he remains responsible for his society's criminal enterprises, but much of the leg- and donkey-work is done by 49s or officials below him. He is increasingly less likely to be involved in choppings or internecine warfare, unless his involvement is called for through personal loss of face or the need to remind the victim there are other, bigger men watching him than a group of lowly 49s.

His income now increases quite rapidly and, the more senior he becomes, the larger it gets, the bulk of the money earned by the 49s coming to him. He pays them their cut, takes a larger one for himself and passes the residue to his superiors. He is also in a position to sponsor initiates, charging introduction fees and receiving a share of initiation fees. As his income grows, he has to conceal its origins from the police or tax authorities. To do this, he usually establishes a cash-rich front business, which might be anything from owning a taxi to running a number of street stalls, a restaurant or similar establishment where much of the take is in hard cash.

These businesses may also be used to launder money belonging to others in his society: in this way, the authorities find it difficult to unravel the tangled skein of finances. Although some Triads flaunt their wealth, most do not live ostentatious gangster-style lives. A lifestyle of limousines and concubines only arises if and when the front businesses succeed, and it is not unknown for very senior Triads to live unpretentious existences. This is not just a modern defence: it is a traditional approach to great wealth harking back to the rich merchants of the fourteenth century feigning poverty to avoid taxation and the discovery of their illegal overseas trading ventures.

In addition to setting up front businesses, the wealthy Triad invests in companies run by entirely legitimate organizations or individuals. By the time he has reached the stage enabling him to so diversify, he is probably a shrewd businessman with an expert commercial team behind him. Investments are usually made in businesses where the return is not necessarily going to be spectacular. A steady profit is preferred to a fluctuating one. However, some investments can be in high-risk, speculative commercial activity such as the stock, commodity or currency markets and, if the risk seems worthwhile, may be venture-capital undertakings. In this last case, the Triad investor may well take over any successful venture, by force if necessary. No-one is ultimately safe if their company is dubiously financed and many businessmen do not know their investors until it is too late.

Profits made from legitimate business activity are more often than not invested only in legal enterprises: illegal investments are made from illegal income before laundering. Keeping the two apart confuses the authorities and thwarts the seizure of assets.

By the fourth phase, the Triad is in a position of

considerable power. Outwardly, he appears respectable and probably moves in high social circles. He may well become an important benefactor of charities, a figure of standing in the community, for the sake of kudos and camouflage. The more credibility, the better.

In his legitimate business dealings, he is quite straight and honest, within the parameters of high finance, his disguise so good he has no need to be otherwise. Furthermore, he has what legitimate businessmen do not have – a safety net of hidden, virtually continuous, untaxed income.

Whilst legitimate and criminal activities are kept far apart, it is not unknown for a Triad tycoon to turn to his society for assistance when he needs it. This is rarely financial back-up. What he may need is enforcement. If a competitor is cutting up rough, forcing a deal, making commercial life hard, the Triad can call up the cavalry. The competitor may then find his factory broken into and key machinery smashed; he may have his Rolls-Royce sprayed with paint-stripper; in extreme cases, his son may be kidnapped or his wife assaulted. The lesson is soon learned. Of course, the competitor can never prove who caused these events. He can only hazard a guess and play along, knowing he is beaten but not daring to speak out.

Once a Triad becomes a tycoon or, perhaps more appropriately, a *taipan*, he is not jealously protective of his legitimate businesses. He will invariably invite some of his criminal comrades on to the board of his legal companies. In this way, legitimate business is invisibly infiltrated by illegal elements. An estimate of the size of this aspect of Triad activity can be gauged from a study of the composition of the executive boards of major modern Hong

Kong companies. It is estimated that 40 per cent of all Hong Kong businesses have Triad members amongst their directors and, at a minimum, 80 per cent of all commercial real estate has dirty money as part of its financing package. The total is many billions of US dollars, in Hong Kong alone. If these statistics are extrapolated across other cities where Chinese commercial activity is considerable – Singapore, Jakarta, Vancouver, Toronto, San Francisco, New York – the percentage of criminal money generated by Triads and invested in the infrastructure of the international commercial life is beyond calculation.

In four stages, therefore, a youth on the streets of any Chinatown can, with luck, perseverance and criminal assistance, reach the top not only of the criminal but also of the legitimate business world and this may happen virtually anywhere on earth.

PART FIVE

CONQUERING BARBARIA

1

THE SIEVE, THE UNICORN
AND 'MAO TSE-TUNG'

By the 1960s, the Triads in the Malay peninsula and Indonesia were under pressure. The police hounded them as subversive criminal elements and the indigenous population resented them. It soon became clear to many societies that they would have to leave in order to survive and prosper. There was also another reason for their decision to expand overseas. Heroin was becoming the international drug of choice, alongside cocaine. It seemed only sensible to spread their client base. Their first port of call was The Netherlands.

The Netherlands was not randomly chosen. The Dutch being a maritime people, their seaports amongst the most important in Europe, there had been a small Chinese population in the country for many years. Chinese from Sumatra had traditionally crewed Dutch merchant ships since the days of the Dutch East India Company and in Rotterdam and Amsterdam there were small enclaves of Chinese and Surinamese, Dutch citizens from the East Indies. The mainstay of these communities was Chinese sailors who had either been dismissed from their ships during the Depression or stranded by the First World War. Keeping to themselves, maintaining their own language and culture, and shunning integration into Dutch society, they were known as 'peanut Chinese' because up to 1939 they eked out an existence selling sugared peanut biscuits, an Indonesian sweetmeat, in the streets.

Where there were Chinese, of course, there were Triad societies. Several existed in Rotterdam and Amsterdam before the Second World War, operating under the guise of the Overseas Chinese Association. They were not criminal but religious or patriotic and, during the Nazi occupation of The Netherlands, were inactive. Chinese in The Netherlands kept a very low profile during the war and were generally left alone by the Nazis, although a small number disappeared into the concentration camps in the process of ethnic cleansing.

In 1945, Dutch ships once more started to use Chinese sailors to make up for the wartime loss of manpower and mini-Chinatowns grew out of the former enclaves. The occupants were principally Chinese from the Dutch East Indies, Malaya and Singapore. Some were Triads, who eradicated the pre-war societies and were soon behaving in their usual criminal manner.

By 1965 the country had become ideal Triad territory. The Dutch had a tolerant attitude towards narcotics, the police force was inexperienced in organized crime and The Netherlands was centrally situated for the whole of Western Europe. As the Dutch withdrew from their Far Eastern colony and Indonesia gained independence, Amsterdam and Rotterdam became a haven for tens of thousands of Indonesian Chinese refugees. The Triads arrived unobtrusively with them. As usual, the insularity of the Chinese community protected them from discovery and they were soon running gambling dens, protection and numbers rackets. The proliferation of Chinese restaurants gave them adequate cover: a small number were owned by Triad societies as legitimate fronts and used as meeting places, Triad lodges, safe houses and centres of general criminality. Entry visas were easy to come by: any Chinese claiming he was coming to work in a restaurant was let in. Through their fraternities and networks of *guanxi*, the Triads quickly became well established and powerful within their community.

It was not long before a small Chinatown formed in Amsterdam along a street called Zeedijk, on the periphery of the *walletjes* 'red-light district'. Despite the proximity of sex shops, sex shows, sex museums and brothels, the Chinese did not engage in vice, although – as we have seen – since the 1980s they have been instrumental in providing the European sex industry with whores from Thailand and China. This uncharacteristic lack of interest in vice was deliberate. The Triads had a bigger business to run than whores.

The relaxed Dutch attitude towards drugs meant that not only were the narcotics laws liberal, but there were even legal obstructions in the way of effective policing. The police were forbidden to entrap drug dealers by posing as buyers; telephone-tapping was permitted but could not be used in evidence; plea bargaining was permitted; carrying narcotics was illegal but the police powers of stop-and-search were highly restrictive. Short of catching someone with a hypodermic jammed into a vein, prosecution was well nigh impossible. Soft drugs were virtually ignored and cafés licensed to sell them. The maximum sentence for possession of or trafficking in heroin, prior to 1977, was four years' imprisonment: in 1977, it was increased to twelve years but rarely passed down. Even those convicted for a full term could be free in eight years and jail was neither a deterrent nor a brake on dealing. Dutch prisons were famously comfortable and most dealers could continue their business from their cell through visitors and the unrestricted use of outside-line telephones. To cap it all, the Dutch police had not a single Chinese officer on their roll and no concept of Triad societies.

Opportunities for smuggling heroin were legion. Customs officers in other European countries referred to The Netherlands as 'The Sieve'. Search procedures at Schiphol airport were slack, Rotterdam so big that customs surveillance of ships was very difficult; the coastline was easy to land upon and the border with Belgium was open. Heroin shipped through Rotterdam could be on its way to Germany, France or Britain within hours of arrival.

The first seizure of heroin in The Netherlands was made in 1971 when a Chinese gambler was picked up with 50 g in his pocket during a raid on a Triad-run illegal gambling den. It was only the third time the Dutch police had come across the drug, the previous two occasions having been the discovery of addicts' individual fixes the year before. Yet heroin had been imported into The Netherlands since 1965.

It was not just a case of the Dutch police being unaware of the drug. When they did come across it they failed to recognize it. Narcotics training was at best rudimentary. There is a story, probably apocryphal but indicative of the situation, which tells of some Dutch policemen inspecting a Chinese restaurant in the kitchen of which they saw a basket containing plastic bags printed with a red circle, Chinese characters, two lions and a globe. On enquiring what the bags contained, they were informed that the contents were Chinese cooking herbs. Shortly afterwards, they happened to see the same trademark on a photograph of a block of Double UO Globe Brand heroin from the Golden Triangle. They returned to the restaurant. The bags had vanished and the restaurateur suggested they had mixed up his premises with another.

The primary destination for heroin smuggled through The Netherlands was West Germany, and especially the US army and air-force bases which were awash with dope. On the streets of cities in the proximity of garrisons such as Hamburg, Heidelberg, Frankfurt, Ulm, Stuttgart, Munich and Wiesbaden, heroin was readily available. Servicemen couriered heroin into Germany from the Far East and Amsterdam, mailed it to the USA in the military postal service and shipped it home in baggage. In the servicemen the Triads had an eager market. Soldiers who had taken heroin in Vietnam to blot out the horrors of war now took it to counteract the boredom of peace. New conscripts were often addicted under the peer pressure of comrades. In time, however, as the military authorities cracked down on drug use and addicts either left the service or were put through drug rehabilitation, demand declined and dealers had to find another outlet. They did. They targeted civilians. The European heroin-addiction epidemic had begun.

Although the Ma brothers and Ng Sik-ho were central to the supply of heroin to Europe – the latter owned a number of front companies in Amsterdam, including at least one restaurant, and organized what was referred to as the Dutch Connection – they were never major Triad figures in The Netherlands. The Dutch Triads had their own Dragon Head.

Thick-set and only 5 feet 6 inches tall, Chung Mon had a rounded simian face and large hands out of proportion to his body. He wore his hair thickly Brylcreemed and was always contemplatively smiling. He was a Hakka, born on 10 September 1920 at Po On in Guangdong province. Also sometimes known as Chen Hsien, he was referred to by the Chinese of Amsterdam as Fo Kee Lun, the Unicorn, an animal of great magical power in Chinese mythology. In 1936, he joined the Kuomintang but went AWOL within a year and, at the age of eighteen, arrived in Hong Kong to be employed as a ship's cook on a Rotterdam-bound freighter. Once in The Netherlands, he deserted and vanished into the small Chinese community. He survived the Nazi occupation, it is conjectured, by making a living as a Gestapo informer. Unusually, he married a Dutch woman, Ann Hess, probably to acquire her nationality as much as her affection. She took a Chinese name and bore him a daughter in the late 1940s. The marriage lasted twenty years, much of it spent living in an apartment on the second floor of Ilperveldstraat 139 in the Amsterdam suburb of Nieuwendam.

When the 14K started to establish itself in Amsterdam is uncertain, as is the date of Chung Mon's joining it. What is certain is that the society was operating in The Netherlands by 1951. Within five years, it was the dominant Triad society in Amsterdam and Chung Mon was running it. Ostensibly, he was a local businessman, entrepreneur and benefactor, but in fact he was The Netherlands' biggest criminal mastermind. By 1960, due to his administrative skills, he had reorganized all 14K operations in Amsterdam – especially the illegal Chinese gambling casinos – to such an extent that the city was the most profitable 14K venture outside Hong Kong.

When heroin started to arrive in 1965, Chung Mon became an importer. His men couriered, received, cut, repackaged and distributed it. This further boosted 14K and his own income and gave him the idea of expanding. In 1968, he moved to Düsseldorf, but his plans failed there and the 14K hierarchy in Hong Kong ordered him back to The Netherlands, sending him a sizeable budget to fund Dutch criminal activity.

Back in Amsterdam, Chung Mon opened a new restaurant called the Sze Hoi (Four Seas) and an exclusively Chinese gambling casino, both financed by the 14K with local Chinese businessmen coerced into investing. From offices in a building at Prins Hendrikkade 105–6, close to the Chinese quarter in Zeedijk, Chung Mon ran other businesses, including an importation company and a travel agency, the Overseas Chinese Travel Service. His position as elected president of the Overseas Chinese Association was the tip of his benevolent iceberg, for he also ran a number of other charities, caring for down-and-out Chinese, providing them with food and paying for their medical treatment. His charitable activities earned him a public honour from the Dutch government.

Not everything went Chung Mon's way. Soon after his gambling club opened, it was the venue for a shooting for which Chung Mon was arrested. He was held without bail for three months then released for lack of evidence. No witnesses came forward but, besides that, Chung Mon had friends in the Amsterdam police for whom he acted as an informer, betraying low-level drug dealers to bolster his respectability.

Some time around 1968/9, the 14K in Hong Kong decided to appoint Chung Mon their pan-European controller. He started to travel widely, using passports in different names proclaiming him to hold British, Taiwanese, Malaysian or Indonesian nationality; the Taiwanese passport afforded him diplomatic immunity. Within a year, he was identified by Hong Kong police as a known associate of criminals, including the Ma brothers. Their suspicion was further aroused when agents reported that Chung Mon had been given an official welcome in Taiwan and entertained by the vice-president.

When Chung Mon flew back to Amsterdam, he took control of heroin distribution throughout Western Europe. Couriers arrived with up to 2 kg at a time, whilst more substantial deliveries came by sea. Two varieties of heroin were imported: No. 3 lower-grade smoking heroin for Chinese addicts across Europe and for some Dutch who had acquired the habit in the former colonies, and No. 4 injectable heroin for American GIs and the burgeoning addict populations of Germany, France, Italy and Britain. Some heroin was even collected from Schiphol airport or the Rotterdam docks by Chung Mon's private bulletproof Mercedes.

The year 1972 was a landmark for Chung Mon: the Vietnam War was drawing to a close; the Turkish government banned opium-poppy farming, which had been

432

producing more than 40 per cent of Europe's supply; and the notorious French Connection, the Mafia-controlled drug route into Europe which was Chung Mon's only real competition, was busted. As we have seen, the Ma brothers and Ng Sik-ho reacted by sending massive shipments to meet rising demand. Purity standards rose, prices dropped. The 14K were selling low to hook more addicts.

To keep his empire secure, Chung Mon established a relationship with the Amsterdam police commissioner, Gerard Toorenaar. He offered to inform for the commissioner and to prevent Chinese gang fighting in the city if the police gave him a free hand. Toorenaar accepted. It was not that Toorenaar was corrupt: he was naïve. At one point, he arranged for the recovery of Chung Mon's Mercedes from Belgium, where it had been impounded. It is said he also gave him a testimonial, clearing him of narcotics involvement, which Chung Mon used to avoid detention in Hong Kong. No trace of this can be found in Hong Kong police files, but some officers attest to its one-time existence.

The next year Chung Mon – sometimes nicknamed '5 per cent Man' because of the cut he took – started exporting to the USA. This brought him under DEA surveillance, which established Amsterdam as the transit point for all Europe's heroin and, targeting the city, they made their first heroin bust there. Word spread quickly to Hong Kong and Chung Mon flew to the colony to undergo Triad training in how to deal with the situation. He also visited the USA and, in Nevada, bought a quickie divorce from Ann Hess before, under a false name, marrying a young Chinese woman, said to have been one of his top drug couriers, who bore him a son.

The success of Chung Mon's operation encouraged other Far Eastern Triads to try their luck in Europe. The Wo Shing Wo arrived in Amsterdam in force. Other societies set themselves up in Rotterdam, Koblenz and Antwerp. It was not long before the various groups were at each other's throats. In Amsterdam there was open warfare, including a number of shoot-outs using the Triads' favourite weapon in The Netherlands, the sawn-off shotgun. Chung Mon, determined to keep his territory free of Wo Shing Wo competition, tipped off the police.

Next to try a takeover was Ng Sik-ho, who sent three men from Hong Kong to start a luxury casino in opposition to Chung Mon's. He again tipped off the police, who raided it and found heroin hidden in hollow mahjong tiles, almost certainly planted there by Chung Mon's followers. A number of arrests were made, but Ng's men had skipped the country hours before. Angered by their temerity, Chung Mon followed them to Hong Kong and is thought to have blown the whistle on Ng Sik-ho. It is likely that the 14K encouraged him: they had been having problems with Ng, who was already under police surveillance. Chung Mon paid for his actions. On 3 March 1975, he was approached by three Chinese as he stepped towards his Mercedes outside his office in Prins Hendrikkade. They shot ten bullets into him at point-blank range. The assassins, flown in from Hong Kong for the hit, were never caught or firmly identified, but it was confirmed that they were members of Ng Sik-ho's former syndicate. Chung Mon's death served some purpose, alerting European police forces to the Triads, but it was ten years before they took them seriously.

In just a few short years, on behalf of the 14K and the Ma brothers, Chung Mon had set up the heroin scourge which has plagued Europe ever since and put into motion the conduit for importation into the eastern seaboard of the USA. To this day, Triads consider him the instigator of the global heroin trade.

With the Dutch police clamping down on the Amsterdam Triads in the aftermath of Chung Mon's murder, many members fled. Some went to Germany, some returned to the Far East, but the majority moved to Britain, where the 14K was already active in the Chinese communities of London, Birmingham, Liverpool and Manchester.

The 14K sent a replacement for Chung Mon from Hong Kong. Chan Yuen-muk, nicknamed 'Mao Tse-tung' because he looked so much like Chairman Mao, was a Red Pole from Kowloon. A coarse, brutal and maladroit gangster, he taxed the illegal gambling casinos, raised levels of protection money, ordered other gangs running heroin into The Netherlands to pay a 'landing fee' to the 14K and generally swaggered about. It was not long before the entire Chinese community had had its fill of him: the law-abiding members, who had not resented paying Chung Mon the obligatory Triad squeeze, loathed him and criminals distrusted and disliked him. Apart from anything else, he drew police attention. This disaffection was noted by the 14K's competitors, who decided to use it to their advantage.

First to fan the fire was the Singaporean Ah Kong

syndicate – the name means 'The Firm' – which had been narcotics dealing for some years, allowed to do so by Chung Mon in exchange for his 5 per cent. Chan tried to foreclose on them, demanding that they work through 14K operators, paying a greater percentage. The outcome was inevitable. Chan was murdered outside a Chinese gambling joint on 3 March 1976: no-one missed the significance of the date. The assassin was a hit-man from Singapore.

Chan's death threw the 14K into temporary disarray. The Ah Kong seized the day, putting word about that they would henceforth be the sole Amsterdam heroin dealers: anyone else bringing narcotics into The Netherlands had to employ them as distributors. Those who tried to evade them were tortured with cigar butts then stabbed to death – a variation on the Triad five thunderbolts and a myriad of swords. As the heroin business increased, independents started up with permission from the Ah Kong. Rivals decided to try their luck. One of these was an enterprising Singaporean Chinese, Tan Suan-chin, more commonly known as Johnny Tan. He had a home in Sweden and was married to a Swede, but worked out of Amsterdam until he was apprehended in September 1977, the police tipped off by an Ah Kong informer.

The 14K were upstaged and not in a position to retaliate. They were losing ground in Hong Kong, the newly sanitized police force and the ICAC snapping at their heels. The Wo Shing Wo were gaining strength in the colony and the 14K were compelled to pay this new threat their full attention. An agreement was reached whereby the Ah Kong kept its domain in Amsterdam and Germany whilst the 14K retained control of Rotterdam, Paris and London. This did not cause either faction too much dismay, for the trade was now so large and profitable there was room for more than one player.

A good deal of inter-faction fighting was still caused by individuals establishing their territories or gaining face. From 1975 to 1980, the streets of Amsterdam were periodically riven by Chinese going after Chinese. Half a dozen Triad officials were butchered, with many more chopped. It was not long before both Dutch and Chinese citizens had had enough. The authorities clamped down. The maximum sentence for narcotics trafficking was trebled to twelve years, police drug squads were enlarged, liaison with the Hong Kong police, the DEA, the FBI and British customs was extended, immigration procedures were made stricter, illegal Chinese gambling dens were closed and a number of Triad members were arrested and imprisoned or deported.

These measures looked good to the public but did not make much of a dent in the drug dealers' armour. Heroin continued to flow in and business might have continued unchecked were it not for the failure of the poppy crop in the Golden Triangle in both 1977 and 1978. With production reduced, the Triads were usurped by Turkish, Iranian and Pakistani producers operating out of the Golden Crescent – primarily Afghanistan – where poppy growing was financing not only criminality but also political unrest. The Mujahaddin's civil war against the Russians was substantially funded by heroin.

With their narcotics base undermined, the Netherlands Triads relied once more on protection rackets, gambling and armed robbery. The crime rate rose as the 1980s rolled by and those Triads who had been imprisoned were progressively released. Proceeds from crimes not only kept the Triads in money but helped finance an increase in narcotics trading in Thailand, where new producers were coming on line, bringing in heroin from Laos via Bangkok. The Ah Kong, reduced in numbers and influence by police action, were dispossessed of their position as their former Malaysian or Singaporean traffickers and dealers reverted to couriering for the 14K, who were coming to prominence once more.

The 14K had learned important lessons. They were no longer the Dutch underdogs but a well-organized group, importing not only heroin but also morphine base, which they refined into heroin in secret refineries in the Dutch countryside, in apartments in towns such as Utrecht and Hilversum or in isolated spots in the northern Netherlands, north and west of Groningen. With Amsterdam's Chinese community dispersed, there were no Chinese ghettos left, so the 14K operated out of small units centred on Chinese restaurants. In the mid-1980s Dutch police discovered seven heroin factories spread over a wide area of The Netherlands. The 14K's dominance gave the Dutch a peaceful interlude from gang warfare, but it did not last. A new Chinese underworld group was on the way.

The Tai Huen Jai, or Big Circle Boys, first appeared in the late 1960s. This was not strictly a Triad society. It was run roughly on Triad lines but did not rely upon rituals, had no connection to the traditions and was not a single society but a loose alliance of criminal gangs. The founding members were former Red Guards from Mao Zedong's brutal Cultural Revolution and demobilized soldiers from the People's Liberation Army (PLA). Like the 14K, they started in Guangzhou and neighbouring districts in Guangdong province. The name derived from two sources: Guangzhou is called by criminals 'the Big Circle'; and detention camps in China, in which many criminals and Red Guards were sent for political re-education, are marked on maps by a large circle. The Big Circle Boys were professional criminals, often labour-camp escapees, who arrived in Hong Kong then often migrated to North America, sometimes being given political refugee visas but usually smuggled in as aliens. Those who remained in Hong Kong made a living by violent armed robbery, hitting banks, gold dealers and security vans or similar targets. With access to PLA armouries, they were equipped with Chinese assault rifles and grenade launchers. Their high-profile criminality upset the Triad societies, which usually avoided such manifest activity.

The Big Circle Boys moved into The Netherlands in 1986, most of them living under false identities. In less than two years, they controlled Chinese crime. Their number grew rapidly. Organized with military efficiency and infamously violent, they took over the 14K narcotics monopoly, marginalized the Ah Kong and were soon Europe's most disciplined, complex and co-ordinated criminal group, based upon Amsterdam but with members living as autonomous cells throughout Europe. Infiltrating or gaining reliable intelligence about them was well-nigh impossible. As well as heroin, they took over the illegal gambling joints and protection rackets, and became heavily involved in illegal immigration. So prevalent were they by 1988 that the Dutch police went public with their concern at the rise in violent Chinese-originated crime and made a forthright request to the Chinese community throughout the country to assist in bringing the Big Circle Boys – which they named specifically – to book. Incredibly, this public appeal was instigated by the Chinese themselves: a number of restaurateurs had clubbed together to write, albeit anonymously, direct to the Dutch government. With Chinese community leaders and deposed Triads assisting the police, the Big Circle Boys came under considerable fire. One major cell was uncovered and broken, and their grip on Amsterdam weakened.

This success, however, was no more than the severing of one of an octopus's tentacles. The Big Circle Boys remained internationally powerful, ranging throughout Europe with impunity – the more so when European Community passport controls and customs inspections were relaxed in the 1990s. To avoid detection, they diversified their heroin imports and their heroin refineries, some mobile and moving from place to place on a regular rota, were operated by Chinese narcotics 'cooks' flown in from the Far East. As a result of their organizational skills, Big Circle Boys remain a serious problem in Europe, with Amsterdam still their 'headquarters'.

In many respects, Amsterdam remains a Triad 'headquarters' too. Dutch laws are still considered lenient compared to those of other European countries, the city is strategically placed, easily approached across national borders, and has a wide multi-racial, cosmopolitan community in which Chinese do not seem apparent. Triad murders continue in The Netherlands. In 1995, nine Chinese were assassinated, whilst in February 1996 a

Chinese was found murdered in Haarlemmermeer, his body riddled with forty-three bullets from four separate weapons. Recently, a new Chinese criminal group has appeared in The Netherlands consisting of Chinese from Wenzhou in Zhijiang. They concentrate on extortion and robbery, operating throughout the central European Economic Community (EEC) nations with their main base in Paris, and are considered the most potent of Chinese organized-crime threats.

Across Western Europe, Triad societies maintain 'branch offices' and engage in all their traditional exploitative crimes wherever there are sufficient Chinese businesses to make it worthwhile. In France, which has a large Vietnamese population, they often work alongside Vietnamese Triad-style gangs, whilst in Italy they sometimes combine activities with Mafia families or organized-crime syndicates in Naples, Rome, Milan and Turin. For many years they operated in accord with the Mafia, smuggling heroin with the illegal immigrants they ran into Italy from Albania. More often, however, they were kept in check by Italian gangs willing to trade with them but not risk being taken over by them. In Spain, where the Chinese ethnic minority is comparatively small, there is none the less Triad activity. In 1994, the Spanish authorities reported that there had been a marked increase in illegal immigration and general Triad criminality over the previous six years. Due to a loophole in Spanish law, there was an upsurge in the number of Chinese asylum-seekers for some years until 1993, most of them applying for entry whilst in the company of a supervising Snake-head. The leak has now been plugged.

In Germany, Triad activity is substantial. As already stated, the country faced the heroin problem early on through the presence of US military bases on its soil. Its magnitude can be seen from US military statistics. It was estimated at the time that 27,000 US troops in Germany were regularly using hard drugs; in 1979 alone, 9,000 American personnel were arrested on drugs charges and heroin worth US$60 million was confiscated.

For a while in the 1980s, the Chinese in Germany faced severe competition from the Turks, of whom there are over a million 'guest workers' in the country. By 1983, they were importing heroin from the Golden Crescent in opposition to the Triads, yet they were not a real threat. Most trafficking was conducted by individuals lacking the efficiency, dedication and thoroughness of the Chinese; and, for all their contacts, they lacked their own *guanxi*. Furthermore, Turkish heroin was not of the same high purity as the Triad product. The Chinese maintained the bulk of the trade.

Elsewhere in Europe Triad activity has been slight, if present at all. They are virtually unknown in Scandinavia, hardly more than a nuisance in Denmark and absent from Greece and Portugal. In the former Eastern Bloc countries they hardly existed, for the Communist regimes regarded them as socially subversive and secret-police forces made it impossible for them to operate – although recent research has shown that the KGB did, on a number of occasions, assist with or ignore heroin shipments coming through the USSR, travelling by way of Chinese advisers and diplomats. The only Communist countries which allowed Chinese to smuggle heroin were Albania, where Enver Hoxha, the reclusive dictator, took a personal cut, and Bulgaria.

From the early 1950s, Bulgaria was systematically involved in organized crime. The KDS, the Bulgarian KGB, dealt in Turkish morphine base and heroin, as well as arms. They occasionally purchased heroin from the Chinese, selling it through Turkish and, later, Pakistani traffickers in Europe and into the USA, using the income to provide weapons for Palestinian and Middle Eastern terrorist groups. All transactions passed through Kintex, a state-owned export company run by the KDS in league with the Sicilian Mafia, Lebanese criminals and corrupt Swiss bankers. Today, renamed KoKintex, it is still suspected of dealing in narcotics.

Whilst Europe has active Triad societies at work, and The Netherlands is the main Triad-infested state, there is one European country where they have been established longer than anywhere else and where for a time it looked as if they would become a dominant criminal force. That country is Great Britain.

2

A NOT-TOO-DISSIMILAR ISLAND

Chinese have lived in Britain since at least the start of the nineteenth century. With the expansion of trade to the Orient and the activities of the East India Company, a minute number lived in London, then the nation's main seaport. They were sailors hired in the Far East, perhaps to fill the space of a man lost on the outward journey. In 1814, a small group was living in the area around the docks. They were an impermanent population who did not like living in Britain and were only biding their time until they could get a ship out. As the decades passed and trade with China increased, more Chinese were employed by shipping companies. Some were sailors but others were stewards, cooks and laundrymen on the passenger vessels sailing to the colonies in the East.

With this increase in the employment of seamen, a tiny Chinese community sprang up in London around Limehouse Causeway and Pennyfields, between Stepney and Poplar, close to the docks. In the census of 1861, it was found that 147 Chinese lived in the entire country. Twenty years later, the number was still only 665, but over 75 per cent of them lived in London.

In narrow streets, they lived quiet, hugger-mugger existences much as they did in the alleys and *hutong*s of Guangzhou or Tai Ping Shan, from whence most of them originated. Catering for Chinese sailors in transit, the residents ran boarding and eating houses, laundries, gambling joints, brothels, a tiny temple to Tin Hau (goddess of the sea) and opium dens. They tended not to mix with their neighbours and became something of an exotic curiosity. Victorians visited the area to ogle at the men with their hair plaited and the sailors eating with chopsticks. The Chinese, ignoring these tourist intrusions, were law abiding and aloof, suffered little racial prejudice and were left alone. The community being virtually devoid of Chinese women, their brothels were staffed by white whores, the only non-Orientals to live in 'John Chinaman's quarter'.

As the Chinese prospered, so they became ready for exploitation. By 1890, there was at least one Triad society in Limehouse, collecting protection money, running several opium dens, gambling houses and a loan-shark racket. Opium was their biggest earner. Although the drug was legal, for a Chinese sailor it was expensive. As most of the sailors were frequent opium smokers, demand was high, so the Triads imported their own supplies, smuggling them in to avoid duty. The police never heard of them because the Chinese did not report them and they never operated outside the Chinese community.

Other societies followed. The Ghee Hin ran a lodge in Britain's other main seaport, Liverpool. About 1900, the Che Kung Tong also set up a branch in Liverpool, where it still exists at 10 Nelson Street, operating as a Chinese social club and referring to itself as a Chinese freemasonic organization. A non-criminal association, it is probably the oldest Chinese secret society in Europe, able to trace itself directly back, and adhering to traditional values.

Whilst they were often exploitative, Triad societies in Britain before the Second World War were socially supportive and patriotic, providing venues such as mahjong schools which brought the Chinese together, offering legal assistance when they came upon problems from people outside their communities, arbitrating in disputes between Chinese, loaning money at market rates to pay for funerals or weddings, funding education for children and health care for the elderly or poor. When Sun Yat-sen was seeking finance, they contributed towards the republican cause and, during the civil war against the Communists, sent money back to Chiang Kai-shek to help fund the Kuomintang.

From around 1900 until the defeat of the Kuomintang in 1949, the Chinese population in Britain fluctuated but never averaged more than 4,000. In the early 1950s, this changed. With Mao Zedong's victory, hundreds of thousands of refugees fled to Hong Kong. They were permitted entry because Britain recognized Chiang Kai-shek's government-in-exile in Taiwan and believed it was its duty to accept them as political refugees. The British government was also keen to bolster its colonial reputation by volunteering such shelter. With other colonies pressing to be given independence, and with India having gained self-rule in 1947, it was considered diplomatic to show generosity.

The influx had a knock-on effect: many Chinese moved on from Hong Kong, a substantial number heading towards the home of their colonial masters. It was a natural destination, for they were British Commonwealth passport-holders. Many arrived hoping to find an island larger but not too dissimilar from Hong Kong, a place to make a fortune, for Britain was leaving behind the post-war austerity years, business was growing and industry picking up.

The Chinese who moved to Britain brought with them their culinary skills and the first Chinese restaurants opened in major cities. Business boomed. Sweet and sour pork, egg-fried rice and chicken with cashew nuts caught on, an exotic alternative to fish and chips. More restaurateurs and waiters arrived, followed by retailers ready to supply the restaurants. The Chinese population of about 4,000 in 1949 had swollen to nearly 300,000 by 1995.

Many of the immigrants were young men who had left wives and families in Hong Kong. They had little or no contact with the English other than to serve them meals, picking up the language as they went along, working long hours in the restaurants and, in time-honoured tradition, keeping their heads down. The police regarded them as the most law-abiding section of society. They were right.

As more Chinese arrived, so new Chinatowns began to appear without any of the indigenous population being inconvenienced. West Indian, Pakistani and Asian immigrants, who were racially intimidated and abused, were unpopular because they were thought to be insidiously infiltrating British society, taking British jobs and moving into 'white' neighbourhoods. The parochial Chinese did not try to acquire such properties but concentrated on run-down, urban buildings no-one wanted, their communities springing up in war-ravaged cities such as Liverpool, Birmingham, Southampton, Cardiff and Glasgow.

In London, Limehouse no longer existed. It had been bombed out during the war and, the docks in decline, there was no need for the Chinese to congregate there; besides, most of them were no longer sailors. About 1960 the Chinese suddenly found a new opportunity. In Soho – the Bohemian red-light district of strip clubs, brothels, artists' studios, jazz dives and coffee bars – rents were low on short-lease properties, especially in the area around Gerrard Street. With a nose for a bargain, the Chinese started to move in. Restaurants opened and other businesses appeared catering for the Chinese, including food stores, bookshops, travel agents, hairdressers, lawyers, accountants, banks, traditional Chinese doctors, acupuncturists, herbalists, hardware merchants and furniture importers. Out of sight were illegal gambling dens, Chinese brothels and mahjong schools. The police ignored them as they caused no trouble, none other than ethnic Orientals were involved and they were unofficially regarded as part of Chinese life. The general consensus was that the presence of the Chinese was beneficial to the country at large. Of course, these establishments were run by Triads, but the police had little notion of what a Triad was and no-one was prepared to explain.

Into the 1960s, Triad societies in Britain carried on as usual. Every Chinese business paid protection, waiters short of funds were cheated by loan-sharks and lonely men visited Triad whores. The situation might have stayed like this but for two factors – the Swinging Sixties and heroin.

With the boom heralded by the Labour government in 1964, the influx of Hong Kong Chinese increased sharply. With them came new Triad groups looking for expansion, especially in relation to heroin. Britain was an ideal market for narcotics. Society was undergoing radical changes. Young people were becoming an important social unit, morals were challenged and the old order was being overturned. In the liberalism of the time, free love was being made, authority was being rebelled against and cannabis was being smoked. Heroin was the next step towards liberation.

Until about 1967, the 14K was Britain's only criminal Triad society. When they first arrived is unknown for sure, but they were in the country by 1952. They had three main power-bases in London, Liverpool and Bristol, with a lesser presence in Manchester and Southampton. They were autonomous and, whilst they had links to 14K societies back in Hong Kong and throughout the rest of the world, they were not part of an overall organization. There was no binding fraternity between them: even within Britain, they were and are still essentially rivals. Any relationship existing between them, such as the provision of heroin by a Hong Kong 14K society to a Manchester 14K society, is not fraternal but a business contract.

Which society first imported heroin into Britain – and when – is not known for certain, although its source is: it came from Hong Kong, sent via Amsterdam by Ng Sik-ho. It may have been the 14K, who certainly had the infrastructure and contacts, but it could well have been the Wo Shing Wo, who arrived at roughly the same time. The stage was being set for trouble.

The police were unprepared for this new problem, despite being robustly warned by the Federal Bureau of

Narcotics and Dangerous Drugs (later to become the DEA) and the FBI, through the US embassy in London, who were more than aware of the heroin flooding into the USA via Britain. The embassy even maintained a resident officer whose task was to gather intelligence on drug traffickers, infiltrate their operations and identify couriers. He worked in collaboration with the British authorities, who were aghast at his methods: he paid informers to pose as buyers and actually bought narcotics with a federal government slush fund in order to establish his agents' bona fides with the dealers. To this day, police informers in Britain are not paid, receiving only expenses, and, in the new era of governmental accountability, are ridiculously obliged to sign a contract of employment as informers.

The British drug squad was at a disadvantage: it was minute, underfunded and undermanned. It received a further setback in 1973 when one of its senior officers was accused of conspiracy to pervert the course of justice and resigned on grounds of ill-health; several of his colleagues, found guilty of perjury, were dismissed or transferred to other departments. Anti-narcotics policing was stripped of its most experienced officers and took two years to become fully instituted again. In the meantime, the Triads' only opponents were customs officers, who, like the police, were on a steep learning curve.

Simultaneously, on the other side of the world, things were changing. The Hong Kong police were being cleansed by the ICAC. With their protection gone, many Triads considered Hong Kong a dangerous place and decided to get out. Britain, with no real drugs squad and ignorant of Triads, promised a safe harbour.

The Hong Kong police were quick to appraise immigration officials in London of the situation, but the Triads neatly side-stepped it. They sequestered Chinese seamen's passports, changed the photographs and entered Britain on the falsified documents, airmailing them back to Hong Kong where the rightful owners' photos were reinserted so they might return to work. Access to passports was easy: the Hong Kong seamen's union had been run by the Triads since the nineteenth century.

The Triads who settled in Britain soon instigated societies with full hierarchies and it was claimed that the 14K had a permanent lodge in Soho, a luxury they could not have indulged in Hong Kong. Within months, they were shaking down every Chinese business in London. Before long, the inevitable conflicts arose. Matters reached a climax in February 1976. A squad of 14K 49s, under the command of a Red Pole, attacked a gambling den in the basement flat of 10 Gerrard Street, looking for – amongst others – a man called Wong Pun-hai, whom they thought had played a part in the gunning down of a relation, Li Kwok-pun, in The Netherlands. Li was also said to have been implicated in the killing of Chung Mon and to have double-crossed the 14K over a heroin shipment. Quite what the squad's motives were are unclear. On the face of it, they were avenging a relative's death and yet they were also seeking to kill those who had, in effect, themselves wrought revenge for the killing of Chung Mon. They were almost certainly acting on an underworld tip-off, but their informant got it wrong. Wong Pun-hai was not in the gambling joint, but his father Wong Kam, a restaurateur from Basildon in Essex, was: he regularly played mahjong there. The gamblers were manhandled and beaten up. Wong Kam was kicked to death.

The police, under Detective Inspector David Oakley, were called in but made little initial headway. Not one of the gamblers had seen a thing. Wong Kam, the police were told, had fallen down the basement steps. After exhaustive questioning, Oakley's team finally identified some of the attackers. One was Li Kwok-shui, a waiter from Burnham-on-Sea in Somerset. Three others, sharing the same patronymic, came from nearer London. All were 14K members and expert kung-fu and Chinese-boxing fighters. Arresting them was difficult. After the murder, they had travelled to Leeds, then moved to Belfast where they hid in a safe house operated by a Chinese restaurateur. From Belfast, they crossed the border to Dublin, were given money and split up. Two went to Belgium, then Amsterdam, whilst the others lived in a safe house in Larne. The police persisted, tracking them until the wanted men surrendered. They were charged with murder and tried at the Old Bailey in November 1976, but the jury found them guilty of manslaughter and they were sentenced to between five and fourteen years' imprisonment.

Other incidents in Soho followed. Several Chinese waiting in a late-night cinema queue at the Odeon in Leicester Square were chopped; no-one identified their assailants. A recalcitrant Chinese gambler with heavy debts was found cut up in an alley between Rupert Street and Wardour Street; although hospitalized, he refused to name his attackers. There were several instances of property damage, including an arson attack just around the corner from the main fire station in Shaftesbury Avenue. No complaints were made.

The authorities found all these incidents illuminating, for they showed professional Oriental gangsters operating in Britain within what was considered a quiet, law-abiding community. What was more, they indicated the fear with which the Chinese regarded them, their utter ruthlessness and their organization. It was also clear that the police needed expert assistance with Triads and there was only one organization capable of providing it – the recently renamed Royal Hong Kong Police.

The officer sent over was Senior Superintendent Douglas Lau Yuk-kuan, who arrived in May 1976. Although only twenty-nine years old, he was head of the intelligence section in the Triad Society Bureau. The intention was to infiltrate him into the London Chinese underworld, but news of his impending arrival preceded him. A corrupt officer in Hong Kong tipped off his brothers in Soho and the British press ran stories of how Lau was going to become a top undercover agent fighting Triad heroin barons. Despite having his cover blown, Lau was still of immense value. He shared his considerable Triad knowledge with the British police, stressing the importance of infiltration. London's Metropolitan Police already knew the value of penetrating gangs, for they had planted informers in the East End mobs in the 1950s. Where the Triads were concerned, however, they faced a problem. Triad societies never enrolled non-Chinese and there were no Chinese officers on the force. Even if there had been, the chances of one being able to worm his way into a Triad society were remote. Any Chinatown newcomer was viewed with suspicion by the Triads and thoroughly quizzed about his past. If anything did not quite fit, or just to check his credentials, all they had to do was telephone the Far East to investigate his background.

Lau adapted his plan. He trained Metropolitan police officers to become hippies. As such, they could mingle in the drugs scene – for most pushers and addicts were non-Chinese – and come into contact with Triad traffickers. Nicknamed by their colleagues 'the Unwashables', these counterfeit hippies soon paid off. Within three months, over a dozen Triad drug dealers had been apprehended.

One major early success of this new tactic was the capture of a twenty-nine-year-old Malaysian woman, Shing Moori Wong, known as May Wong. She and her associate, Li Jafar Mah (also known as Li Mah), were allegedly members of a Malaysian Triad society which trafficked heroin for a Chinese, Ricky Chan, who lived in Ipoh. Before their arrival on the scene, Chan's heroin was distributed by a Hong Kong Chinese Wo Shing Wo member called Anthony Lam. For a while, Lam operated effectively, but he became addicted and was replaced by a Malaysian Chinese, Mervyn Chin Keong-yong who had come to Britain from Amsterdam in 1972. By 1975 he was doing well, but he was also skimming the profits to feed his gambling habit. When his superiors in Malaysia learned of this, his fate was sealed. Knowing this, he and Lam staged a number of deliberately unskilled robberies in order to be arrested, believing their best sanctuary was prison. After breaking into the London home of the Thai military attaché, they were arrested, Lam turning witness and being sentenced to five years in prison. Chin, who had been under Unwashable surveillance, received more than he bargained for and was sentenced to ten years for robbery and narcotics trafficking.

454

With Chin put away, Ricky Chan had to move fast to maintain his market niche. He sent for Li Mah, an experienced dealer and skilful smuggler, who came with his companion, May Wong. Roedean-educated, very pretty and intelligent, she claimed to be the daughter of a wealthy Malaysian gold dealer allegedly killed by Triads in December 1971. This was not entirely true. Her dead father was in fact her stepfather and a successful bullion smuggler who had been brutally murdered by a trusted henchman out to take over his operation. According to her story, she had established a Singapore beauty salon and boutique after leaving school, then became a nightclub hostess in order to come into contact with Triads and revenge her father; that her stepfather's killers had been arrested, and seven of them executed, seemed beside the point. Through the nightclub, she met Li Mah, whom she claimed was Triad connected but in debt due to the failure of a business venture. To repay his debts, he agreed to traffic heroin into Britain, May Wong admitting that she joined him in the hope of identifying who had ordered her stepfather's death. Together, they frequently flew from Singapore to Amsterdam, arranging heroin deliveries to London, paying Chan his share of the take in cash. To further protect their network, they used Singaporean couriers unknown to the police.

At this time, the police in London were coming up to speed under Douglas Lau's tuition. Their intelligence showed the couple associating with two of Chin Keong-yong's acquaintances, a boutique-owner called Molly Yeow and a man known as Chi Sang. When Molly Yeow's apartment in Montpelier Grove, Kentish Town, was raided, notebooks of contacts and narcotics accounts were discovered. They showed, over a six-month period, a turnover exceeding £500,000 and gave the location of a heroin-cutting factory-cum-distribution-centre in Islington, then a run-down part of north London. Molly Yeow, Li Mah, and a number of others were arrested. May Wong was in Singapore when the raids took place. The police enforced a press embargo then telephoned her with the news that Li and Yeow had been badly injured in a car smash. May Wong hurried on to the next London flight and was arrested as soon as her aircraft landed. Her apartment was searched and two unlicensed handguns found, one showing signs of having been recently fired. In October 1976, fourteen people were tried for narcotics offences. May Wong and Li Mah received sentences of fourteen years, although May Wong's term was later reduced to twelve. Molly Yeow got ten years and an Australian drug runner working for them five and a half years.

The sending down of May Wong and her colleagues was not the Metropolitan Police's only success. Another was the conviction of Jason Ng Kok-lian, the son of a Malaysian Chinese multimillionaire, under Operation Templar, a drive against heroin dealers commanded by Superintendent Alfred Luff. Ng used an old secret-service ploy to protect his ring. On payment, his customers were told to collect their purchases from a 'dead letter box' in a telephone booth or a burial site beneath a tree in Hyde Park. After a long period of surveillance, the police followed Ng and his primary courier, an Arab called Abu Said Bakaar, in a squad car. This developed into a car chase through central London, Bakaar dumping thousands of pounds' worth of dope out of the vehicle on the way. Both were eventually arrested. A search of Ng's home revealed over sixty packets of cut heroin. A further stash worth over £1 million was buried in the garden of a house in Ilford used as a cutting factory.

The success of these prosecutions boosted police morale and dented that of the Triads, who reassessed their narcotics business and started to tread more cautiously. Many withdrew from smuggling drugs into Britain, relying on others to supply them whilst they concentrated on peddling. This change badly affected the 14K, which had been dominant in Britain. With the Triads falling back upon the stocks-in-trade of extortion, loan-sharking, gambling and, increasingly, Chinese video piracy, competition began to grow between them and the Wo Shing Wo, resulting in the latter taking over central London and the 14K being forced to retreat to provincial cities.

The rise of the Wo Shing Wo was due in no small measure to a man who was to become one of the most important Triads in Britain. His name was Yau Lap-yuen, but he preferred to be known as George or Georgie Pai. He was also referred to by the nicknames of Limping George or George the Duck, on account of his walking with a limp: like Ng Sik-ho, he had received a beating during a gang fight early in his Triad career.

Yau, of Hakka descent, was born on 13 July 1946 in Fanling, a small rural town in Hong Kong. His parents moved to Britain in the 1960s to open the China Garden restaurant at 16 Market Place, Glastonbury in Somerset, but their son remained in Hong Kong, where he joined the Wo Shing Wo whilst in his teens. Clever and ambitious, he rose quickly through the ranks to become the head of his own sub-group, responsible for running Wo Shing Wo affairs in the Kwun Tong area of Kowloon. He acquired a reputation for violence, was arrested on a number of occasions and imprisoned in Hong Kong. On 28 February 1975, he arrived in Britain.

The Wo Shing Wo then consisted of a number of groups scattered about Britain. Pai embarked upon a crusade to unite them. He was assisted by three men, Ah Hung, Cheung Kin-wah and Tsui Yung-sang, of whom one was an illegal gambling-den owner with a record of narcotics trafficking and attempted murder. Tsui, a martial-arts expert, was later jailed for heroin dealing. Ah Hung became Pai's right-hand man. After an internal power struggle and a contretemps with the 14K, Pai had assembled a gang of about eighty followers. Disregarding the 14K, they moved in on Soho, putting the squeeze on legal and illegal businesses alike. This led to a skirmish with the 14K from which Pai's new Wo Shing Wo emerged triumphant. Encouraged by success, they expanded outside London.

Triad crime across central and southern Britain suddenly escalated. By September 1975, a gang specializing in armed robbery became active in the Midlands. Calling themselves the Sing War Society, they were thought to be a team of Pai's followers based in Manchester and Birmingham on an in-service training course. They also engaged in protection rackets and it was through these that the police received their first complaint from a delegation of local Chinese businessmen in Birmingham who were being extorted by, as they reported it, the Wo Shing Wo. One of the complainants mentioned the name of 'Georgie' from London. Sums demanded were always multiples or variations of 336, a relevant Triad number. Across the Midlands and into South Wales, there was a rise in attacks on Chinese which were not racially motivated.

Whilst engaged in his power struggle with the 14K in London in the summer of 1975, Pai became embroiled in a fight at the No. 44 Club in Gerrard Street. With others, he was arrested, the case coming before the courts in November 1976. He was fined £50 and given a two-year suspended sentence for causing an affray. His Hong Kong police record was inadmissible. Despite the lenient sentence, the police were not displeased. The whole episode had been a well-studied object lesson in the Triads.

Two of those arrested with Pai were already known to the police. Anthony Lam and Joe Lim were both involved in narcotics. Lam's diary was discovered and named Pai as a Triad. It was then discovered that Li Mah had introduced Pai to his Singaporean associates when he first arrived in Britain. Clearly, the police believed, Pai was an important underworld figure. It was discovered that he was married to a young Chinese woman called Sandy, had a small son and lived in a flat in Birmingham, although he gave his address as his parents' restaurant. He travelled the southern half of Britain, staying most frequently in Manchester, Portsmouth and Southampton, where he ran protection rackets and, on occasion, it is thought, drugs. Only Liverpool, under the control of the 14K, was forbidden to him.

Throughout 1976, Pai was rarely seen in London, where Ah Hung was taking a percentage from every Chinese gambling den on his behalf. All the while, Pai was consolidating his position, not always successfully. In Portsmouth, he was set upon by a party of Chinese seamen defending a gambling den they frequented. Organizers of late-night Chinese-language film shows to whom Pai offered protection also occasionally crossed him.

By 1977, he was doing well. Manchester police reckoned every Chinese business in the city was paying an average of £8 per week in protection money. Pai was said to claim that he collected £250 a week from just one gambling club. In London, an informer reported he was earning £20 a week from restaurants but up to £200 a week from unlicensed gambling establishments.

Bit by bit, police knowledge of Pai was accrued and assessed, and suggested his implication in a wide range of offences. Yet no-one would testify against him. He was not just feared but respected. Unlike many Triads, he was approachable and possessed considerable charisma. Within the Triad code, he was forthright and trustworthy, never shirking fraternal responsibility for the welfare of his brothers or their families. Anthony Lam's wife held him in high esteem and business associates who were not Triads enjoyed his company, for he was witty and a good conversationalist. In many respects, he was a traditional Triad who accepted the obligations his position gave him.

Police attention did not hamper Pai's career. One of his 49s, arrested in the Gerrard Street fight, skipped bail and fled to Amsterdam with an Irish girlfriend. Together they set up what was, for its time, a sophisticated smuggling route, flying heroin from Bangkok to Amsterdam via Moscow then sending it to Britain by courier from The Netherlands or by mail from Belgium, to an address in

Kettering, Northamptonshire. From there, it was allegedly distributed by Pai. How much truth there is in this is debatable. Much of Pai's life is now clouded by the mythology which rises around important underworld figures. It is unlikely. The heroin, it was reported, was sold to London and Liverpool, but the latter was in the grip of the 14K and Pai was anathema to them. Furthermore, he was making good money from protection rackets and may not have wanted to jeopardize this by dealing in heroin when he had seen the length of sentence handed down for narcotics trafficking. He also knew the police were more likely to target narcotics traders than extortionists. On the other hand, police intelligence gained from informers suggested he was in the heroin game, though this may have been deliberate misinformation given by Pai's competitors.

The tables began to turn. First of all, Pai overlooked renewing his visa to Britain, which drew him to the attention of both the police and the immigration authorities in July 1977. That November, he was arrested by Hampshire police and charged with blackmail and conspiracy to demand money with menaces, as a result of complaints made by film-show organizers in Portsmouth and Southampton. When the case came to trial in June 1978, the court heard that he had a previous conviction for affray. Pai was found guilty and sentenced to two years' imprisonment. Upon his release on 27 March 1979, he was deported to Hong Kong. Police records at the time stated that he was very dangerous, highly influential and the top Wo Shing Wo official in Britain.

Where Pai went in addition to Hong Kong, how long he spent in the colony and when he returned to Europe is not known for certain, but on 5 October 1983 he was stopped by immigration officers at Dover, re-entering Britain from Brussels on a false passport, and turned back. Early in 1984, he illegally entered the country and was arrested in April, but released pending an appeal against deportation. He was, by now, considered to be the most powerful and important Triad in Britain. He fought deportation until the summer of 1992 when the Home Office, despite police intervention and a review of his criminal career, granted him temporary right of abode. In January 1993 this was ratified. Rumours circulated that he not only had astute but also well-connected lawyers who had lobbied key figures in the Conservative government on his behalf. It was thought they had persuaded the authorities that, if Pai was returned to Hong Kong, he would face political retribution when China regained sovereignty over the colony in 1997. There was no foundation for this assumption.

Not long after the announcement of Pai's permission to remain in Britain, he came under the scrutiny of Roger Cook, the investigative television journalist, who made him the subject of a *Cook Report* exposé. This, not surprisingly, infuriated Pai and he issued a writ for libel against Granada Television, the programme producers. To date, this has not been acted upon.

Today, Pai is thought in law enforcement circles to be the undisputed head of the Wo Shing Wo in Birmingham, if not in Britain, and under more or less constant police observation. What criminality he is involved in is not fully known. It is said he now acts as a true *shan chu*, mediating in Triad disputes and keeping the Triad peace. In 1994, the London head of the Wo Shing Wo was ferociously attacked and clinically died three times whilst undergoing surgery. His attackers were never identified and no arrests were forthcoming. Curiously, no revenge attacks were made either, possibly due to Pai's overriding arbitration. Police forces across Britain believe Pai still holds the key to much of the country's Triad activities but they cannot prove it and, although they keep an eye on him, they are now preoccupied with men who are not as traditional as Pai and, whilst not necessarily any more cunning, are far more ruthless.

Throughout the 1980s, Britain's Triad societies jockeyed with each other for supremacy, the ebb and flow of power shifting from one to the other as territorial control moved, the Chinese criminal world in a state of flux. The only constant factor was the victims, who had to put up on demand and shut up. Crimes ranged wider than before and now included such activities as VAT fraud, often perpetrated through a legitimate business which was obliged to break the laws and risk being caught. If tax inspectors discovered the fraud, it was the law-abiding Chinese who suffered and were stigmatized as tax embezzlers. Drugs were trafficked, but these tended not only to be the 'class A' dangerous drugs like heroin but also the 'softer' varieties such as cannabis and the new 'designer drugs', many of them manufactured in The Netherlands and Germany then imported into Britain by Triad couriers, against stiff competition from European dealers.

New societies arrived in Britain. In the years after the British government signed the Joint Declaration in 1984 for the reversion of Hong Kong sovereignty to China, an atmosphere of uncertainty hung over the colony and this impinged itself upon Triads as much as on traders and tycoons. A number of Triad societies, hitherto unknown in Britain, moved in. Amongst these, the two main arrivals were the Wo On Lok (colloquially referred to as the Shui Fong, or Water House) and the San Yee On.

The Wo On Lok is highly organized and very professional, many of its hierarchy being successful businessmen with legitimate companies who use the society to extend their profits, avoid taxation and launder illegal earnings. Centred on London and Southampton, they maintain links with other Wo On Lok groups in Eire, The Netherlands, Germany and France and tend to prefer to make their money from 'victimless' crimes such as gambling, counterfeiting and video piracy, although they also engage in extortion.

An insight into their activities in Britain was gained in 1993 when a Triad informer and self-proclaimed Wo On Lok hit-man, George Cheung Wai-hen, gave evidence to the Old Bailey trial of six Chinese charged with possession of a firearm with intent and conspiracy to cause grievous bodily harm to a rival, Lam Ying-kit. Cheung – who had been instructed to kill Lam but, with other accomplices, had botched the attempt on 7 September 1991 – outlined for the court his initiation ceremony, which had been held at 2 a.m. in the basement of the Princess Garden Chinese restaurant in Greyhound Road, Fulham. The ceremony more or less followed the traditional pattern, and Cheung stated that he had to pay his proposer and *dai lo* – an actor called Tang Wai-ming – £36.60, the usual traditional initiation fee in Britain. Cheung was given a reduced sentence of five years because of his co-operation.

The San Yee On in Britain is run along very business-like lines and appears in structure as much like a well-run company as a criminal syndicate. It owns legitimate businesses, deals in white-collar crime and specializes internationally in the Oriental entertainment business, setting up concerts and theatrical plays by artistes from the Far East, not necessarily for exclusively Chinese audiences.

The second-biggest Triad society in Britain is the 14K. Still prevalent in Liverpool and London, with a presence in other cities, it preys upon Chinese businesses and, to a lesser but still measurable extent, other immigrant companies such as small West Indian and Asian firms, usually corner shops and small factories. Pakistani and Indian businesses are the more likely targets, as West Indians tend to fight back or report instances of intimidation to the police, whereas Asians are more docile and eager to avoid trouble. 14K membership is drawn from the Chinese community, attracting disaffected teenagers of school age or young men from the growing population of illegal immigrants from mainland China. Reports of non-ethnic Chinese youths joining the 14K have circulated, but their veracity is as yet unproven.

What is proven is that British urban youth gangs not infrequently emulate Triads, hero-worshipping them after watching Chinese kung-fu and gangster movies. These quasi-'triad' gangs – which go by such names as the Gremlins, the Nam Boys and, in the Fulham area of London, the SW Triads – sometimes have Chinese members who may introduce their peers to real Triads. Gang membership is mostly made up of white or racially mixed – usually Eurasian rather than Afro-European –

teenagers and men in their early twenties. They may be imitations, but they are just as vicious, their targets frequently other youths whom they bully and rob, and whom, on occasion, they attack. They also force young girls into prostitution, keeping them 'loyal' with threats of considerable violence to both themselves and their families. These prostitutes frequently work not just for the gang but for a Triad-run brothel where they can charge as much as £250 an hour.

Chinese youth-gang graffiti has adorned London subways and railway embankments since 1988, vying for space with the scrawl of vandals and football hooligans. In October of that year, a Vietnamese youth was garrotted, his body dumped into the Thames. When his corpse was found, it was wearing a T-shirt bearing a spider-and-web design, thought to be a Vietnamese Triad-style gang uniform.

The most infamous act of violence involving pseudo-triads was the murder of a much-respected London headmaster. Philip Lawrence, principal of St George's Roman Catholic secondary school in Maida Vale, west London, was fatally stabbed a few weeks before Christmas 1995, when he went to the defence of a pupil being beaten with an iron bar in the street outside his school gates. As he remonstrated with his pupil's attackers, Learco Chindamo, a fifteen-year-old of mixed Italian–Filipino parentage, turned on the teacher, kicking him and slapping his face before stabbing him in the chest. Lawrence was given open-heart surgery in a school corridor and underwent a six-hour operation in hospital, but died from his wounds. It transpired that Chindamo and his gang had been called in at the request of a pupil at the school to sort out a younger student with whom he was in dispute.

Chindamo was infatuated by the Triads. He and his comrades, one of whom was atypically black, adopted Triad mannerisms, dressed in dark clothes with bandannas at their throats and carried weapons. Chindamo was reported as possessing a range of knives, a baseball bat and a set of Chinese martial-arts fighting staves. Truanting from school, where he was listed as a disruptive student, he spent his time wandering the streets of London with his gang, extorting money from other teenagers and engaging in acts of criminal damage and petty theft. He was sentenced to be detained at Her Majesty's pleasure, an open-ended sentence the completion of which rests upon the discretion of the courts and the government.

At the time, there was much press speculation that Triads had carried out the attack, but this was wrong. Indeed, the word went out that the Triads not only had nothing to do with the incident but decried it. No Triad member would ever lose control of himself in such a way: Triad victims may be chopped, but those who interfered to save them would more likely just be pushed aside or beaten up to discourage their involvement or their turning witness later.

The largest British Triad society today is the Wo Shing Wo, based in Manchester but with sub-branches in Birmingham, London and Glasgow and smaller operating groups in Bristol, Newcastle and Cardiff. It has a substantial force of 49s and a co-ordinated cohort of Red Poles. Recruits are acquired in the usual Triad way, but the Wo Shing Wo also contains businessmen who have either allied themselves with it for their own security or are (for want of a better term) associate members who use the society's criminal activities as an occasional investment opportunity. The various units of 49s, usually centred on a Chinese cultural club or martial-arts association, work in tightly defined urban districts, rarely poaching on another's territory. They will, however, cross turf boundaries in the country at large where they may extort Chinese businesses over a very wide area. It is not unknown for them to seek protection money from Chinese restaurants as far afield as Truro and Great Yarmouth.

Manchester is known as a Dragon City. This is the modern extrapolation of a centuries-old Imperial Chinese edict which allowed important centres to display a dragon at major religious and cultural ceremonies. There are only three other official Dragon Cities outside the Orient – Perth in Australia, San Francisco and Vancouver.

In the 1980s, Manchester was home to one of the most rapidly expanding Chinese communities in the world. From a population of 7,000 in 1980, it numbered over 35,000 by 1990 and is now the second-largest British Chinese community after London. The Chinese are spread across the city, having taken advantage of cheap land prices resulting from the swift decline in heavy industry in the years of the Thatcher government. Trade incentives brought in to address the decline provided added impetus for Chinese businessmen. However, most Chinese businesses are concentrated in a city-centre Chinatown, about 1 km square. So important is the community that it has its own Chinese consular office, a Chinese-language newspaper and a local current-affairs radio programme broadcast in Cantonese. Cathay Pacific, Hong Kong's national airline, flies a daily 747–400 service from the city's airport to the Far East.

The Wo Shing Wo is central to life in the Mancunian Chinese community, where members are so brazen as openly to wear society T-shirts. They have an iron grip on the Chinese labour market and few new arrivals obtain employment without joining them or paying an 'employment agency' fee. Companies are threatened with withdrawal of labour and pay to keep their businesses going. Illegal immigrants form a virtual Wo Shing Wo criminal workforce.

According to Greater Manchester police intelligence, the Wo Shing Wo is led by Georgie Pai as *shan chu*; his *fu shan chu* is a successful restaurateur and merchant with businesses across northern England and as far south as Birmingham. The central structure of the society consists of thirteen senior office-bearers and up to 200 49s. Police believe the society earns much of its income from protection rackets aimed at restaurants and casinos frequented by Chinese, many of which are legally licensed, and at the Chinese video-rental trade.

Rivalry between any of the San Yee On, 14K, Wo On Lok and Wo Shing Wo is common, but is most bitter between the last two. In the south of England, the Southampton-based Wo On Lok and a Wo Shing Wo society in Portsmouth are in frequent conflict. In Cardiff, Glasgow, Belfast and across the Midlands from Birmingham to Nottingham, their internecine struggles are especially rancorous, mainly centred on the Chinese video-entertainment business, which, in the late 1990s, is big business. The two societies control or have significant

469

holdings in 85 per cent of the market. The products over which they fight are the latest Chinese-language films, television soaps and dramas, Chinese rock-music videos and Cantonese or Beijing opera.

Original cassettes or laser discs are legally purchased in the Far East, the contents then pirated and distributed around the world to feed expatriate desires for Chinese home entertainment. It is possible to make up to 5,000 copies of a VHS video cassette before losing picture quality; with laser discs, the number of copies is unlimited. In Britain in 1997, a video cassette of a recently released Chinese movie is rented out for between £3 and £7 a night. Three copies of one film can, therefore, gross on average £105 a week, £2,700 over the expected six-month life of a new movie. Multiply this by the number of films released each month and the several hundred Chinese video shops around Britain, then take into account the initial unit production and distribution cost of about £5 for each cassette, and the profitability of the business can be appreciated. The Chinese video trade in Britain in 1997 grossed approximately £18 million. It provides an excellent means of laundering money and is not regarded as a high priority by police. The tax authorities regularly investigate the trade, but rarely bring a successful prosecution as evidence of tax evasion is hard to prove.

A Triad murder in Glasgow is thought to have been connected to this trade. In October 1986, Philip Wong was hacked to death before a crowd of Chinese witnesses, his murder not only an act of revenge but a warning to the community. Wong was a successful restaurateur, well respected in both the Chinese and

470

the wider community, but he was also the *pak tsz sin* of the Wo On Lok. He had crossed a Wo Shing Wo member who had been pirating cassettes to which Wong had purchased the rights. In 1985, Wong was brash enough to instigate legal action against the Wo Shing Wo man, as a result of which, it is said, he was called to an arbitration meeting at which, it is thought, he was informed that the Wo Shing Wo were henceforth going to run the Glasgow Chinese-video market. The arbitrator also allegedly requested a payment of £2,000 by way of apology for the insult of the intended court action. Wong seemingly refused to comply and settled the 'debt of honour' with his life.

As the 1980s progressed, police awareness of and action against Triads increased. The Triads responded to this with tougher measures aimed at their victims, partly to gain face and partly to make up for lost revenue. Chinese businesses, whilst still very much afraid of Triads, started to become less compliant and, although Britain does not maintain a witness-protection programme, more willing to come forward with complaints or 'anonymous' tip-offs.

Needless to say, Triad violence continued. In 1987, a number of Chinese were tried in Glasgow for the chopping of John Cheng Pik-wai. Cheng, a restaurant-owner, was middle aged and had lived in Scotland since 1974. Much respected in the Chinese community, he was a martial-arts master and considered by many Glaswegian Chinese as a sage-like figure to whom they turned for advice on religious and cultural matters and even help with traditional medicine. He frequently acted as an arbitrator in minor disputes and, through his martial-arts mastership, had a large following across Britain. Some of his disciples were Triads, although he was not.

An astute businessman, Cheng had set his eye on owning one of Glasgow's best Chinese eating-houses, the Loon Fung, which came up for sale. Another would-be purchaser was the owner of a chain of Chinese video-rental shops from Southampton called George Tsang. Nicknamed Fat Man, he was a leading Wo On Lok member and his society was eager to gain a foothold in Glasgow where there was no particular Triad society in overall control. Tsang was out-bid, however, and the vendors sold the Loon Fung to Cheng. Tsang, having lost face, threatened Cheng to try to make him sell the establishment, but Cheng stood firm. At that point, Tsang acquired a hit squad which travelled north to Glasgow and hacked Cheng with meat cleavers so badly that he came within an inch of losing his life. After the attack, Tsang vanished, probably overseas.

The affair was nothing out of the ordinary for a Triad hit save in two respects. Cheng survived what was intended to be a lethal attack, probably because of his ability to defend himself and focus his inner strength, and he was prepared to take the stand in court. He presented the judge with a fascinating insight into the Triad under-world, not just in Glasgow but nationwide. And he named names. 'Golo' Ming, whose real name was John Cheung Wai-ming, a one-time Hong Kong prison war-der and a Wo On Lok member already wanted in Manchester for a chopping incident, was found guilty of the attack and sentenced to twelve years' imprisonment for attempted murder.

The repercussions of the John Cheng attack reached

beyond a conviction and intelligence-gathering. Cheng's bravery in acting as a witness steeled the resolve of many more Chinese and they started to report crimes to the police.

In Liverpool in November 1989, Lau Kam-keung (known as Freddie Lau or Crazy Kim) was sentenced to ten years for conspiracy to blackmail. The victim, Wong Mai-cheung, who ran a restaurant in Nelson Street, had been the victim of Lau's extortion since 1986. He had dutifully paid up until he heard of the John Cheng case and of a complaint to the police made by another Chinese resulting in an arrest. Wong decided that he had had enough and, at meetings with Lau, secretly tape-recorded his threats. Other Chinese subsequently followed these examples and suddenly the Triads were not only no longer as secure from arrest as they had been, but they also suffered a loss of face and, worse, income.

As a result, the Triads began looking for new opportunities. By the early 1990s they had found one – or, rather, they reactivated one. It was heroin.

For well over a decade, since the high-profile busts of the mid-1970s, the British Triads had only dabbled in heroin, leaving the trade to others. Despite continuously improving standards of police and customs operations, large shipments of heroin were still imported. Regardless of anti-drugs campaigns, the danger of AIDS and the increase in cocaine and designer-drug usage, heroin remained the drug of choice for many. To cater for them, traffickers adapted their systems to cope with changing law enforcement methods and tactics.

Much of what came into Britain was not from the Golden Triangle but originated in the Golden Crescent, smuggled by Pakistani and Middle Eastern syndicates in collusion with European organized-crime gangs. However, a percentage was of Triad origin, arriving by way of Amsterdam or Central America.

In the past, it had been comparatively easy to catch a Triad smuggler. For one, he was Chinese and stood out. By the late 1980s this racial aid was defunct. The Triad smugglers adapted. They abandoned Oriental couriers, Chinese seamen or airline staff and, for a while, used Nigerians or Ghanaians before concentrating upon Westerners. Backpackers, always keen to earn some money to return home or move on, were a good target but somewhat obvious: they bore, in a customs officer's eyes, the stigma of hippydom. Tourists were also a good bet. Some agreed to risk carrying heroin to pay for their holiday or make a sudden windfall. Others were duped into the trade by having their bags tampered with by Chinese staff in hotels or airports. Not a few were befriended by Chinese whilst on holiday and persuaded to take a small present back to a relative working in Britain. However, the heroin trafficker of the 1990s is an altogether new animal. He (or she) is now more likely to be well educated, widely travelled, intelligent, cosmopolitan, efficient and astute, with a good head for figures and, usually, looks like what he or she really is – a businessman working in a multinational commodities market.

In the 1990s, there has been a revival in heroin usage in Britain and Triad participation in it. It began in 1985 with the arrival in Britain of a Hong Kong Chinese called Li Koon-mui. The *shan chu* of the 14K in Amsterdam, where he ran a gambling club, he had been deported from The Netherlands with a string of narcotics convictions to his name, starting with a four-year sentence for trafficking in 1977. He also had a reputation for violence and was associated with a machine-gun attack on Triad opponents. Shortly after his appearance in London there were several Triad shootings. These were unusual: British Triads, living under tight gun-control laws, tend not to use firearms.

Once he was settled, Li was joined by some of his 14K brothers from Amsterdam and began to encourage the society to build itself up, especially in London. His motivation seemed to be twofold. First, he wanted to become dominant in London, where he started a new gambling joint, and, second, he needed a fit fighting force to take on the Big Circle Boys who were threatening 14K heroin dealing on the Continent. In other words, Li had retrenched to Britain to regroup. Whether or not he was successful in ousting the Big Circle Boys is unknown, but he did become head of the 14K in London although he did not stay long. In the early 1990s, having fallen foul of the immigration authorities, he was superseded by a newcomer and left Britain. Unconfirmed reports had him moving to Belgium. His successor is now the undisputed head of the 14K in Britain and the most influential man in London's Chinatown.

In early 1995, a new phenomenon appeared on Gerrard Street: mainland Chinese immigrants, predominantly men from Fujian. Compared with the resident Chinese, they were as obvious as Chinatown's two ceremonial lion statues around which they gathered. They wore cheap, old-fashioned suits or anoraks made in Communist China, spoke only Putonghua and begged from other Chinese. The lions became referred to by locals as the

Unemployment Exchange. Chinese who offered them jobs found them lazy and unreliable. When the police arrested them for vagrancy or as illegal aliens, they immediately applied for political asylum, although few received it.

Most of these opportunist asylum-seekers were ill equipped to apply for sanctuary. They had broken all the cardinal rules for seeking refugee status. Better prepared were the Chinese dissidents who were granted residency in Britain after the Tienanmen Square massacre. In London they established 'democratic societies' and, for £5,000, would provide a full set of fake, but very genuine-looking documents to support an asylum request. These included such papers as copies of Chinese arrest warrants, letters from friends warning the bearer not to return to China, reports of family members being harassed for information, even wanted posters. Immigration officials were taken in and asylum granted.

In the mid-summer of 1995, two mainland Chinese illegals from Fujian province, Fei Lin and Tao Zhang, were found murdered. Investigations suggested that they had tried to muscle in on an illegal immigrant-smuggling racket. This was not unusual. A number of the lion-lingerers had changed, chameleon-like, from shabby down-and-outs into snappily dressed, mobile-phone carriers with money in their pockets. They were the lucky ones, recruited by the Triads or employed by immigrant smugglers to receive new arrivals.

The smuggling racket grew over the next few years, police regularly raiding establishments in London to discover up to thirty men living in a three-bedroomed council flat, sleeping by turn on mattresses on the floor, packed together like sardines. The coolie tenements of nineteenth-century Hong Kong had metamorphosed into cramped squats in modern London. Immigration officers found dozens at a time squashed into container lorries from The Hague or Antwerp, loaded with flowers or dry goods. At times, so many were discovered that the authorities could arrest only a small number because they simply had insufficient accommodation for them all. Those not arrested promptly vanished, whilst those who were apprehended applied for housing and welfare benefits and got them. Even after being housed, they remain unemployed and unemployable in the long term. As such, they are ready recruits for Triad societies.

For a while, in the years leading up to the British withdrawal from Hong Kong in 1997, there was a fear that the Triads might move out of the colony before the Communists moved in. The fear was allayed by a parliamentary commission in 1985 which declared, 'We are satisfied that there are no Triads operating in the UK, simply gangs using Triad nomenclature, to inspire fear. Thus the shadow of the threat of retribution is disproportionately larger than its substance. The word "Triad" could be usefully dropped from the police vocabulary.' Although a pre-1997 mass Triad exodus did not occur, the commission conclusion was a miscalculation of astounding proportions.

By 1988, it had become clear that the Triads were still very much part of the vocabulary. Police forces started to hold regional and national conferences specifically on the subject, officers were sent to Hong Kong on specialized Triad training courses and the presence of undercover officers was increased. The John Cheng attack opened many eyes and prompted Superintendent John Sharkey of the Strathclyde police, which dealt with the Cheng case, to address an inter-force conference with the words:

> I do not share that [government] spokesman's clairvoyant confidence to make such a generalization. Triads, gangs, groups, whatever you wish to call them, do exist and operate within the British–Chinese community within the United Kingdom. They are distinguished from ordinary gangs by their ritual, degree of organization, and order. They are identifiable by sub-groups within a rank structure, their codes of practice, and their allegiances to their bosses in Hong Kong. The Chinese criminal world is almost an impenetrable secret community on its own.

In part, Sharkey was wrong. Triads in Britain do not owe an allegiance to Dragon Heads in Hong Kong and their interest in ritual has long since faded to the very basics, but he was utterly correct in his assumption that they have a criminal presence in every aspect of Chinese life in modern Britain.

As the century turns – after a period of insensibility to the problem caused by innocence rather than indolence – police action against the Triads is increasingly successful, if only in certain forces. The Metropolitan Police have developed a particular expertise in combating Triad and, more recently, ethnic Chinese crime caused by non-Triad Chinese syndicates. Infiltration of the Triads is far more sophisticated and effective, relying upon informers and a select number of intelligence-gatherers within the Chinese community, and playing upon the perpetual rivalry between different groups: quite often, intelligence is obtained from one Triad seeking to depose a competitor. As a result of competent policing, Triad activity in Britain is no longer as serious a threat as it once was and control over their crime is being maintained. However, the Triads are far from being defeated.

3

CLIMBERS ON THE GOLDEN MOUNTAIN

In the mid-nineteenth century, a name was coined in southern China. In Cantonese it was pronounced Kau Kum Shan. It offered hope to hundreds of thousands and a dream to millions. Meaning the Golden Mountain, it was the colloquial name for San Francisco and became the generic name for America, the destination of the adventurous and the desperate.

Chinese traders from the Sam Yap first arrived in what is now California in the 1830s, but it was not until 1848 that the real influx began, thousands emigrating to escape poverty in China. When gold was discovered in California, gold fever struck Guangdong and Fujian. Shipping companies published broadsides stating that coolies would be as rich as mandarins in a year, in a land where food was cheap, illness rare and danger absent. In 1848, 2,000 Cantonese emigrated; four years later, over 20,000 entered California at San Francisco alone. Most arrived as labourers in the goldfields or on railroad construction, working freelance or for Chinese or American concerns.

They were ripped off from the moment they landed. Triads operating the travel agencies in China were in league with confederates in San Francisco. Once the immigrants arrived, they had to register with the appropriate Triad-affiliated *hui guan*, which welcomed them, temporarily housed them and if necessary found them work, but also kept an eye on them, making sure they paid their debts. By 1862, there were six *hui guan* which joined together to become the Chinese Consolidated Benevolent Association, also known as the Six Companies.

The Chinese were an ideal labour force, hardworking, resilient and uncomplaining. Within five years, 65 per cent of all mine workers west of the Rockies were Chinese. When the gold started to run out, they transferred to railroad-construction companies: were it not for the Chinese, the west coast would not have been opened up so early or so rapidly, nor have flourished as it did – but at a human price, for 70,000 died on the railroads from disease, Indian attacks or abuse.

America might have looked liked a golden mountain from Guangdong, but it was not. Life was cruel, accommodation squalid and the long hours of work exhausting. The promised high salaries never materialized because 'deductions' were made for board and lodging and even tools were sometimes 'hired' to the coolies. White miners drove Chinese prospectors off the best lodes and the government clamped down on them with racially discriminating legislation. No Chinese females were allowed through immigration, nor any children unless they were old enough to work.

When the railroads were completed, few Chinese had the financial means to return home. Their plans for making and saving a fortune had evaporated. With no labouring to do, they did as Chinese have always done. They adapted. Some set up chop-houses and bakeries, some general stores. Chinese laundries appeared in the streets and Chinese servants in the homes of the rich. Chinese barbers cut hair whilst, by 1890, over half of San Francisco's fresh vegetables were grown by Chinese market gardeners. The more successful they became, the more discrimination they faced.

In July 1877, San Francisco erupted in violence aroused by white working-class anti-coolie clubs accusing the Chinese of taking all the menial jobs. Gangs of white youths ran amok, killing Chinese in the streets, looting and torching Chinese homes and businesses. Elsewhere across the American west, Chinese were murdered, lynched and run out of town in a campaign of racial hatred which was to continue for years.

Politicians saw the race ticket as a vote winner. No sooner were the railroads completed than Congress moved against the Chinese. They had served their purpose and were now surplus to social requirement. In May 1882, the Chinese Exclusion Act was passed, to be extended two years later. All Chinese labour immigration was halted. No Chinese was eligible for US citizenship. However, Chinese merchants and their families were permitted entry and labourers already resident were permitted exit and re-entry visas, although this provision was later annulled. As late as 1924, Chinese women were refused permanent residence even if their husbands possessed it and it was not until 1943 that the Act was repealed and Chinese given the right to naturalization. Even then, it was only the need to keep Chiang Kai-shek and the Kuomintang on side in the war against Japan that prompted the move. Chinese immigration was still restricted, a new law limiting it to an intake of exactly 105 per annum. State legislatures made their own laws. In California, ethnic Chinese were barred from marriage to Caucasians until 1948. Chinese businesses were more highly taxed than others and financial transactions with Chinese were liable to surcharge. No Chinese could catch fish or trap furs for resale or trade with Indians, own a plot of more than 20 acres or testify in court (they were considered liable to lie under oath). No company was permitted to employ Chinese.

In the face of such conditions, the Chinese had had only one option: to form self-help societies. These were colloquially known as 'tongs'.

The tongs – the word means an assembly hall – started as mutual societies but were soon central to the life of Chinese communities, becoming the unofficial local Chinese administration providing a social legal framework, arbitrating in disputes, operating a credit union and banking structure, offering welfare in needy cases and running schools. As members were frequently unrelated by place or clan, they pledged their allegiance to each other with an oath-taking ceremony backed up by religious ritual, a secret code and body language. In other words, they were secret societies.

Amongst the first was the Che Kung Tong. Whilst founded by criminals, it was not at first a criminal organization, although it did represent travel agents back in China involved in the illegal-immigrant coolie trade. Gradually, however, it bought immigrants' debts from the travel agents and soon had a large number of timorous creditors whom it placed in employment, extorted and then used as a criminal workforce. Other tongs followed the example, until there was virtually no Chinese who was not a tong member.

Wherever Chinese communities sprang up, tongs provided services for them, organizing primitive sanitation, a watchman corps to look out for racist goons and even streetlighting, yet their main provisions were gambling and opium dens, brothels and doss-houses. Legal opium was shipped in, illegal whores smuggled in hidden in boxes or bales of cloth, or brought in overland from Vancouver. Women were a prized commodity in a 95 per cent male community and were openly sold at market like slaves. After gambling, prostitution was the biggest earner. The whores operated in two types of establishment. The first was typically Chinese, consisting of a 'crib' – a one-bed cubicle surrounded by wooden panels, the entrance hung with a curtain. The occupant traditionally wore black silk. The second was the Western-style 'parlour house', a well-appointed bordello with bedrooms and a saloon bar.

The supposedly dissolute nature of Chinese communities earned them an unsavoury reputation. Racist propaganda published risqué accounts of debauchery, white slavery and narcotics use. All Chinese were declared opium addicts or 'hopheads', although the true figure was about 40 per cent of the population. The tongs were rarely mentioned because the official administration knew little if anything of their existence. The raciness of Chinese quarters, now officially termed Chinatowns, attracted non-Asiatics. White criminals found safe shelter there and, although they rarely joined one, were soon hand in hand with the tongs, helping to spread vice outside the Chinese domain. Chinese whores became much sought after in saloons as far west as Kansas and Nebraska and as far south as the Texas–Mexico border.

By 1900, there were a dozen tongs operating along the western seaboard. As well as running 'services', they taxed Chinese businesses, bribed government officials not to investigate Chinatowns, thereby slowing down the integration of Chinese into the community at large and supported Sun Yat-sen's republican movement, thus proving their patriotism and increasing their power. One of these, the Hip Sing Tong, started in San Francisco as a small mutual-protection association but grew to be the only tong with branches across the entire USA at one time. A century later, it still remains a force to be reckoned with.

Inevitably, Chinatowns were volatile places, the tongs increasingly competing with each other, maintaining gangs of meat-cleaver-armed thugs known as *boo how doy*, or 'high binders', as lookouts and muscle. Conflict was unavoidable and, in 1875, the first tong war broke out in San Francisco, quickly spreading to other cities.

It all began when Lo Sing, a Suey Sing Tong member, was chopped. He reported his attacker to his comrades as being one Ming Long, a Kwong Dock Tong man with whom he was vying for the affections of Kim Ho, a prostitute Lo Sing was trying to buy. Face lost and honour breached, the Suey Sing Tong threw down the gauntlet. The gangs met at midnight at a prearranged road junction and joined battle. Eddie Gong, of the Hip Sing Tong, witnessed the battle and described it in his co-authored book, *Tong War!*, published in 1930:

On one side of the street were the boo how doy of the Suey Sing Tong and on the other the boo how doy of the Kwong Dock Tong. The high binders, who were the best fighters of both tongs, had wound their queues about their heads, wore black slouch hats well down over their eyes, walked with their hands folded indolently across their abdomens and with their knives, daggers, clubs and hatchets stuck in their six-foot-long silken belts beneath their large blouses.

A huge crowd watched the fighting. By the time the police arrived, nine men were seriously injured, four fatally. The authorities investigated the affair. No-one talked. The spectators were blind. The Suey Sing Tong won, gaining much face and renown. Lo Sing married Kim Ho.

For the next half-century, tong wars flared up, caused by territorial disputes, personal animosity and inter-tong grudges. Some were sustained instances of *xie dou*, others short and bloody scraps. Life was cheap, choppings and murders commonplace. The authorities rarely understood the cause and were only infrequently effective in addressing it.

Of the tong leaders, the most successful was a San Franciscan Chinese called Fung Ching-toi, or Little Pete. Notorious through the 1880s, he led the Sum Yop Tong. He had travelled to America from Guangzhou as a child. By the age of twenty-five he was a tong leader, owned a number of gambling and opium dives and was infamous for his ruthlessness: rumour has it that he ordered at least fifty murders in his career. He was eventually arrested for attempting to bribe a jury and district attorney, and sentenced to five years in San Quentin prison, during which time his reputation increased. On release, he teamed up with an Irish gang boss, 'bought' some police officers and became the undisputed Dragon Head of Chinatown. The other tongs, and some lower-ranked Sum Yop Tong members, wanted him dead, but he was too well protected. Yet his time came and, as if prophesying future American mob hits, he was murdered in a barber's chair.

Another famous figure in 1880s San Francisco was a *boo how doy* who was also a poet. Hong Ah-kay was noted for his lyrical verse, scholarship and gentle mien. In battle, however, he was a ferocious master of the chopper. In one affray, he was said to have cracked open seven skulls with seven consecutive blows: this may be hearsay, for seven is an auspicious number. Nevertheless, his tong honoured him for the exploit. The police had a different view. He was arrested and hanged.

After San Francisco, the second Chinatown of any size to appear was in New York. By 1872, it contained 700 Chinese, most of whom had headed east after the boom in railroad-building ceased. They were joined by others, swelling the population to about 15,000 by 1890. As in San Francisco, gambling, opium and prostitution were the main industries. Only two tongs existed in New York, the On Leong Tong and the Hip Sing Tong.

Their tong war began in 1899. Tom Lee, for years the On Leong Tong boss and main gambling-joint owner, ruled Chinatown until confronted by Mok Duk (also known as Mock Duck or Mark Dock), a merciless Hip Sing Tong *boo how doy* who wore a chain mail vest, was armed with two revolvers and a meat cleaver, and carried the ambition of ousting Lee and the On Leong Tong. In collaboration with Lem Tong-sing (also known as Scarface Charley Tong), the Hip Sing Tong leader, he torched an On Leong Tong boarding house on Pell Street, taking control of the street, and informed the authorities of the whereabouts of their gambling dens. Thereafter, the Hip Sing Tong owned Pell Street and the On Leong Tong possessed Mott Street until the late 1940s.

Battles and assassinations raged on and off for some years. In 1904, the war intensified with a smaller gang, The Four Brothers Tong, joining in. In 1906, Judge Warren W. Foster brokered a peace but it lasted only seven days. Another truce was forged six months later which held until 1909, when violence flared again with random choppings and shootings and a few more spectacular murders such as the killing of five On Leong Tong members in a theatre, the gunfire masked by firecrackers, and that of a famous Chinese comic opera singer called Ah Hoon. An On Leong Tong man, Hoon was shot in a locked and guarded room by a Hip Sing Tong hit man who was lowered from the roof of the building in a sling to shoot him through the window. In all, 350 Chinese were reckoned to have died in 1909 alone, their deaths interspersed with frequent but transitory peace treaties brokered by a judge. Another peace treaty was forged by the Republic of China's ambassador and the New York Police Department which established the Chinese Peace Society in 1913, all the tongs and the Chinese Merchant Association being signatories. The peace continued until 1924 when some disgruntled On Leong Tong members absconded to the Hip Sing Tong with the former's funds.

As for Mok Duk, he survived a contract of US$1,000 put out on him by Tom Lee: in fact, the two hit men brought in from San Francisco to waste him, Yee 'Girl-Face' Toi and Sing Dock, wound up in their own quarrel, with the former killing the latter. Mok Duk was never indicted for any violent crime, his only stretch inside being in 1912 when he was locked up in Sing Sing for six months for operating a *chi fa* racket and gambling den. His term of imprisonment caused a lull in the fighting, which continued on his release. Eventually, he retired to Brooklyn, a rich man.

Every outbreak of tong violence hit the national headlines and pulp magazines. Gory tales of Oriental mayhem captured and coloured the public imagination, reaching a climax in the Fu Manchu stories of Sax Rohmer. They did the Chinese community no good, showing them to be brutal, lawless and corrupt although, the tong fighters aside, the Chinese were the most law-abiding ethnic group in America. Caucasians generally avoided Chinatowns. In June 1889, Rudyard Kipling narrowly avoided being shot in a San Francisco Chinatown gambling den, but this was coincidental as he was not the intended target but caught in the middle of a tong dispute. Most whites were usually unmolested in Chinese communities and only at risk from pickpockets or, after dark, criminals of their own race.

The tong wars focused public attention on the problems of organized crime, not run just by Chinese but also by Irish, Jewish and, later, Italian gangsters. Yet despite this awareness, little was done to curb the tongs and they grew more entrenched and successful, expanding their criminal activities and sinking their tendrils deeper into the fabric of Chinese life across the nation.

As the Chinese gradually came to be more accepted into society as a whole, attitudes towards Chinatowns and the tongs altered. By the early 1930s, Chinese families were moving in, the ratio of the sexes started to equalize and the demand for whores dropped. The Second World War also took away so many young white men that the parlour houses were made redundant, the tongs losing much of their income. After Pearl Harbor, the Chinese were viewed sympathetically as fellow sufferers of Japanese aggression and the tongs further marginalized. They had to adapt and, by 1946, under pressure from Chinese community leaders and merchants in league as the Chinese Consolidated Benevolent Association, many were transformed into the American equivalent of *kai fong* associations. The Ying On Tong, for example, became the Ying On Labor and Merchants' Benevolent Association. As such, they took on social responsibilities and respectability. They also regarded themselves as patriotic and substantially contributed to Chiang Kai-shek's Kuomintang anti-Japanese fundraising initiatives. Madame Chiang Kai-shek, née Mei-ling Soong, and an associate of Big-eared Du, was voted 'Woman of the Year' by women in the USA year after year.

Some tongs remained criminal, but even their crime was modified. Vice, opium and gambling dens were restricted to the Chinese. Where whorehouses had been, eating-houses appeared and Chinatowns, far from being avoided, became tourist attractions. The tongs, criminal or otherwise, started to make money from the tourist and entertainment industries.

The criminal tongs may have had to adapt to the times, but their leaders remained feared. They carried on their extortion rackets, taking more money as the Chinese communities grew wealthier. Their criminality was insidious, rarely reported to the police and involved only Chinese. To the outsider the Chinese communities appeared prosperous and stable, but they actually seethed with crime. It was not until 1951 that any state recognized the tong situation, when the California regional office of the Federal Bureau of Narcotics and Dangerous Drugs published a report into the complexities of Chinese ethnic crime. Doing something about it, however, was another matter. The tongs were institutionalized and thought to be impossible to eradicate.

From 1965, Chinese immigration to the USA intensified with the lifting of immigration quotas and restrictions. Chinatowns expanded fast. New York's Chinese population rose from 20,000 in 1960 to over 400,000 in 1995. The tongs increased in size and expanded their activities to meet the new demand, especially in gambling joints. Similar numbers of Vietnamese and Triads from Hong Kong and Taiwan arrived. They were a breed apart from the tongs, which, even if criminal, were still charitable institutions. The Triad newcomers quickly infiltrated the tongs. An FBI report in 1985 declared that, whilst most tong members were law-abiding, community-minded citizens, they were increasingly being manipulated by Triads who hid behind them.

One of the first outward manifestations of the Triads was the appearance of youth gangs made up of streetwise *fei jai* determined to establish themselves in the eyes of

Chinese Americans with whom they had little in common. Custom-made 49-type enforcers, the tong leaders and Triad officials were quick to adopt them. The first gang to come to official notice was the Wah Ching, meaning Chinese Youth. Founded in 1964 in the Bay area of San Francisco, its primary objective was to defend members from Chinese American aggression. They were followed in San Francisco by the Joe Boys, named after their Macanese leader, Joe Fong; the Ghost Shadows of New York City, established in 1972; and other New York gangs, including the Flying Dragons, the White Eagles, the Cheung Ching Yee and the Black Eagles, which was a Vietnamese Chinese group.

Under tong control, the gangs evolved into fighting units, each working for a specific master. The Ghost Shadows became the strong arm of the On Leong Tong, the Flying Dragons working for the Hip Sing Tong. They protected loan-sharks, guarded gambling dens, peddled narcotics and collected protection money. In return, they were allowed to own monopolies such as the sale of firecrackers and joss-sticks.

The Ghost Shadows' early leader was a charismatic youth from Kowloon, Hin Pui-lui, known as Nickie Louie. Efficient and fearless, he led his gang against the Flying Dragons whom he was determined to quash. Over a dozen attempts had been made on his life by the time he was twenty-six and, for a while in the 1970s, it looked as if the tong wars might return to New York.

As more immigrants arrived through the 1970s and 1980s, more gangs formed, competition increased and the murder rate rose. The year 1977 was particularly brutal. The Wah Ching fought a series of battles with the

Cheung Ching Yee, which was trying to take over their lucrative firecracker business. At first, the Wah Ching were victorious but, in September, the Cheung Ching Yee hit back. Three masked men entered the Golden Dragon restaurant in San Francisco and opened fire on Wah Ching diners with a .38 pistol, two shotguns and an assault rifle. One of the hit-men, 'Crazy Melvin' Yu, emptied the assault rifle into a seated man whom he assumed to be the Wah Ching leader: he was, in fact, a Japanese law student. He then turned the weapon on three Chinese girls at a nearby table, killing them before spraying the entire dining room. The two men armed with shotguns ran upstairs to where the Wah Ching were eating, murdering a waiter *en route*. They, too, opened fire indiscriminately, killing two teenage school pupils. When they fled the carnage, five lay dead and eleven wounded. Not one Wah Ching member was scratched. The city authorities were aghast. Within days, the San Francisco police department set up a dedicated task force but, although they made arrests six months later, they were still out of their depth.

The massacres continued. In 1983, thirteen people were slain in a gambling den in Seattle; the same year, eleven were killed when Flying Dragon members hit Ghost Shadow members in the Golden Star bar in New York. On both occasions, innocent spectators became victims. Behind the massacres, the rate of individual murders relentlessly climbed.

Still, it seemed that few people made the link between these gangs, the tongs and Triad organized crime: indeed, the term 'Triad' only came into use with American law-enforcement agencies from about 1985. As soon as the link was realized, conspiracy theories abounded. Were they controlled by Far Eastern societies? Was there a central criminal commission? Were they real or pseudo-triads? Studies revealed them to be autonomous but in touch with overseas societies; there was possibly a loose confederacy or a commission; and they used rituals, though these were less than shadows of real Triad ceremonies.

It was gradually realized that their connection with overseas Triads existed for one primary reason: to obtain narcotics, particularly heroin, from Teochiu Triads in Hong Kong and Thailand. The relationship had been building since the 1970s when FBI successes against the Mafia altered the face of the US narcotics market.

The growth of New York's Chinatown had long since led to an increase in friction between the Triads and the Mafia. They had an almost special mutual animosity, which lay partially in the fact that the common boundary between the areas of Chinatown and Little Italy was Canal Street. The Chinese had stayed to the south, the Italians to the north: no Chinese had dared cross into Mafia territory and no self-esteemed Italian would be seen slumming it with the 'slants', as the Chinese were colloquially known in Mafia circles.

The Mafia attitude towards the Triads is well illustrated by the recording obtained from a listening device planted in the home of Mafia godfather Paul Castellano, quoted in *Boss of Bosses* by Joseph F. O'Brien and Andris Kurins, the two FBI agents who ran the bug. A mafioso was heard to remark: 'You gotta be strong with the Chinese. They sense weakness, they get brave. You gotta push their skinny asses into a chair and stick your fingers in their face.

Keep your fucking chopsticks outa my plate, you little slant cock-sucker. You savvy?'

Yet now the Chinese were growing in power and organization and moving uptown. As the Italians were removed from the scene, a vacuum formed and it was this, more than anything else, that helped the Triads and the Chinese gangs to power. Not only had they access to product, but they also had a well-developed organization through which to smuggle and distribute it. At first their heroin was unpopular, for they cut it too thinly, but from 1977 they raised purity levels so that, by 1987, heroin of 85 per cent purity was available. When the fear of AIDS increased, the Triads brought out an even purer, cheaper heroin which could be smoked instead of injected, thus avoiding needle-sharing, hepatitis and possible HIV contamination. For some years, until 1994 when Colombian cocaine barons entered the market, the Triads controlled 95 per cent of the American heroin trade.

The authorities at last started to accept the situation. In 1987, the FBI and the DEA jointly launched an all-out assault on Chinese organized crime, pulling agents off other assignments to create specialist teams. Once on the case, the magnitude of Triad narcotics trafficking became apparent.

In December 1987, three Chinese were arrested in Queens, New York, having been followed from Kennedy airport where they had disembarked from a flight from Bangkok. Their car contained US$1 million in cash and 75 kg of heroin. Two months later, six Hong Kong Chinese and Thais were apprehended smuggling heroin worth over US$150 million in hollow terracotta figures, also flown in from Bangkok. Bigger consignments came by sea container, hidden in a wide variety of general cargo. It was usually landed in California then distributed nationwide, the bulk going to New York. Government agents reported that the Ghost Shadows were one of the main internal heroin traffickers. The link between the tongs and the Triads and the gangs was finally forged.

As if further proof were needed, the On Leong Tong was taken over in the late 1970s by a man whose criminal education, both literally and figuratively, was gained in Hong Kong. Chan Tse-chiu had been a Hong Kong police sergeant serving under the Five Dragons who fled from Hong Kong to Taiwan in 1975 ahead of the ICAC, and, not being able to establish a criminal toehold in Taipei, arrived in New York later that year. He joined the On Leong out of preference to the Hip Sing because the latter had just come under the leadership of Benny Ong Kai-sui, taking over from his brother Sam, who had led it for fifteen years. The Ongs were powerful and Chan was ambitious, but not stupid: the Ongs were too well established.

Investing in a number of legitimate businesses, including several restaurants, a jewellery store and a Chinese funeral parlour, Chan took the name of Edward; the police called him Fast Eddie. Befriending Nickie Louie, he employed the Ghost Shadows to protect his and the On Leong's businesses; he also contacted former comrades in Hong Kong. By 1980, Fast Eddie was head of the On Leong, chairman of the National Chinese Welfare Council and busy ingratiating himself with New York City officials and the police. To enhance his public image, he hired a top New York PR consultancy firm. In 1984, he contributed a large sum, rumoured to be US$10 million, to an American vice-presidential candidate. His motivation was double-pronged: he hoped to lift immigration restrictions and he wanted to 'own' a politician.

Eddie went from strength to strength. When Benny Ong reached the age of seventy, Fast Eddie took over as the leading light of Chinatown. He bankrolled more politicians, one of whom stabbed himself to death whilst being investigated for corruption, 'owned' police officers, set up the Oriental Bank of New York, bought a cinema chain and was elected president of the Continental King Lung Commodities Group, a suspected Triad money-laundering front. He also engaged in heroin importation from Bangkok via Hong Kong: by 1983, it was alleged that he was a drugs baron.

The FBI and the DEA had him in their sights and he was subpoenaed to appear before the President's Commission on Organized Crime in October 1984. He failed to appear. Government testimony named him as the crime overlord of New York's Chinatown. Where Eddie Chan went no-one knows. His legitimate businesses continued to function, but he had flown. Rumours abounded: he was heroin dealing in France, hiding in the Dominican Republic, returned to Taiwan, setting up afresh in Canada, operating a Malaysian heroin syndicate. He has not been traced since, but his fame lives on in fiction: he was the model for Joey Tai, the Chinese gang boss in Robert Daly's novel *The Year of the Dragon*.

With Chan gone, Benny Ong, now in his late seventies, resumed leadership of the Chinese community. A pragmatist of the old school, he kept the lid on Chinatown. When he died, aged eighty-seven, his funeral was one of the last great gangland events. It lasted three days and was attended by Triads from all over the world, giving the FBI an unprecedented photo opportunity.

The tongs and Triads not only received income from crime and legitimate activities. They were also financially and politically supported by the Kuomintang-controlled Taiwanese government. In exchange for this support, the tongs and Triads guaranteed that pro-Kuomintang attitudes prevailed in Chinese communities in the USA and rooted out any left-wing elements. The government strenuously denied the connection, but this was prevarication. In recent years, since the influence of the Kuomintang has waned in Taiwan, the Taiwanese government, eager to eradicate what it can of Triad influence, has leaked or published information confirming the association.

Opponents of the Kuomintang were shown no quarter. Henry Liu, a San Francisco journalist, noted critic of Taiwan and author of a scathing attack on President Chiang Ching-kuo, Chiang Kai-shek's son, was shot in front of his home in October 1984 by a United Bamboo Society hit squad. CIA agents discovered that the hit had been ordered by the United Bamboo Society leader, Chen Chi-li, and the USA demanded his extradition. Taiwan refused but tried him in Taipei. In the trial, Chen declared that he had been ordered to commission the hit by Admiral Weng Hsi-ling, head of the Taiwanese secret service. Both were sentenced to life imprisonment, but the FBI subsequently found out that Chen was continuing to lead the society from his cell, masterminding its heroin business affairs.

Once they had focused on the problem, the authorities went into battle armed with the American Racketeer Influenced and Corrupt Organizations legislation, nicknamed the RICO statutes, which had been founded in 1970 to hit at the organized-crime infiltration of labour unions. Federal agencies such as the FBI, Internal Revenue Service, US Immigration and Naturalization Service, DEA and US customs liaised, in some instances for the first time. The first case to come to court in 1985 was against twenty-five Ghost Shadow members, including Nickie Louie; sentences ranged up to thirty years.

The bedrock of Triad crime in the USA is traditional, with narcotics, illegal immigrant smuggling, extortion, gambling, prostitution and loan-sharking prevalent. Kidnapping is also common. Victims may be wealthy Chinese or members of their families, or illegal aliens who have reneged on debts. The modus operandi is to snatch the victim and hold him in a secret location where he is savagely beaten or, in the case of young women, repeatedly raped. No latitude is given in paying the ransom and many victims are in the end murdered. The business is so profitable that some gangs compete for victims. Thirty-four cases were reported in New York City alone in 1995, but an official guestimate is that only 10–15 per cent of kidnaps are reported. House invasions, where a gang raids a family home, brutalizes the inhabitants, smashes the place up and steals all items of worth are also increasing. Once again, only a percentage are reported.

New crimes coming to the fore in the USA are similar to those conducted elsewhere. Computer-software piracy is one, another proof of the existence of pan-Pacific organized-crime connections. In mid-1997, fake

Microsoft software worth over US$6 million, plus US$3.5 million in cash, were discovered in Los Angeles and Orange County, California. These included 23,000 counterfeit Microsoft Windows 95 CD-ROMs and 26,500 counterfeit Microsoft authenticity certificates manufactured in southern China. Many were indistinguishable from the genuine product. Hi-tech credit-card and counterfeit-currency scams are also engaged in and so – unique to the USA – is hi-tech robbery.

Computer-industry production often flies close to the wind and there is always a danger that microchip supply will falter or fall behind demand. When this occurs, as it did in 1995, computer manufacturers become desperate and chip prices rise sharply. The Triads know this. They spy on silicon-chip companies, often placing an informer in the firm, and kidnap a key personnel member whom they hold in their home or, more often, at the factory. Staff are terrorized and restrained with tape. The chip gangs usually comprise a hard core of efficient gunmen armed with automatic military weapons, together with a smaller group of highly trained thieves who, like professional fine-art robbers, know exactly what to steal. The latest central processing units – the 'brain' of a computer – are the favoured commodity. These gangs are mobile and, because of their specialist nature, may put aside inter-society or inter-gang rivalries in order to select the best operatives available. In California, computer-industry analysts project that the illicit market for microchips will exceed the legitimate market by 2010.

The income from Triad crime, of course, requires laundering. As in most countries, American Triads invest heavily in property and maintain layered, interrelated bank accounts, but in this they encounter a problem. American banks are strictly controlled to prevent their becoming dirty money washing machines and the Department of the Treasury has created the Financial Crimes Enforcement Network (FinCEN), described by its senior financial specialist, Lucrezia Rotolo, as 'neither an intelligence, nor a regulatory, nor a law-enforcement organization. It is all three and more . . . We follow the money because we have learned that this is what hurts such criminal organizations the most.' Supporting legislation demands that all US banks report every transaction over US$10,000 dollars, criminalizes money laundering and forces federal registration of all money transmitters, cheque-encashment agencies, remittance corporations, money changers and giro houses. However, foreign banks not incorporated in the USA are able to avoid such rigorous policing. Over 100 Chinese-owned banks exist in California alone, many of them conducting business in Chinese to hamper investigation. A major conduit for Triad finance and difficult to regulate, they cater exclusively for Chinese customers and are often outwardly small offices, yet the volume of business they conduct is staggering. An example lies in the Monterey Park suburb of Los Angeles. In an area of 7 square miles with an overall population of 60,000, of which a good proportion are Chinese, there were fourteen Chinese banks in 1988 with an estimated daily turnover of US$1.5 million in dirty money alone. Not only money avoids regulation. Gold, platinum, jade, diamonds and other gemstones are also purchased with dirty money, exported and sold.

Another means of avoiding detection is by using the chitty system. Devised during the eighteenth century by merchants in China avoiding tax, this is an underground banking network loosely based upon *hui guan* and *guanxi* but cutting across clan boundaries so that any Chinese may employ it. The centre of the system is the chitty, Cantonese pidgin slang for a small piece of paper. The chitty can be purchased in one country and encashed in another, through Triad contacts. A sort of uncrossed, unendorsed banker's draft, it may be made out in any currency or commodity. In other words, a chitty bought in Bangkok for a million *baht* may be exchanged in Amsterdam for a million *baht*s' worth of heroin. Notification of transactions is today sent globally by coded e-mail or fax. Chitties are rarely discovered by law enforcers and, if they are, they are often either dismissed or not understood for most are innocuously coded. The network, of which many authorities and police forces are totally ignorant, has never been infiltrated.

The old tongs are not yet extinct. The largest, the On Leong, operates nationwide, as does the Hip Sing. In addition, there are the Ying On in southern California and Arizona, the Suey Sing in San Francisco and Los Angeles, and the Ping On in Boston. New York has seen the arrival of a new Triad society, the Tung On, which is connected to the San Yee On in Hong Kong. One of its leaders, a respected businessman and adviser to the state governor, was indicted in 1997 for murder, conspiracy and racketeering. He was claimed to have extorted up to US$100,000 per week from restaurants and earned in excess of US$200,000 a week from protecting gambling clubs.

Other recent law-enforcement successes have hit hard

at the gangs, who have expanded their range. The Wah Ching are represented in most major cities with Chinese communities and are in contact with the 14K in Hong Kong. The Ghost Shadows also operate nationally. Their leader, Chan Wing-yeung, was indicted for racketeering in 1995, the charges referring in part to his being the mastermind behind the Bahamas-based Evergreen Bullion Company which embezzled some US$10 million from 300 investors whilst purportedly trading in precious metals and foreign currency. Much of the evidence against him derived from a phone-tap on his mother's house on Mulberry Street, in the heart of New York's Chinatown. The following year, he turned prosecution witness, his and three others' testimony clearing up seventeen unsolved murders, many of them arising from a Ghost Shadows vs. Tung On war in the early 1990s.

Hong Kong Triads have also moved to America, partly to join in the looting of the Golden Mountain and partly as insurance against the economic uncertainties of the post-British years in the territory. As Far Eastern currencies tumbled over the winter of 1997–8, and the Hong Kong stock market wavered, Triad money moved. Societies known to have branches in the USA include the United Bamboo Society from Taiwan, the 14K, the Wo Shing Wo, the San Yee On, the Wo On Lok and the Wo Hop To. This last unseated the San Yee On from San Francisco; its leader, Raymond Chow, was convicted of narcotics offences in 1996.

The wealth of the Golden Mountain has attracted more than the Triads. Other Asian gangs have appeared, the largest of which are the Vietnamese and the Vietnamese Chinese. Although the former are not Triads, they

mimic them, using ritual initiation and a similar hierarchical structure in which the *shan chu* is called the *dai lo
dai* (literally translated from the Cantonese as Big Brother
Big), his assistant is the *dai lo*, with underlings known as *ma
zhai*.

Refugees from Vietnam began to arrive in the 1970s.
Predominantly Western-educated and wealthy, they included businessmen escaping Communism, politicians,
professionals like lawyers and doctors and former military
officers, some of whom had been active in narcotics
trafficking. They were followed by 'boat people', economic and often criminal migrants escaping poverty or
the law, who later brought over their families. Many of
the migrants were unaccompanied youths, sent overseas
to become US citizens and, therefore, an immigration
lifeline to families in Vietnam. Housed in orphanages,
fostered out or living alone in a strange land, alienated and
lost, they formed burglary gangs, sometimes with friends
they had made in Hong Kong's crowded and secure
refugee camps, in order to survive and give themselves
a sense of identity. Inured to violence by the Vietnam
War, they were exceedingly ruthless and, as the Chinese
youth gangs had been before them, were utilized by
Chinese criminals.

The gangs adopted Western names, the best known
being the Black Eagles, Saigon Cowboys (who had
relocated from Vietnam after the war), Thunder Tigers,
Pink Knights and Viet Ching or Vietnamese Youth.
One gang, the Frogmen, comprised ex-South Vietnamese army special forces personnel, trained by the US
army as saboteurs and assassins. During the 1980s, they
developed from street gangs into criminal syndicates and

are now in conflict with the Chinese. The Viet Ching compete in California with the Wah Ching, into whose rackets they are forever seeking to elbow their way. In New York, the Vietnamese Born to Kill gang (known as the BTK) went on a killing spree and, in 1986, sided with disaffected Ghost Shadows and Flying Dragons members to form the Canal Business Association, known for its ignoring of criminal territorial rights. In July 1990, when their *dai lo* was murdered in New York, his funeral cortège passed through an opponent's territory on the way to the cemetery. With the funeral under way, three men opened up on the mourners with machine pistols. The bereaved returned fire. No-one was killed but seven were wounded. Two years later, the gang suffered a major setback when nine senior personnel were indicted under the RICO laws. Now much weakened, the gang has re-formed as, it is said, the BTK, meaning Back to Kill.

Since the 1980s, America has also seen the advent of the Tai Huen Jai, the Big Circle Boys. They flew in from Hong Kong as refugees, often on bogus papers and claiming to be dissidents. A large number appeared in the months after the 1989 Tienanmen Square massacre, but they were frauds, for they had been resident in Hong Kong since at least 1987. Others were smuggled in. Mostly wanted men in China, they were quick to commence organized-crime activities, especially heroin trafficking. Having learned the need for secrecy in China, they work in small cells of up to ten and do not, as many believe, exist as a single entity. In many places, their name is erroneously used to refer to any non-Triad gang consisting of Chinese from China. They are not Triads, having no fixed hierarchy and using no form of ritual, but they are well in with them.

As with the tongs and gangs, the Big Circle Boys have produced some noted characters, amongst them Johnny Kong Yu-leung. He first came to prominence around 1982 as leader of the heroin-dealing Flaming Eagles in New York – a gang made up of a mixture of Communist Chinese, Hong Kong Chinese and a few Chinese American. Kong was a Shanghainese who had made a large sum of money in the Vietnam War selling GIs fur coats smuggled or stolen from fur businesses in Hong Kong, investing the profits in a New York cinema, a factory in Paraguay and commercial properties in San Francisco. He also possessed a luxurious house in Panama. When the Vietnam conflict ended, he went to New York and traded heroin, using armed robberies to obtain venture capital. As a major drug smuggler, who it was believed had run heroin worth US$2 billion, the DEA and the FBI concentrated on him and in 1986 he was arrested and imprisoned. In 1997, however, it was reported that he was back in business.

The Big Circle Boys do not just smuggle narcotics: they also run people. The alien smugglers are colloquially referred to as Snake-heads and, unusually in Chinese organized crime, may be women. One of these was Cheng Chui-ping, who ran illegals over the US border at Niagara in 1990. It is virtually impossible to assess how many aliens these gangs run, but the US immigration authorities believe the figure to be around 100,000 per annum. According to the US census, the Asian population rose by 108 per cent in the decade from 1981, reaching 7.2 million; by 2000, it is projected to stand at 12 million, about 5 per cent of the nation. Aside from heroin and humans, the Big Circle Boys are involved in kidnapping, armed robbery, arms dealing and commercial fraud. Those who have reached middle age have in some instances quit the USA to live in the Far East, remaining in league with those in America to whom they supply heroin and afford other general assistance.

The 1990s have seen the arrival of yet another wave of Chinese criminals. Gangs from Fujian have appeared in Los Angeles and, especially, New York, made up of illegal immigrants. Some have joined existing gangs such as the Flying Dragons, but others have formed autonomous units which operate alongside Triads, other gangs and the Big Circle Boys. The Fuk Ching (Fujianese Youth) is already the most notorious. One of their leaders, Paul Wong Kinfei (known as Fuzhou Paul), is considered responsible for a wide range of crimes in New York City. Named by the DEA as a heroin and illegal-immigrant trafficker, he fled the USA to live in some style in Fuzhou. Extradition from China seems improbable. Another senior figure from New York, Guo Liangqi (called Ah Kay), whose younger brothers were slain in a gang squabble, was extradited because he was apprehended in Hong Kong before the change of sovereignty.

Most American cities contain Triad or Triad-affiliated (or imitative) gangs. In Dallas, the Horse Gang or Oriental Boyz engage in all the usual criminal activity, from protection rackets to narcotics peddling. Atlanta (Georgia) contains Born To Kill, Hip Sing Tong, Ghost Shadows and On Leong Tong gangs and Boston the San Yee On. In Washington DC, the Fuk Ching run guns and drugs. Chicago has long been 'owned' by the Hip Sing Tong in collaboration with the Flying Dragons. In 1993 there were seven tongs or Triad groups vying with each other for business in Atlantic City (New Jersey) while two years before, in Cleveland (Ohio), there was a spate of armed robberies and burglaries masterminded by one Chin Kin-fun, a Ghost Shadows member from San Francisco. Yet it is not only metropolitan areas that endure Triad and related criminality. The gangs have been discovered as active in such places as Biloxi (Mississippi), Fall River (Massachusetts) and on the Hawaiian island of Oahu, where they have worked alongside Korean and Filipino gangs in the manufacture and distribution of 'ice', the slang name for crystalline methamphetamine hydrochloride.

America faces an uphill task in combating such a complex criminal underworld. Intelligence is difficult to gather and even harder to collate and interpret. The old-style tongs, the Triads, the street gangs, the Vietnamese, the Vietnamese Chinese, the Big Circle Boys and the Fuk Ching are now being joined by Putonghua-speaking Taiwanese and Shanghainese syndicates, as well as Japanese Yakuza, Filipino gangsters and Koreans. They all speak different languages, which makes intelligence gathering a nightmare, have different codes of behaviour and fall in and out of alliance, making it well nigh impossible to keep abreast of developments. In addition, they are increasingly doing business with Italian, Dominican, Russian and Colombian syndicates. They are well organized, ruthless, difficult to infiltrate, opportunist and entrepreneurial. In the recent past, a Triad societies' meeting was convened in Los Angeles to attempt to marry a new Taiwanese society, the Hung Moon, with

508

the United Bamboo Society, 14K, Four Seas (Sze Hoi) and Wah Ching into a sort of Mafia-style commission. It is not known whether the meeting was successful in forming a united alliance. Furthermore, in 1996, it was discovered that the Wo Hop To was actively poaching members from other gangs, the first instance of such a move in the USA. As for New York's Little Italy, it is now all but surrounded by Chinatown, a metaphor of the success of Chinese gangsters in the metropolis. In short, Chinese organized criminals seem undefeatable.

The USA is not, of course, alone. Canada shares a similar history and, nowadays, the same problems. Chinese arrived there as coolies heading for the British Columbia goldfields in 1858. With the gold rush over they, like their countrymen south of the border, built the railroads, were racially abused and subjected to discriminatory taxation and immigration restrictions. Conditions, however, were still better on the northern ridge of the Golden Mountain than they were in China and immigration continued. A Chinatown started to form in Vancouver. Whites feared for their jobs and the Chinese became even more hated. In September 1907, Vancouver's Chinatown was the scene of horrific race riots.

Where the Chinese went so, of course, did the Triads. The first known existence of a Canadian Triad society was in 1863 in the gold-mining settlement of Bakerville. It was called the Hung Shan Tong (Red Mountain Tong) and was said to be an offshoot of a San Franciscan tong whose members had travelled north to avoid racial abuse in California. Other societies followed, many of them legally constituted as freemasonic associations. They were less belligerent than their American counterparts and there were no tong wars. They ran their Chinatown gambling, whores and illegal opium dives, collected dues and looked after their countrymen in trouble.

The Chinese population flourished and, therefore, so did the tongs. One particularly successful man was Shu Moy, leader of Vancouver's Chinatown from around 1905 until the late 1930s. Canada's first Chinese criminal supremo, his word was law in the Chinese communities of the Pacific coast. Opium, made illegal in 1908, was one of his major businesses. He smuggled it in from Hong Kong, where it was still legal, and sold it on to the USA, his couriers being Chinese cabin crew on Empress and Blue Funnel Line passenger ships.

The next Chinese settlement of any size to coalesce was in Toronto in the 1880s, begun by coolies who moved east along the Canadian Pacific railroad they had recently finished building. Although it numbered only a few thousand Chinese, Toronto's Chinatown contained the usual high proportion of dives and bordellos alongside laundries, bakeries and general stores. Public animosity ran high, encouraged by the popular press. At first, there were tongs in Toronto but, surprisingly, they had faded out by the 1930s. In general, Toronto's Chinese were a quiet, law-abiding community involved in what the police colloquially termed 'fanny, fan-tan and fumes'.

So long as Chinese criminality stayed within the Chinese communities, the authorities were not too concerned, but they were worried by illegal immigration. Chinese 'bum-runners' (as they were nicknamed) had been importing illegal immigrants since the turn of the century, using fake passports and work permits, smuggling not only their own kind but also Europeans, especially Italians and, later, Jews escaping Nazi Germany. In 1946, with the restrictive entry laws repealed, Chinese immigration increased. As the population grew, so did the criminality and, in 1960, the word 'triad' came into use as a non-specific term to describe racketeering by Asiatics.

Seven years later, the Canadian authorities inadvertently blundered. They relaxed the immigration laws further and 91,000 Chinese emigrated to Canada between 1967 and 1972. Most were Western-educated Hong Kong Chinese, who, being British Commonwealth citizens, required no entry visas. Some were Triads who, after setting up legitimate fronts, took over the Chinatowns of Vancouver and Toronto in their usual intimidatory fashion. By 1970, heroin addiction was on the increase.

Matters took a new turn two years later when Hong Kong cleaned up its police force and the Five Dragons – and a lot of smaller dragons – headed for Vancouver, where they were naïvely welcomed because they had money to invest and Vancouver was expanding fast. When the Five Dragons left, many others stayed.

The Canadian tongs were by now all but extinct. The Triads were in control and new societies established. The most successful was the Luen Kung Lok, which had started in the late 1940s as a small society made up of workers in the Royal Naval dockyards in Hong Kong. In Canada, it was reborn under the leadership of Lau Wing-keung, better known as Lau Wing-kui.

Lau was said to be a member of the Hong Kong Tung Lok Tong society and an expert gambling operator. He left Hong Kong in 1974, despite having no criminal record – although the police were investigating him at the time, partly because of his known association with the Five Dragons and Ng Sik-ho. Arriving in Canada, he moved to Toronto where the Luen Kung Lok was inaugurated, bringing several smaller groups under its umbrella. Operating under cover of a martial-arts club, the society established links with societies in Hong Kong, across Canada and in the USA. Recruiting was allegedly the responsibility of Danny Mo, a martial-arts expert from Hong Kong. By 1977, Lau was said to control Toronto's Chinatown and to have business dealings across the nation, as well as with Fast Eddie in New York. He travelled extensively around Canada, to Hong Kong, Macau and the Dominican Republic. All might have stayed well for him had it not been for a Canadian magazine article published in 1979 which accused him of being a narcotics dealer and Triad Dragon Head. This was exacerbated by a police investigation which, although it proved no criminality, was seeking to have him deported under immigration laws as a potential threat to society.

As he had done from Hong Kong, Lau departed before any action could be taken and went to the Dominican Republic, where he operated a casino at the Hotel Embajador in Santo Domingo. The hotel was owned by Simon Yip, a Hong Kong Chinese associate who was instrumental in persuading the Dominican government to sell Dominican nationality to Hong Kong Chinese eager to gain foreign citizenship before Hong Kong reverted to Chinese sovereignty. The casino made good money for both Lau and the hotel, but there was a problem. Lau had a small entourage of Luen Kung Lok 49s who started throwing their weight about and it soon looked as if the hotel, which was otherwise respectable, was associated with organized crime. The government was dismayed and Simon Yip annoyed. In 1981, he requested that Lau resign from the casino and leave the country.

Returning to the Far East, Lau settled in Hong Kong but went into business running gaming tables at the Lisboa casino in Macau. He maintained his connections in North America and, in 1983, allegedly convened a meeting in a private dining room at the Miramar Hotel in Kimberley Road in Kowloon. Present were Triad leaders from Kau Kum Shan. The Hong Kong police, given advance warning by the Royal Canadian Mounted Police, raided the meeting and questioned those present, but no charges were laid. It was assumed that the meeting was concerned with the consolidation and co-ordination of Triad activity in North America.

By 1991, Lau was living in .Kowloon while he continued to operate several high-roller private gaming tables at the Lisboa. His presence in Macau was important, for it is said that he acted as an ombudsman in disputes between Triads involved in the Macau gambling scene. If true, Lau has played – and may continue to play – a vital role in the stability of the enclave. He is a Dominican citizen, but his wife and children are reputed to live in Canada. Despite international police surveillance, as well as DEA observation instigated because of his known association with Ng Sik-ho, Lau has never been convicted of a criminal offence in any country.

With Lau in self-imposed exile from Canada, it is believed the Luen Kung Lok came under the command of Danny Mo Shui-chuen. No proof exists of his Triad membership, although the Hong Kong police consider him to be one and the Toronto police have associated him with a number of Luen Kung Lok crimes. In 1985 he was sent to trial for armed robbery, but acquitted on appeal after key prosecution witnesses absconded. By 1991, Mo was established as a very successful Canadian impresario with a legitimate entertainment company.

As the 1990s progressed, the Luen Kung Lok seemed to wane, especially in Toronto. It appeared as if the Triads were now *passé*, with street crime moving into the realm of gangs. In Vancouver, however, their position was strengthening. Crime in the city, where one in three citizens of the 1.5 million population is Chinese, began to change around 1975. The existing Triads were joined by new criminal associations from California, Hong Kong, Taiwan, China and Vietnam, as well as by Luen Kung Lok factions from Toronto. Being Canada's primary seaport on the Pacific coast, the city became and remains a major heroin-importation point. According to a DEA stool-pigeon, the narcotics business was organized by the 14K in Hong Kong. Other Triads organized a huge illegal immigrant trade through the port, many of these doubling as 14K heroin couriers.

By 1980, Vancouver was home to seven Chinese street gangs, the most prominent being the Hung Ying (Red Eagles), which specialized in extorting restaurateurs and Chinese students. The latter have long been, and remain, a target for gangs and Triads. They are young and easily identified, often flaunting their wealth by way of expensive cars or jewellery and are often in Canada alone and therefore vulnerable. They are not only extorted but sometimes kidnapped, the police not being informed and the ransom being paid overseas in Hong Kong or

Malaysia. For a time, the Red Eagles' main rival was the Lotus Family, until in 1982 the Vietnamese Chinese gang, the Viet Ching, arrived from the USA, resulting in intermittent gang conflicts.

The Viet Ching, whilst not a traditional Triad society, is structured like one, with an ordered hierarchy. In some places, such as Toronto, they waxed as the Luen Kung Lok's power waned. By 1992, the Viet Ching and other – Chinese – gangs held sway. Or so it seemed. In fact, they were only prominent in the Chinatowns because they were running the traditional protection, gambling and loan-sharking rackets. The Royal Canadian Mounted Police believe the serious crime, such as narcotics importation, was still being carried out by the Luen Kung Lok. This was no longer thought to be Danny Mo's society but to be run by others, using the Big Circle Boys to transport heroin across state lines and into the USA through small border-road crossing points between Saskatchewan and Montana and Manitoba and North Dakota.

Since 1991, the Vietnamese Chinese gangs, gangs of Chinese illegal immigrants from Communist China and the Big Circle Boys have been of increasing concern to the Canadian authorities. They terrorize Toronto's Chinese and small Vietnamese communities. No-one will report them for fear of retaliation. Murders in the Asian community are common and the police have gone so far as to admit that they consider the ethnic criminals to be the biggest single threat to public order in the metropolitan area.

The current situation is confusing and volatile. As well as the Luen Kung Lok, the 14K and the San Yee On are active. Fujianese gangs are setting up in Toronto in competition not only with Chinese and Vietnamese but also Cambodian and Laotian gangs. A Vancouver police report in January 1998 lists nearly two dozen unsolved homicides within the Asian community since mid-1996. They have little chance of being solved. The Big Circle Boys are consolidating their power-base, expanding their enterprises, forming alliances of convenience with competitors and causing the authorities significant concern. Police intelligence suggests they are splitting in two, with older members becoming narcotics importers whilst the youngsters are keeping to the usual rackets.

Yet the Big Circle Boys are evolving in another, much more dangerous direction. Until now, Asian criminals have acted predominantly within their own community; the Big Circle Boys, however, are breaking with this tradition. They have infiltrated banks with undercover moles, who have studied banking technology, then purchased credit-card manufacturing equipment with which they make duplicate credit cards which are undetectable. They are also beginning to extort non-Chinese businesses and are conducting home invasions on other ethnic minorities, especially blacks. Of the other businesses in which they are involved, the smuggling of illegal immigrants is earning them probably as much as narcotics. They also have a monopoly on the hot car trade, feeding the demand for luxury cars in South-east Asia and China in particular. When the Hong Kong *dai fei* runners were curbed, the trade altered. Cars – conveniently standard left-hand-drive models which may be licensed in China – are stolen in the USA and Canada then shipped in cargo containers, often via Hong Kong's Kwai Chung container port, the busiest in the world. It is a multi-million-dollar business. A car that sells new in Vancouver for C$50,000 is worth ten times as much secondhand in Guangzhou. Payment for the cars is not infrequently made in heroin.

Throughout North America, Chinese organized crime is officially regarded as one of the biggest threats to law enforcement today. It is considered to be potentially far worse than Mafia crime ever was, and a greater threat to law and order than any other organized-crime structure on earth. The Golden Mountain, it would seem, has lived up to its name.

4

POCKET RATS, LIONS' BONES
AND WAKING BEARS

The emperors of China had an abiding penchant for
exotic beasts. Cheng Ho brought home a giraffe and
an elephant from Africa in the fifteenth century, and
foreign rulers gave animals in tribute. Lions, leopards,
tigers, even rhinoceros and a hippopotamus all appeared
in Beijing, to be marvelled at by the court. Yet even they
found it hard to envisage what in Cantonese was called
the *doi lo siu*, the 'pocket rat', which was taller than a man,
ate with its hands and kept its young in a hole in its belly.
Reports of the creature surfaced from time to time, but
no-one believed in it or in its home, Australia. All that was
to change in October 1851, when the barque *Nimrod*
arrived in Sydney from Xiamen with 120 Chinese coolies
on board.

There had been a very few Chinese craftsmen and
servants in Australia before 1851, but the *Nimrod* carried
the first true migrants. They were welcomed because
Australia needed them. Expanding agriculture required
labour and the Aborigines were considered too stupid
and, above all, too lazy for manual work. The industrious

Chinese, employed as contract labour, were ideal. However, it was not long before the immigrant trickle, as in other parts of the world, swelled to a flood.

In 1851 a failed Forty-Niner returned from the Californian gold rush and struck gold in New South Wales. The news flashed around the world. Thousands headed in from all corners of the globe, including southern China. Some came as contract labourers and promptly broke their contracts; some came on 'sail now, pay later' credit tickets; and some bought their passage outright. In 1855, 11,000 credit-ticket emigrants landed in Victoria, the majority coming from the Sze Yap. On arrival, they headed for the mining camps, erected their tents, pegged out their plots, kept themselves to themselves and dug. Within two years, 22 per cent of all goldminers were Chinese. Racial tensions ran high and there were anti-Chinese riots. A few found wealth, most found nothing and drifted away to alternative work or, in 1866, to New Zealand where gold was struck in Otago.

Those Chinese who settled in Australia worked as carpenters, furniture-makers, coolies, laundrymen or market gardeners. Some set up stores. By 1860, 40,000 lived in the city of Victoria alone. Socially ostracized, they mostly lived in slum ghettos. Racial tension increased. The Chinese were referred to as 'Celestial Scum', 'Mongolian Filth' and 'Locusts'. Riots were not infrequent and lynchings not unknown. In 1881, 1,000 white miners, who regarded the Chinese as competition for the dwindling gold, attacked Chinese miners at Lambing Flat. A number of Chinese were killed, their bodies left to turn to dust, and many were injured. The authorities sided with the whites and Chinese immigration restrictions were imposed.

519

As the Chinese grew wealthier, they started to evolve Chinatowns in such locations as Lower George Street in Sydney and Little Bourke Street in Melbourne. Here, they retained their cultural identity, smoked opium, gambled and, lacking Chinese women, associated with poor white women who worked for them as servants or prostitutes. Some of these married Chinese men. White society was scandalized and the Chinese were hated even more. When the *Afghan* sailed into Port Melbourne in 1888 with 250 Chinese passengers, the docks were picketed to prevent their landing.

Once again, in the face of sustained racial condemnation, the Chinese had good reason to unite and protect themselves. They achieved mutual protection through their *hui guan*, by forming new associations and, inevitably, tongs or Triad societies. These were not criminal, but they did run gambling dens, lodging-houses and whorehouses and they imported opium through licensed merchants; when, after the turn of the century, it was prohibited, they smuggled it.

For fifty years from 1900, the Chinese population in Australia lived quietly. They prospered and, within the constraints of a white-dominated society with an active policy of white supremacy, played their part. Australian Chinese in small numbers fought alongside whites in both world wars. Integrating into society, they became policemen, schoolteachers and, eventually, professionals. Of all the sectors of Australian society, they were the most conservative and law abiding. The secret societies rarely quarrelled and remained non-criminal, although they did not turn down the opportunity to extort the occasional illegal business. They gained their income from joining fees and subscriptions, looked after their members' welfare and were accepted. Non-Chinese knew nothing of them.

Matters began to change in the early 1950s. When the Triads fled from newly Communist China, some went to Australia. Even then, they hardly rippled the social pool, preying only upon the Chinese; the authorities remained ignorant of them. It was not until the 1960s that they started to appear on crime sheets.

It was heroin and the comically named Corset Gang that, in 1967, brought the Triads to public attention. Operating out of Hong Kong, the gang was a co-operative of Teochiu Triads and retired Australian police officers, masterminded by a Hong Kong Chinese millionaire *shan chu*. Using Australian couriers, the gang ran heroin from Hong Kong to the Mafia in the USA, the couriers using duplicate passports to cover their tracks. They flew from Sydney to Hong Kong, collected their heroin, hid it in specially tailored body corsets or vests, travelled on to Europe, then transited through to New York. In six months, they smuggled narcotics worth over A$22 million.

The Corset Gang's eventual capture alerted Australians to the Triads, but they still did not realize their full criminal potential. It took the escalation of the Vietnam War really to awaken them.

US troops in Vietnam went to Australia on R-and-R (rest and recreation) trips and took their heroin addiction with them, a street culture of whores and hustlers springing up around them in Sydney. At first the troops sold heroin to acquaintances, but it was not long before the Triads got in on the game. In 1970, narcotics abuse was all but unknown in Australia: between 1974 and 1977, heroin busts rose 3,000 per cent. In just one summer month in 1978, heroin worth A$100 million was seized.

The Teochiu Triads in Thailand were the main source. They had overproduced in the Golden Triangle and were looking for new markets. Australia, with its inexperienced customs officers, undefended coastline and burgeoning youth culture, was ideal. By 1980, Triad syndicates were flourishing in Sydney, running all their usual scams on the local Chinese population and trafficking narcotics to white Australian dealers and organized-crime gangs.

To combat the heroin epidemic, three Royal Commissions were set up. A federal narcotics unit was founded, penalties increased, powers to freeze assets introduced and covert operations such as telephone-tapping, mail interception and bugging permitted. These produced a wealth of Triad information, but did not disrupt the heroin trade.

As heroin addiction statistics climbed, so too did crime. In Sydney, the Chinatown district expanded rapidly, Triad-related crimes rocketing. The Australian Federal Police (AFP), admitting it was impotent, put the blame squarely and unfairly upon Hong Kong for not halting the criminal exodus. Yet they, too, were powerless. Australia was the second most popular emigrant destination after Canada; immigration visas issued to Hong Kong citizens doubled between 1986 and 1988, many seeking a bolt-hole before 1997's Communist takeover. Chinese from other South-east Asian countries also headed for Australia, attracted by its economic potential. Most, but not all, immigrants were legal. And in their midst came Triads, some bringing new societies with them, others joining societies which had been in place for up to thirty-five years. As far back as 1950, Australia featured in Triad traditional history as a land to which they were moving.

In September 1988, the Australians seized a staggering 31 kg of heroin, found in a suitcase in the Sydney home of a former Hong Kong Chinese, John Chai Nam-yung, who was described at his trial in 1991 as head of the Australian branch of the Wo Yee Tong Triad society and owner of an illegal gambling club. He was sentenced to twenty-four years' imprisonment. In a joint Hong Kong–Australian police follow-up operation, thirty more suspects were apprehended. Within weeks, narcotics agents boarded a yacht, the *Zoë*, sailing from Hong Kong to Sydney, discovering another $43\frac{1}{2}$ kg. AFP morale ran high, but it was also sobered by the thought that this much heroin was reaching Australian shores, all of it Triad controlled.

The Triads were up to other business in Australia too. They moved into vice in a big way, importing mainly Thai or Malay girls on the promise of legitimate work as domestic servants and waitresses. Most were smuggled in, but some, doubling as heroin couriers, were issued with visas by a corrupt clerk working in the Australian High Commission in Hong Kong. Prostitutes, when caught, were deported. Other undesirables were not so easily removed.

Not all Australian Triads are in fact undesirable. Like the Che Kung Tong in Liverpool, there is a legally constituted, non-criminal Triad society in Melbourne. A forty-year-old lodge building at 7 Waratah Lane is the registered headquarters of Mun Ji Dong, the People's Governing Society. With an associated lodge in Sydney,

523

the Ji Gung Tong (Public Society), it has been registered as a masonic-type charity for nearly a century, having been founded as the Yee Hing Society in the Victoria goldfields in the 1860s. Originally a self-protection society, fighting racism and arranging burials, it is now a freemasonic organization which went public to counter the Triad criminal reputation. Its members are local businessmen including, it is reported, a number of non-Chinese, who are proud of their Triad heritage and scornful of criminals. They claim their only criminality occurred in the early 1900s when they extorted illegal Chinese gambling houses. Stressing that they are a cultural and patriotic society with secrets, not a secret society, they have published photographs of senior members, one of whom, Edmond Louey, has rather naïvely claimed that Australia has no criminal Triad societies but only Triad-related syndicates. He is wrong.

Triad criminality in Australia today is identical to that anywhere else and, just as elsewhere, they are still involved in narcotics, although probably not to the same extent as in other countries. By 1997, there were well over 100,000 addicts in Australia, their habit being fed by the arrival of at least 2,000 kg of heroin per annum, of which about 85 per cent originates through South-east Asian Triad syndicates. In Australia, however, Triads are the importers but seldom the distributors. Once a bulk cargo of heroin is landed, it is immediately sold to non-Chinese distributors who cut it, package it, then pass it on to ethnically non-Asiatic street peddlers, often recent immigrants. In February 1994, for example, the Triads were selling to a Romanian émigré heroin network working Australia's eastern seaboard.

Since the mid-1980s, the AFP has increased its targeting of Triad groups. In 1988, Peter Lamb, an AFP assistant commissioner, declared that there were up to ten Triad societies operating in Australia, with a total estimated membership of 2,000, of which the 14K was the best organized. It was based in Sydney but had a branch in Melbourne. Three years later, Carmel Chow, a former National Crime Authority official, stated that the San Yee On, 14K, Wo Yee Tong and Big Circle Boys were all operating in Sydney and Melbourne, joined in the latter by the Wo Shing Wo. Other Chinese criminal elements existing alongside them sometimes claim Triad affiliation, which has led to a muddying of the law-enforcement waters.

The Australian Asian crime scene is further complicated by its fluid nature. Crime syndicates, often set up by an individual or small coterie, appear for particular criminal purposes, then, once these have been achieved, break up to re-form for another enterprise, perhaps with new key personnel. This implies that the Australian Triads lack staying power, continuity of purpose or overall organization. This is a misconception. They are enduring because they are flexible. Like any astute business, they bend to accommodate changing circumstances.

There has been a suggestion that Triads in Australia are developing links with other organized-crime groups, such as the Italians and Vietnamese, of whom there are large numbers in the country. Some observers dismiss this supposition for lack of evidence, yet it exists under their very noses. The Triads have used Australia as a heroin transit point in alliance with the Mafia, have established links with Romanian gangsters and have, for at least ten years, been using Vietnamese Chinese as 49s. Although there is reason to believe the Vietnamese are now running their own heroin through Ho Chi Min City, the Triads are still dominant. How much longer this will last is unknown, as the Vietnamese and the Triads are at loggerheads in some places. In Brisbane, they work in partnership, but in Perth there has been Sino-Vietnamese infighting, the price of heroin halving as a result of the competition. The Sydney suburb of Cabramatta holds the largest Vietnamese community in Australia and is a major distribution base for the wholesaling of heroin, the business dominated by Vietnamese Chinese. The police seem largely oblivious to the fact, assuming Cabramatta to be just an ordinary Vietnamese ethnic enclave with little Chinese or Triad infiltration.

The prevailing successful socio-economic and stable political environment in Australia is attracting more and more Chinese criminals – including those from Fujian – whose biggest asset is the ability to disappear within a Chinese community which now numbers approximately 300,000, most of whom have emigrated since 1985. Their proliferation is such that, in the Sydney metropolitan area, Chinese is now the most commonly spoken language after English.

There is also in Australia an unknown but substantial number of illegal immigrants from China, brought in by Fujianese criminals. On 13 June 1997, a ship carrying 139 such illegal aliens ran aground in northern Queensland, every passenger supplied with fake Australian identification papers, whilst early in 1998 a Chinese national was apprehended with 500 counterfeit Queensland driving licences in his possession. The number of illegal immigrants is likely to increase in coming years. Australia is to be designated the Chinese government first official overseas tourist destination and will be the subject of a dedicated travel infrastructure, providing an easy target for organized-crime infiltration.

Fujianese crime in Australia is already serious, with kidnapping and extortion its specialities. In May 1997 a Fujianese, Yao Yin, was sentenced to six years' imprisonment for the planned abduction of a wealthy Chinese family's son, the ransom demand insisting on A\$6.5 million to be paid in China. As an adjunct to kidnapping, with abduction used as a threat, Chinese schoolchildren in top Australian private schools are being blackmailed or extorted. Sums demanded are in multiples of the traditional 36. Some pupils, or their parents, meet the demands, whilst others simply withdraw their children from the Australian education system. In at least one instance, the Triads have actually enrolled one of their own youths in a school as a paying pupil in order to rip off his classmates. As well as carrying out crimes against the person, the Fujianese are also beginning to organize hi-tech crime and fraud and, through this, are coming up against other Triad and Chinese groups which have already embarked upon a wave of sophisticated criminal activity. The authorities fear this may lead to gang warfare over territorial rights and a need to establish face and power.

One important figure stands out in the current Australian law-enforcement system. Mark Craig is a former police officer with the Queensland Police Service who has not only studied the Triad menace in Australia in considerable depth but is also an authority on it worldwide. His

527

book, *Chinese Organised Crime*, written with the financial assistance of the Winston Churchill Memorial Fellowship and published in 1996 for restricted distribution amongst international law-enforcement agencies, is as disturbing as it is fascinating. Through this work and its attendant publicity, Craig has gained a well-earned reputation as a seminal whistleblower and, as such, has suffered at the hands not of the Triads but of the Australian authorities, whom he believes still refuse to acknowledge fully or to come to terms with the problem the country faces with Asian in general, and Chinese in particular, organized crime. His mail has been intercepted and efforts have been made to silence him in the media.

It is Craig's assessment that, particularly at federal level, Australian politicians and the law-enforcement community are actively against any raising of tricky or contentious issues. He believes an environment now exists in Australia similar to that of San Francisco in the late 1970s and New York in the 1980s, with the scene set to develop in the same way as in the USA, culminating in gang wars and public massacres. Signs of this potential have been present for most of the 1990s, the pivotal moment being on 4 July 1991 when Victor Chang, an internationally acclaimed heart surgeon, was murdered in Sydney by two Malaysian Wah Kee members during an incompetent extortion attempt. Craig's contention, which is not without considerable supportive validity, is that politicians and bureaucrats are reluctant to draw attention to any ethnic minority group in Australia at a time when multicultural political correctness and the eruption of Aboriginal rights issues are the order of the day. With liberals avoiding the issues, Chinese and other Asian organized criminals are taking full advantage of the situation to play the anti-racist card.

A further benefit coming the criminals' way is being fostered by the groundswell of Australian republicanism. In the process of breaking from the British monarchy and establishing itself as a republic, the Australian government is doing its utmost to expurgate any bad press and show that the nation is mature and stable enough for full political self-determination. Criminals know this and are making the most of the federal head-in-the-sand approach to social problems. Should the republic become a reality, as it most likely will, the country will immediately experience a huge surge in economic growth and vitality, providing a rich environment for Triad exploitation.

These factors, linked to Craig's assertion that the federal authorities are complacent with regard to the extensive problem of illegal immigration from China, bode ill for the future, with Australia becoming a primary organized-crime target.

The complacency of the authorities is compounded by accusations of police incompetence and even corruption, especially in urban areas. Craig cites an apocryphal story of an Italian *mafioso* once being asked why his 'family' had not established itself in the Italian community in Sydney, to which he replied that they could not gain a foothold because the cops had got there first. Indicative of the situation is the fact that Queensland's former police chief is currently serving a fourteen-year prison sentence, and it is alleged that a number of his corrupt fellow officers, still on the force, have escaped detection and detention.

*　　*　　*

Australia is not the only new world nation the Triads have invaded. New Zealand is another, although their presence is not as significant there as in Australia, with Asians in general making up only 1.5 per cent of the population. New Zealand has the advantages of not having such a thriving economy and of being geographically isolated. Triad crime is largely restricted to the usual running of video-rental stores and the shakedown of Chinese businesses, some of which are family firms begun by 1860s gold-hunters, though it does also encompass narcotics and, to a smaller extent, vice. However, the Triads there are in league with those in Australia and Hong Kong, and have forged links with Maori criminals. In early 1996, it was discovered that a NZ$140,000 contract had been put out on Sergeant Api Fiso, commander of the national Asian Crime Unit. It was thought the contract was being placed by the 14K Ngai group in Hong Kong, on behalf of the 14K *shan chu* in New Zealand, a naturalized Hong Kong Chinese called Ricky. The hit was placed with the Mongrel Mob, New Zealand's most infamous Maori gang. Under the codename Operation Strike, Hong Kong, New Zealand and Australian police carried out co-ordinated raids on properties in Hong Kong, Wellington, Auckland and Sydney. Arrests were made, including those of Ricky and the Mongrel Mob leader. Subsequently, it was discovered that the 14K in Hong Kong had had nothing to do with it and that the hit was being paid for by a single individual with a grudge, a relationship having been built up in prison between him and some fellow Chinese and a number of Maori gangsters from whom they had sought protection from other prisoners.

*　　*　　*

530

More recently, the Triads have moved into South Africa. With the end of apartheid and international sanctions, the country has opened its borders. The economy, though rocky, has grown and the majority black population, for decades repressed, breathes a new air of freedom. It is a freedom they are buying at a price, for South Africa has a lot to offer the Triads.

Geographically, it is ideally placed to be a heroin transit point, halfway between the Golden Triangle and the USA, and the police and customs service are unused to organized crime, their main experience restricted to criminal gangs operating in the sprawling townships which are ideal potential heroin markets. Other factors making South Africa an attractive target are the lawlessness, unemployment, lax border controls with tens of thousands of miles of unguarded boundaries, and the absence of public awareness of the dangers of drug abuse.

Drug trafficking is rife in Africa. Cocaine arrives from Colombia via Nigeria. Mandrax and *dagga* (cannabis) circulate around the sub-Saharan countries. Dar es Salaam in Tanzania and Beira in Mozambique are transit ports for heroin from both the Middle East and South-east Asia, run predominantly by Pakistanis and Chinese respectively, in partnership with narcotics rings in Lusaka and Harare. Zimbabwean dealers are protected by – and often are – senior government officials. Comparatively wealthy South Africa is the traffickers' destination, especially the Triads'.

South African Narcotics Bureau statistics suggest there are well over 100 drug syndicates operating in the country, with 127 organized-crime groups in the greater Johannesburg area alone. The majority deal in cocaine, but heroin use is increasing. It is sold in the townships under the nickname 'flower': dealers purvey it in small bunches of blossoms available from roadside stalls or in the *shebeen*s and beer halls. The Triads, whilst not controlling the market, own a substantial share.

Triad societies as such seem not to have existed in South Africa in the past. Although there has been a Chinese population there for over eighty years, they do not make up a substantial ethnic sub-group, with only some 15,000 in the country as a whole, and they have not established dense communities, although in Johannesburg there is a small Chinatown. The existence of tongs or *hui guan* has never been acknowledged, and it may well be that they have never existed because they were not socially needed or because the Chinese population was too small and dispersed. Chinese did not flood to the South African goldfields as they did to the Australian and North American, nor did they provide a cheap labour force. When the railways were being built and the country opening up, it was the Indians who moved in rather than the Chinese. However, the Chinese, especially those from Hong Kong, have always had easy access to the country by dint of being British colonial and, later, British Commonwealth passport holders. In recent decades, with South Africa withdrawn from the Commonwealth, their entry was still unhampered. Hong Kong having been a major South African trading partner since the 1960s, its citizens have been granted access for over twenty years either on a British passport or on an ordinary Hong Kong identity card. Taiwanese Chinese have also been welcome for the same reason. There is no doubt that Triads have used this facility, for South Africa is a source of three items the Chinese particularly want: game products, abalone and gold.

For years, Hong Kong Triads have laundered money in South Africa, legally buying gold in Johannesburg and shipping it back to Hong Kong or Taiwan to sell on the thriving domestic gold markets. They have similarly purchased diamonds and, to a lesser extent, ivory, which has been treasured in China for centuries. Hong Kong has been the world's fine-art ivory-carving centre since the 1890s, many of the carving firms operating in Kowloon and paying protection to the 14K, which has been heavily involved in importation. The trade in this commodity continues, albeit much reduced since the global moratorium on ivory dealing has been in force.

In addition to ivory, Triads also trade in other game products, such as big-cat bones, glands and dried flesh, and that most sought-after of animal parts, rhino horn, all destined for the traditional Chinese medicine market. Rhino horn, considered a cure for TB, is weight for weight worth more than heroin; it is smuggled out by sea through Durban and Cape Town or by road to Mozambique, then on by air. Abalone fishing is now heavily restricted: the Chinese regard this increasingly rare shellfish not only as the source of mother-of-pearl but as a gourmet delicacy. It is smuggled by Triads, who employ fishermen to rob the beds off the coast of Namibia. Shark's fin and, to a much lesser extent, snakes are also traded, but these are not illegal.

Gradually, the Triads are bringing their own criminal activities into the urban areas. Vice is increasing, Thai and Chinese girls arriving by road from Zimbabwe. The prevalence of AIDS in Africa means that they are often carriers, for many have already been 'broken in' in Harare and Lusaka. In some places, Triads or Chinese racketeers are setting up gambling casinos for African clienteles.

Triad violence has also arrived in South Africa. It first appeared in 1994, when Cape Town police were called to the docks to stop a fight between Taiwanese and Hong Kong Chinese. Next, a Taiwanese who refused to pay protection money was shot nine times at point-blank range with a revolver. A Chinese businessman, Chun Jen-chun, was found near Cape Town airport: he had been shot in the head. The following year, an unidentified Chinese was found floating down a river in the Orange Free State with a crossbow bolt lodged in his skull. Another was found burned beyond recognition on a roadside, then, in a shooting in a Johannesburg restaurant, another was killed and several more wounded. The South African police, inured to violence through the apartheid years, were shocked and baffled.

According to the police, there are several Triad or Triad-style gangs in South Africa, including the 14K, the Flying Eagles and the Table Mountains. One of the most wanted leaders is a Taiwanese seaman who jumped ship in Cape Town in 1991 and made a fortune dealing in ivory, rhino horn and bullion. Although an illegal immigrant, he is often seen in Johannesburg, but seems to have settled in Gaborone just over the border with Botswana.

South Africa is today what Australia was thirty years ago. Inexperienced in the ways of international organized crime, its law enforcement undermanned and ill-trained for the problem, its population socially unsettled and its borders undefendable, it is ripe for the taking.

★   ★   ★

Just as new to organized crime is the old empire of the USSR. The Russian 'mafia' is now more prevalent in the Western press than the Italian one – even James Bond has had dealings with them. So, too, have the Triads.

Triad societies in Europe, particularly in Germany, are well connected to the Russians, running narcotics, whores and illegal immigrants through the Commonwealth of Independent States, or CIS. Immigrants are an especially lucrative business: it is estimated that over 250,000 have passed through Russia since 1992. In 1997, searchers 'looking for the moon' paid US$35,000 to travel from Guangzhou to Germany via Moscow, St Petersburg, Warsaw, Budapest or Prague. As long as they were in Russia, they were 'protected' by Russian gangsters. Former Eastern Bloc governments have even encouraged the trade. In 1992–3, the Hungarian authorities offered residence permits to Hong Kong Chinese for US$100,000, even advertising the fact in the press. Many Triads accepted the invitation: it gave them legitimate citizenship in the new, post-Communist Europe.

Yet the Triads are not just running their traditional rackets through Russia: the Moscow mobsters, sometimes referred to by Triads as 'waking bears', are teaching them new tricks.

Russia is in chaos and, where chaos reigns, crime flourishes. One example is the vehicle trade. Many European gangsters steal cars in prosperous countries, drive them into former Eastern Bloc nations and sell them. That Triads work in this business is indisputable and may be seen clearly in Albania where there has been a busy stolen-car market just outside the port of Durrës since the overthrow of Communism. Operated by Italian *mafiosi* and Albanian criminals who were formerly secret policemen, the market has several Chinese salesmen who deal in cars when they are not smuggling immigrants. Another activity is the arms trade. Russia, no longer needing a vast army in the post-Cold War era, is awash with high-quality weapons filched or purchased from barracks. These are sold to Third World countries by Russian criminal gangsters with active Triad involvement. Worse, they also deal in nuclear materials, of which US$20 billion worth was stolen in 1991–2 alone.

There is a story – which no-one will corroborate but which is certainly not beyond the realm of truth – concerning an event in Switzerland in 1994. A party of schoolchildren were doing a science project in a town near the Austrian border, their work involving the measuring of background radiation with a Geiger counter. In a car park, their counter started clicking furiously and they called their teacher. He found the counter to be working properly and called the police. They cordoned off the car park and searched it. In a car with Austrian plates, they discovered a comatose Chinese and, in the trunk of his car, a plastic box containing over 1 kg of enriched, weapons-grade plutonium. The Chinese died without regaining consciousness. From his papers, it was found that he had travelled from the Ukraine through Romania, Hungary and Austria. Where the plutonium was going, no-one knew, but Libya or Israel were considered possibilities. He had no onward papers and it is thought that he was heading for a rendezvous in Switzerland.

Whether this story is truth or not is irrelevant. It is known that Chinese gangsters are running with the

Russian 'mafia' and that the latter deal in nuclear materials: it takes no leap of the imagination to put the two together. Furthermore, it came to light in 1998 that the Russian military had invented a suitcase-cased, one-kiloton plutonium-fuelled nuclear bomb and had built 132 of them. When an audit was made of these in the process of nuclear disarmament, only forty-eight could be accounted for. The chances that some of the missing eighty-four have been sold to terrorist or foreign governments through criminal networks is considered not just probable but likely. If this is true, Triads have almost certainly been involved.

This Sino-Russian criminal alliance is considered such a serious threat, not only to international law enforcement but to national security, that some countries are directing their secret-service organizations away from military to criminal spying – not before time. How successful they will be remains to be seen, but hopes are not high. Even national secret services are undermanned compared to the criminal syndicates.

Fortunately, the Sino-Russian relationship does not always run smoothly. This was well illustrated in Macau in 1993–4 when a Russian 'mafia' ring from Vladivostok, allegedly headed by a man called Sergei Sukhanov, started to operate a vice ring in the enclave. They flew in some very high-class whores and started working them through the casinos. Wealthy Chinese punters took to these leggy, blond White Russians: the Triads were not only peeved but lost face. There was a series of confrontations, stopping just short of all-out gang warfare, but the Russians stood their ground. What really did for them was a rich New Zealand lawyer from Hong Kong, Gary Alderdice, who fell in love with one of the hookers, Natalie Samosalova. He proposed marriage to her and then went to Vladivostok with her to buy her out from her employers for US$150,000. There, both he and Samosalova were murdered. The Hong Kong and Macanese police started investigations and the Russian gangsters lowered their profile. How much help the Triads gave the police is not known, but it is to be assumed that they positively assisted with the investigations.

Such amicable facilitation is not always forthcoming. Long famous for its decadence, Macau is in essence a Triad city. Only 16 square kilometres in area, with a population of about 500,000, it has an estimated Triad population of around 10,000, most of whom are involved in gambling and associated vice: the police are reckoned to be outnumbered by Triad gang members to the ratio of 3:2. They operate in all ten of the Macau casinos and manage approximately 10,000 prostitutes. When one considers that 40 per cent of Macanese government revenue and 50 per cent of the gross domestic product arises from gambling, and that Stanley Ho earned an estimated US$2 billion in 1996 from his Macau casinos, of which 30 per cent was paid to the government in taxes, one can see why the Triads are so heavily involved. Macau means big bucks to them.

For at least three decades, and probably much longer, the Triads have thrived in an uneasy coexistence alongside the Portuguese administration, running loan-sharks, smuggling and operating whores in and near to the casinos. For most of the 1990s the 14K, with about 5,000 members, has held sway over seven of the casinos, the Wo On Lok, with about 3,000 members, being active in two more. The former is highly organized, to such an extent that its leaders can call out a force of 100 49s in a matter of minutes, whilst the latter is growing in influence locally. The Hong Kong-based San Yee On also has a sizeable presence in Macau, but it is believed to be restricted to specific gambling-related businesses and not a part of the general scene. Police sources in Hong Kong claim that San Yee On gambling interests, which are legitimate, are overseen by Thomas Heung, another of Heung Wah-yim's family. Between the 14K and the Wo On Lok, a loose pact has been in operation for some years to preserve the Triad peace and keep the San Yee On from increasing its foothold in Macau. However, in 1996, the pact collapsed and the enclave was rocked by gang warfare.

The core of the matter centred upon the 14K and Wo On Lok jockeying for position before the agreed hand-over of Macanese sovereignty from the Portuguese colonial powers to the Chinese government in 1999: although Portugal has no treaty obligation to return Macau to China, it has agreed to relinquish it. In readiness for the political change, each Triad society is seeking to gain the upper hand in order to strengthen its bargaining position with the Beijing government in the hope of taking over the gambling franchise in the next century. Another factor in this power struggle is the drop-off in economic activity and prosperity in Macau, which began to take effect in late 1994 and, increasingly, through 1995, leading to a massive property crash in 1996. By the end of that year, there were tens of thousands of residential units, mostly apartments, without buyers or any hope of a sale.

At the centre of the war was control of the provision of private or VIP gaming rooms. With names like the Jade Room, the Golden Palace, the Emerald Pavilion and the Diamond, they cater for high rollers, most of them wealthy Hong Kong, Malaysian, Indonesian, Taiwanese and Japanese businessmen, professional gamblers and well-heeled Triad officials. With stakes at each game capable of reaching well into six figures, if not higher, whoever controls them is on to a highly lucrative business.

Triad control of VIP rooms exists because, when Stanley Ho first decided to open private rooms in his casinos, he chose not to run them himself but franchised them out to the most competitive tender, taking a royalty on the earnings. It was a chance no Triad could miss, for each room could easily net HK$250,000 a weekend, just from the gambling; on the side, their hostesses, hookers and loan-sharks could also make a killing. Suddenly, they were presented with a legal stake in the gambling scene and the delicate balance that existed between the interests of organized crime, legitimate business and law and order was undermined. The situation was exacerbated further by the Macanese government's attitude towards the Triads. With Macau to revert to Chinese sovereignty, the Portuguese administration has essentially withdrawn from seeking to control the enclave. They have, by their semi-surrender of responsibility, virtually handed control to the Triads, Chinese criminal syndicates from Guangzhou and corrupt Chinese government security personnel, all of whom are busy wheeling and dealing. Macanese legislator Ng Kuok-cheong has publicly stated that he believes Portugal is to blame for the troubles, accusing it of treating Triads as a Chinese problem, to be tolerated so long as matters do not get out of hand, and criticizing the Lisbon government for not providing adequate laws to address Triad criminality, such as exist in Hong Kong.

The gang war started in November 1996, when a hit was attempted upon Lieutenant Colonel Manuel Antonio Apolinario, the senior Macanese government security officer responsible for the gambling industry. He was shot twice by an assassin riding pillion on a motorcycle: one bullet wedged in his jaw, a second narrowly missed severing his spine. In Macau's narrow, traffic-congested streets, a small motorbike is an assassin's favoured escape vehicle. On 19 April 1997, Lam Pui-chang, a rich Hong Kong businessman, shareholder in a high-roller room, gambling-tour travel agent and jewellery shop-owner with connections to the Triads, was shot three times in the stomach near the Hyatt Regency Hotel. His assassin also rode pillion on a motorbike. Three days later, a nurse who was related to a police officer investigating the gambling rooms was murdered as a warning, and eleven schoolboys were stabbed in an amusement arcade, one of their attackers being shot dead by the police. The home of the policeman who killed the attacker was fire-bombed a week later. Over the next few weeks, the streets of Macau saw several grenade and fire-bomb attacks, a number of choppings or stabbings and drive-by shootings. Then, during the evening rush hour on 4 May, hit-men on motorcycles sprayed a car on the Rua da Praia Grande. The three occupants, Shek Wing-cheung, Fong Mou-hung and Lo Wing-hwa, were killed. Shek was the right-hand man of the head of the 14K in Macau. Rumour on the streets said the assassins, whom some claim were actually PSB operatives on an anti-Triad hit mission and who came in from China to fulfil the contract, were paid HK$50,000 a corpse.

The situation was getting out of hand. Macau's reputation was suffering. Tourist numbers dropped away, gamblers stopped coming from Hong Kong. Business was being hit. In the light of this, the 14K and Wo On Lok entered into peace discussions. For a short while, the killings stopped: at least, the gambling-war murders did. Nonetheless, a dismembered body was found in an empty factory and an interior decorator on his way to the bank with a large sum of money died from loss of blood when a number of Triads, probably squeezing him for protection money, tried to chop off his arm to get the bag handcuffed to his wrist.

In June, it was reported that the peace talks had broken down. Early in August, Stanley Ho – who had previously complained about the local judiciary being too lenient with gangsters and had called for the reinstatement of the death penalty, and who had recently signed an agreement with the Macanese and Chinese authorities which gave STDM the right to run the casinos until 2001, after the change of sovereignty – went public. He stated that organized crime was not involved in the casinos and that the two sides were reaching a settlement, predicting the violence would end within a few weeks. It did not.

A bomb exploded outside the Governor's Palace, cars were petrol-bombed and three workers were shot outside the New Century Hotel on Taipa Island, which was about to open a new casino. On 19 October, two men were killed in a gunfight outside the Hyatt Regency, then the following week Leung Kwok-hung, said to be a 14K, was murdered in the lobby of the apartment block in

542

which he lived. In his hand were clutched his car keys. An elderly caretaker-cum-security guard was also shot.

By now, business was badly hit. Tourism was down 23 per cent, with some hotels running at 20 per cent occupancy. The US and Australian foreign ministries warned their nationals to avoid Macau and some foreign companies withdrew on-going plans to invest. The international press dubbed Macau the 'Chicago of the Orient' and the 'Nineties' Casablanca', although the 'new Shanghai' might have been more apposite. Residents stopped going out to restaurants in the evening for fear of being caught up in the violence. Retail shops, usually open until 10 p.m., closed in the early evening with receipts well down. Cab drivers reported trade after dark reduced by two thirds. Earnings from prostitution slumped.

The Macau Legislative Assembly hurriedly ratified a tough anti-Triad bill which promised a clampdown on violent crime. Replacing a 1978 bill, it defined a Triad society and specifically proscribed nineteen crimes, including murder, pimping, kidnapping, robbery and extortion. Triad membership, hitherto not illegal, was now subject to a three-year prison term, with up to twelve years for proven senior members. Foreign Triads were forbidden entry and witness protection was offered to any Triad giving evidence against his leaders.

The PSB across the border, which had been involved in discussions with the Macanese police on a number of issues, stepped up border patrols and proposed a joint strategy to address the issues of marine policing, travel and identification documents and exchange intelligence. Some Macanese observers voiced the opinion that Chinese officials in contact with the Triads had been behind, or had encouraged, the attacks to destabilize local security. Under the terms of the Sino-Portuguese handover agreement, China is obliged to leave the local Macanese to run their own police force. If they were unable to do so, they would have to turn to China for help, giving the Beijing authorities the excuse to move in and fully control the enclave. The veracity of this theory, however, remains unproved.

The Triads' reaction was to send a threatening round-robin letter to Macau's eight Chinese language dailies and the local television channel, stating: 'Warning, from today it is not allowed to mention Wan Kuok-koi, (alias) Bang Nga-koi, or the 14K, otherwise bullets will have no eyes and knives and bullets will have no feeling.'

Also known as Broken Tooth Kui, Wan was the subject of one of the first arrest warrants under the new law: he was reported to be the self-proclaimed *shan chu* of the 14K. Three of his supposedly close followers had been arrested in May and charged with Triad membership and extortion. Serving the warrant was not easy, for Wan promptly took a holiday overseas; then, suddenly, it was immaterial. On 28 July, his last day of service before retiring to Portugal, a colonial judge voided the warrant and dropped the charges. Not long after, however, the PSB in Zhuhai, the neighbouring Chinese city to Macau, issued a warrant for Wan's arrest on narcotics charges. This, too, was dropped when it was found that the Chinese judge was corrupt, and it subsequently transpired that both warrants had been instigated by Wan's biggest rival. Whether the judge's alleged bribe was paid to issue or quash the warrant is not clear.

More had been going on than a 14K vs. Wo On Lok

fight. Internal strife was seething in the 14K. The cause was the rivalry between Broken Tooth Kui and Ng Wai, also known as Kai Sze or Market Wai because he allegedly started off his criminal career running protection rackets in Hong Kong's Mong Kok market street. For over a year, the true story of the Macau gang war was clouded by rumour, misinterpretation and supposition, but this was somewhat clarified in 1998 when Broken Tooth Kui gave an exclusive interview to John Colmey, the Far Eastern correspondent of *Time* magazine, in which he more than set the scene of the current gang strife.

According to Kui, Kai Sze Wai, a senior 14K official, had arrived in Macau in 1987 from the Philippines where he had been engaged in running casinos. After ousting the leading 14K *shan chu*, Ping Mo-ding, with Broken Tooth Kui's assistance, Kai Sze Wai became the Dragon Head himself and bought the franchise to a number of VIP gaming rooms. As time passed, Broken Tooth Kui's power increased. He acquired more followers and became the target of Wo On Lok 49s, who were ordered to eradicate him. He survived two shootings and a chopping which has left several of his fingers crippled and cost him nine teeth, now replaced by false ones and the source of his nickname. With yet further kudos and face gained from his survival, he started to become a threat to Kai Sze Wai and the two fell out. Broken Tooth Kui's men were hit, he struck back and war was declared. According to Broken Tooth Kui, Kai Sze Wai lost and became the subject of a sustained campaign to oust him from business.

Broken Tooth Kui quickly moved in on the VIP rooms, taking over those Kai Sze Wai had run in the Lisboa Hotel and establishing his own Wan Hau VIP

Club: together, these are said to earn him US$6 million a month. In addition, he owns a successful and popular discotheque, the Heavy Club: although in his forties, Broken Tooth Kui is a keen fan of disco-dance music. Not satisfied with undermining Kai Sze Wai's businesses, he posted bills all over Macau accusing him of being a narcotics trafficker. Kai Sze Wai's response was to open a new casino in the New Century Hotel on Taipa Island. Three days before the grand opening, it was splattered with machine-gun fire and Broken Tooth Kui announced that anyone patronizing it would automatically be his enemy. Kai Sze Wai took to holing up in the hotel, from which, according to Broken Tooth Kui, he dare not move. His support is said to be steadily dwindling and his followers gradually deserting him. It will be only a matter of time before Broken Tooth Kui is, in his own eyes, supreme.

Supremacy is, of course, his aim. Thrice married with six children, he is heading for criminal stardom in more ways than one. An avid baccarat player, owner of a fleet of expensive cars (including a mauve Lamborghini) and sporting a gold diamond-studded Rolex, he has financed a feature-film bio-pic based upon his life. Entitled *Casino*, it is essentially just another Triad movie, but it is nevertheless fascinating, for Broken Tooth Kui has been involved at every level of production and, according to the producer, the screenplay went through a number of rewrites to hide the real story and stave off litigation. Ironically, the star of the film, Simon Yam Tat-wah, is the brother of Peter Yam Tat-wing, head of the Hong Kong Police Tactical Unit and one-time commander of the Organised Crime and Triad Bureau. Most of the main

546

characters' names are homophones or puns on those of real characters: no doubt Hong Kong and Macanese police and Chinese PSB intelligence officers have closely studied it.

With the war seemingly over, it now appears that the Macanese Triads are just going to get on with making money as long as Stanley Ho's gambling concession holds. It is generally felt that, after the 1999 handover, Macau will be run by an unofficial 'committee' of Triads, corrupt Chinese politicians and bent PSB officers. Some observers reckon Macau will be to the next fifteen years what Shanghai was to the Roaring Twenties and Thirties – a den of iniquity and criminal activity under the control of a charismatic, powerbroking, deal-making twenty-first-century Du Yueh-sheng. Whether or not this figure will be Broken Tooth Kui remains to be seen, for his designs have been somewhat upset by his being apprehended in a high-profile arrest at the Lisboa Hotel in May 1998, after the car belonging to the Macanese chief of Judiciary Police, Dr Antonio Marques Baptista, was firebombed whilst its owner was jogging near by. Charged with a number of Triad crimes, Broken Tooth Kui may yet, however, walk free. Within a fortnight of his arrest the sub-director of the jail holding him, Jose Maria Hui, resigned in fear of reprisal attacks and Lieutenant-Colonel Jose Lourenco, commander of the Public Security Police information department, also quit when, it is thought, he was ordered to testify.

Elsewhere in the world, Triad criminal presence is thought to be insignificant – for the time being. Central America is barely affected although Triads still run narcotics and illegal immigrants through Mexico into the USA and they have, in the past, assisted indigenous narcotics dealers with technical knowledge. The Caribbean is devoid of their criminality, although their money launderers operate in offshore banking centres. Triads are now known to be in business with South American drugs cartels. In Colombia, the cocaine barons have for some years been growing opium poppies in between rows of coca bushes: they are now manufacturing heroin under the initial tutelage of Triad chemists. How far the Triad syndicates will succeed in extending their tentacles into Latin America remains to be seen.

5

OLD EMPERORS, NEW EMPIRES

Despite worldwide anxiety that, with the return of Hong Kong to China in 1997, the Triads would abandon their traditional centre and become a global, integrated organization, as the 1980s passed a Triad exodus seemed less likely. The Sino-British Joint Declaration and the Basic Law were set to stabilize Hong Kong for fifty years. Little would change save politically.

Then came the Tienanmen Square massacre of 1989. China already executed drug pushers and corrupt officials, brothel-keepers and embezzlers. If tanks were sent against unarmed pro-democracy students, what, some asked nervously, would be aimed at criminals? This apprehension was no better seen than in Hong Kong's Stanley prison, where convicted narcotics dealers began to fear the firing squad as soon as the British administration left. Eager to rehabilitate themselves, many started to sing and a wealth of criminal intelligence was gathered as the prison warders made no efforts to allay their charges' concerns.

Rather than fleeing Hong Kong, the Triads took a more rational view of the Chinese takeover. The mass exodus could be postponed. Little was going to be different: the police, the ICAC and the customs and excise staff would be the same. Business was booming and likely to continue, so opportunities would remain for criminal enterprise and investment. Furthermore, China itself was evolving.

Since 1985, China has unequivocally, irreversibly changed under Deng Xiaoping's radical liberalization towards a market economy. Mao Zedong's *Little Red Book*, high-collared jackets, stirring workers' marching songs and drab blue cotton *fu* trousers have vanished. Peasants labouring in the fields wear jeans, office girls mince through Guangzhou in mini-skirts. Older folk still play mahjong, but the young go to karaoke bars or the cinema to see action movies, not politically correct dramas. Western rock and roll is still frowned upon, but teenagers don't need it: they have their own pop music. Farmers sell their produce at market and keep the profit. Ancestral graves have been repaired and temples renovated after years of neglect begun by the Cultural Revolution. State-owned businesses have been privatized, factories opened with foreign investment. The capitalist is no longer a social pariah.

Where business thrives, so does crime. Between 1993 and 1995, violent crime in China rose 16 per cent, with robbery increasing by 15 per cent and fraud by 27 per cent. In Shenzhen, crime leapt by 66 per cent, with vice increasing by a staggering 92 per cent. Much of this is Triad related or instigated, for they are becoming increasingly active in China. Several factors have assisted them. First, already shown, China has a massive unemployment problem with its estimated 300 million without regular work. This disaffected, socially mobile mass provides a perfect criminal workforce. Those who do not work for the Triads and other criminal gangs are ripe for exploitation. Second, China is in social ferment, the chaos providing good camouflage for criminality. Third, China is riddled with corruption: nothing cannot be bought, from a parking ticket to a Chinese assault rifle. Fourth, with the privatization programme, there are businesses available for investment by 'patriotically inclined' entrepreneurs and government departments, which are being permitted to start up their own companies. The PSB, the Justice Department and the People's Liberation Army are amongst those becoming involved in making money through unbridled capitalism. The PLA is particularly active and has investments in as wide a range of activities as professional basketball teams and regional airlines created when China's national carrier was rationalized.

As North America and, later, Europe were in the past, so China is now: it is providing potential and opportunity on a massive, unprecedented scale.

In Shenzhen, Triads control a considerable vice, gambling and narcotics empire which is rapidly expanding across southern China and up the coast to Shanghai. According to PSB sources, a number of gangs operate in Shenzhen, including the Sha Tou, the Flying Eagles and the Fei Hong, the members being Communist Chinese criminals under the leadership of Triads from Hong Kong. In Guangxi, a gang called the Qi Bing Shi (the Cavalry Division) has the regional cities of Wuzhou and Nanning sewn up with protection rackets and gun-running. The PSB, which has long been reticent about the prevalence of organized crime in China, now routinely refers to Chinese gangs with 'mafia-like characteristics'.

For the first time since 1951, large-scale opium production is under way in Szechuan and Yunnan, with heroin addiction rapidly increasing nationwide. The heroin is manufactured in remote areas with the connivance of corrupt officials and trafficked by Teochiu Triads from Hong Kong, Taiwan and Thailand. The narcotics couriers are frequently engaged on the side in illegal-immigrant smuggling into Hong Kong, the border having remained closed after the change of sovereignty to avoid a flood of economic migrants. They also operate cigarette-smuggling rackets, engage in massive counterfeiting enterprises and continue to smuggle Chinese antiques and antiquities, as they have done for some years, contrary to Chinese law. Not only small *objects d'art* are being smuggled: entire pieces of furniture are being secreted out of China, carefully dismantled and hidden in bales of cloth or barrels of rice. In Guangzhou, they are hand in glove with the military, siphoning off army funding into both legitimate and criminal businesses. Corruption is rife and the Triads, flush with foreign currency, are busy purchasing favours, establishing *guanxi* and buying every government official they can.

Just as they did in the days of Chiang Kai-shek, Big-eared Du and Pockmarked Huang, the Triads are moving in on the government. Before he entered his dotage, Deng Xiaoping referred on several occasions to the Triads as patriots. He declared that most of them were good, with only a small percentage bad, and those that were bad were not as bad as they were painted. He even went so far as to suggest they were descended from the Yellow

Emperor, which is to say they are the successors of the first emperor of China. Such a statement is tantamount to saying they are central to Chinese tradition. On more than one occasion, several of Deng's children and close relatives have visited Hong Kong to be wined and dined by top Triad officials. Tao Siju, minister of state security and head of the PSB, has echoed Deng's remarks, stating to news reporters in 1993 that the Triads are patriots who love Hong Kong and their motherland and, as such, are welcome and regarded as someone with whom to unite. He has additionally thanked the Triads for 'protecting a state leader' on an overseas visit. Rumours abound that he has actually joined a Triad society. If so, it will most likely have been the San Yee On, which is the most active Hong Kong society in China.

Wong Man-fong, a very senior Communist Party official and former Chinese diplomat in Hong Kong, has said publicly that a secret deal was forged with the Hong Kong Triads in the early 1980s to the effect that, if they did not cause political unrest after the transfer of the colony's sovereignty, their criminal activities would be tolerated. It is Chinese government policy not to antagonize the Triads. In some diplomatic circles, it is being suggested that the Triads are, on occasion, being asked to engage in 'wet work' (assassinations) on behalf of the Communist Chinese secret service, just as they have, in the past, similarly acted for the Kuomintang in Taipei. The 14K has already assisted China by abducting two 'wanted' persons. In 1993, they kidnapped a Chinese of Australian nationality, James Peng Jiandong, from Macau to Shenzhen where he was being sought for alleged fraud. He was sentenced to eighteen years' imprisonment, although it seems as if his real crime was not fraud but crossing one of his business partners who was Deng Xiaopeng's niece. In 1995, they similarly kidnapped Li Hui, the mistress of Chen Xitong, the Communist Party leader in Beijing. She was taken from Hong Kong to Beijing to encourage her lover to confess to crimes against the people. During the years running up to the Hong Kong handover, Triads were used as spies for Xinhua, the official Chinese news agency in the territory and *de facto* Chinese 'embassy'. The Wo On Lok in Hong Kong works for the Second Department of the General Staff, China's equivalent to the CIA.

This toleration will spell disaster. Chinese criminologists estimate that the number of organized-crime gang members in China escalated from 100,000 in 1986 to over 500,000 in 1994: the figure is now likely to be in the region of 1.5 million. Li Sunmao, a senior PSB investigator, has publicly blamed this astronomic rise on corrupt officials and the rural migration of peasants looking for work in the industrial cities. Over 75 per cent of those arrested were recruited into gangs from amongst the peasant migrants. The corruption of officials goes beyond mere bribery, as was shown in 1994 when the PSB in Yucheng County, Henan, moved against a sixty-nine-strong gang which had been engaged in extortion and manipulating village committees and local businesses. The leader of the gang, He Changli, ultimately came to 'own' the entire town of Limin, of which he was, in fact, the government-appointed deputy chief administrator.

The extent to which Triads have gained a foothold in China is illustrated by the recent exploits of the San Yee On from Hong Kong. Well entrenched in Guangdong, they have even founded their own sub-society in Guangzhou called the Hei Tai Yang, or Black Sun Society. As a group, the San Yee On has for years invested in entertainment and leisure businesses in Hong Kong, where they own and operate a number of top-rank nightclubs, such as the China City in Tsim Sha Tsui East, in Kowloon. So confident are they in their position that the China City was, according to the Hong Kong police, used for a San Yee On initiation ceremony in 1995. Their nightclub investments, however, cover more than Hong Kong, for they are now involved in similar businesses in China. The Broadway nightclub in Shenzhen and the huge Top Ten nightclub in Beijing, opened in 1993, belong to them in partnership with Tao Siju. In Shanghai, they have gone into business with senior PSB officers to share the proprietorship of the Shanghai Gentlemen's Club, a very select and high-class bordello for senior Communist Party officials; ironically, the club occupies the building in which Big-eared Du once had his offices. They also own a half-share in the Seagull Bar and the Shanghai Hotel in which it is situated. The PSB additionally owns another high-class whorehouse, appropriately called the Protected Secrets Club. Further coventures with the PSB include the joint ownership of cinemas in Guangzhou.

The age-old paradox remains. Triads are executed for dealing in narcotics whilst their societies are officially recognized. Corruption thrives. The peasants provide the criminal workforce. The *shan chu*s and bent officials reap the profits. Nothing much, it seems, has changed since imperial times, although in 1996 the Chinese government did announce the launching of a 'Strike

Hard' campaign against crime and corruption. Since 1998, it has also started to take a tougher line with organized-crime gangsters, conducted targeted operations and high profile trials leading to executions or long prison sentences, but just how efficient these initiatives may prove to be is uncertain. Many observers believe them to be largely cosmetic, too little and too late.

As it is in China, so it is becoming in her latest mini-province, the Special Administrative Region of Hong Kong, where Triad criminality is also gradually being condoned. This is despite an assurance in 1996 by Chinese officials, attempting to defuse Tao Siju's pro-Triad remarks, that no Triads would be permitted to 'buttress their roots' in the territory after the change of sovereignty.

In post-colonial Hong Kong, Triads and organized crime are flourishing and, whilst there is no overtly direct connection, the Far Eastern press has circulated unsubstantiated rumours that descendants and allies of Triads are gaining considerable political power. The president of the Provisional Legislative Council, the unelected pro-tem ruling council set up by Beijing in 1997, was Rita Fan Hsu Lai-tai. Born in Shanghai, she fled to Hong Kong as a child in 1949 when her father, Tse Ta-tung, moved out of the city ahead of the victorious Communists. Under the British, she was a senior legislator, a British appointee to the Legislative Council, who was awarded the honour of Commander of the British Empire (CBE) by the Queen. In 1991, she fervently endorsed the Bill of Rights that the British were trying to append to the terms of the handover of the colony, introducing a semblance of democracy ahead of the 1997 transfer of power. The following year, however, she turned her political coat. It has been rumoured, but never substantiated, that her father was not only a successful Shanghai businessman but also an important Green Gang member. It has even been suggested in some quarters, no doubt with politically malicious intent, that she is a blood descendant of Du Yueh-sheng himself.

Fan and her husband have maintained close business relations with Albert Yeung, the middle-aged Teochiu multimillionaire former chairman of the Emperor Group, a large conglomerate with substantial investment interests in China. Her husband has been one of the Emperor Group auditors and she herself worked for the company for several years before leaving to tend to her sick daughter in Canada, to whom she donated a life-saving kidney. Yeung – a flamboyant entrepreneur who paid HK$1.7 million in 1994 for the car licence plate 9, which is deemed by the Chinese to be a very lucky number – was convicted in 1980 of attempting to pervert the course of justice by seeking to persuade a defendant in a physical-assault trial from testifying against his attacker, a professional jockey with the Royal Hong Kong Jockey Club, of which Yeung was a member. He was sentenced to six months' imprisonment. Six years later, he was convicted of running an illegal gambling business and given a suspended sentence. He was charged with criminal intimidation and the false imprisonment of a former employee in 1994, but when the case came to trial the prosecution witnesses completely lost their memories and Yeung's alleged victim, a currency dealer named Michael Lam, said that he was too frightened to testify. The prosecution collapsed. The judge, dismissing the case, stated he was not sure if justice had been done, whilst the Hong Kong press was scathing in its condemnation of the outbreak of mass amnesia. The following March, Stephen J. Solarz, a US congressman, was asked to withdraw from seeking appointment as US ambassador to India when it became known that he was associated with Yeung. Solarz vociferously defended Yeung, but was allegedly obliged to back down when confidential US government intelligence was passed to him by the US consul in Hong Kong, which suggested that Yeung was a Triad member.

Early in 1997, Yeung's conglomerate was given a licence to trade in foreign-exchange currencies, but the government regulator, the Hong Kong Securities and Futures Commission, would grant it only on condition that Yeung and his two brothers were not involved. Yeung has strenuously denied being a Triad member, but his various convictions have all been as a result of both ICAC and police investigations.

There is a further dimension to this story. It took the police three days to apprehend Yeung for the alleged criminal intimidation of Lam. It was not that he went into hiding but that permission had to be sought from very high levels for his arrest. Indeed, his arrest actually caused the postponement of a meeting he was scheduled to have with Jiang Zemin, the president of China.

Yeung's fostering of senior Chinese politicians goes back to 1989. In the aftermath of the Tienanmen Square massacre, China was in international political purdah and needed friends. The time was ideal for anyone who wanted to make an impression in Beijing. Yeung started to invest heavily in China. In the winter of 1992, the Emperor Group and a subsidiary of the Ministry of

Justice jointly set up China's first private bank. In June 1993, the Ministry bought 84 million shares of Emperor Group stock, making it the biggest shareholder in the conglomerate after Yeung himself. Today, Yeung trades extensively with and in China, using this as vindication of his non-Triad involvement. His argument is that the Chinese would not deal with him were he a gangster. His political allies, however, are not all-powerful: in 1998, Yeung was fined HK$20.6 million after admitting to a charge of insider dealing. He was simultaneously barred from holding a directorship in a listed company for two years.

Whatever the facts may be, it remains the case that if tycoons with criminal records can be so well connected in China then it requires no leap of the imagination to assume that the Triads are similarly highly placed.

The Triad threat in China is not restricted to that country. Using factories privatized under Deng Xiaoping's reforms, Triads are embarking upon new crimes. Having successfully pirated computer software and wristwatches, and counterfeited credit cards, they are moving on to bigger things. Amongst these is the manufacture of fake aircraft parts. All spare parts for aircraft are made to a very high specification and most are individually certificated: no 747 has a part fitted that is not of authentic Boeing manufacture and that has not undergone rigorous quality testing. The fakes, to some of which false certification is attached, are made out of sub-standard metal and, although fashioned to high engineering tolerances, are liable to failure. At present, circulation of fake aircraft parts is restricted to China, but aeronautical industry analysts confidentially fear it is only a matter of time before they are available worldwide.

With the end of the Cold War, China has less need to maintain a huge army, except to preserve internal security. The army has therefore been reduced, leading to a large number of former troops who, being unemployed but skilled in fighting, are ideal Triad recruits. Furthermore, the armouries across China are now in part redundant. Arms are being stolen (or sold by corrupt officers) and not only used by Chinese criminals and Triads in China but also passed into the international arms trade.

A potentially very lucrative and highly dangerous sideline of the narcotics and counterfeit trades is medicine. In Third World countries, proprietary medicines are often sold dose by dose, packets being split up to maximize profit but also to cater for the poor. Where a Westerner buys a packet of aspirin and keeps it on the shelf, the poor Chinese peasant will buy three pills rather than tie up money in a whole packet for just one headache. Triads have for years bought Western medicines – often obtaining supplies from Hong Kong pharmacists discarding stock beyond its sell-by date – and sold these by the dose in China or exported them to poorer nations, especially in eastern and central Africa. Now they are starting to make their own, selling them under Western-looking brand names (such as Klazo for Glaxo) to give them kudos. In some cases, the medicines are mere placebos.

Heroin and fake medicines aside, Triads are becoming involved in the Far Eastern designer-drugs trade. The Yakuza have long manufactured amphetamines, the Japanese leisure drug of choice. More recently, they have embarked upon the production of 'ice', which the Triads are now buying or making in China. The drug is readily available in Hong Kong and Singaporean nightclubs and discos, alongside Triad-manufactured Ecstasy and cannabis grown in Thailand or the Philippines and imported by Triads, sometimes with Yakuza involvement.

Triad links with the Yakuza go back a long way. A confederacy of secret fraternities, the Yakuza are not just criminal. They are historically ultra-right-wing and involved in terrorism, political corruption and extremist politics. Until about 1930, they operated primarily in Japan, but as Japanese expansionism grew, they moved overseas to Japanese-occupied territories, not infrequently assisted by Triad societies which sold them opium, provided them with women and, in some countries, aided them in the systematic pillaging of national banks, monarchies, rich merchants, religious organizations and criminal fraternities. Under the guidance of Yoshio Kodama, a secretive Japanese billionaire, the Yakuza and Japanese military together accumulated the biggest treasure ever assembled, known now as Yamashita's Gold. Consisting of tons of thousands of metric tons of gold, as well as gems and other rare metals, it was buried all over the Philippines in 1944–5. About one third has been discovered, much of it by Ferdinand Marcos, who is thought to have used Hong Kong Triads to sell part of it on the gold market.

Today, the Yakuza exists wherever there is an expatriate Japanese community, especially in Hawaii and California. Inevitably, they have come into contact with the Triads, but how closely is hard to establish, although in

Hong Kong there have been instances of positive liaison. In 1978, Japanese police arrested Yakuza couriers importing amphetamines from the 14K and, in 1985, the 14K were found to be associated with a 'speed' and heroin shipment seized from the Yakuza in Honolulu, who had taught 14K chemists how to make it in Hong Kong. In Taiwan, the Yakuza are closely associated with the Triads, with whom they share anti-Communist sentiments. Closer criminal co-operation is now being forged and bodes ill for the future.

A recent police report produced by the Taiwanese government, which is trying to rid itself of its Triad associations and distance itself from Triad affiliation, states that the country has a population of 21 million of which over 10,000 are known gangsters, and that the crime rate has jumped 80 per cent in six years. With social order deteriorating nationwide, organized crime groups have infiltrated business and political circles. A second report alleges that violence has been used to pressure support for Triad-friendly political candidates, with public-works projects having been undermined by corruption. Typically, gang members purchase farmland then bribe or coerce officials into passing it for industrial, commercial or residential use, thereby substantially increasing its value. The report further outlines the establishment of chitty-system-type underground banking networks and details Taiwanese nationals' involvement in international narcotics trafficking, vice and other crimes.

The climate in Taiwan is such today that, although the government is trying hard to clean up the country, it is none the less dangerous to speak out against organized crime. The independent Taiwanese lawmaker Liao Hsueh-kuang was reported in May 1997 to be playing safe after having been kidnapped the previous year by a criminal gang. He and his family receive round-the-clock police protection at their home in suburban Taipei, whilst his legislative office is heavily guarded by both uniformed and plainclothes officers. How safe he is is debatable, for sections of the Taiwanese police are as corrupt as the Hong Kong police before the opening of the ICAC. Furthermore, Liao is not unique, for a good many of his fellow politicians and legislators have also requested or received police protection. Amongst these is the opposition politician Michael Tsai, who has challenged one of Taiwan's most prominent organized-crime syndicates, naming another politician, Luo Fu-tsu, as being in league with them and subsequently trying to force him to resign from the administration in the public interest. Luo has refused to stand down, despite declaring himself to be the 'spiritual leader' of the Tian Dao Man, or Heavenly Way Alliance. It is conservatively estimated that 10 per cent of elected officials to the National Assembly have criminal affiliation or covert backing. A government source has gone public by declaring that an estimated one third of all local-assembly members have Triad affiliations or criminal records. These elected officials frequently use gang members as *chuang chiao*, middle-men who go out into the community to buy votes.

Legislator Liao may count himself fortunate. Retaliation against critics of organized crime and those who cross the syndicates is swift and merciless. A magistrate, Liu Pang-yu, and seven others were murdered in November 1996 at Liu's home. Liu had been impeached on corruption charges and it was thought that he had somehow double-crossed criminal associates. One of those killed with him, a local councillor called Chuang Hsun-his, had already received death threats for seeking to pull down Triad-owned nightclubs and brothels in Chungli city. Earlier in the year, an opposition lawyer was knifed by organized-crime members in revenge for his investigation into a commercial-contract scandal involving the United Bamboo Society and a US$210 million project.

In the spring of 1997, the Taiwanese government set up Operation Self-Renewal, a sixty-day amnesty for organized gangsters. One in seven surrendered to the police, making a total of 1,528 confirmed and reformed recalcitrants. Amongst these were Wang Kuo-ching, leader of the Heaven Division of the United Bamboo Society, and Tung Ke-chen, deputy leader of the Four Seas Society. Wang echoed many of his comrades-in-crime's sentiments when he declared, 'I just want to stop bearing the cross of being a gang member and be a normal businessman.' However, many observers believe the amnesty has simply given the gangsters the opportunity to legalize their criminality.

There are four main Triad groups operating in Taiwan, the Sung Lian and the Tian Dao Man existing alongside the Four Seas and United Bamboo Societies. These last three plus the United Pipe Gang, are currently seeking to form a political party. There may be little to stop them, for in Taiwan membership of a Triad society is not proscribed. Their intention is to form what they call a union for justice to address the government crackdown on organized crime and they have powerful allies both in

Taiwan and overseas. Amongst these is Yamaguchi Gumi, Japan's largest Yakuza organization, representatives of which attended a summit meeting with Triad leaders and sympathetic legislators in Taiwan in July 1996. If the 'united justice' alliance were to succeed, Taiwan would be the first country to have a legally constituted organized-crime political association.

In the area of white-collar crime, the Triads are becoming increasingly sophisticated. A Triad might in some instances be described as a highly educated and motivated criminal yuppie. Where his forebears twenty years ago counterfeited 50-cent pieces, he now counterfeits securities documents, bonds, stocks and share certificates. At his desk, he is as likely to be insider dealing as laundering money through the stock market, or masterminding an insurance fraud. Insurance crimes can be audacious in the extreme. A building may be losing money, be too old, need redevelopment. The owner employs Triads to torch it. He receives an insurance pay-out of which the Triads get a cut, his plot is cleared by the fire and ready for rebuilding with Triad investment. Cargoes shipping out of Hong Kong are 'lost' at sea. Sometimes, entire cargo vessels go 'missing', presumed sunk in the southern oceans' mountainous seas or by a passing typhoon, only to turn up several years later under a new flag and a new name.

Tight bank security and the uncertainty of Far East financial markets have caused some Triad societies to spread their risk. Unable to infiltrate the banks effectively, as they did in Shanghai in the days of Big-eared Du, they now hold deposits in offshore havens like the Bahamas, hedging inflation and operating innumerable shell companies to stave off the increasing instability of the Asian tiger economies which is likely to affect them adversely. This is ironic, as much of the instability is caused by corruption and graft, of which they operate a fair share, and poses the question of what might happen if they increased their presence in other as yet stable financial markets.

Of the Triads' new criminal enterprises, one that is best called 'cyber-crime' has as great a potential for profit as narcotics with hardly any of the risk, and it could go bigger, for the targets are the computers upon which international commerce is utterly reliant. It started in the 1970s with simple hacking. Computer access codes were bypassed down telephone links allowing the illegal electronic transfer of funds at the speed of a keystroke. It was bank robbery without explosives or the combination of the vault. In time, computer-software engineers invented 'fire-walls' – programmes and systems which prevented access to sensitive areas of a computer network; these changed daily, even hourly, and were therefore virtually unimpeachable. Today, hacking is outmoded. In its place are DoS (Denial of Service) attacks.

DoS is a highly secretive criminal activity. Law-enforcement agencies are tightlipped about it and finance companies refuse to admit they have been cyber-robbed for fear of losing customer confidence. It involves state-of-the-art military weapons and programs at the cutting edge of computer technology. Three means of attack are used: the HIRF (high-intensity radio frequency) gun, the EMP (electromagnetic pulse) cannon and the logic bomb. HIRF and EMP weapons were used in the Gulf War to disable

Iraqi communications systems and avionics computers. No bigger than anti-tank bazookas, they 'fire' bursts of electronic power which disrupt computer circuitry, even from a distance of hundreds of metres, and can destroy hard disks. Logic bombs are encrypted algorithms (tiny programs akin to computer viruses) which are 'hidden' in computer systems by 'sleepers', usually temporary office staff who infiltrate companies. When activated by a telephone call, or upon a predetermined date, they 'lock out' the computer system by encrypting data held on hard disks so no-one may access it. The computer has been hijacked, the company denied access to its business. At this point, the hijacker contacts the system's owner and demands a ransom in exchange for the code which will reverse the encryption process. Sometimes the mere threat of DoS is enough to force a victim to pay up. In effect, it is the ultimate twenty-first-century protection racket.

In a fortnight from 6 January 1993, two stockbroking firms and a merchant bank in London were blackmailed out of £32,500,000. Since then, over sixty successful blackmailings of international finance companies in Europe and the Far East have occurred, with a total ransom in excess of US$800,000,000 being paid. One of the blackmailers is thought to be a Russian crime syndicate run by one-time KGB agents; the others are unknown but seem to have emanated from the USA. Rumours suggest that at least one is Triad related.

It is not known for sure if Chinese DoS criminals exist and are Triad linked or not, but there are persistent reports that they are and that they operate with the assistance of former Romanian Securitate agents in collaboration with ex-KGB officers. Whatever the truth, the Triads have the technical expertise – or access to it – to embark upon this highly lucrative and almost unpreventable crime and many believe this will be a growth area for them.

Still in the area of cyber-crime, the Triads have taken full advantage of the development of the Internet. They operate a large number of hard-core pornography sites on the World-Wide Web and use e-mail as a means of communication in every aspect of their international business, from narcotics to the chitty banking system. By using encryption software such as PGP (Pretty Good Privacy), they send messages without the least worry. Even if they are intercepted, they are indecipherable.

Another area of recent Triad expansion is into the international paedophile business. A diabolic extension of the illegal-immigrant racket, this trade is new to the Triads and has surprised some observers. The Chinese generally respect children and, whilst concubines and *mui tsai* were traditionally sold, they were never abused, and cases of child abuse are still comparatively rare in Chinese society. For the Triads, however, profit overrides every concern.

Children are either abducted in China, purchased from poor families or removed from state orphanages. They are then attached to a courier, frequently a woman, and added to her passport as her own child. She and the victim fly to Moscow or St Petersburg before travelling on to Germany or The Netherlands. Immigration officers see nothing amiss: the child is on its 'mother's' passport and, to an untrained Western eye, looks like her offspring. Once in Europe, the child is sold into a paedophile ring, at which point it vanishes, its long-term fate unknown for the trade is still too new. It is presumed the child, after some time as a captive sex slave, will be killed, perhaps as the 'star' of a snuff video. Alternatively, it will be sold on into prostitution.

Counteracting the Triad societies tests the mettle of every law enforcement officer and legislator. The most basic action is the undermining of any potential for Triad recruitment. Youths, easily inculcated with the criminal ethos, are targeted with advertising campaigns. Martial-arts clubs and similar youth associations are observed and street youth gangs broken up. The prevention of youth involvement in Triads is nevertheless difficult: the police face not only peer pressures but also, thanks to the movies, the perceived glamour of the Triads, which is hard to overcome in rebellious urban youths.

Another more effective stratagem is making member-ship, even passive, an indictable offence with a suitable deterrent, which need not be detention. Many countries have a wide range of alternatives. The seizure of assets, the infliction of substantial fines and deportation are but a few. Yet these do not break the Triad will: a Triad is a Chinese and, as such, has a stoical approach to life and a determination to succeed against all odds. Rehabilitation of offenders is an option, but this is seldom effected. The 36 oaths have a strong power over a Triad.

The policing of Triads must be specifically apportioned, a realization learned by the Hong Kong police which instigated definitive Triad measures in stages in the mid-1980s, after they had come to terms with the fact that the secret 1976 report had seriously misinterpreted the situa-tion. Whilst the police have the usual complement of dedicated units – criminal intelligence, vice, traffic, homicide and so on – each police district has its own Triad unit which collates information and relays it to a central Organized Crime and Triad Bureau (OCTB) in police headquarters. So great had the problems of organized and Triad crime become that the OCTB is partitioned into four separate divisions, each addressing a particular area of criminality. Division A deals with vehicle crime and the smuggling of stolen cars to China, whilst Division B handles firearms trading, Triad involvement in the film industry and liaises with Taiwanese police on Triad matters. Division C addresses major crimes involving firearms and investigates white-collar crime, and Division D liaises with the PSB. The OCTB as a whole is in permanent liaison with other units likely to encounter Triad-related crime, such as the Criminal Intelligence, Commercial Crime and Anti-Narcotics Bureaux. An overview is thereby achieved which co-ordinates police action, a structure since imitated to good effect in other countries.

Ideally, infiltration must be an ambition of all police forces, backed up by bugging and telephone-tapping. Intelligence gathering at the very heart of Triad organizations is essential. These measures may well curb civil rights, but this must be accepted, for there can be little room for liberal sentiment in dealing with organized crime. Zero-tolerance policing is also desirable. Triad crime being so brutal, there can be no three-strike policy: a first crime must receive a substantial sentence. This not only punishes but can cause loss of face which may be a unique police weapon. Other criminals shrug off arrest as an occupational hazard but, for the Triad, it may be construed as a mark of failure, demeaning him in the eyes of comrades and victims.

Addressing the reluctance of a Chinese community to move against the Triads in their midst is a more daunting challenge. Witnesses at Triad trials have a propensity for amnesia or absenteeism and the threat of contempt of court proceedings is nothing compared to death by a myriad of swords. Appealing to a man's civil responsibility, when his son might be kidnapped or daughter raped, has little effect. Yet there are ways to counteract the grip the Triads hold over their victims. Witness-protection programmes are highly effective. They need to be: when a chopping may be commissioned for as little as $200 or £250, the going rate in New York and London respectively in 1997, witness safekeeping is vital. Stool-pigeons and informers, especially those who are active Triads but who elect to turn prosecution witness, also require protection, particularly if, by plea bargaining, they still receive a minimal custodial sentence: a turncoat's former comrades can reach into every prison cell. Another alternative is the introduction of an American-style Grand Jury system which offers witnesses immunity from prosecution. The drawback to these alternatives is, of course, the financial cost and, in the final analysis, the best encouragement to a community is effective policing. Once the Triads' mythological immunity to prosecution is broken, courage will grow and the cycle of predation crumble.

Legislation expressly tailored to Triad crime is another requirement. Laws against bribery and extortion are vital, as so much Triad crime is corruption-based, and legislation along the lines of the highly effective RICO statutes is essential. RICO brought down the Italian mobs and, in their latest revisions, are of considerable value against any organized-crime syndicate. They allow for swingeing asset-confiscation, investigation into the financial affairs not only of the convicted but also of their associates and even relatives, heavy prison sentences and massive fines. Despite their proven efficacy in the USA, such laws either do not exist or are still in their infancy in most other countries. Furthermore, surprisingly few countries have followed the Hong Kong model of making Triad membership an indictable offence. For example, Triad membership is not a criminal offence in Britain, a flaw in the legislation which it seems could and should be promptly addressed.

Whilst individual countries may have laws relevant to the combating of Triad crime within their national boundaries, specific international legislation is lacking. Effective laws directed against international narcotics trafficking do exist, but otherwise concerted co-operation against comprehensive criminal activity is sadly wanting. The Triads are surviving not only by their own considerable wiles but because their enemies are disunited.

There is an international reluctance to admit the potential of Triad societies. Too many governments regard them as a local problem and – where they seem to be little more than an accumulation of thugs ripping off restaurant-owners – deal with them accordingly. Yet the wider implications, narcotics aside, tend to be ignored and it is too often forgotten that the Triads are much more than streetwise 49s. They have the expertise, organization and will to undermine the fabric of any country's commercial wellbeing and are just as likely to manipulate the stock market as they are a street vendor.

It seems there is a conspiracy of ignorance amongst

many governments, a head-in-the-sand attitude towards Triads and international organized crime in general. Its existence is admitted, but little is done to address it. Insufficient funding is allocated and inadequate resources assigned to the problem, whilst the Triads have almost inexhaustible financial and material backing.

Organized crime in general has to be a major priority of all governments. Those of the developed countries must fight it to maintain their stability, whilst developing nations have to guard against the threat to prevent their progress being retarded by corruption – a fact now becoming increasingly recognized by the United Nations. In late 1994, the UN held a conference on organized 'transnational' crime. The Secretary General, Boutros Boutros-Ghali, addressed the conference in unequivocal terms. He regarded international organized crime as a serious threat to world peace and the security of humanity, and stressed the need for the founding of an international criminal jurisdiction. In furtherance of this aim, the International Law Commission was appointed to address international crime and consider the establishment of a permanent international criminal court with UN support. It is still in its infancy. Boutros-Ghali concluded, 'I am convinced that today much more must be done . . . it is necessary to co-ordinate national means and develop international means. In co-ordinating national action, states must harmonize the means at their disposal to combat transnational crime, both in the area of legal instruments and on a practical level.' He added that it was imperative for UN member states to share criminal intelligence, facilitate cross-border investigation, provide legal and technical assistance to countries lacking adequate law-enforcement systems and reach bilateral agreement on criminal extradition.

It is no longer sufficient to pit only police forces against the Triads. They are now such a threat as to be worthy of the attention of secret services and similar agencies. The USA has directed the CIA at organized crime, although at times it has also collaborated with it for its own ends. Britain's MI5 security system is also addressing the problem, in collaboration with other secret services such as BOSS, the South African service, and those of other Western nations. National customs and police forces communicate with each other where they have a common interest or problem. FinCEN is proving effective both as a policing measure and a deterrent. European governments, with the insecurity of the Cold War behind them, are beginning to follow suit with the setting up of TRACFIN in France, CTIF in Belgium and the National Criminal Intelligence Service (NCIS) in Britain; Australia has developed its own system, AUSTRAC. Yet there is no unanimous, specifically directed global co-operation.

Interpol, the international police liaison organization based at Lyons in France, established a special organized-crime unit in 1990 to study the problem, create a database of criminal syndicates, co-ordinate and analyse intelligence submitted by Interpol member states and circulate the findings. As a central intelligence agency it is very valuable, but it is not, as many believe, an international law-enforcement body and that is what is needed.

Europol, the European Community version of Interpol set up in 1993, might provide the necessary international police force, but it still has no uniform or established headquarters and its legal status has yet to be ratified. The

British government's stalling of the agreements because of non-co-operation on other matters, such as the new European currency and the BSE beef crisis, is putting Europol into a political backwater at just the time when it should be forging ahead. Other nations, despite the EC open-border policy, balk at the thought of cross-border arrests of each other's nationals. How an Italian can arrest a Belgian in London is a problem as yet unanswered.

With the de-Communization of the Eastern Bloc nations and the lowering of the military threat, now is the time to gather forces to confront global organized-crime syndicates, for they are far more dangerous than opposing political systems. Armies are governed by political will and constrained by political expediency. Gangsters are loose cannons, with no controlling ethos other than the making of money. When they do engage in politics, they do so amorally and only for profit.

The prognosis is not good. The world now holds two highly internationalized criminal groups: the Russian 'mafia' and the Triads. They are already co-operating. Contacts between the Triads, organized Chinese criminals outside the Triad system and international terrorist groups are rumoured to exist though no knowledge has yet been made public.

Suffice to say that with the current lack of international resolve and the Triads' penchant for secrecy, their organizational skills, brutal determination and considerable experience, the future does not augur well.

BIBLIOGRAPHY

Books and Publications

Andrew, Kenneth, *Hong Kong Detective*, The Adventurers' Club, London, 1962.

Auden, W. H., and Isherwood, Christopher, *Journey to a War*, Faber, London, 1939.

Bak, Janós M., and Benecke, Gerhard (ed.), *Religion and Rural Revolt*, Manchester University Press, Manchester, 1984.

Ball, J. Dyer, *Things Chinese*, Kelly & Walsh, Shanghai, 1925.

Barber, Noel, *The Fall of Shanghai*, Macmillan, London, 1979.

Barr, Pat, *To China with Love*, Doubleday, New York, 1973.

Barnes, Irene H, *Behind the Great Wall*, Marshall Bros., London, 1896.

Baschet, Eric, and Han, Suyin, *From the Warlords to World War*, Swan, Germany, 1989.

Black, David, *Triad Takeover*, Sidgwick & Jackson, London, 1991.

Bland, J. O. P. and Backhouse, E., *China under the Empress Dowager*, Heinemann, London, 1910.

Blythe, Wilfrid, *The Impact of Chinese Secret Societies in Malaya*, Oxford University Press, London, 1969.

Booth, Martin, *Opium: A History*, Simon & Schuster, London, 1996.

————— *The Triads: The Chinese Criminal Fraternity*, Grafton Press, London, 1990.

577

Bresler, Fenton, *The Chinese Mafia*, Weidenfeld & Nicolson, London, 1981.

Cameron, Nigel, *An Illustrated History of Hong Kong*, Oxford University Press, Hong Kong, 1991.

Candlin, Enid Saunders, *The Breach in the Wall*, Macmillan, London, 1973.

Ch'en, Chieh-ju, *Chiang Kai-shek's Secret Past*, Westview Press, Boulder, Colorado, 1993.

Chesneaux, Jean (ed.), *Popular Movements & Secret Societies in China 1840–1950*, Stanford University Press, Stanford, 1972.

————— *Secret Societies in China in the 19th and 20th Centuries*, Heinemann, London, 1971.

Chin, Ko-lin, *Chinese Sub-culture and Criminality*, Greenwood Press, New York, 1990.

————— *Human Snakes – Illegal Chinese Immigrants in the United States*, research dissertation for School of Criminal Justice, Rutgers University, Newark, 1997.

Ching, Frank, *Ancestors*, Harrap, London, 1988.

Coates, Austin, *Macao and the British*, Oxford University Press, London, 1966.

————— *A Macao Narrative*, Heinemann, Hong Kong, 1978.

Coble, Parks M., Jr, *The Shanghai Capitalists and the Nationalist Government, 1927–37*, Harvard University, Cambridge, Mass., 1980.

Collis, Maurice, *Wayfoong*, Faber, London, 1965.

Comber, L. F., *Chinese Secret Societies in Malaya*, Augustin, London, 1959.

Cooper, John, *Colony in Conflict*, Swindon Book Company, Hong Kong, 1970.

Craig, Mark, *Chinese Organised Crime*, the 1996 Winston Churchill Memorial Fellowship, Queensland Police Service, Brisbane, 1996.

————— *The Rising Threat to Australia from Chinese Organised Crime*, Australian & New Zealand Society of Criminology, Brisbane, 1996.

Crisswell, Colin, and Watson, Mike, *The Royal Hong Kong Police 1841–1945*, Macmillan, Hong Kong, 1982.

Croizier, Ralph, *Koxinga and Chinese Nationalism: History, Myth and the Hero*, Harvard University Press, Cambridge, Mass., 1977.

Deacon, Richard, *A History of the Chinese Secret Service*, Muller, London, 1974.

Deraul, Arkon, *A History of Secret Societies*, Citadel, New York, 1961.
——————— *Secret Societies: Yesterday and Today*, Muller, London, 1961.
Dubro, James, *Dragons of Crime – Inside the Asian Underworld*, Octopus, Toronto, 1992.
Dutton, Michael R., *Policing and Punishment in China*, Cambridge University Press, Cambridge, 1992.
Endacott, G. B., *Hong Kong Eclipse*, Oxford University Press, Hong Kong, 1978.
Farmer, Rhodes, *Shanghai Harvest*, Museum Press, London, 1945.
Fong, Mak Lau, *The Sociology of Secret Societies – A Study of Chinese Secret Societies in Singapore and Peninsular Malaysia*, Oxford University Press, London, 1981.
Franck, Harry A., *Wandering in China*, Fisher Unwin, London, 1924.
Freemantle, Brian, *The Octopus*, Orion, London, 1995.
Glover, Archibald E., *A Thousand Miles of Miracle in China*, Pickering & Inglis, London, 1904.
Han, Suyin, *Eldest Son: Zhou Enlai and the Making of Modern China 1898–1976*, Jonathan Cape, London, 1994.
Hahn, Emily, *China to Me*, Doubleday, Doran, New York, 1945.
——————— *The Soong Sisters*, Robert Hale, London, 1942.
Hauser, Ernest O., *Shanghai: City for Sale*, Harcourt Brace, New York, 1940.
Hewlett, Sir Meyrick, *Forty Years in China*, Macmillan, London, 1943.
Hook, Brian (ed.), *The Cambridge Encyclopaedia of China*, Cambridge University Press, Cambridge, 1982.
Jarvie, Ian C. and Agassi, Joseph, *Hong Kong: A Society in Transition*, Praeger, New York, 1969.
Kesson, John, *The Cross and the Dragon*, Smith, Elder, London, 1854.
Keswick, Maggie, *The Thistle & The Jade*, Octopus, London, 1982.
Kipling, Rudyard, *Something of Myself*, Penguin, London, 1977.
Lamour, Catherine, and Lamberti, Michel R., *The Second Opium War*, Allen Lane, London, 1974.
Lethbridge, H. J., *Hard Graft in Hong Kong*, Oxford University Press, London, 1985.
——————— *The Hong Kong Guide 1892*, Oxford University Press, Hong Kong, 1982.
Ling, Pan, *Old Shanghai – Gangsters in Paradise*, Heinemann, Hong Kong, 1984.

579

Loewe, Michael, *Everyday Life in Early Imperial China*, Batsford, London, 1968.

MacKenzie, Norman (ed.). *Secret Societies*, Aldus Books, London, 1967.

Mason, Richard, *The World of Suzie Wong*, Collins, London, 1957.

McCoy, Alfred W., *The Politics of Heroin* (revised edition), Lawrence Hill Books, New York, 1991.

Miles, Milton E., *A Different Kind of War*, Doubleday, New York, 1967.

Miller, G. E., *Shanghai: The Paradise of Adventurers*, Orsay, New York, 1937.

Morgan, W. P., *Triad Societies in Hong Kong*, The Government Printer, Hong Kong, 1960.

Mother St Austin, *Fifty-Six Years A Missionary in China*, Burns, Oates & Washbourne, London, 1935.

Murray, Dian H., *The Origins of the Tiandihui*, Stanford University Press, Stanford, 1994.

O'Brien, Joseph F., and Kurins, Andris, *Boss of Bosses*, Simon & Schuster, New York, 1991.

O'Callaghan, Sean, *The Triads*, W. H. Allen, London, 1978.

Ownby, David, and Heidhues, Mary Somers (eds.), *"Secret Societies" Reconsidered*, Sharpe, New York, 1993.

Pan, Lynn, *Sons of the Yellow Emperor*, Secker & Warburg, London, 1990.

Pickering, W. A., *Chinese Secret Societies and their Origin*, The Royal Asiatic Society, Straits Settlements, 1878.

Posner, Gerald L., *Warlords of Crime*, Queen Anne Press, London, 1988.

Pratt, Sir John T., *War and Politics in China*, Jonathan Cape, London, 1943.

Rafferty, Kevin, *City on the Rocks*, Viking, London, 1989.

Rattenbury, Harold B., *Face to Face with China*, Harrap, London, 1945.
————— *This is China*, Muller, London, 1949.

Robertson, Frank, *Triangle of Death*, Routledge & Kegan Paul, London, 1977.

Robinson, Jeffrey, *The Laundrymen – Inside the World's Third Largest Business*, Simon & Schuster, London, 1994.

Sante, Luc, *Low Life: Lures and Snares of Old New York*, Farrar, Straus & Giroux, New York, 1991.

Sayer, Geoffrey Robley, *Hong Kong 1841–1862*, Hong Kong University Press, Hong Kong, 1980.

Schiffren, H. Z., *Sun Yat Sen and the Origins of the Chinese Revolution*, University of California Press, Berkeley, 1970.

Schlegel, Gustave, *The Thian Ti Hwui, the Hung League or Heaven–Earth League*, University of Leyden, Leyden, 1866.

Seagrave, Sterling, *Lords of the Rim*, Transworld, London, 1995.

————*The Marcos Dynasty*, Ballantine, New York, 1988.

————*The Soong Dynasty*, Sidgwick & Jackson, London, 1985.

Sergeant, Harriet, *Shanghai – Collision Point of Cultures 1918/1939* Crown, New York, 1990.

Shi, Nai'in, and Luo, Guanzhong, *Outlaws of the Marsh*, Allen & Unwin, London, 1986.

Sinclair, Kevin, *Asia's Finest*, Unicorn, Hong Kong, 1983.

Sinclair, Kevin, and Ng, Nelson, *Asia's Finest Marches On*, Kevin Sinclair Associates, Hong Kong, 1997.

Sivin, Prof. Nathan, et al., *The Contemporary Atlas of China*, Weidenfeld & Nicolson, London, 1988.

Soothill, W. E., *The Three Religions of China*, Oxford University Press, London, 1929.

Spence, Jonathan, *God's Chinese Son*, HarperCollins, London, 1996.

Spence, Jonathan, and Chin, Annping, *The Chinese Century*, Harper-Collins, London, 1996.

Stanton, William, *The Triad Society*, Kelly & Walsh, Hong Kong, 1900.

Sterling, Claire, *Crime without Frontiers*, Little, Brown, London, 1994.

———— *Thieves' World: The Threat of the New Global Network of Organised Crime*, Simon & Schuster, New York, 1994.

Smedley, Agnes, *Battle Hymn of China*, Gollancz, London, 1944.

———— *Chinese Destinies: Sketches of Present Day China*, Hurst & Blackett, London, 1934.

Sues, Ilona Ralf, *Shark's Fin and Millet*, Garden City, New York, 1944.

Tan, Chester C., *The Boxer Catastrophe*, Octagon Books, New York, 1983.

Thompson, H. C., *The Case for China*, George Allen & Unwin, London, 1933.

Townsend, Peter, *China Phoenix*, Jonathan Cape, London, 1955.

Tu, Elsie, *An Autobiography*, Longman, Hong Kong, 1988.

Turner, J. A., *Kwang Tung or Five Years in South China*, Partridge, London, 1894.

Wakeman, Frederic Jr, and Yeh, Wen-hsin, *Shanghai Sojourners*, Institute of East Asian Studies/University of California, Berkeley, 1990.

Ward, Iain, *Sui Geng: The Hong Kong Marine Police 1841–1950*, Hong Kong University Press, Hong Kong, 1991.

Ward, J. S. M., and Stirling, W. G., *The Hung Society*, Baskerville Press, London, 1925.

Wilson, Dick, *China's Revolutionary War*, Weidenfeld & Nicolson, London, 1991.

Without stated authors

Organised and Serious Crimes Ordinance, Hong Kong Government (update 1995).

Societies Ordinance, Hong Kong Government (various dates).

Annual Reports (1987–96), Independent Commission Against Corruption, Hong Kong.

Journalistic and Broadcast Sources

Asiaweek, BBC-tv, *Atlantic Monthly*, the *China Mail*, the *Chinese Journal* (Shanghai), the *Chinese Repository*, the *Boston Globe, Eastern Express* (Hong Kong), *Far Eastern Economic Review*, *Fortune Magazine*, Granada Television, *Hong Kong Tiger Standard*, the *Independent*, the *Journal of the Royal Asiatic Society of Great Britain and Ireland*, the *Los Angeles Times*, *Newsweek*, the *New York Times*, *Newsweek*, *Nexus* (NCIS Bulletin), *Philadelphia Inquirer,* the *South China Morning Post*, the *Straits Times*, the *Sunday Times*, *Time*, *The Times*, the *Washington Post*, the *Washington Times*.

INDEX

589

Hager, D. Charles, 96
Hague, William, 295
Hai San, 337–8, 342, 343
Hak Chai, 315
Hak Sh'e Wui, 41
Hakka, 60–1, 81, 115
Han Chao-shun, *see* Soong
Han Shan-tung, 38
He Changli, 554
Heaven and Earth Society
    (T'ien-ti Hui), 38, 42, 44–
    51, 52–3, 328
Heavenly Kingdom of Great
    Peace, 63
Heavenly Way Alliance (Tian
    Dao Man), 563
Hei Tai Yang, *see* Black Sun
    Society
heroin: addiction rates, 292,
    511, 522, 552; Australian
    market, 521–3, 524; British
    distribution, 460–1;
    Canadian market, 511;
    Chinese market, 552;
    Colombian production,
    548; Du's production, 154–
    5, 156; Hong Kong
    laboratories, 264–5, 269,
    302–3, 562; Hong Kong
    retailing, 361; Japanese
    production, 163;
    Netherlands operations,
    425, 426–43, 460; Ng Sik-
    ho's operations, 296–307;
    smoking, 154; South
    African market, 531–2;
    Teochiu Triad dealers,
    285–95, 494, 521–2, 552;

US government tool, 278,
    288; US market, 495–9
Hess, Ann, 430, 433
Heung, Charles, 397–8
Heung, Jimmy, 397
Heung, Thomas, 539
Heung Chin, 318
Heung Chin-sing, David,
    322–3
Heung Wah-yim, 317–24,
    397, 539
Heung Wing-yee, Anita, 318
Hin Pui-lui (Nicky Louie),
    492, 496, 499
Hing Ah Kee Kwan, 253
Hing Chung Wui, 204
Hip Sing Tong, 485, 488,
    492, 496, 502, 507
Ho Hung-sun, Stanley, 380–
    5, 538, 540, 542, 547
Ho Kai, 97
Ho Kan-t'ang, 72
Ho Seng, 339–40
Ho Tung, Sir Robert, 72,
    380
Hok Beng Society, 341
Hon Kwing-shum, 282
Hong Ah-kay, 487
Hong Hei, emperor, 210
Hong Kong: anti-Christian
    attacks, 77–8; anti-Triad
    police activities, 306–26;
    arms trade, 62; Basic Law,
    549; bookmaking, 312–13;
    British colony, 62, 73, 241;
    British lease (1898), 83,
    267, 463; car thieves, 400–
    1; Chiang Kai-shek's plans,

596

Malaya: anti-Triad operations, 340–1, 348–52; colonial rule, 337; coolies, 327–30; Emergency, 348; flag societies, 343–5; Japanese occupation, 346–8; Larut Wars, 337, 338; riots, 334–6; Triads, 304, 332–48, 425, 454

Malayan Communist Party (MCP), 347–8

Man Chi Tong, 258–9

Man On Society, 246, 248, 267

Man Shing Tong, 246

Man Wan-lung, 190, 205, 213

Manchester, Triad presence, 449, 459, 460, 467–9

Manchus, 41, 45, 97, 188, 189

Manufacturers' Bank, 165

Mao Fu-mei, 128, 129, 152

Mao Zedong: attitude to peasant societies, 160–1; drugs policy, 409; relationship with Chiang Kai-shek, 168, 175, 238, 446; relationship with Triads, 178–9, 180, 237–9

Marcos, Ferdinand, 383, 399–400, 561

Marques Baptista, Antonio, 547

martial arts, 249–50, 312

Mason, James, 78

Mason, Richard, 363

medicine: Chinese traditional, 352, 533; fake, 560

Miles, Milton, 170–1

Ming, 'Golo', 472

Ming dynasty: end (1644), 39; foundation (1368), 28, 38; restoration question, 49, 179, 206; secret societies' support for, 40–3; Sun Yat-sen's celebration, 120; Triad traditions, 198, 206; *see also fan q'ing - fuk ming*

Ming Long, 485

Ming Yee Fong Luk, 189, 201

Ming Yeun Tong, 199–204

missionaries, 74–81, 208

Mo Shui-Chuen, Danny, 512, 513–14, 515

Mo Tat, 196

Mok Duk, 487–8, 489

Mongols, 27–8, 37, 38

Mongrel Mob, 530

Morgan, W.P., 187, 204, 209, 217

morphine, 154, 264

Morrison, George, 89

Morrison, Robert, 61

Mountbatten, Lord, 348

Mui, Anita, 394, 396

mui tsai system, 247, 260, 330

Muk Yeung, 198, 209–14

Mun Ji Dong, 523

Muslims, 68, 342, 343, 344

Nam Kong, 282

Nanjing: Chiang Kai-shek's government (1928), 150, 159; fall (1402), 29; fall (1851), 63; fall (1912), 119;

597

598